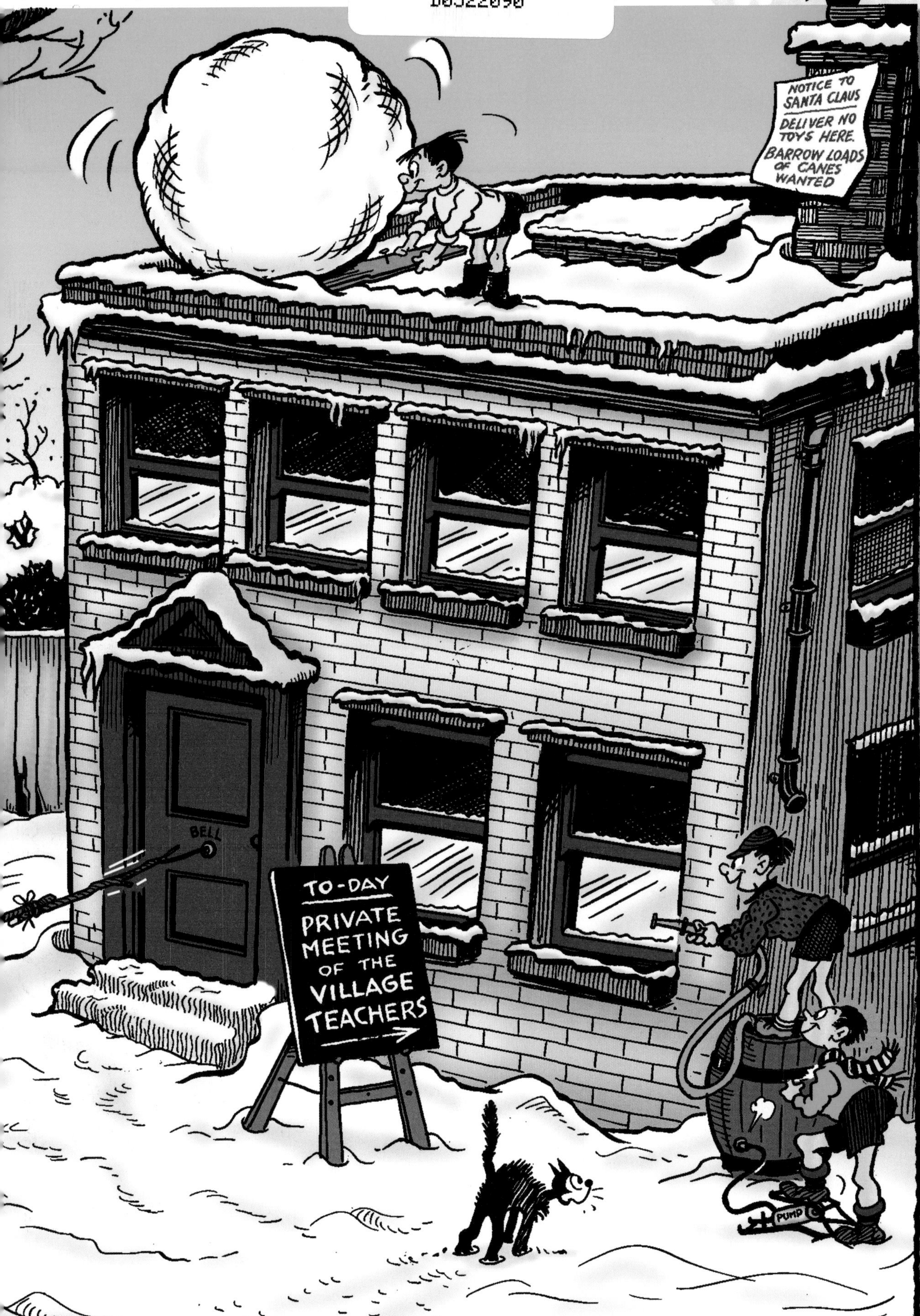
NOTICE TO SANTA CLAUS
DELIVER NO TOYS HERE.
BARROW LOADS OF CANES WANTED
BELL
TO-DAY
PRIVATE MEETING OF THE VILLAGE TEACHERS
PUMP

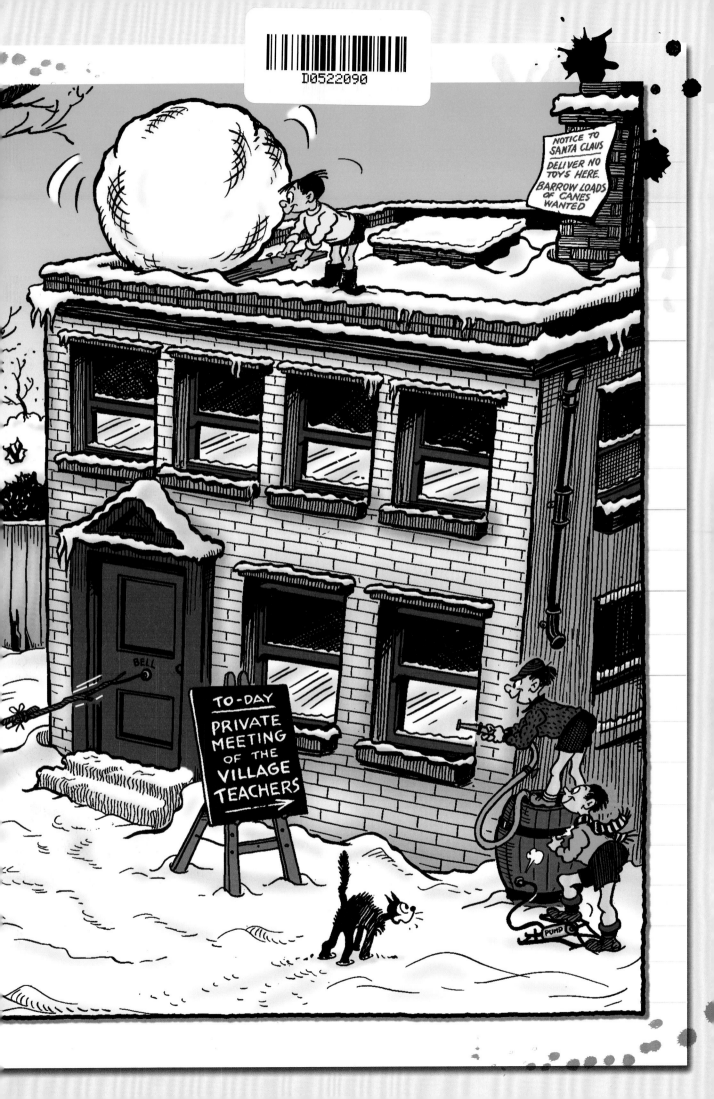

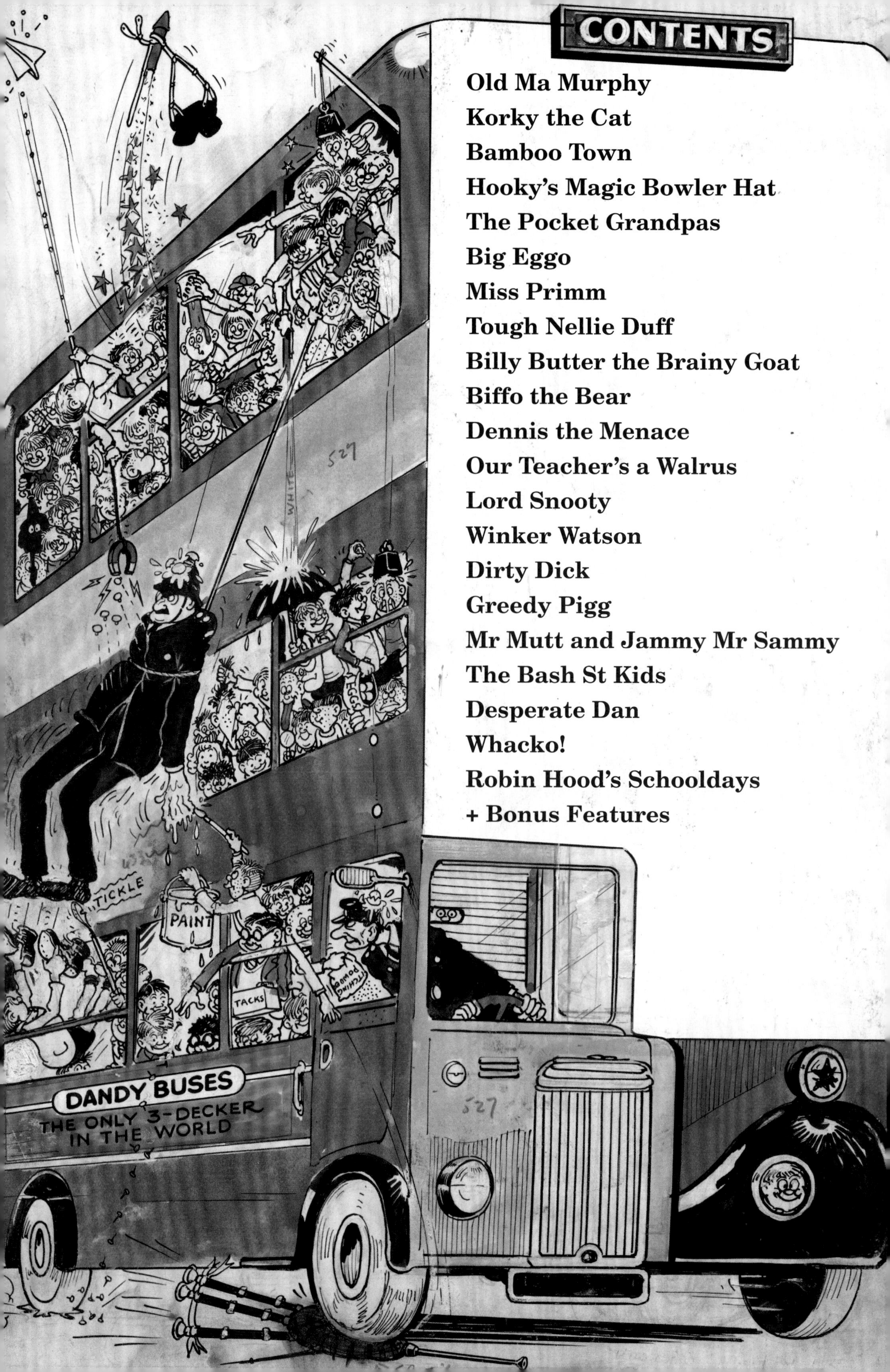

CONTENTS

Old Ma Murphy

Korky the Cat

Bamboo Town

Hooky's Magic Bowler Hat

The Pocket Grandpas

Big Eggo

Miss Primm

Tough Nellie Duff

Billy Butter the Brainy Goat

Biffo the Bear

Dennis the Menace

Our Teacher's a Walrus

Lord Snooty

Winker Watson

Dirty Dick

Greedy Pigg

Mr Mutt and Jammy Mr Sammy

The Bash St Kids

Desperate Dan

Whacko!

Robin Hood's Schooldays

+ Bonus Features

DANDY BUSES

THE ONLY 3-DECKER IN THE WORLD

TICKLE

PAINT

TACKS

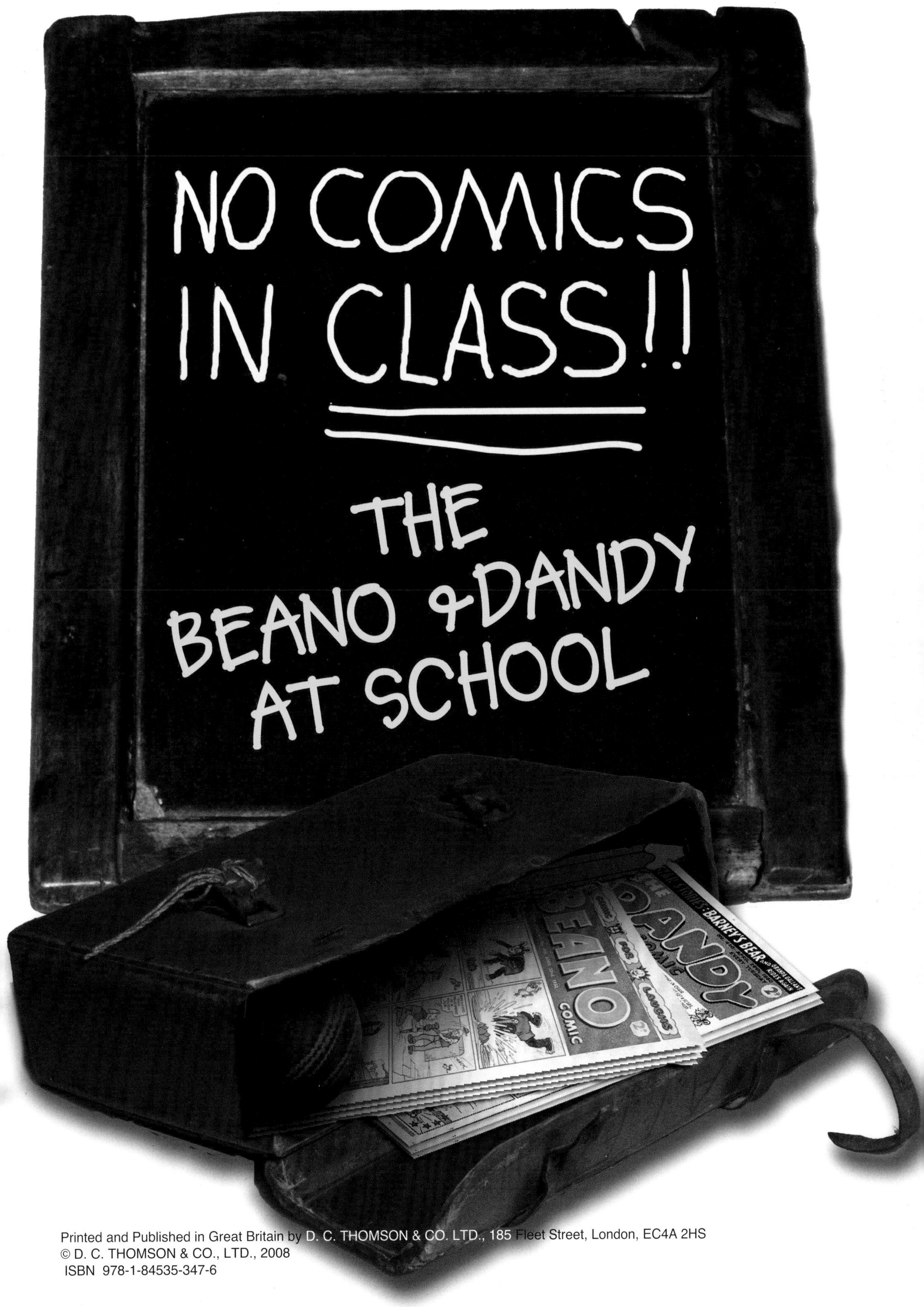
NO COMICS
IN CLASS!!
THE
BEANO & DANDY
AT SCHOOL
BEANO
COMIC
DANDY
BARNEY'S BEAR

Printed and Published in Great Britain by D. C. THOMSON & CO. LTD., 185 Fleet Street, London, EC4A 2HS

ISBN 978-1-84535-347-6

COMICS IN THE CLASSROOM

Over the decades millions of boys and girls have enjoyed The Beano and the Dandy. No matter if they were a fifties teddy boy or a nineties cool kid they all had one thing in common..... they went to SCHOOL!

With the pupils went their two best loved comics, joining the school line, catching the school bus and appearing (often to teacher's disapproval) in classrooms everywhere.

It was not surprising then that school stories and schoolyard storylines appeared constantly in the make-up of both comics.

So, sit up straight, books open at page one and enjoy our selection of comics in the classroom.

THE
EE BOYS ARE PLAYING TRUANT TODAY.
OUT AND BRING IN WILLIE SMITH
MY BROWN AND JIMMY JONES.
ATTENDANCE LIST
MUSEUM
SOOT
BIG EGGO
BLUNDERBUSS
NAILS

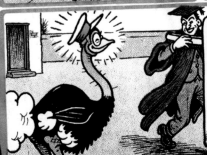

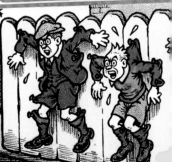

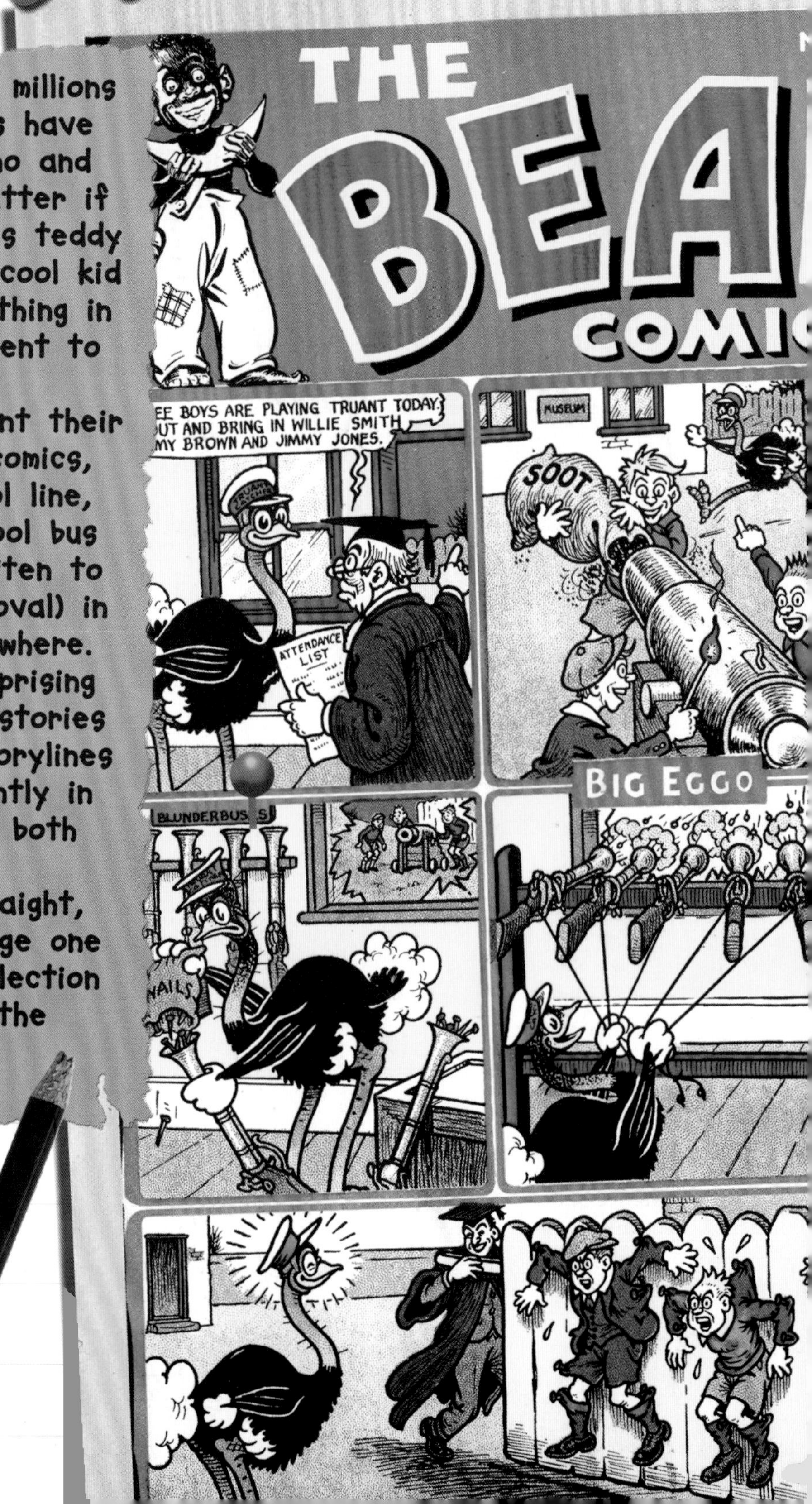

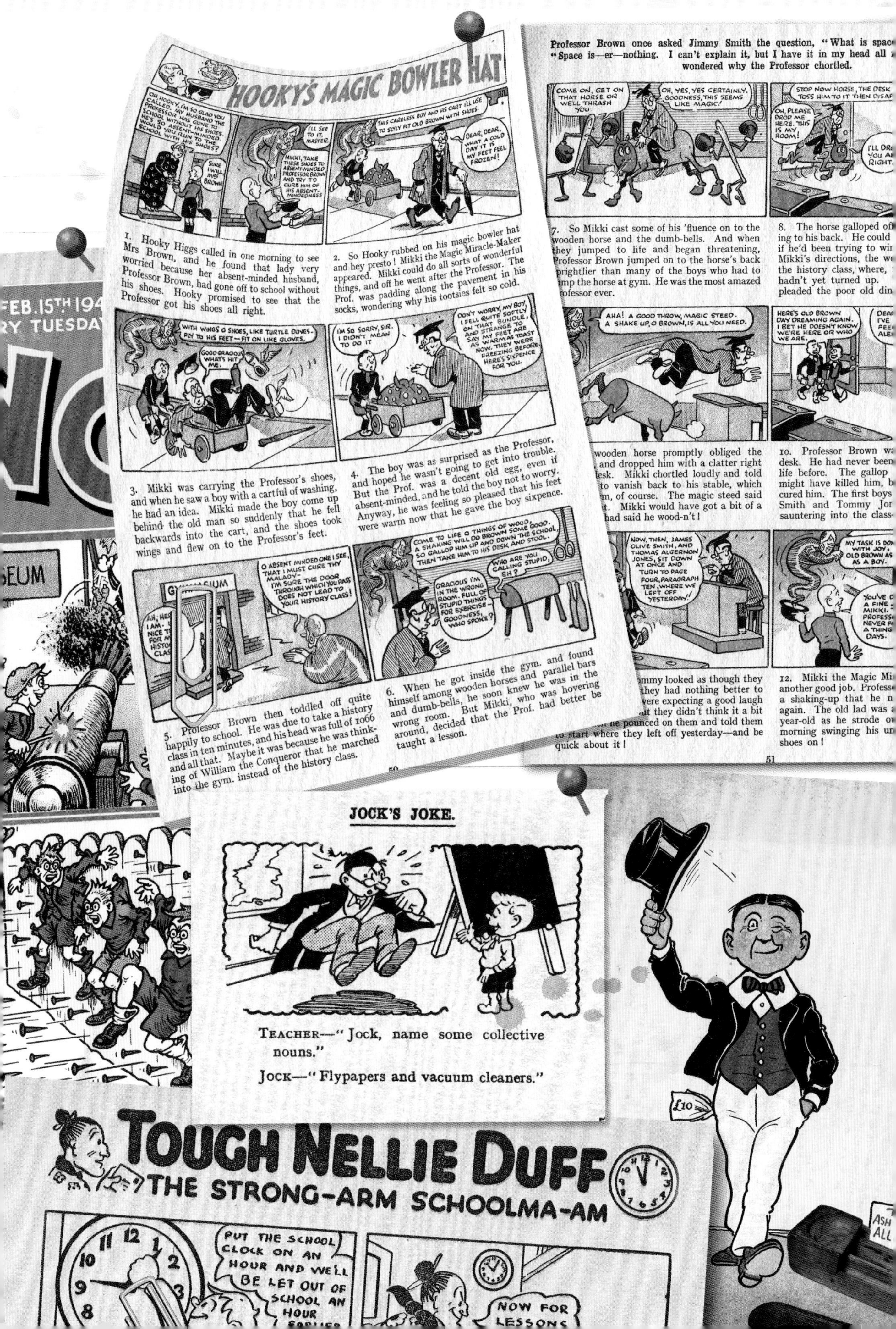

HOOKY'S MAGIC BOWLER HAT
OH, HOOKY, I'M SO GLAD YOU CALLED. MY HUSBAND THE PROFESSOR HAS GONE TO SCHOOL WITHOUT HIS SHOES. HE'S SO ABSENT-MINDED. WOULD YOU RUN TO THE SCHOOL WITH HIS SHOES?
SURE I WILL MRS BROWN.
I'LL SEE TO IT, MASTER.
MIKKI, TAKE THESE SHOES TO ABSENT-MINDED PROFESSOR BROWN AND TRY TO CURE HIM OF HIS ABSENT-MINDEDNESS
THIS CARELESS BOY AND HIS CART I'LL USE TO SLYLY FIT OLD BROWN WITH SHOES.
DEAR, DEAR, WHAT A COLD DAY IT IS MY FEET FEEL FROZEN!
1. Hooky Higgs called in one morning to see Mrs Brown, and he found that lady very worried because her absent-minded husband, Professor Brown, had gone off to school without his shoes. Hooky promised to see that the Professor got his shoes all right.
2. So Hooky rubbed on his magic bowler hat and hey presto! Mikki the Magic Miracle-Maker appeared. Mikki could do all sorts of wonderful things, and off he went after the Professor. The Prof. was padding along the pavement in his socks, wondering why his tootsies felt so cold.
WITH WINGS O SHOES, LIKE TURTLE DOVES—FLY TO HIS FEET—FIT ON LIKE GLOVES.
GOOD GRACIOUS WHAT'S HIT ME.
I'M SO SORRY, SIR. I DIDN'T MEAN TO DO IT
DON'T WORRY, MY BOY. I FELL QUITE SOFTLY ON THAT BUNDLE, AND STRANGE TO SAY MY FEET ARE AS WARM AS TOAST NOW. THEY WERE FREEZING BEFORE. HERE'S SIXPENCE FOR YOU.
3. Mikki was carrying the Professor's shoes, and when he saw a boy with a cartful of washing, he had an idea. Mikki made the boy come up behind the old man so suddenly that he fell backwards into the cart, and the shoes took wings and flew on to the Professor's feet.
4. The boy was as surprised as the Professor, and hoped he wasn't going to get into trouble. But the Prof. was a decent old egg, even if absent-minded, and he told the boy not to worry. Anyway, he was feeling so pleased that his feet were warm now that he gave the boy sixpence.
O ABSENT MINDED ONE I SEE, THAT I MUST CURE THY MALADY—I'M SURE THE DOOR THROUGH WHICH YOU PASS DOES NOT LEAD TO YOUR HISTORY CLASS!
COME TO LIFE O THINGS OF WOOD, A SHAKING WILL DO BROWN SOME GOOD. SO GALLOP HIM UP AND DOWN THE SCHOOL THEN TAKE HIM TO HIS DESK AND STOOL.
GRACIOUS I'M IN THE WRONG ROOM. FULL OF STUPID THINGS FOR EXERCISE—GOODNESS, WHO SPOKE?
WHO ARE YOU CALLING STUPID, EH?
5. Professor Brown then toddled off quite happily to school. He was due to take a history class in ten minutes, and his head was full of 1066 and all that. Maybe it was because he was thinking of William the Conqueror that he marched into the gym. instead of the history class.
6. When he got inside the gym. and found himself among wooden horses and parallel bars and dumb-bells, he soon knew he was in the wrong room. But Mikki, who was hovering around, decided that the Prof. had better be taught a lesson.
50
Professor Brown once asked Jimmy Smith the question, "What is space?" "Space is—er—nothing. I can't explain it, but I have it in my head all ..." wondered why the Professor chortled.
COME ON, GET ON THAT HORSE OR WE'LL THRASH YOU
OH, YES, YES CERTAINLY. GOODNESS, THIS SEEMS LIKE MAGIC!
OH, PLEASE DROP ME HERE. THIS IS MY ROOM!
7. So Mikki cast some of his 'fluence on to the wooden horse and the dumb-bells. And when they jumped to life and began threatening, Professor Brown jumped on to the horse's back sprightlier than many of the boys who had to jump the horse at gym. He was the most amazed professor ever.
AHA! A GOOD THROW, MAGIC STEED. A SHAKE UP, O BROWN, IS ALL YOU NEED.
HERE'S OLD BROWN DAY DREAMING AGAIN. I BET HE DOESN'T KNOW WE'RE HERE OR WHO WE ARE.
NOW, THEN, JAMES OLIVE SMITH, AND THOMAS ALGERNON JONES, SIT DOWN AT ONCE AND TURN TO PAGE FOUR, PARAGRAPH TEN, WHERE WE LEFT OFF YESTERDAY!
... to start where they left off yesterday—and be quick about it!
51
JOCK'S JOKE.
TEACHER—"Jock, name some collective nouns."
JOCK—"Flypapers and vacuum cleaners."
TOUGH NELLIE DUFF
THE STRONG-ARM SCHOOLMA-AM
PUT THE SCHOOL CLOCK ON AN HOUR AND WE'LL BE LET OUT OF SCHOOL AN HOUR
NOW FOR LESSONS
£10

Teachers believed in corporal punishment and dolled

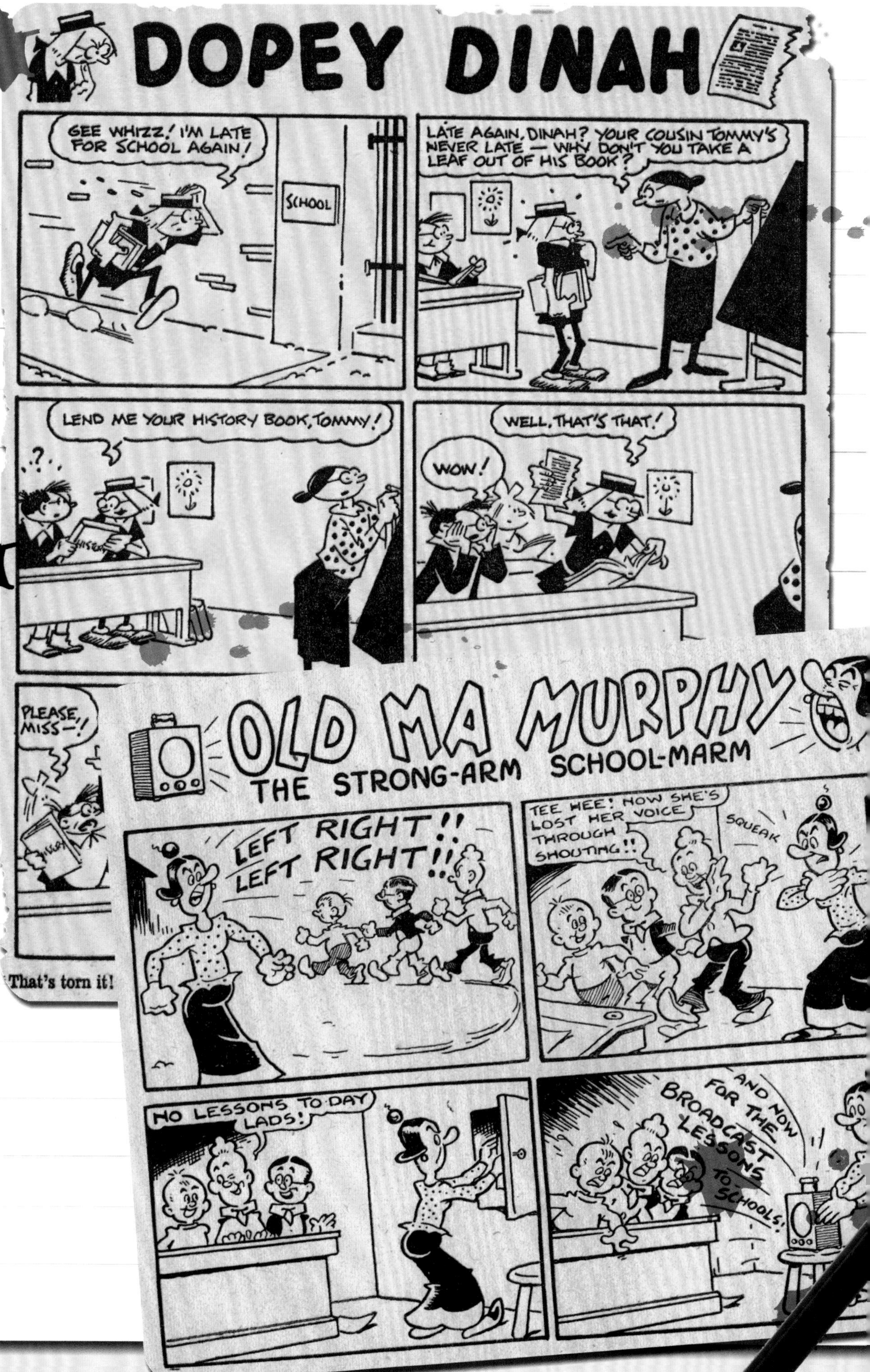
DOPEY DINAH
GEE WHIZZ! I'M LATE FOR SCHOOL AGAIN!
SCHOOL
LATE AGAIN, DINAH? YOUR COUSIN TOMMY'S NEVER LATE — WHY DON'T YOU TAKE A LEAF OUT OF HIS BOOK?
LEND ME YOUR HISTORY BOOK, TOMMY!
?
WELL, THAT'S THAT!
WOW!
PLEASE, MISS—!
That's torn it!
OLD MA MURPHY
THE STRONG-ARM SCHOOL-MARM
LEFT RIGHT!! LEFT RIGHT!!
TEE HEE! NOW SHE'S LOST HER VOICE THROUGH SHOUTING!!
SQUEAK
NO LESSONS TO-DAY LADS!
AND NOW FOR THE BROADCAST LESSONS TO SCHOOLS!

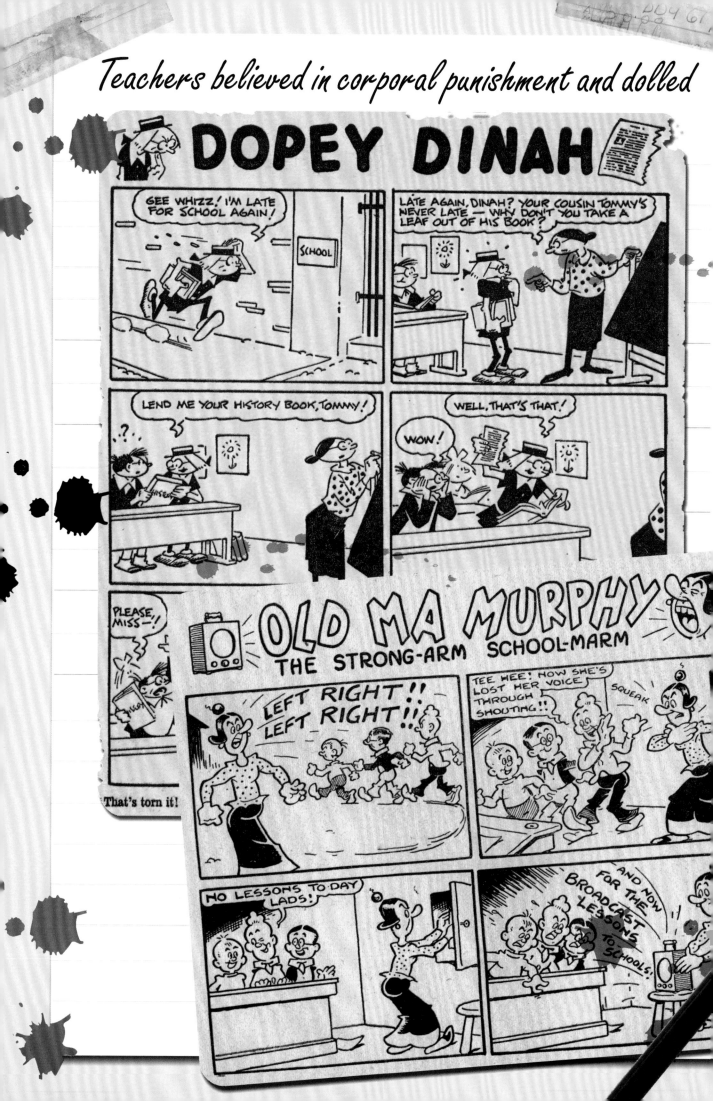

it out in lavish, comic cuts amounts.

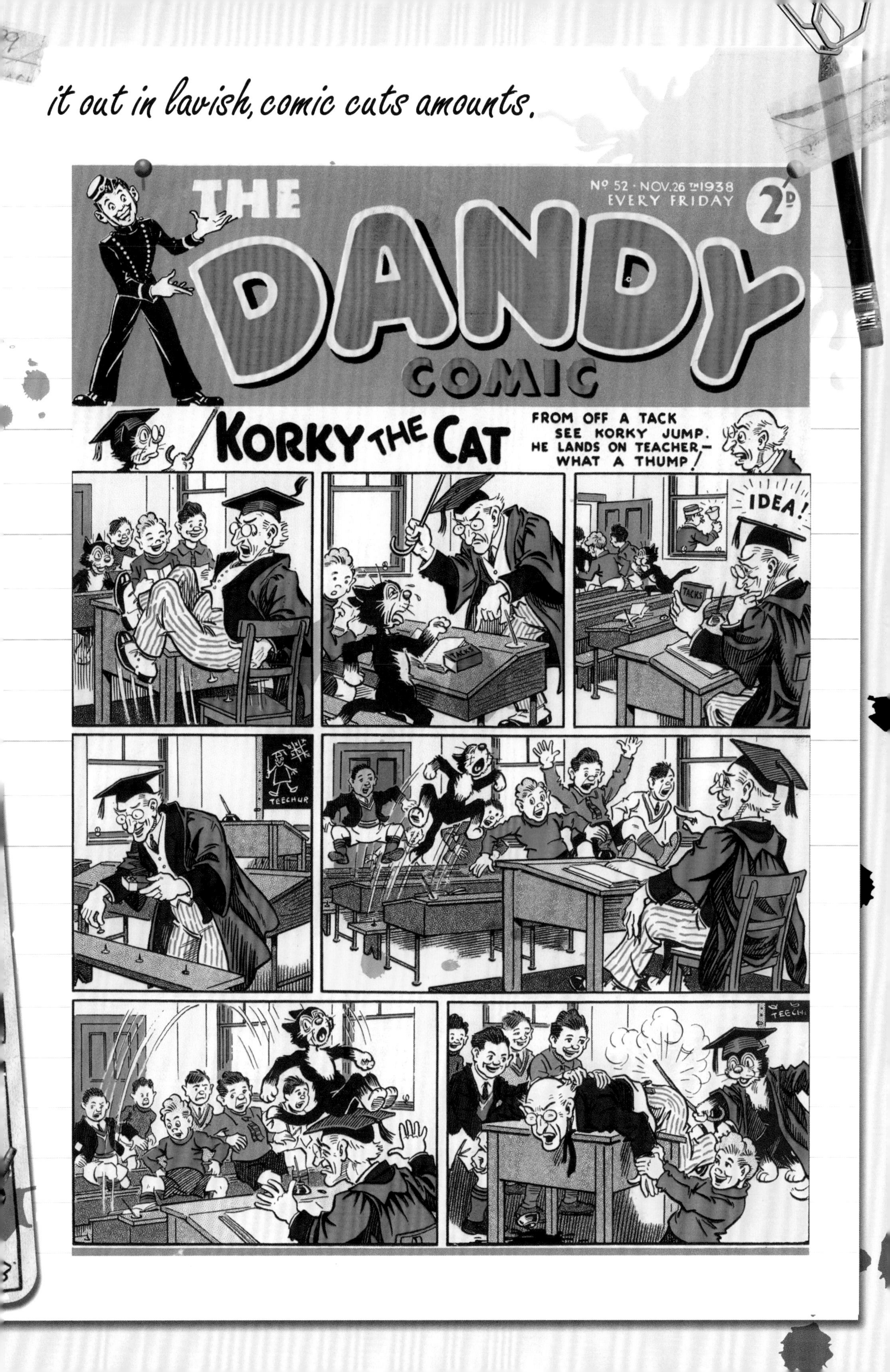

THE DANDY COMIC
Nº 52 · NOV. 26TH 1938
EVERY FRIDAY
2D
KORKY THE CAT
FROM OFF A TACK
SEE KORKY JUMP.
HE LANDS ON TEACHER—
WHAT A THUMP!
TACKS
IDEA!
TACKS
TEECHUR

A classroom riot in Bamboo Town. Never leave an elephant in charge of a class.

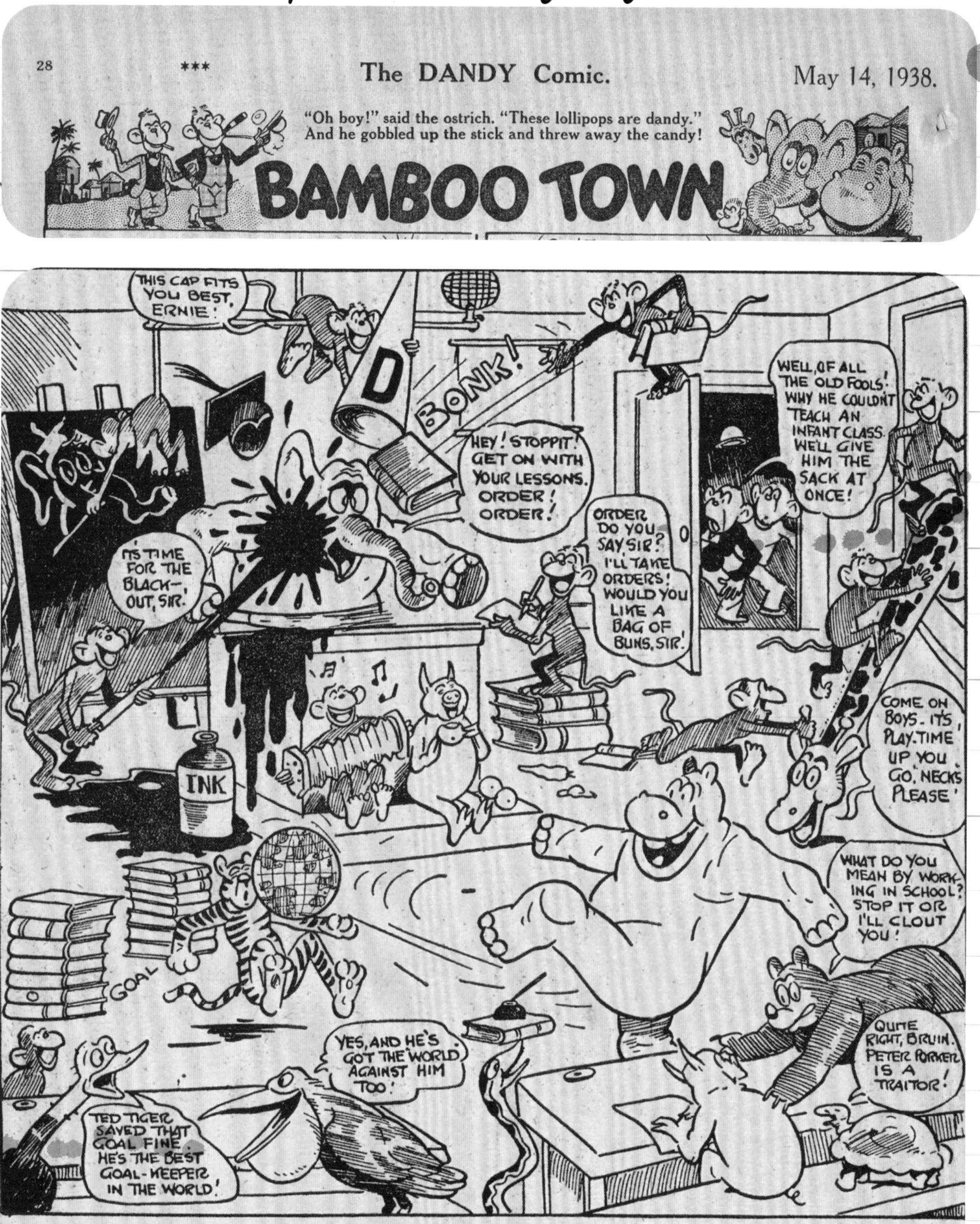

28 *** The DANDY Comic. May 14, 1938.
"Oh boy!" said the ostrich. "These lollipops are dandy."
And he gobbled up the stick and threw away the candy!
BAMBOO TOWN
THIS CAP FITS YOU BEST, ERNIE!
D
BONK!
HEY! STOPPIT! GET ON WITH YOUR LESSONS. ORDER! ORDER!
WELL, OF ALL THE OLD FOOLS! WHY HE COULDN'T TEACH AN INFANT CLASS. WE'LL GIVE HIM THE SACK AT ONCE!
IT'S TIME FOR THE BLACK-OUT, SIR!
ORDER DO YOU SAY, SIR? I'LL TAKE ORDERS! WOULD YOU LIKE A BAG OF BUNS, SIR!
INK
COME ON BOYS. IT'S PLAY-TIME! UP YOU GO, NECKS PLEASE!
WHAT DO YOU MEAN BY WORKING IN SCHOOL? STOP IT OR I'LL CLOUT YOU!
GOAL
YES, AND HE'S GOT THE WORLD AGAINST HIM TOO!
QUITE RIGHT, BRUIN. PETER PORKER IS A TRAITOR!
TED TIGER SAVED THAT GOAL FINE. HE'S THE BEST GOAL-KEEPER IN THE WORLD!

Ernie Elephant couldn't give a grocery order far less keep a school in order. Mickey Monkey gave him a whack with a book, and Pongo and Bongo gave him the sack.

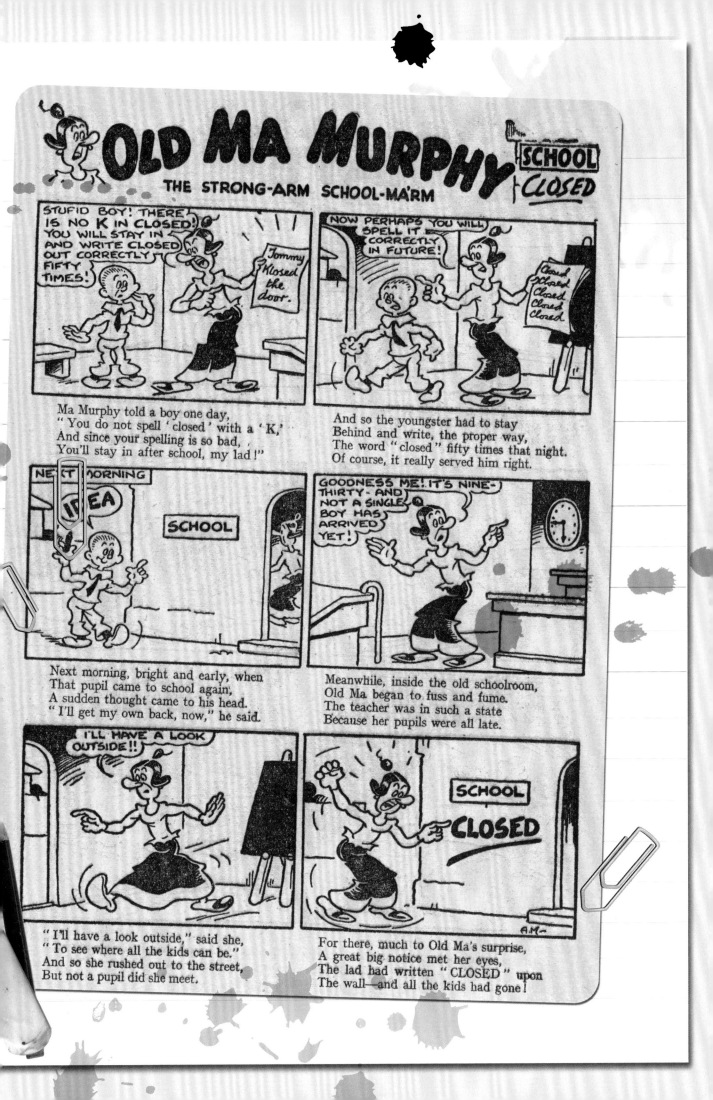

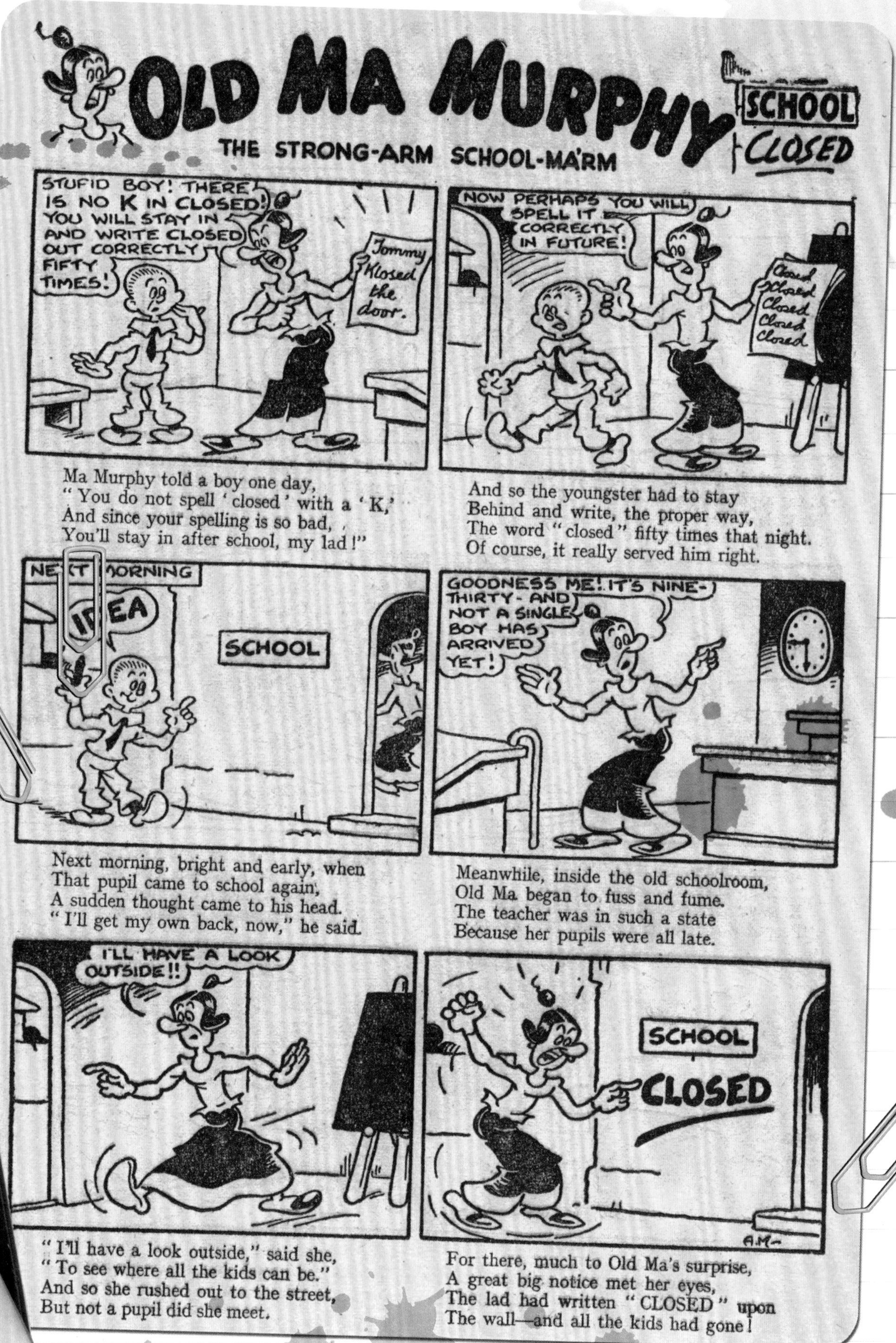
OLD MA MURPHY
THE STRONG-ARM SCHOOL-MA'RM
SCHOOL
CLOSED
STUFID BOY! THERE IS NO K IN CLOSED! YOU WILL STAY IN AND WRITE CLOSED OUT CORRECTLY FIFTY TIMES!
Tommy Klosed the door.
Ma Murphy told a boy one day,
" You do not spell 'closed' with a 'K,'
And since your spelling is so bad,
You'll stay in after school, my lad!"
NOW PERHAPS YOU WILL SPELL IT CORRECTLY IN FUTURE!
Closed Closed Closed Closed Closed
And so the youngster had to stay
Behind and write, the proper way,
The word "closed" fifty times that night.
Of course, it really served him right.
NEXT MORNING
IDEA
SCHOOL
Next morning, bright and early, when
That pupil came to school again,
A sudden thought came to his head.
" I'll get my own back, now," he said.
GOODNESS ME! IT'S NINE-THIRTY - AND NOT A SINGLE BOY HAS ARRIVED YET!
Meanwhile, inside the old schoolroom,
Old Ma began to fuss and fume.
The teacher was in such a state
Because her pupils were all late.
I'LL HAVE A LOOK OUTSIDE!!
SCHOOL
CLOSED
A.M.
" I'll have a look outside," said she,
" To see where all the kids can be."
And so she rushed out to the street,
But not a pupil did she meet.
For there, much to Old Ma's surprise,
A great big notice met her eyes,
The lad had written "CLOSED" upon
The wall—and all the kids had gone!

Hooky's Magic Bowler Hat was drawn in a very

HOOKY'S MAGIC BOWLER HAT

OH, HOOKY, I'M SO GLAD YOU CALLED. MY HUSBAND THE PROFESSOR HAS GONE TO SCHOOL WITHOUT HIS SHOES. HE'S SO ABSENT-MINDED. WOULD YOU RUN TO THE SCHOOL WITH HIS SHOES?
SURE I WILL, MRS BROWN
I'LL SEE TO IT, MASTER.
MIKKI, TAKE THESE SHOES TO ABSENT-MINDED PROFESSOR BROWN AND TRY TO CURE HIM OF HIS ABSENT-MINDEDNESS
THIS CARELESS BOY AND HIS CART I'LL USE TO SLYLY FIT OLD BROWN WITH SHOES.
DEAR, DEAR, WHAT A COLD DAY IT IS MY FEET FEEL FROZEN!

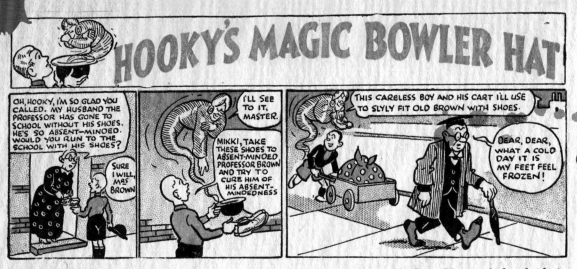

1. Hooky Higgs called in one morning to see Mrs Brown, and he found that lady very worried because her absent-minded husband, Professor Brown, had gone off to school without his shoes. Hooky promised to see that the Professor got his shoes all right.

2. So Hooky rubbed on his magic bowler hat and hey presto ! Mikki the Magic Miracle-Maker appeared. Mikki could do all sorts of wonderful things, and off he went after the Professor. The Prof. was padding along the pavement in his socks, wondering why his tootsies felt so cold.

WITH WINGS O SHOES, LIKE TURTLE DOVES- FLY TO HIS FEET—FIT ON LIKE GLOVES.
GOOD GRACIOUS WHAT'S HIT ME.
I'M SO SORRY, SIR. I DIDN'T MEAN TO DO IT
DON'T WORRY, MY BOY, I FELL QUITE SOFTLY ON THAT BUNDLE, AND STRANGE TO SAY MY FEET ARE AS WARM AS TOAST NOW. THEY WERE FREEZING BEFORE. HERE'S SIXPENCE FOR YOU.

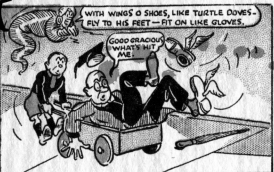

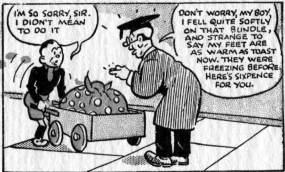

3. Mikki was carrying the Professor's shoes, and when he saw a boy with a cartful of washing, he had an idea. Mikki made the boy come up behind the old man so suddenly that he fell backwards into the cart, and the shoes took wings and flew on to the Professor's feet.

4. The boy was as surprised as the Professor, and hoped he wasn't going to get into trouble. But the Prof. was a decent old egg, even if absent-minded, and he told the boy not to worry. Anyway, he was feeling so pleased that his feet were warm now that he gave the boy sixpence.

GYMNASIUM
AH, HERE I AM. IN NICE TIME FOR MY HISTORY CLASS.
O ABSENT MINDED ONE I SEE, THAT I MUST CURE THY MALADY- I'M SURE THE DOOR THROUGH WHICH YOU PASS DOES NOT LEAD TO YOUR HISTORY CLASS!
COME TO LIFE O THINGS OF WOOD, A SHAKING WILL DO BROWN SOME GOOD. SO GALLOP HIM UP AND DOWN THE SCHOOL, THEN TAKE HIM TO HIS DESK AND STOOL.
WHO ARE YOU CALLING STUPID, EH?
GRACIOUS I'M IN THE WRONG ROOM. FULL OF STUPID THINGS FOR EXERCISE— GOODNESS, WHO SPOKE?

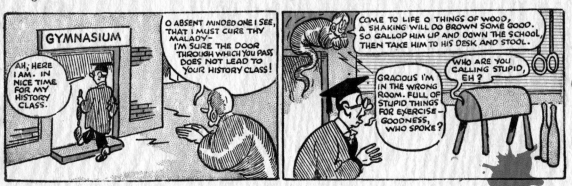

5. Professor Brown then toddled off quite happily to school. He was due to take a history class in ten minutes, and his head was full of 1066 and all that. Maybe it was because he was thinking of William the Conqueror that he marched into the gym. instead of the history class.

6. When he got inside the gym. and found himself among wooden horses and parallel bars and dumb-bells, he soon knew he was in the wrong room. But Mikki, who was hovering around, decided that the Prof. had better be taught a lesson.

crisp style by Beano staff artist Chick Gordon

Professor Brown once asked Jimmy Smith the question, "What is space?" Jimmy replied, "Space is—er—nothing. I can't explain it, but I have it in my head all right." And Jimmy wondered why the Professor chortled.

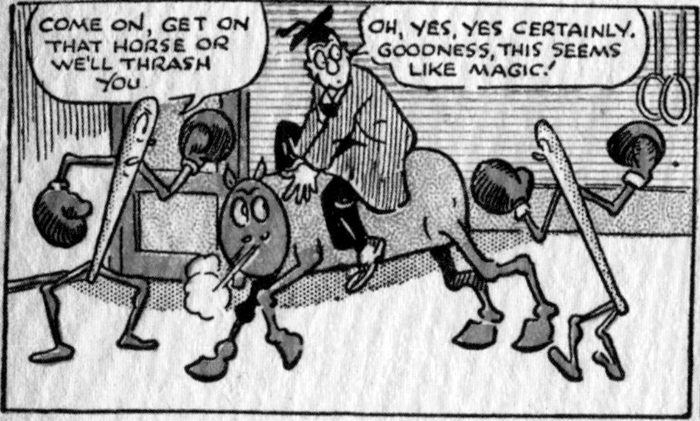
COME ON, GET ON THAT HORSE OR WE'LL THRASH YOU.
OH, YES, YES CERTAINLY. GOODNESS, THIS SEEMS LIKE MAGIC!

7. So Mikki cast some of his 'fluence on to the wooden horse and the dumb-bells. And when they jumped to life and began threatening, Professor Brown jumped on to the horse's back sprightlier than many of the boys who had to jump the horse at gym. He was the most amazed Professor ever.

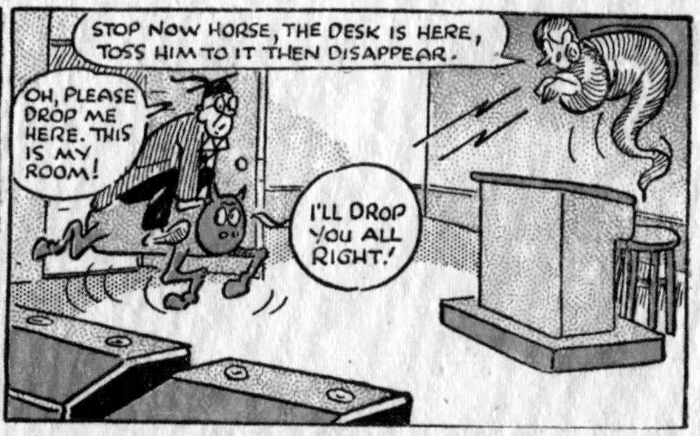
STOP NOW HORSE, THE DESK IS HERE, TOSS HIM TO IT THEN DISAPPEAR.
OH, PLEASE DROP ME HERE. THIS IS MY ROOM!
I'LL DROP YOU ALL RIGHT!

8. The horse galloped off with the Prof. clinging to his back. He could not have gone quicker if he'd been trying to win the Derby. Under Mikki's directions, the wooden steed made for the history class, where, fortunately, the boys hadn't yet turned up. "Drop me, please!" pleaded the poor old dinner-in of dates.

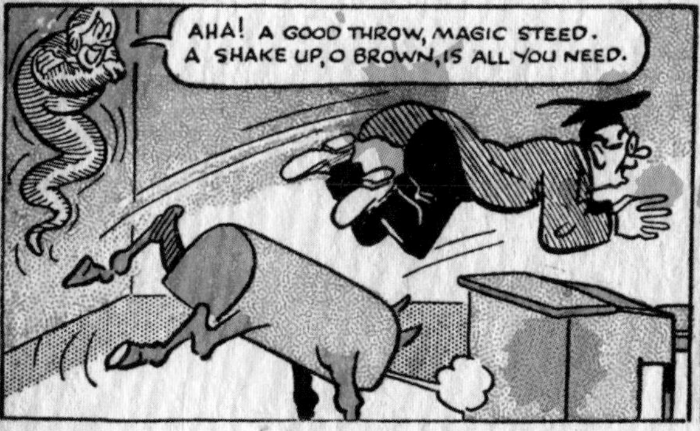
AHA! A GOOD THROW, MAGIC STEED. A SHAKE UP, O BROWN, IS ALL YOU NEED.

9. The wooden horse promptly obliged the Professor, and dropped him with a clatter right into his desk. Mikki chortled loudly and told the horse to vanish back to his stable, which was the gym, of course. The magic steed said he'd do that. Mikki would have got a bit of a shock if he had said he wood-n't!

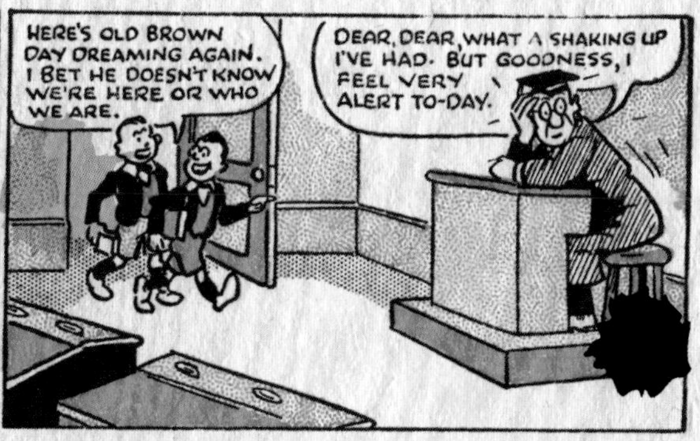
HERE'S OLD BROWN DAY DREAMING AGAIN. I BET HE DOESN'T KNOW WE'RE HERE OR WHO WE ARE.
DEAR, DEAR, WHAT A SHAKING UP I'VE HAD. BUT GOODNESS, I FEEL VERY ALERT TO-DAY.

10. Professor Brown was left sitting at his desk. He had never been so wide-awake in his life before. The gallop from the gymnasium might have killed him, but fortunately it had cured him. The first boys to arrive were Jimmy Smith and Tommy Jones, and they came sauntering into the class-room.

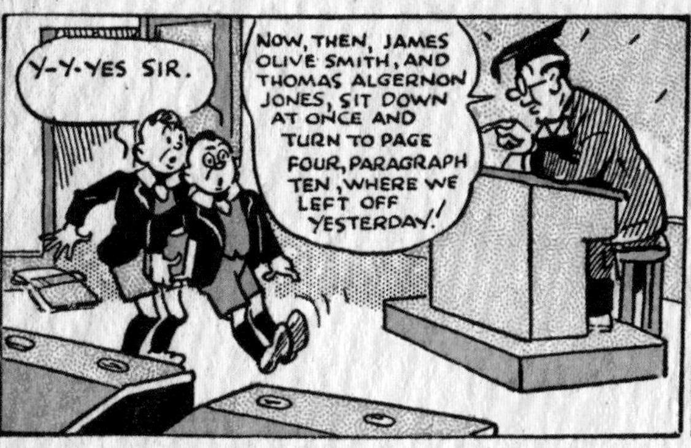
Y-Y-YES SIR.
NOW, THEN, JAMES OLIVE SMITH, AND THOMAS ALGERNON JONES, SIT DOWN AT ONCE AND TURN TO PAGE FOUR, PARAGRAPH TEN, WHERE WE LEFT OFF YESTERDAY!

11. Jimmy and Tommy looked as though they had come because they had nothing better to do. As usual, they were expecting a good laugh at the Professor. But they didn't think it a bit funny when he pounced on them and told them to start where they left off yesterday—and be quick about it!

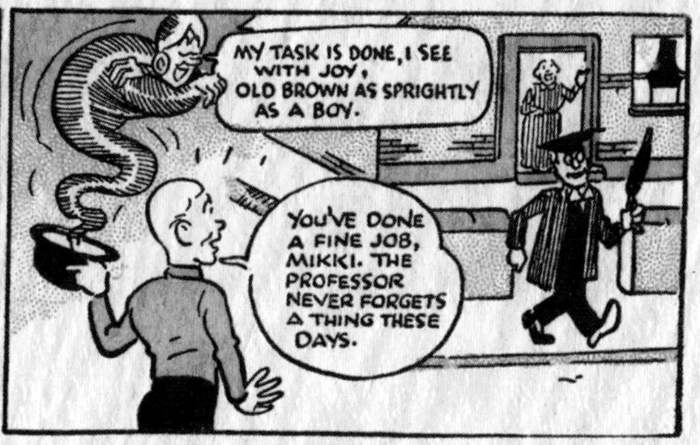
MY TASK IS DONE, I SEE WITH JOY, OLD BROWN AS SPRIGHTLY AS A BOY.
YOU'VE DONE A FINE JOB, MIKKI. THE PROFESSOR NEVER FORGETS A THING THESE DAYS.

12. Mikki the Magic Miracle-Maker had done another good job. Professor Brown had got such a shaking-up that he never forgot anything again. The old lad was as sprightly as a two-year-old as he strode out of his gate every morning swinging his umbrella—and with his shoes on!

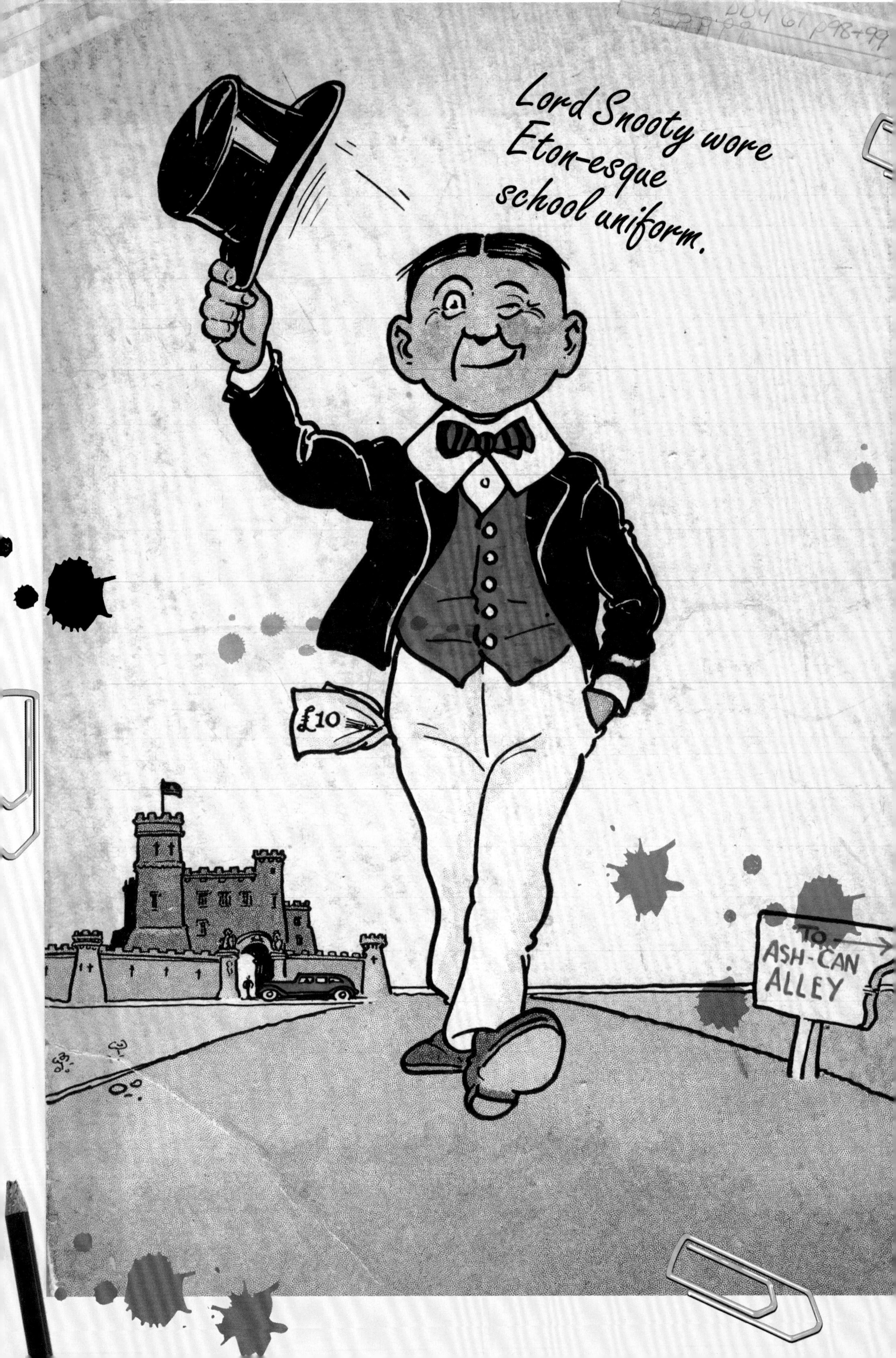
Lord Snooty wore Eton-esque school uniform.
£10
TO ASH-CAN ALLEY

Both Beano and Dandy ran a lot of text stories, they were more popular than the picture strips in the forties. Often they were school based.

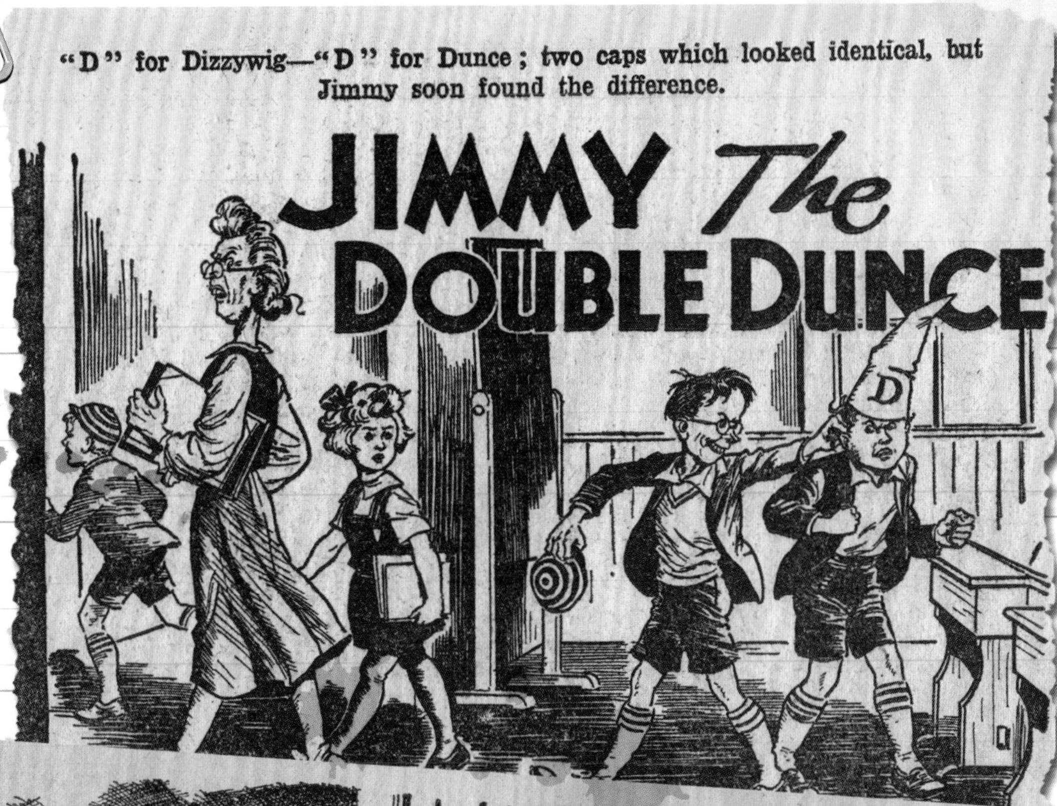
"D" for Dizzywig—"D" for Dunce ; two caps which looked identical, but Jimmy soon found the difference.

JIMMY The DOUBLE DUNCE

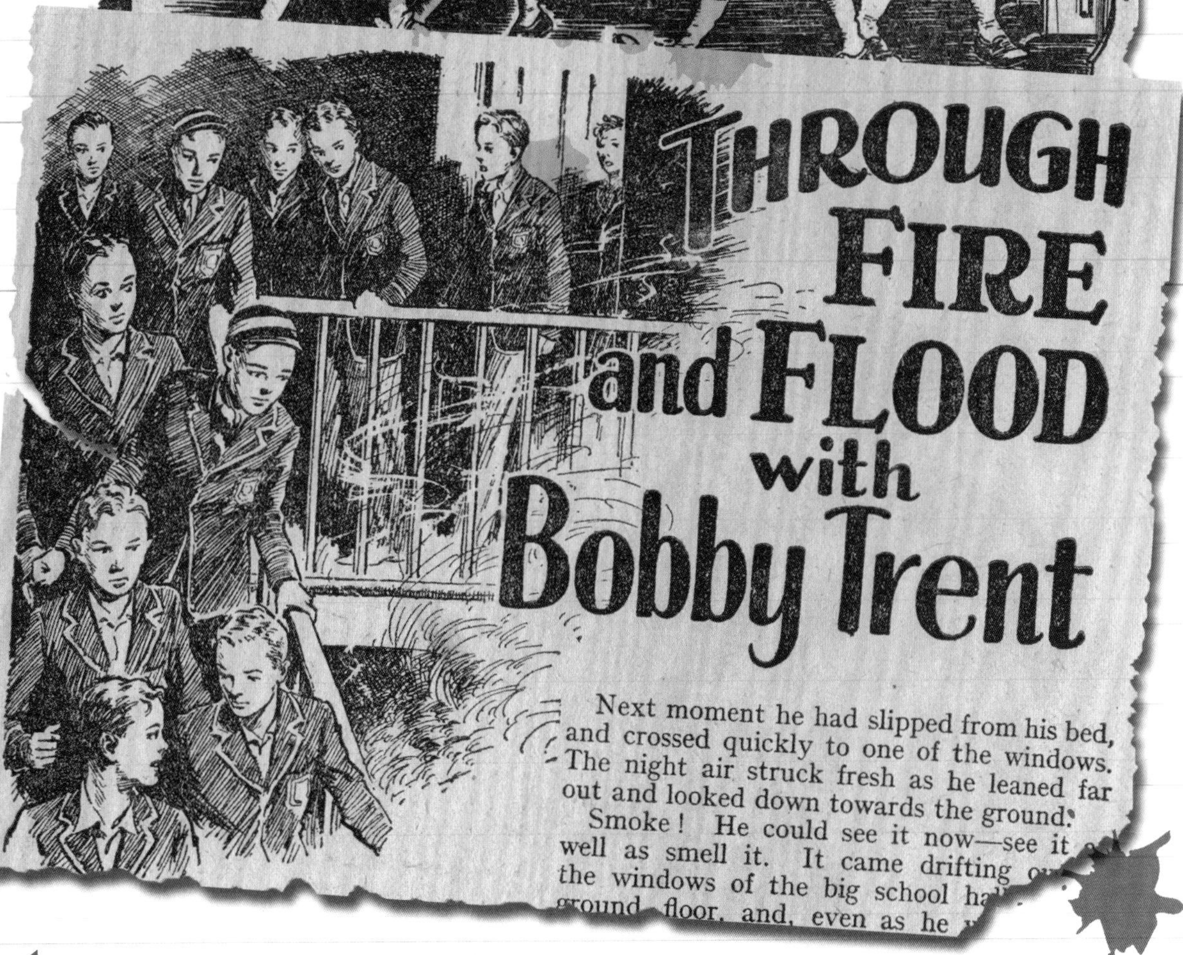
THROUGH FIRE and FLOOD with Bobby Trent

Next moment he had slipped from his bed, and crossed quickly to one of the windows. The night air struck fresh as he leaned far out and looked down towards the ground.

Smoke! He could see it now—see it a well as smell it. It came drifting o the windows of the big school ha ground floor, and, even as he w

POCKET GRANDPA

Schoolboy Jimmy Bruce had a mini sized Grandfather in this story from The Dandy annual 1941. The following year Jimmy and his Grandpa again had a school based story in the annual but it was now titled Jimmie's Pocket Grandpa. This storyline was so strong that years later in 1975, Dandy editor Albert Barnes brought the idea to life again, this time a cartoon picture story drawn by Ron Spencer and titled Peter's Pocket Grandpa. The difference in scale between Peter and his Grandpa caused Ron no end of headaches when laying out the pages, printers too struggled with the very fine lines Grandpa had to be drawn with.

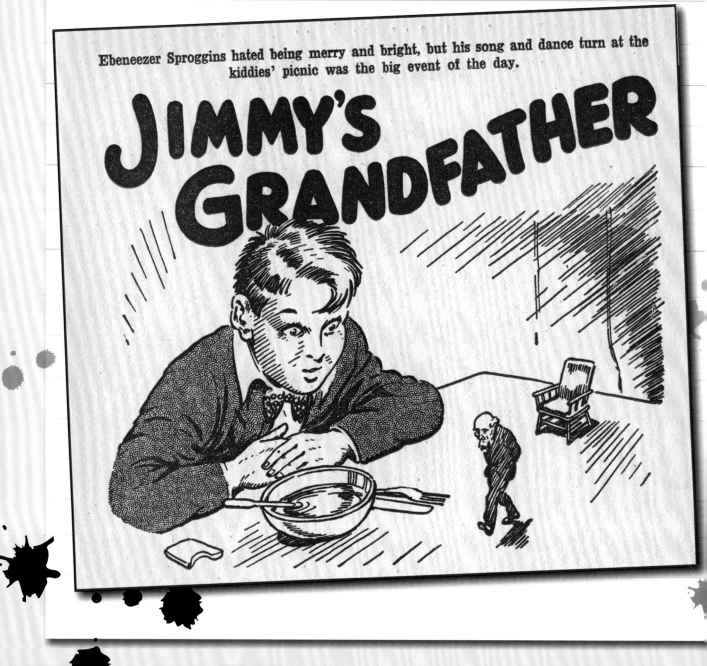

Ebeneezer Sproggins hated being merry and bright, but his song and dance turn at the kiddies' picnic was the big event of the day.

JIMMY'S GRANDFATHER

Mr Bloater toadied to the posh young gents of St Claud's School; but when Jimmie dropped a basketful of the boys on Bloater's front lawn one day, he wasn't very pleased to see them.

JIMMIE'S POCKET GRANDPA

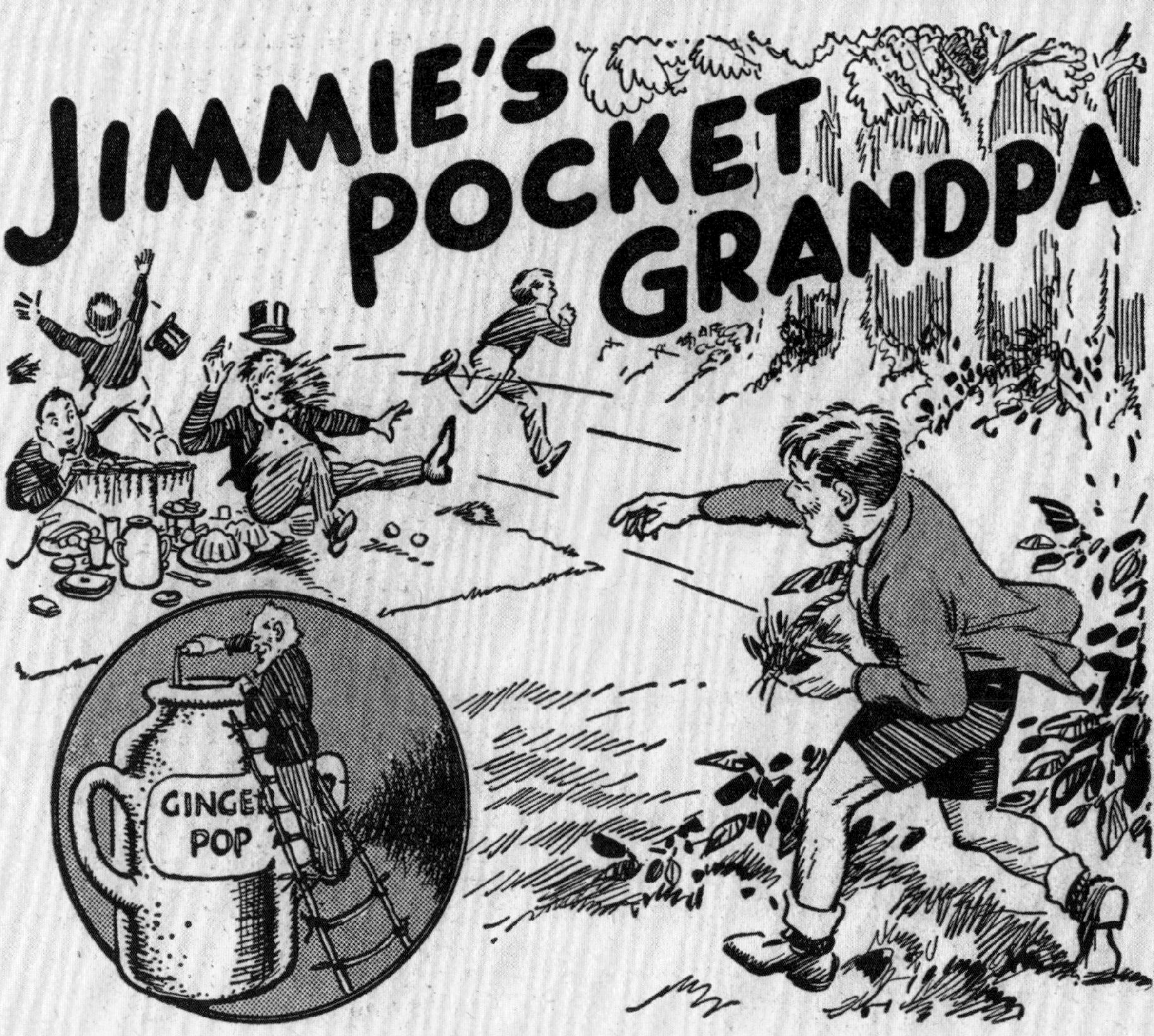
JIMMIE'S
POCKET
GRANDPA
GINGER
POP

JIMMIE BRUCE was strolling along a road which led past a wood when a sudden outcry fell on his ears. Next moment a bunch of small boys came rushing pell-mell out of the wood, hotly pursued by a big, fat, red-faced man wearing a baggy plus-four suit of startling hue.

"Be off with you!" roared the man, shaking his walking stick furiously at the small boys who had halted a little way along the road. "I won't have no slum brats picnicking and trespassing in my woods!"

"Aw, go and boil your silly fat head!" yelled one of the kids, sticking out his tongue. Then the whole bunch of them started to sing in jeering chorus:

"Bloater, Bloater, silly old fool,
Tries to suck in with the swank-pots' school!"

"Oh, my, just you wait till I catch you!" bellowed the fat, red-faced man, fairly dancing with rage. "I'll tan your hides for you. I'll put my game-keepers on to you, that's what I'll do!"

With this parting threat he turned on his heel and strode furiously back into the wood.

"What's up, kids?" asked Jimmie with a grin, strolling along to where the small boys were standing.

"It's that nasty old Bloater!" cried the leader of the bunch hotly. "He's bought all the land around here and he's stopped us playing in the woods. It was different when old Colonel Mather was alive. He let us play in the woods as much as we liked. A proper toff he was!"

"Yes, I know," nodded Jimmie. "And this bloke Bloater isn't, eh?"

"Naw, of course he isn't!" said the other scornfully. "He looks down on us just because we're poor. It would be different if we had plenty of money like them swank-pots along at St. Claud's School. Old Bloater lets them picnic in his woods as much as they blinking well like. He's always trying to suck in with them because their fathers and mothers are rich. Look, here's a bunch of 'em coming now!"

⚜ ⚜ ⚜

Bloater the Snob.

COMING along the road was a party of very posh young gents from St. Claud's School. They were wearing nice clean collars and shiny silk toppers, and were carrying a couple of big picnic hampers at the sight of which the small kids' mouths fairly watered.

As they passed Jimmie and the kids, the St. Claudites stuck their elegant noses in the air as though they were passing something that had fallen off a dust cart.

"Yah, swank-pots!" yelled the leader of the kids after them. Then he said to Jimmie: "Look, there's that nasty old Bloater waiting to welcome the snobs to his rotten old woods!"

The big, red-faced Mr Bloater had re-appeared at the edge of the wood. He beamed all over his great fat face at sight of the St. Claudites and Jimmie and the kids heard him cry:

"So here you are. Welcome to my woods and I hopes you have a real nice picnic. It's a nice day, isn't it?"

"Haw, a very nice day," drawled several of the party, then the whole bunch of them vanished into the wood along with Mr Bloater.

"Well, I guess we'd better be getting along," said the leader of the kids. "There's no use hanging about here. Come on, you blokes!"

They moved away along the road in the direction of the town. The moment they had gone the head of a tiny little old man popped up out of Jimmie's pocket and cried:

"I heard every word, Jimmie. Gosh, but that nasty old Bloater doesn't half need a lesson!"

"You're telling me, Grandpa!" said Jimmie with a grin.

Strange though it may sound, the tiny little old man in Jimmie's pocket was none other than his grandpa.

Jimmie's grandpa was a very clever scientist. He had invented a wonderful liquid for making people little. He had taken a swig of the liquid himself with the result that he had promptly been changed into a little old man only six inches tall.

Now Grandpa was a jolly old cove who loved a lark, and he'd found that by being little he could have heaps of fun and could play some grand pranks on people.

So, although he had invented a liquid which would make him big again, he preferred to stay little and enjoy himself.

"I know all abut old Bloater," he went on wrathfully. "He's well named Bloater, because he's made a fortune out of a lot of fish shops which he owns. He's a low-down, ignorant man and those kids were quite right when they said he's trying to suck in with the toffs around here. I'll give him toffs. I'll settle his blinking hash for him!"

"What are you going to do, Grandpa?" demanded Jimmie quickly, for he knew that jolly old Grandpa could get up to some wizard wheezes when he liked.

"I'll tell you what I'm going to do, Jimmie, lad," chuckled Grandpa. "He, he, he! I haven't half got a brainy idea. You listen to me!"

⚜ ⚜ ⚜

Grandpa's Wheeze.

AS Jimmie listened to little old grandpa's wheeze, he nearly burst with laughing.

"Gosh, Grandpa, what a giddy rag!" he spluttered. "It'll not only fix old Bloater, but it'll teach those St. Claud snobs a lesson as well!"

"You bet it will," chuckled Grandpa. "Okay, Jimmie, let's find out where they're holding their picnic. But mind none of the game-keepers see you."

Jimmie's Pocket Grandpa

"I'll watch that," said Jimmie.

With Grandpa in his pocket, he slipped into the wood and set off in search of the picnickers. He hadn't long to search, for the

big stone jars of ginger-pop.

"I don't see old Bloater," whispered Grandpa, sticking his head up out of Jimmie's pocket. " I reckon he must have gone on to his house. Let's get busy!"

Moving stealthily away from the tree, Jimmie slipped back into the wood, well out

As they passed Jimmie and the kids, the St. Claudites stuck their elegant noses in the air

sound of their haw-haw voices drew him to a clearing in the middle of the woods.

Keeping well under cover, Jimmie stealthily approached the edge of the clearing and took a look at the St. Claudites from behind a tree.

They were unpacking the picnic hampers, bringing out cakes, sandwiches, cold chickens, jellies, ices and, last but not least, two

of sight of the St. Claudites. Then he hunted about until he found a couple of thin twigs about eighteen inches long and fairly straight.

"Will these do, Grandpa?" he asked.

"Yes, fine, Jimmie, lad," chuckled Grandpa.

Jimmie's next action was rather queer. Taking his pocket knife and some string from his pocket, he cut the string into a dozen pieces, each piece being about two inches long.

Then returning his knife to his pocket, he tied the ends of the pieces of string to the two twigs, leaving a space of about an inch between each piece.

When he had finished, he had got what looked for all the world like a roughly made little ladder with string rungs.

"How about that, Grandpa?" he asked.

"That's grand, Jimmie," chuckled Grandpa. "I'll manage that all right."

✣　✣　✣

Panicky Picnickers

RETURNING stealthily to the tree at the edge of the clearing, Jimmie took another look at the St. Claudites. They hadn't started in on the eats yet, but were sitting talking and laughing in their haw-haw voices.

Taking Grandpa from his pocket, Jimmie set him and the little ladder down on the ground behind the tree. Then with a whispered word to the little old man, Jimmie glided silently away amongst the trees until he reached the other side of the clearing.

He quickly cut four or five big turfs with his pocket knife. Then gathering the turfs up in one arm, he stepped boldly into view at the edge of the clearing.

"Hallo, swank-pots!" he jeered.

With the words, he hurled a couple of turfs at the startled St. Claudites, catching one of them a terrific smack full on the face and sending another's nice, shiny topper flying.

With howls of rage the St. Claudites leapt to their feet. As they did so, Jimmie hurled the rest of the turfs at them, catching one of them such a terrific smack on the mouth that it knocked him flat on his back on top of the expensive ices and jellies.

Then Jimmie turned and fled, with the raging pack of St. Claudites chasing madly after him, howling and yelling with fury.

The elegant young gent who had been knocked flat on his back, leapt to his feet with a yell of rage and joined in the pursuit, with the result that the clearing was left completely deserted.

"Good lad, Jimmie!" chuckled little old Grandpa, dodging from behind the tree with the little ladder

and scuttling forward with it to the nearest stone jar of ginger-pop.

Propping the little ladder against the neck of the jar, Grandpa ran swiftly up it. Then, whipping a tiny bottle from his pocket, he poured the contents into the ginger-pop.

Scuttling down the ladder, he picked it up and rushed with it to the second jar of ginger-pop. It was the work of a moment to prop the ladder against the neck of the jar and go scrambling up it.

Whipping another tiny little bottle from his pocket, Grandpa emptied the contents into the jar of ginger-pop. Then, going like lightning down the ladder, he picked it up and scuttled away with it amongst the trees.

He could hear the St. Claudites returning, and a few moments later they came marching back into the clearing, talking furiously.
"Beastly common cad!"
"What a pity he got away!"
"We wouldn't half have scragged the lout if we'd caught him!"

Feeling pretty hot and thirsty after their fruitless chase, they filled their glasses with ginger-pop from the two stone jars and the whole bunch of them started to gulp it down.

As they did so an amazing thing happened. For, to their horror, they started to shrink and shrink with lightning-like speed until the whole bunch of them were just tiny little figures less than six inches tall.

What was more, their posh silk toppers and elegant suits had shrunk with them. For the stuff which Grandpa had poured into the ginger-pop was his wonderful liquid for making people little, and part of its marvellous power was to make people's clothes little as well.

"What's happened?" howled the St. Claudites, staring at each other in pop-eyed fright and astonishment. "Oh, dear, what's the matter? We've all gone little!"

Their voices were as strong as ever they had been, for although the wonderful liquid made people little, it didn't alter their voices.

"Oh, dear, this is awful!" howled the terrified St. Claudites, running round and round in frantic circles, so great was their panic. "What can have happened? It must have been that ginger-pop! Oh, what are we going to do – what are we going to do?"

Jimmie, who had slipped silently back to

84

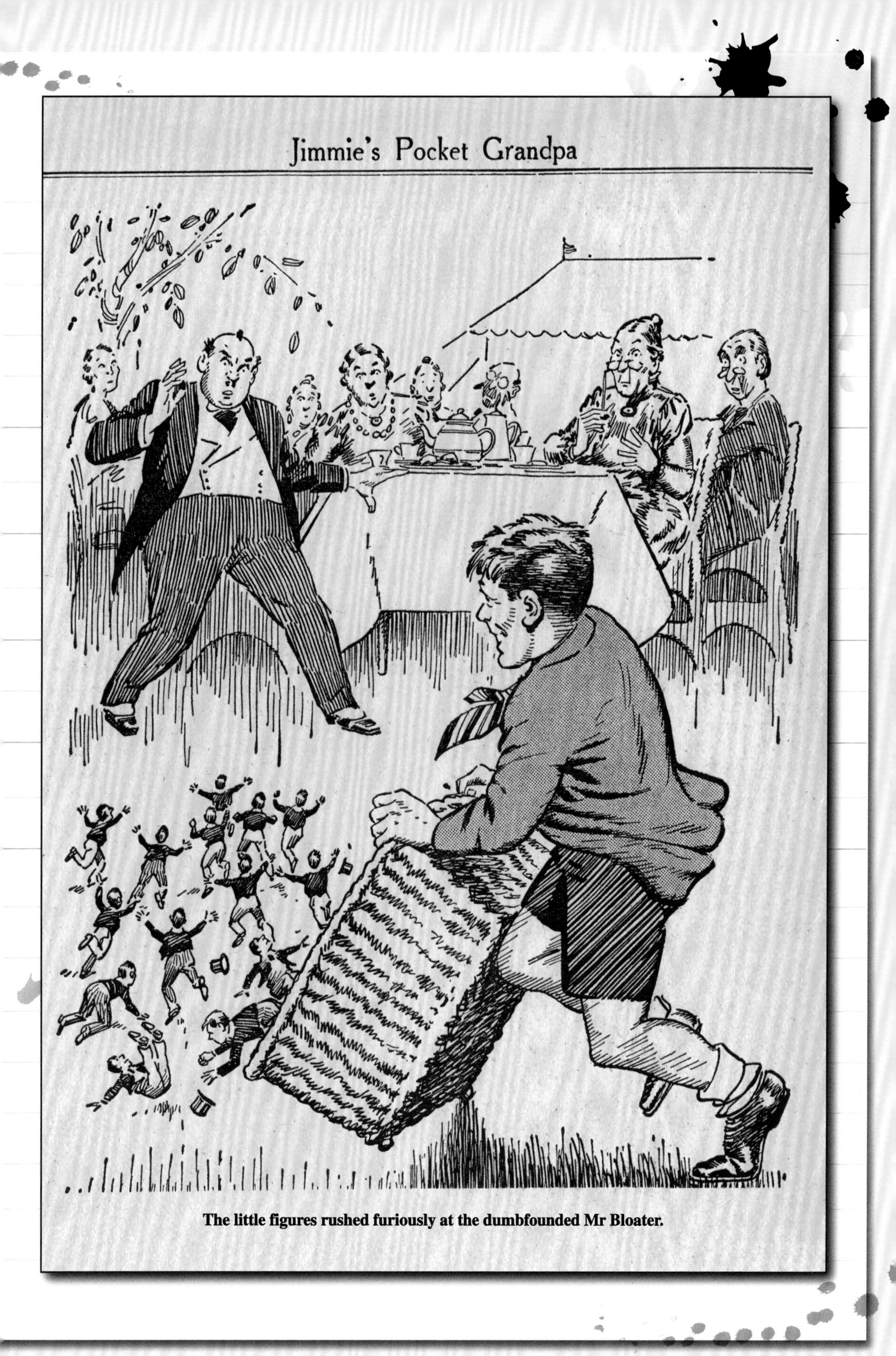

The little figures rushed furiously at the dumbfounded Mr Bloater.

the clearing, was watching the extraordinary scene from behind a tree.

"Good old Grandpa!" he chuckled. "He hasn't half fixed the cocky blighters. They're not feeling so cocky now, I bet!"

This was perfectly true, for so frightened were the tiny little St. Claudites at the strange and dreadful fate which had over taken them, that half-a-dozen or more had burst into tears.

"Boo-hoo-hoo-oo!" they bellowed. "Oh, why did we ever c-c-come on this nasty picnic? Boo-hoo-hoo-oo!"

Then suddenly another strange thing happened. For a voice cried:

"Poor little fellows. Has that wicked old wizard made you little as well as me?"

And into the clearing trotted the tiny little figure of Jimmie's grandpa.

⚜   ⚜   ⚜

The Magic Brew

THE little St. Claudites stared at Grandpa as though they couldn't believe their eyes. Then with one accord they made a rush at him, crying:

"Who are you? Oh, do tell us how we've been made little. Oh, do tell us what's happened. You're little like us, so you must know. Oh, do tell us all about it!"

"Steady, steady, lads!" cried Grandpa, who had nearly been swept off his feet by the rush. "Poor, little fellows. I'm sorry for you. That wicked wizard ought to be hanged!"

"What wizard?" howled the terrified St. Claudites. "Do you mean we've been made little by a wizard?"

"You have indeed," said little old Grandpa, shaking his head. "You've fallen under his cruel spell, the same as I have!"

"But who is he?" cried the St. Claudites. "Who is this wicked old wizard?"

"Why, old Bloater, of course," said Grandpa.

At this astonishing piece of information, the little St. Claudites gaped in open-mouthed amazement at Grandpa.

"Yes, it's a queer story," went on Grandpa, shaking his head. "Seeing him walking about you'd never think he was a wizard. But he is. His name's not Bloater at all. It's Enni Mor Hashma

and he's thousands of year old. Going around as a big, fat man called Bloater is just one of his disguises!"

"What?" gasped his startled hearers.

"Yes," went on Grandpa, enjoying himself hugely. "He can change himself into anything he likes – a bird or an animal or anything. Once upon a time, hundreds and hundreds of years ago, he used to change himself into a great big fiery dragon and go about breathing smoke and flame. Oh, he's a wicked old rascal, is Enni Mor Hashma. I ought to know; I used to be his servant!"

"Did you?" gasped his hearers, scarcely able to believe their own silly ears.

"Oh, yes," said Grandpa. "I was a grand big blacksmith slave and as strong as an ox. But one day I upset a very special magic brew that Enni Mor Hashma was making, and, in his rage, he changed me into the poor, miserable little man that you see now."

"But why should he make us little?" howled the St. Claudites.

"Because he hates boys," said Grandpa. "With an oily smile and cunning words he lures them into his woods or castle – he used to have a castle in the olden days, you know – and then he either makes them little or else changes them into mice or lizards or bow-legged grass-hoppers or something like that."

"But are we to stay little like this for ever?" wailed his hearers in terror.

"I'm afraid so," said Grandpa. Then he pretended to give a sudden start and cried excitedly! "Wait a minute, though. How many of you has he made little?"

"Twenty of us!" cried the St. Claudites. "There's twenty of us here!"

"That's the magic number!" cried Grandpa, more excitedly than ever. "That's the magic number that will break the spell. Listen, if twenty of his victims all tackle Enni Mor Hashma at the same moment and sing this song the spell will be broken."

Lifting his voice, Grandpa warbled:

"Okey, dokey, hiddle-dy hi,
 A cunning old wizard we all of us spy;
 Change us to big, you wicked old man,
 Change us to big as quick as you can!"

"Get along up to his house and all of you sing that song to him together, and he'll be forced to produce the magic brew that will make you big again!" cried Grandpa. "The whole twenty of you must do it, mind, because twenty is the magic number that breaks the spell!"

"But how are we going to reach his house when we're little like this?" cried the St. Claudites in despair.

"I'll take you," said a voice.

The little St. Claudites spun round. Standing grinning down at them was Jimmie, who had come silently up behind them.

"I've heard every word," went on Jimmie, "and I just say it's been a proper shock to me. I didn't think there were any such things as wizards these days. It just shows you, doesn't it! Anyway, I'll forgive you for chasing me and I'll take you to this wicked old wizard's den – or, rather, his house."

"Will you?" cried his hearers eagerly. "Oh, how sporting of you. But how will you take twenty of us?"

"Easy," grinned Jimmie. "I'll take you in one of your picnic hampers!"

⁂ ⁂ ⁂

A Basketful of Boys

MR BLOATER was giving a tea party that afternoon. He had managed to get a lot of the richest people in the neighbourhood to come to tea, and he was standing them a spread on the lawn in front of the house.

Suddenly he scowled, for a boy was striding across the lawn towards him with a hamper on his back.

"The tradesmen's entrance is round the back," snapped Mr Bloater.

"I don't want the tradesmen's entrance," replied the boy, who was none other than Jimmie, of course. "These are for you!"

With the words, Jimmie tilted the hamper and out on to the lawn tumbled twenty elegantly dressed little figures wearing tiny silk toppers.

With cries of astonishment and alarm, Mr Bloater's posh guests leapt to their feet and stared goggle-eyed, as, picking themselves up, the twenty little figures rushed furiously at the dumfounded Mr Bloater, screaming:

"Okey, dokey, hiddle-dy hi,
A cunning old wizard we all of us spy;
Change us to big, you wicked old man,

Change us to big as quick as you can!"

Mr Bloater leapt back, his eyes nearly popping out of his head.

"What the – who the dickens are you and where have you come from?" he gasped.

"You know who we are," screamed the little St. Claudites. "And we know who you are, too. You're Enni Mor Hashma, the wicked old wizard. You lured us into your nasty wood today and made us all little. So make us big again at once, you wicked old monster. Give us the magic brew that'll make us big again!"

"Here it is!" cried Jimmie, darting forward and pretending to snatch out of thin air a bottle of liquid which he had had hidden up his sleeve. "Look, it says on the label:

"If once more you would be big,
Of this brew just take a swig!"

"Hurrah!" screamed the little St. Claudites, capering madly with delight. "Give us some – give us some!"

The bottle was full of Grandpa's wonderful liquid for making people big again. As Jimmie gave each of the St. Claudites a dose, the tiny little figures grew and grew with lightning-like swiftness until they were their proper size again.

Then, scared stiff in case the wizard might change them into something else, the whole bunch of them took to their heels and rushed away as fast as their legs could carry them.

Of course, the whole amazing story was all over the place in no time. In vain Mr Bloater raged and raved, swearing that he wasn't a wizard at all and that he'd have the law on anybody who said he was.

The posh guests at his tea party had seen the tiny little St. Claudites with their very own eyes. They were quite certain that there was something very, very queer indeed about Mr Bloater, and they and their friends and everybody else gave that raging gent such a very wide berth that at length he sold his house in disgust, and went to live in another part of the country altogether.

This pleased everybody very much, particularly the small boys whom he had barred from his woods.

"I told you I'd fix him, Jimmie, lad," chuckled jolly old Grandpa. "It's brains that count, not size!"

"You're telling me," said Jimmie with a grin.

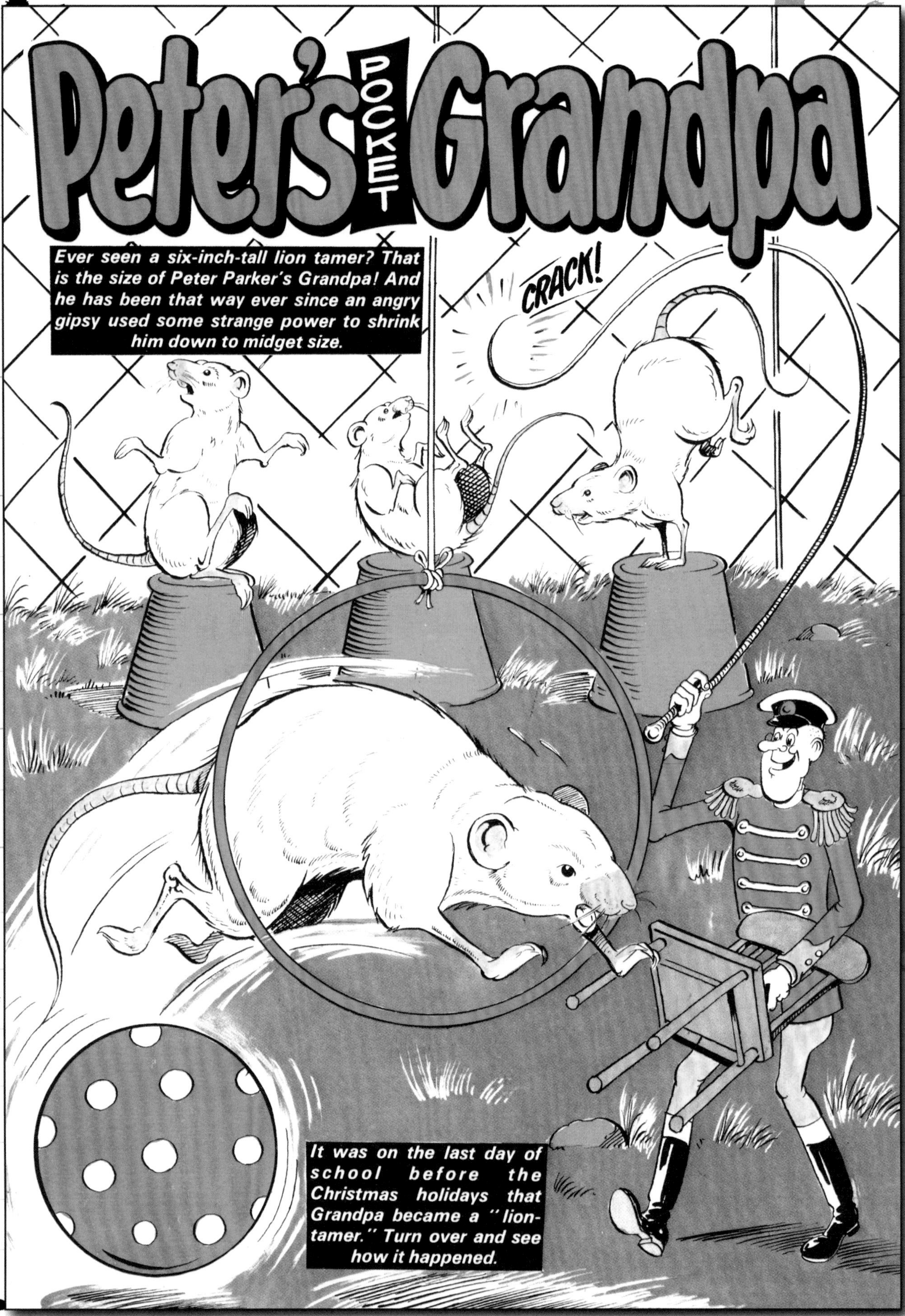

Peter's POCKET Grandpa
Ever seen a six-inch-tall lion tamer? That is the size of Peter Parker's Grandpa! And he has been that way ever since an angry gipsy used some strange power to shrink him down to midget size.
CRACK!
It was on the last day of school before the Christmas holidays that Grandpa became a "lion-tamer." Turn over and see how it happened.

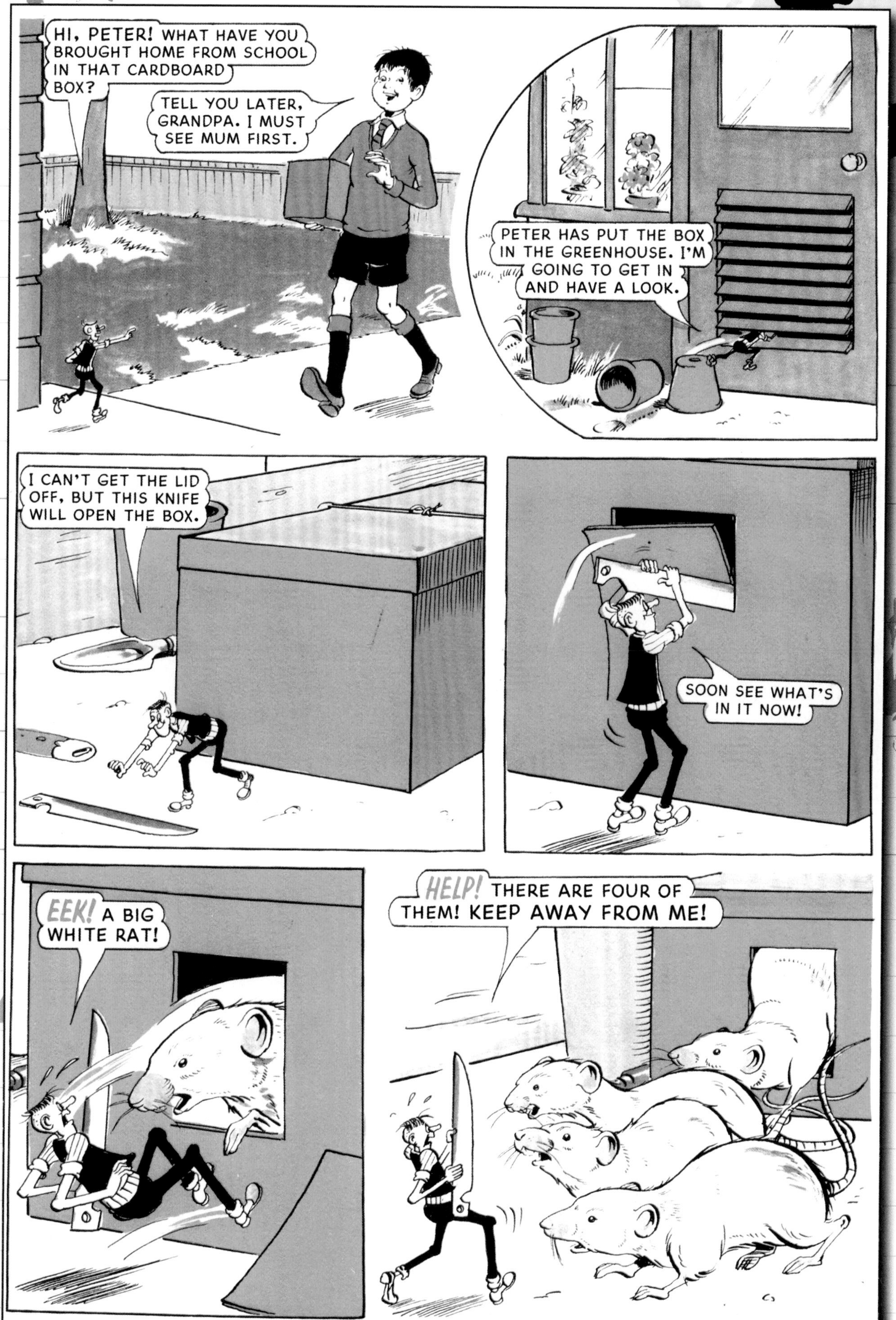
HI, PETER! WHAT HAVE YOU BROUGHT HOME FROM SCHOOL IN THAT CARDBOARD BOX?
TELL YOU LATER, GRANDPA. I MUST SEE MUM FIRST.
PETER HAS PUT THE BOX IN THE GREENHOUSE. I'M GOING TO GET IN AND HAVE A LOOK.
I CAN'T GET THE LID OFF, BUT THIS KNIFE WILL OPEN THE BOX.
SOON SEE WHAT'S IN IT NOW!
EEK! A BIG WHITE RAT!
HELP! THERE ARE FOUR OF THEM! KEEP AWAY FROM ME!

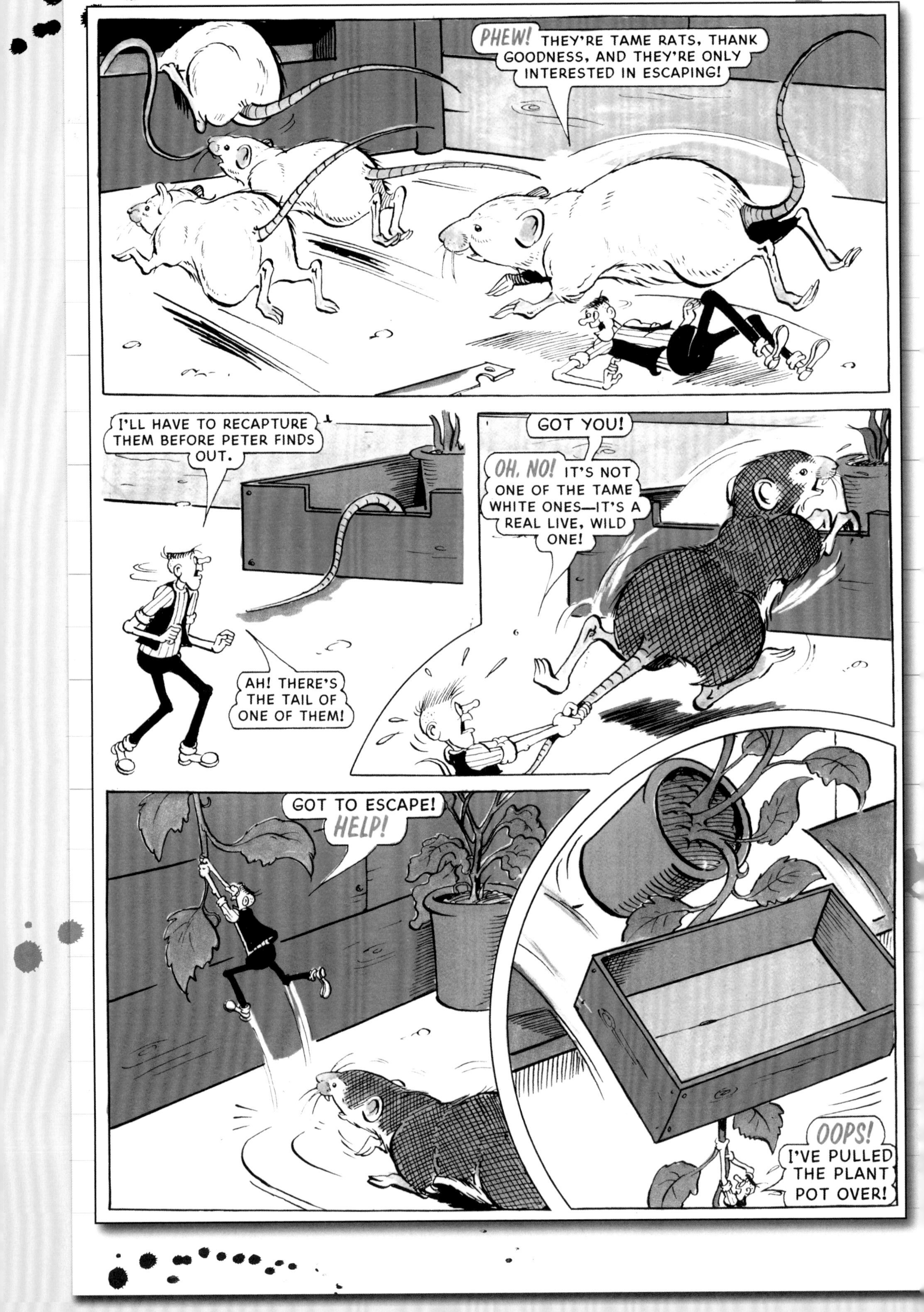
PHEW! THEY'RE TAME RATS, THANK GOODNESS, AND THEY'RE ONLY INTERESTED IN ESCAPING!
I'LL HAVE TO RECAPTURE THEM BEFORE PETER FINDS OUT.
AH! THERE'S THE TAIL OF ONE OF THEM!
GOT YOU!
OH, NO! IT'S NOT ONE OF THE TAME WHITE ONES—IT'S A REAL LIVE, WILD ONE!
GOT TO ESCAPE! HELP!
OOPS! I'VE PULLED THE PLANT POT OVER!

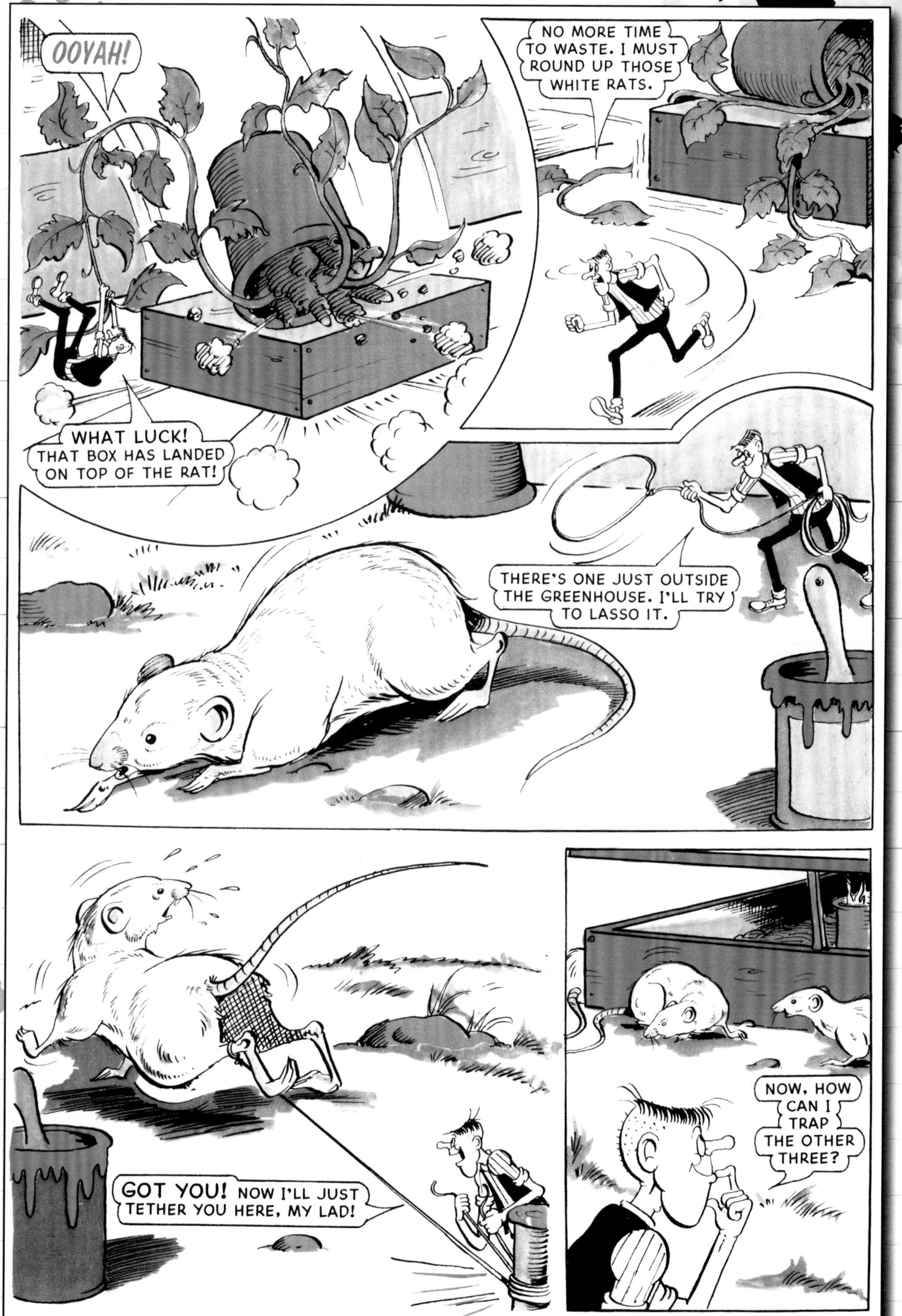
OOYAH!
WHAT LUCK! THAT BOX HAS LANDED ON TOP OF THE RAT!
NO MORE TIME TO WASTE. I MUST ROUND UP THOSE WHITE RATS.
THERE'S ONE JUST OUTSIDE THE GREENHOUSE. I'LL TRY TO LASSO IT.
GOT YOU! NOW I'LL JUST TETHER YOU HERE, MY LAD!
NOW, HOW CAN I TRAP THE OTHER THREE?

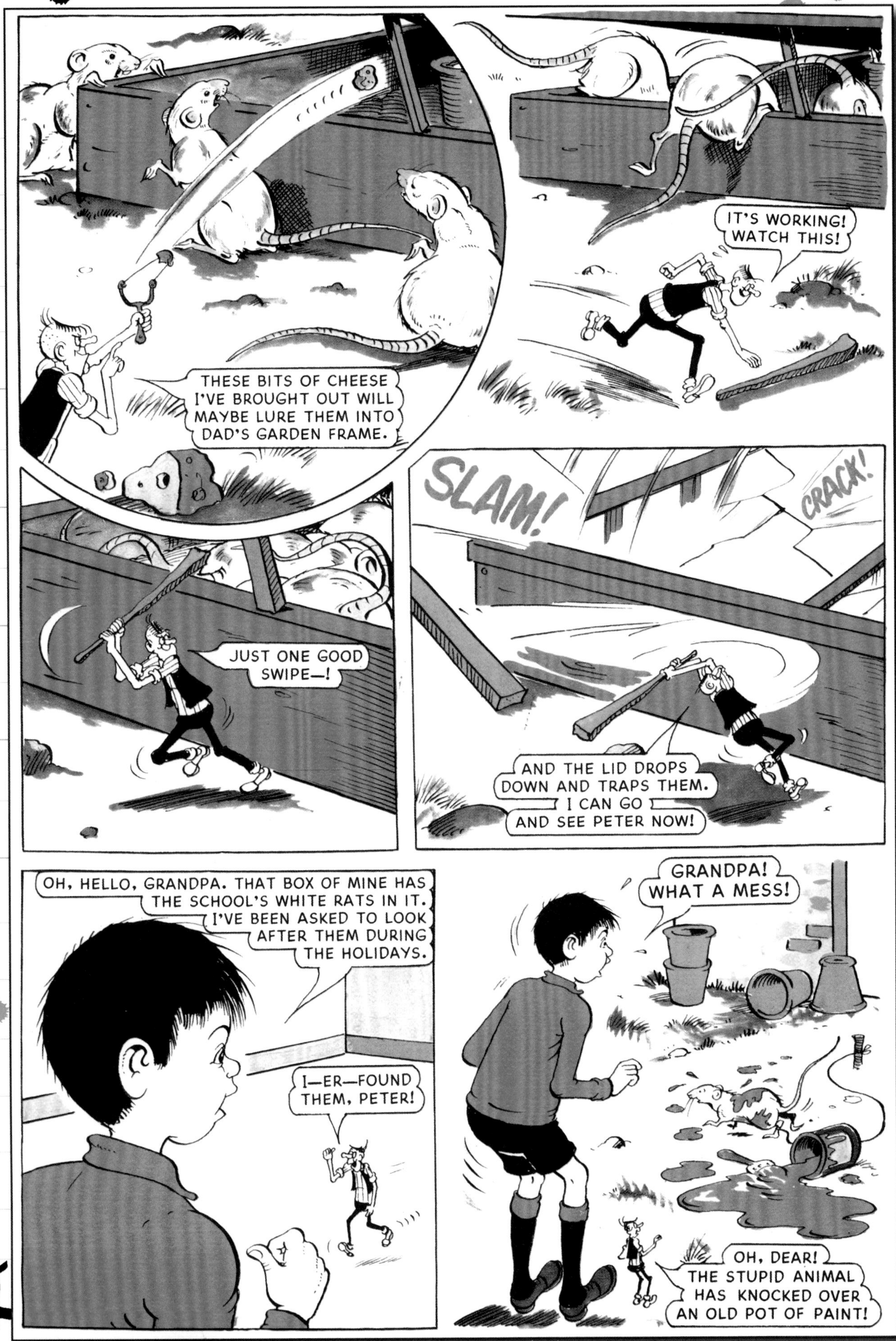
THESE BITS OF CHEESE I'VE BROUGHT OUT WILL MAYBE LURE THEM INTO DAD'S GARDEN FRAME.
IT'S WORKING! WATCH THIS!
JUST ONE GOOD SWIPE—!
SLAM!
CRACK!
AND THE LID DROPS DOWN AND TRAPS THEM. I CAN GO AND SEE PETER NOW!
OH, HELLO, GRANDPA. THAT BOX OF MINE HAS THE SCHOOL'S WHITE RATS IN IT. I'VE BEEN ASKED TO LOOK AFTER THEM DURING THE HOLIDAYS.
I—ER—FOUND THEM, PETER!
GRANDPA! WHAT A MESS!
OH, DEAR! THE STUPID ANIMAL HAS KNOCKED OVER AN OLD POT OF PAINT!

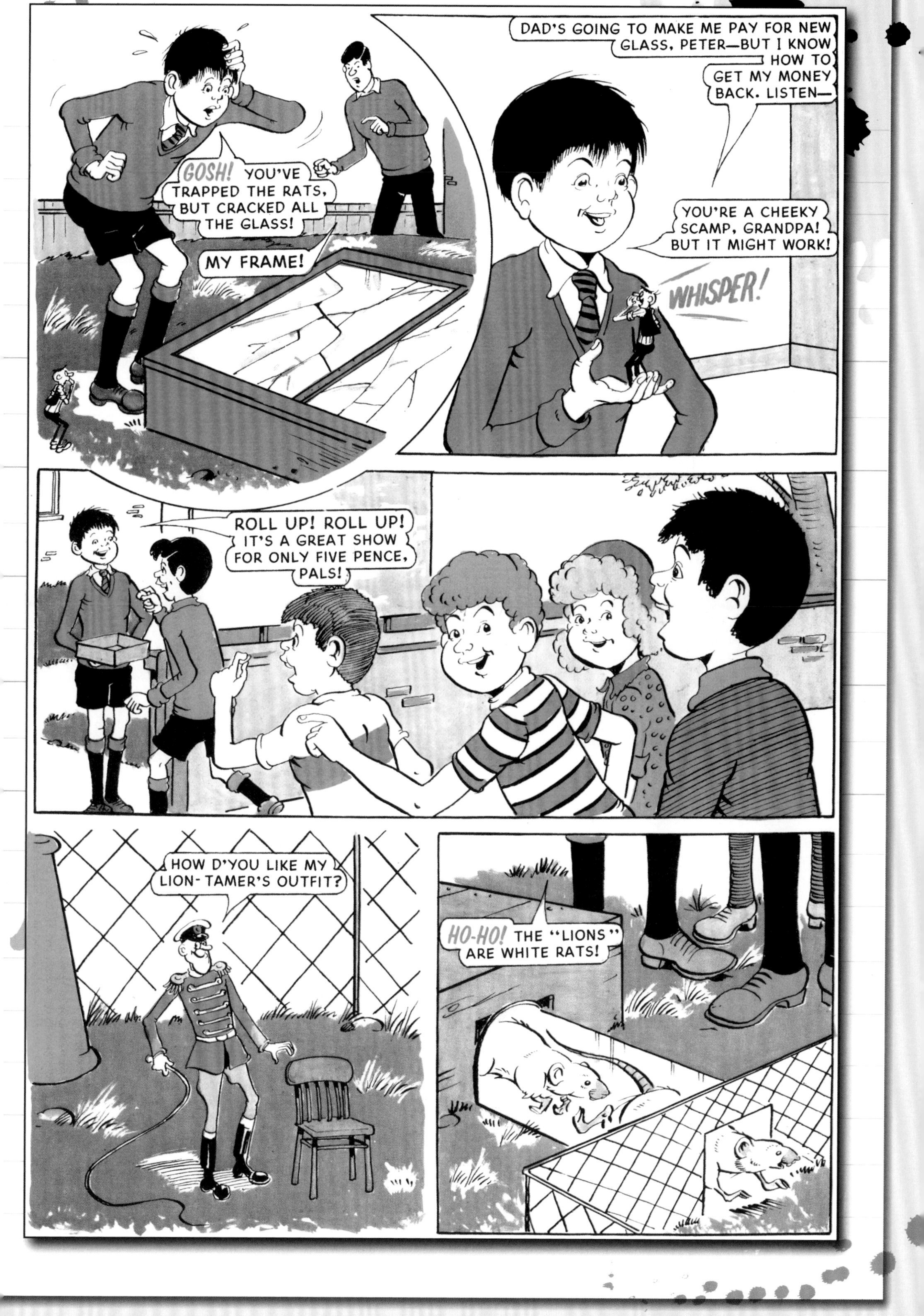
GOSH! YOU'VE TRAPPED THE RATS, BUT CRACKED ALL THE GLASS!
MY FRAME!
DAD'S GOING TO MAKE ME PAY FOR NEW GLASS, PETER—BUT I KNOW HOW TO GET MY MONEY BACK. LISTEN—
YOU'RE A CHEEKY SCAMP, GRANDPA! BUT IT MIGHT WORK!
WHISPER!
ROLL UP! ROLL UP! IT'S A GREAT SHOW FOR ONLY FIVE PENCE, PALS!
HOW D'YOU LIKE MY LION-TAMER'S OUTFIT?
HO-HO! THE "LIONS" ARE WHITE RATS!

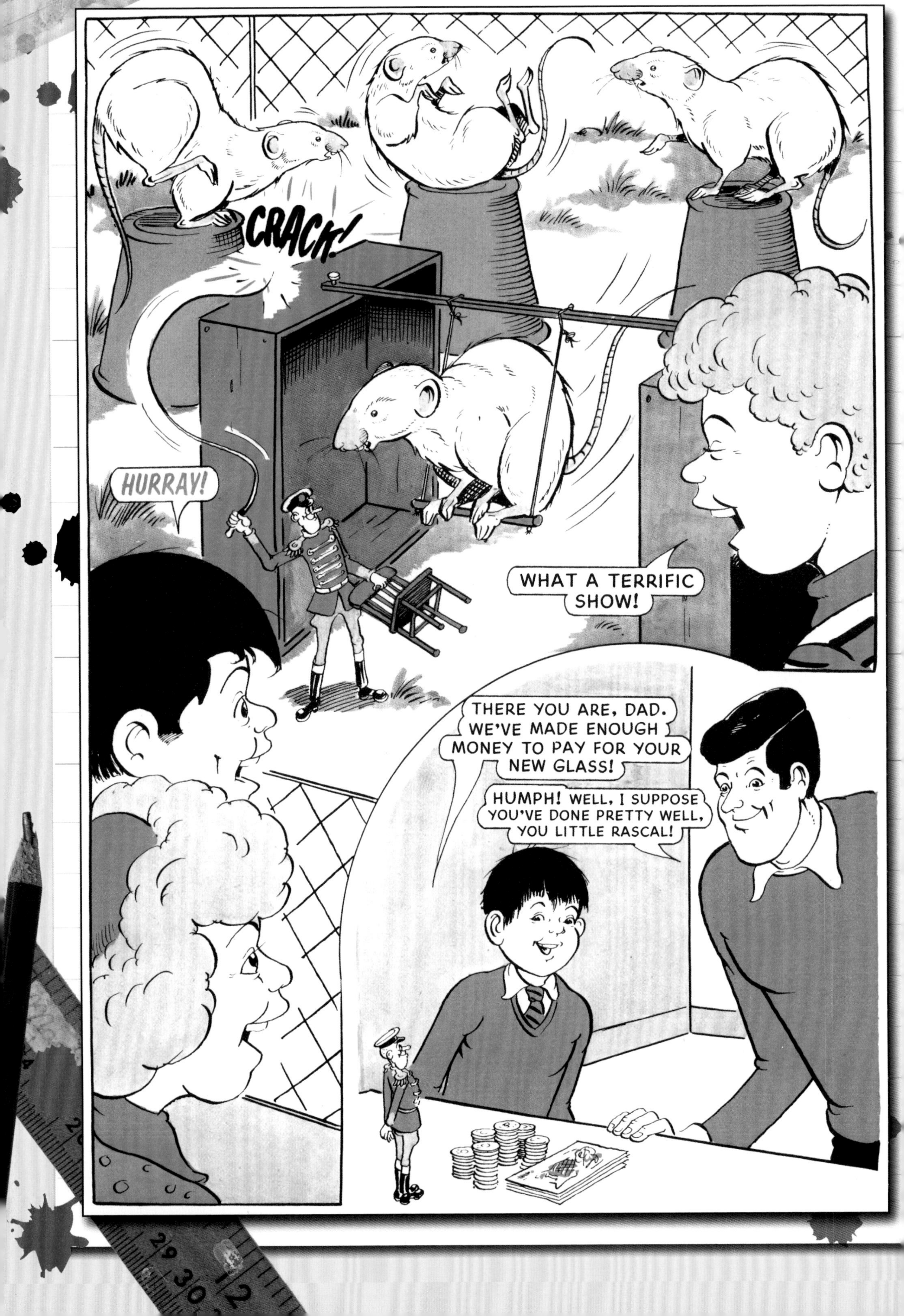
CRACK!
HURRAY!
WHAT A TERRIFIC SHOW!
THERE YOU ARE, DAD. WE'VE MADE ENOUGH MONEY TO PAY FOR YOUR NEW GLASS!
HUMPH! WELL, I SUPPOSE YOU'VE DONE PRETTY WELL, YOU LITTLE RASCAL!

The eat-anything Ostrich is made to pay in the END!! (sorry).

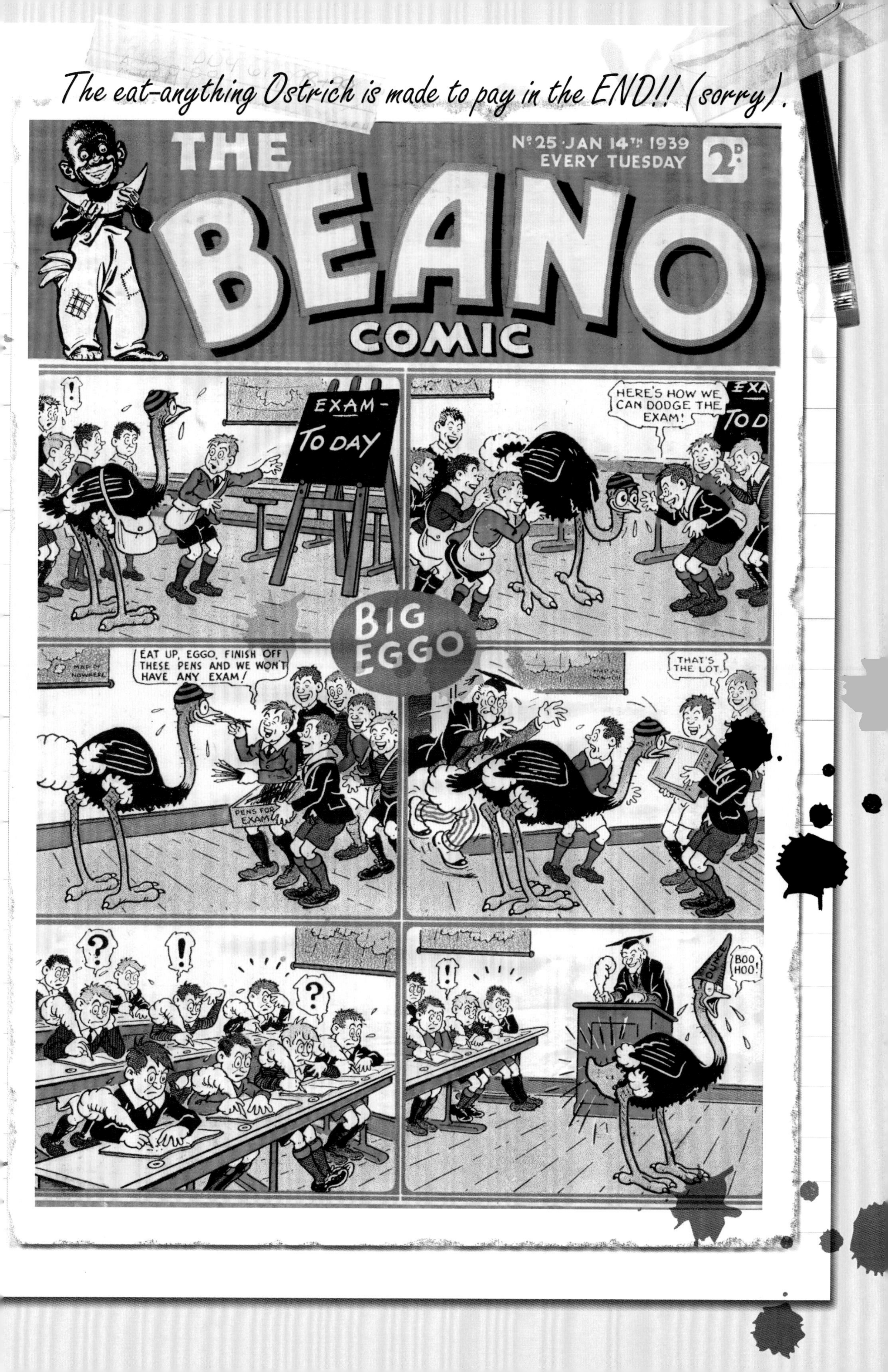
THE BEANO COMIC
Nº 25 · JAN 14TH 1939
EVERY TUESDAY
2D
EXAM — TO DAY
HERE'S HOW WE CAN DODGE THE EXAM!
BIG EGGO
EAT UP, EGGO, FINISH OFF THESE PENS AND WE WON'T HAVE ANY EXAM!
PENS FOR EXAM
THAT'S THE LOT.
DUNCE
BOO HOO!

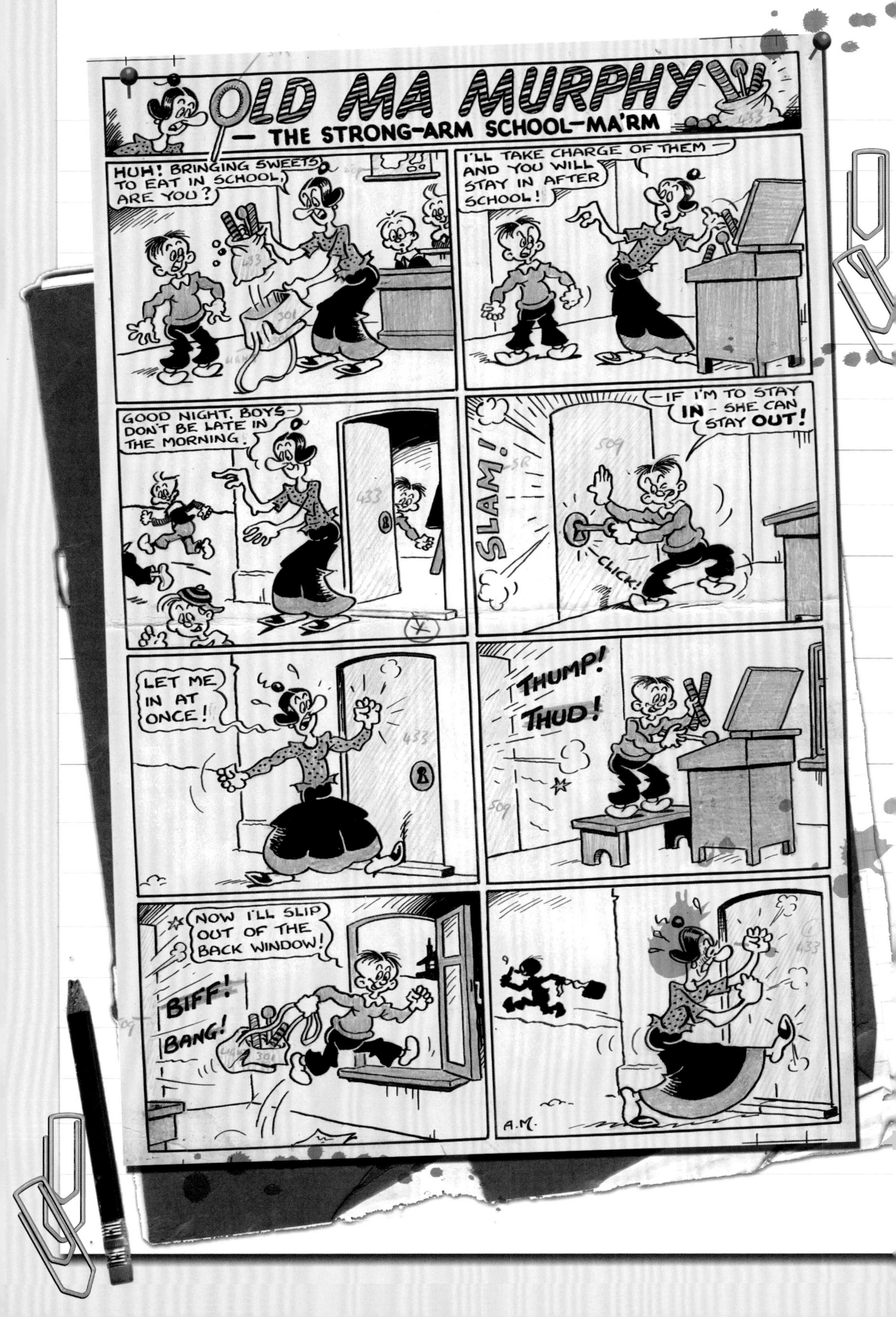
OLD MA MURPHY
— THE STRONG-ARM SCHOOL-MA'RM
HUH! BRINGING SWEETS TO EAT IN SCHOOL, ARE YOU?
I'LL TAKE CHARGE OF THEM — AND YOU WILL STAY IN AFTER SCHOOL!
GOOD NIGHT, BOYS — DON'T BE LATE IN THE MORNING.
— IF I'M TO STAY IN — SHE CAN STAY OUT!
SLAM!
CLICK!
LET ME IN AT ONCE!
THUMP!
THUD!
NOW I'LL SLIP OUT OF THE BACK WINDOW!
BIFF!
BANG!
A.M.

Going by looks Ma Murphy and Miss Prim are family. Both from the pen of Alan Morley, who initialled most of his stylised sets.

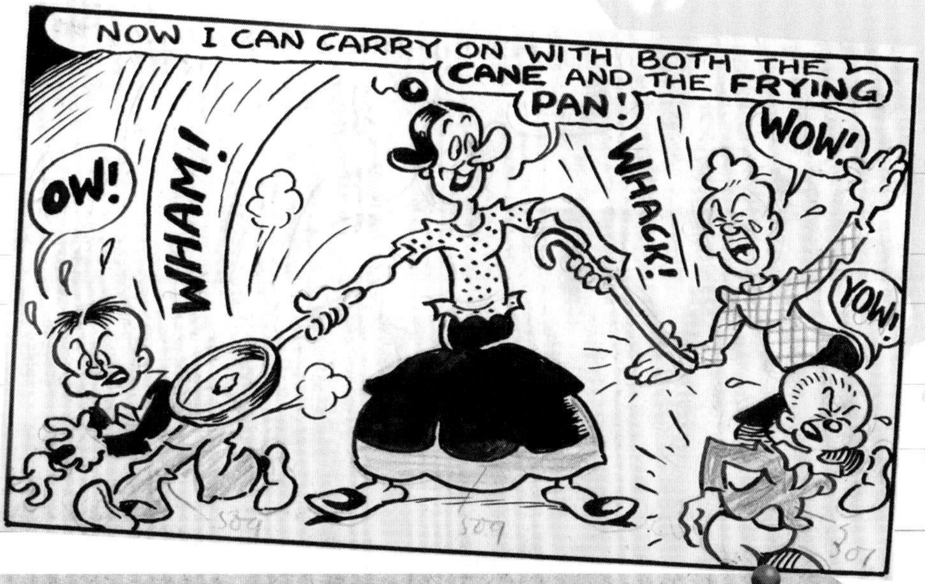
NOW I CAN CARRY ON WITH BOTH THE CANE AND THE FRYING PAN!
OW!
WHAM!
WHACK!
WOW!
YOW!

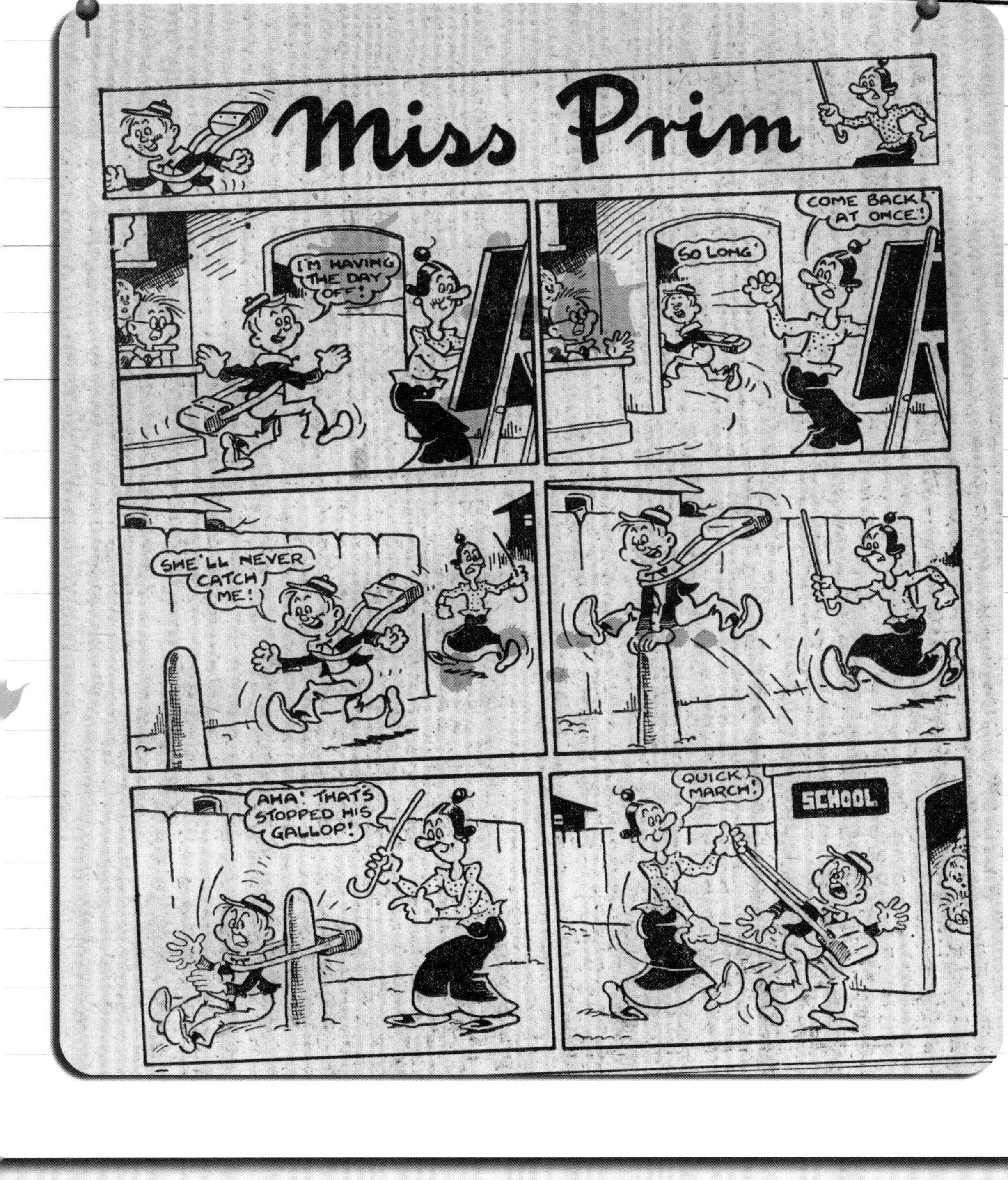
Miss Prim
I'M HAVING THE DAY OFF!
COME BACK AT ONCE!
SO LONG!
SHE'LL NEVER CATCH ME!
AHA! THAT'S STOPPED HIS GALLOP!
QUICK MARCH!
SCHOOL

Nosiest schoolgirl in the land, Keyhole Kate.

A brilliant title and another strong-arm teacher. No problem with classroom discipline in Beano Book 1941.

TOUGH NELLIE DUFF

THE STRONG-ARM SCHOOLMA-AM

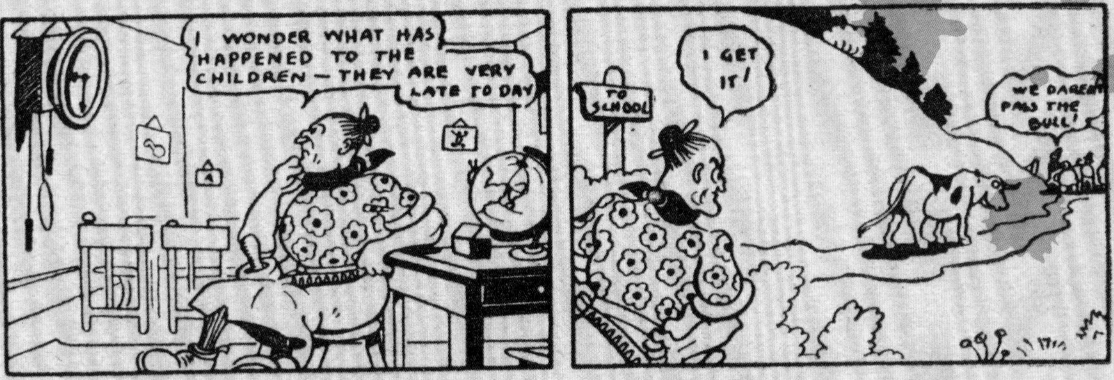
I WONDER WHAT HAS HAPPENED TO THE CHILDREN — THEY ARE VERY LATE TO DAY
TO SCHOOL
I GET IT!
WE DAREN'T PASS THE BULL!

Thoughtful Nellie strokes her chin.
" Time these children were all in."

Children daren't pass the bull,
So they cannot get to school.

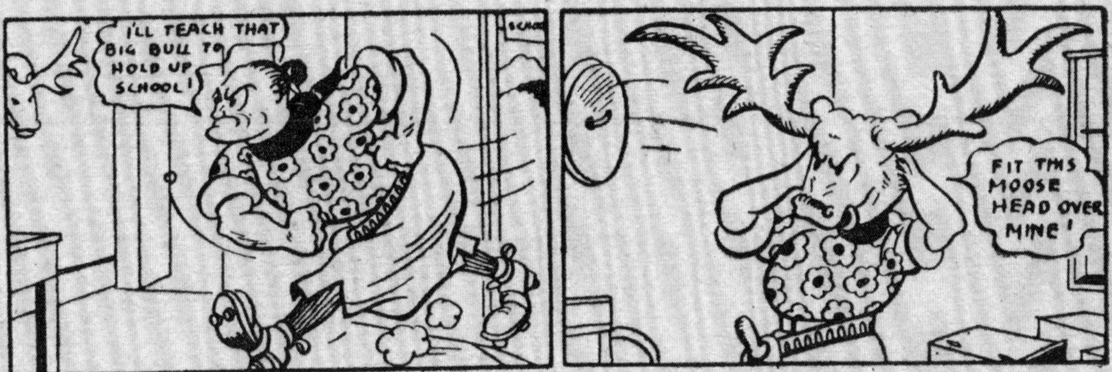
I'LL TEACH THAT BIG BULL TO HOLD UP SCHOOL!
FIT THIS MOOSE HEAD OVER MINE!

Nellie's anger knows no limit.
Bull will tremble in a minute.

" This moose head will do me fine.
I shall fit it over mine ! "

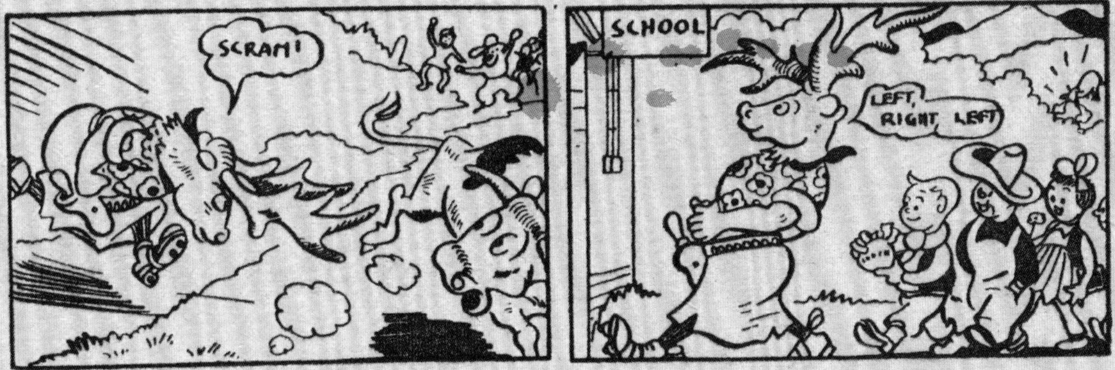
SCRAM!
SCHOOL
LEFT, RIGHT, LEFT

Bull is scared at fearsome creature,
Though it's only angry teacher.

" Left, right, left "—the danger's past.
Children get to school at last.

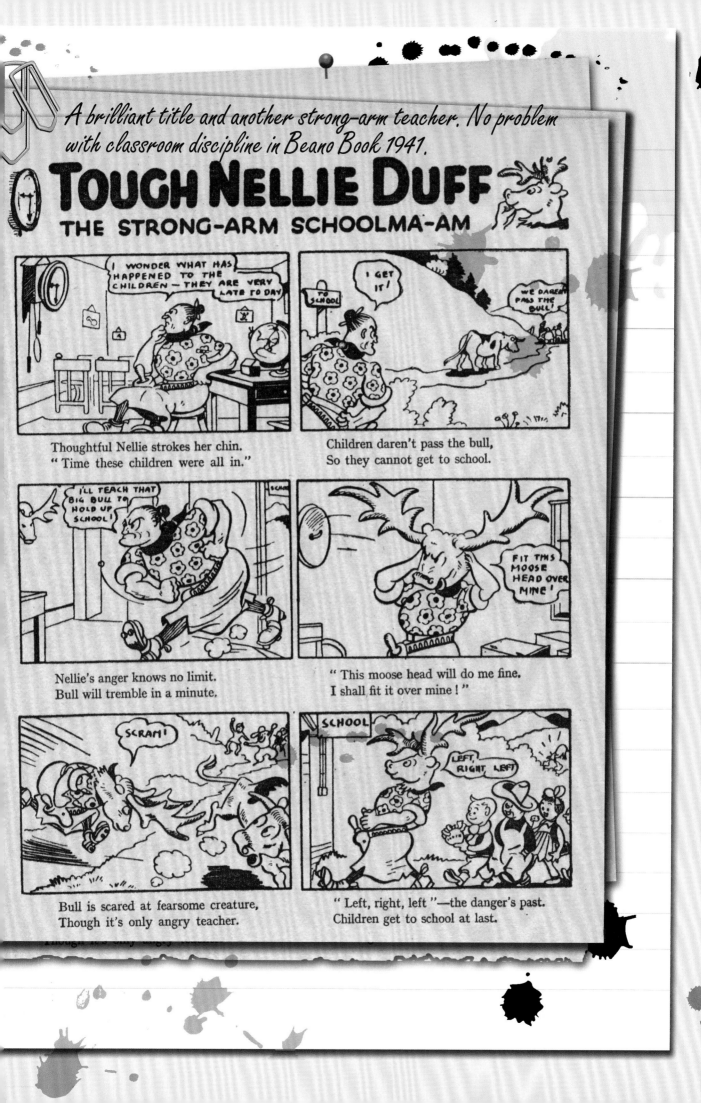

Another Miss Prim, another tough teacher. In the best Dandy tradition

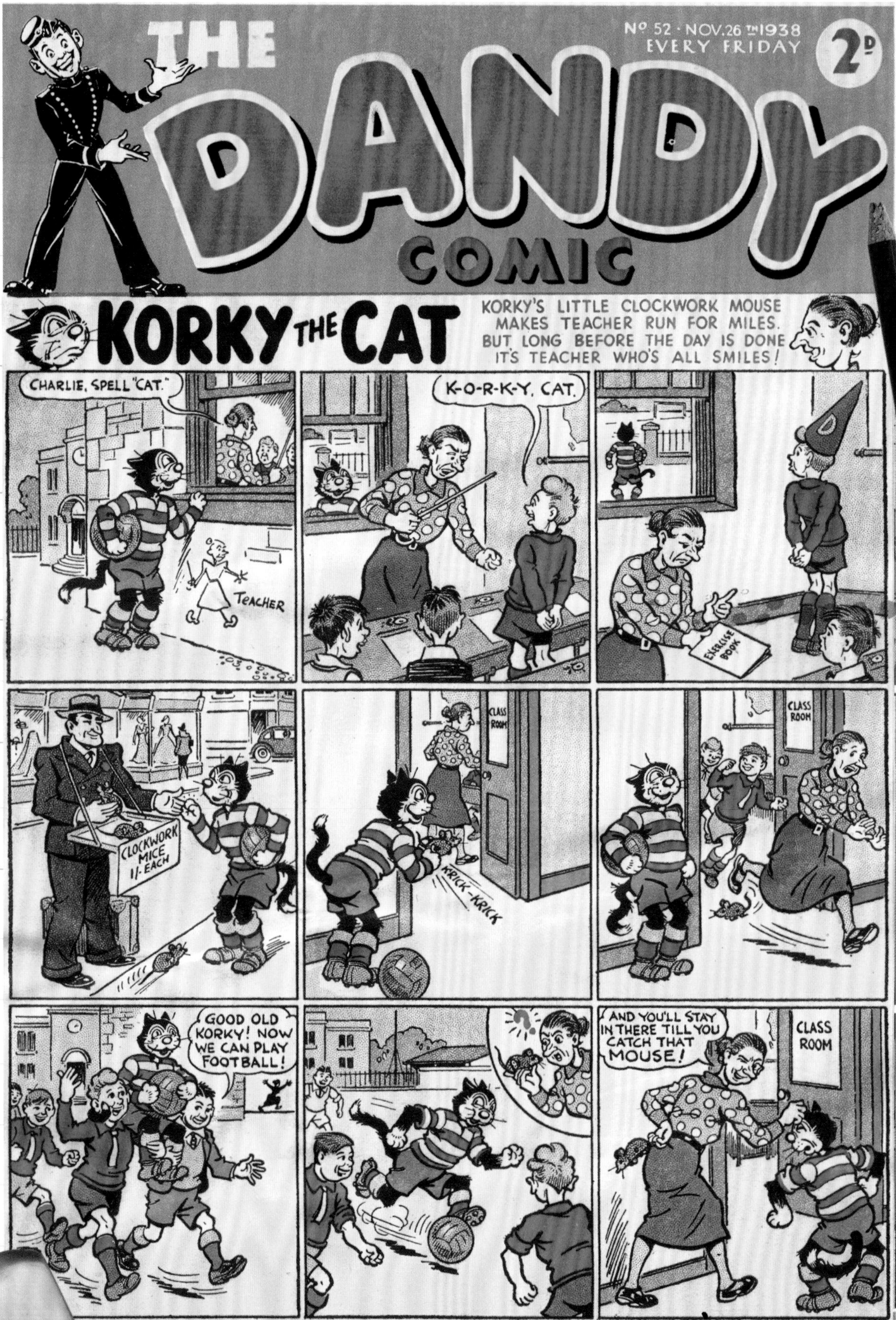
THE DANDY COMIC
No 52 · NOV. 26th 1938
EVERY FRIDAY
2d
KORKY THE CAT
KORKY'S LITTLE CLOCKWORK MOUSE MAKES TEACHER RUN FOR MILES. BUT LONG BEFORE THE DAY IS DONE IT'S TEACHER WHO'S ALL SMILES!
CHARLIE, SPELL "CAT."
TEACHER
K-O-R-K-Y, CAT.
EXERCISE BOOK
CLOCKWORK MICE 1/- EACH
CLASS ROOM
KRICK-KRICK
CLASS ROOM
GOOD OLD KORKY! NOW WE CAN PLAY FOOTBALL!
AND YOU'LL STAY IN THERE TILL YOU CATCH THAT MOUSE!
CLASS ROOM

she pays no attention to the fact there **is a goat in her classroom!**

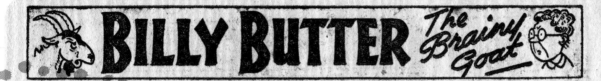

BILLY BUTTER
The Brainy Goat

HERE YOU ARE—HAVE A SWEET, BILLY.
AH! EATING SWEETS IN CLASS, EH?
I'LL TAKE CHARGE OF THESE, MY LAD.

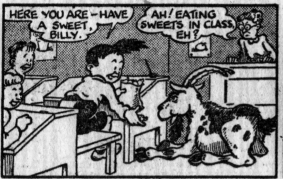

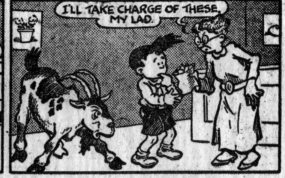

Billy was in school with Pete,
Who offered him a lovely sweet.
But teacher spied them, and, alas,
She said, "Ah! Eating sweets in class!"

The teacher wasn't pleased, so she
Said, "Bring that bag right up to me."
She took the sweets, and Billy Goat
Looked far from pleased, as you will note.

I'LL JUST PUT THEM AWAY IN MY HANDBAG WHERE NOBODY WILL BE TEMPTED BY THEM.
AND NOW THIS WILL TEACH YOU NOT TO EAT IN SCHOOL.
WOW!

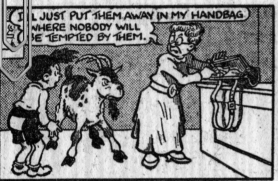

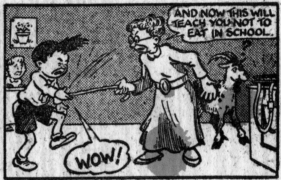

Said teacher, "I'll put them away
Inside my handbag for to-day,
Then no one will be tempted to
Eat them if they're in there, it's true."

Miss Prim said, "Now you know, my lad,
To eat in school is very bad."
While teacher caned Pete, Billy thought
He'd eat the sweets—yes, all the lot.

GOODNESS GRACIOUS! WHAT'S GOING ON HERE?
CRUNCH! CRUNCH!
OOOH! MY HANDBAG!
TEE-HEE! SHE CAN'T STOP BILLY EATING SWEETS IN SCHOOL!

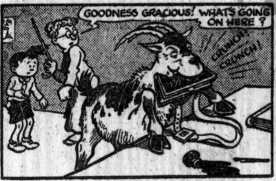

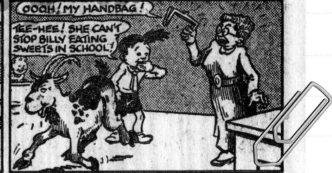

Then suddenly the teacher spied
Young Billy. "Goodness me!" she cried.
"What is he doing over there?
He's got my handbag, I declare."

Miss Prim was really very mad,
Her handbag now looked rather sad.
"Tee-hee!" laughed Bill. "She can't stop me
From eating sweets in school, you see."

Beanotown school did not seem to think it odd that a bear attended class.

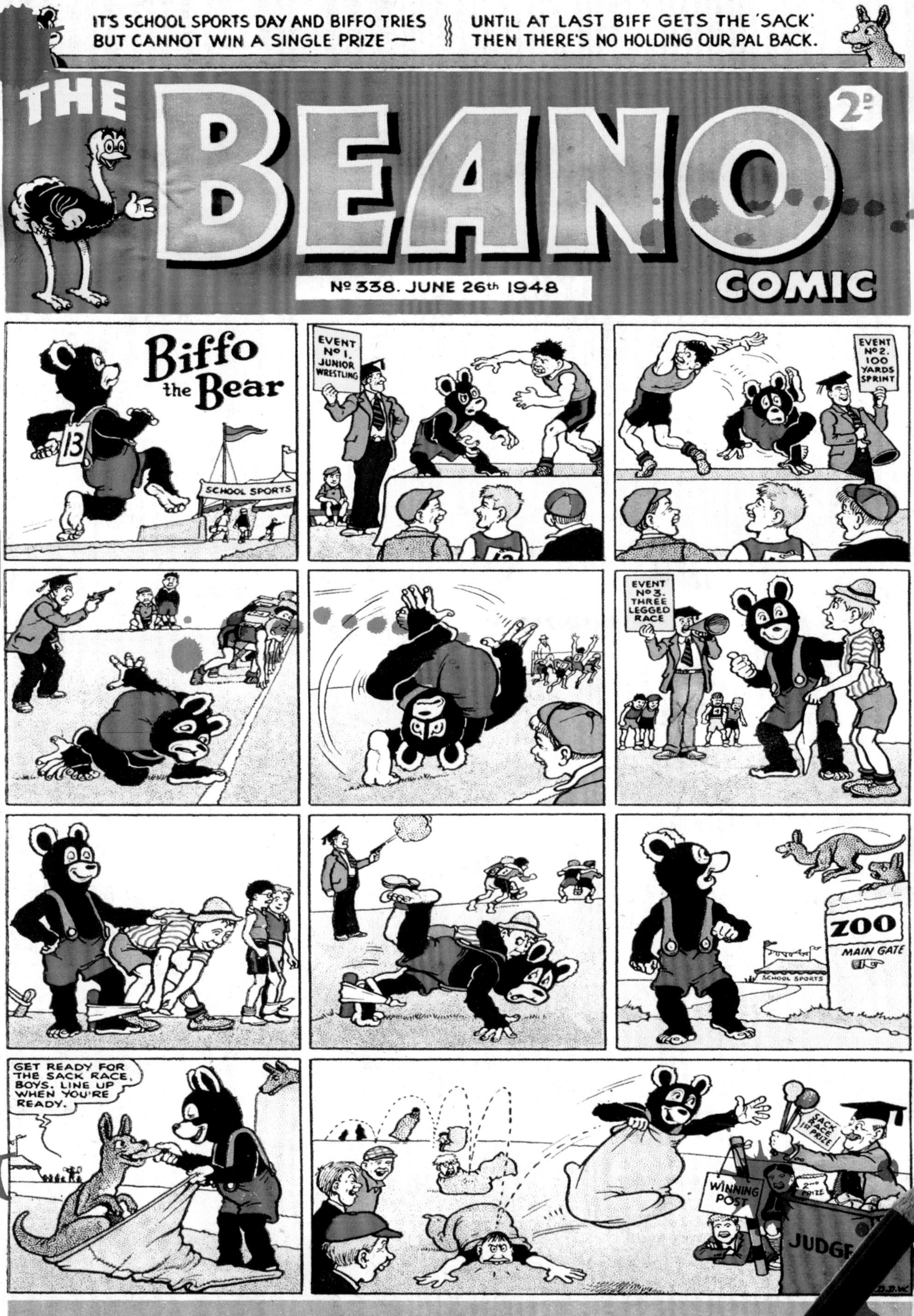
IT'S SCHOOL SPORTS DAY AND BIFFO TRIES BUT CANNOT WIN A SINGLE PRIZE —
UNTIL AT LAST BIFF GETS THE 'SACK' THEN THERE'S NO HOLDING OUR PAL BACK.
THE BEANO
2D
Nº 338. JUNE 26th 1948
COMIC
Biffo the Bear
13
SCHOOL SPORTS
EVENT Nº 1. JUNIOR WRESTLING
EVENT Nº 2. 100 YARDS SPRINT
EVENT Nº 3. THREE LEGGED RACE
ZOO
MAIN GATE
SCHOOL SPORTS
GET READY FOR THE SACK RACE, BOYS. LINE UP WHEN YOU'RE READY.
SACK RACE 1ST PRIZE
2ND PRIZE
WINNING POST
JUDGE

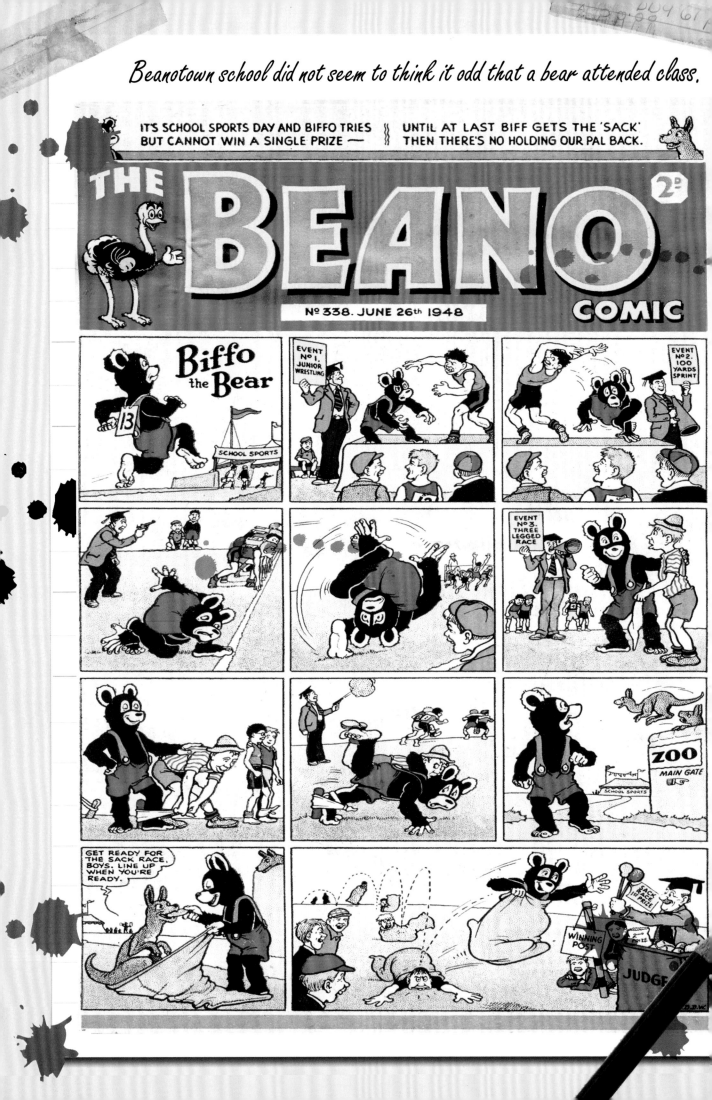

A number of excellent strips are based around the local school.

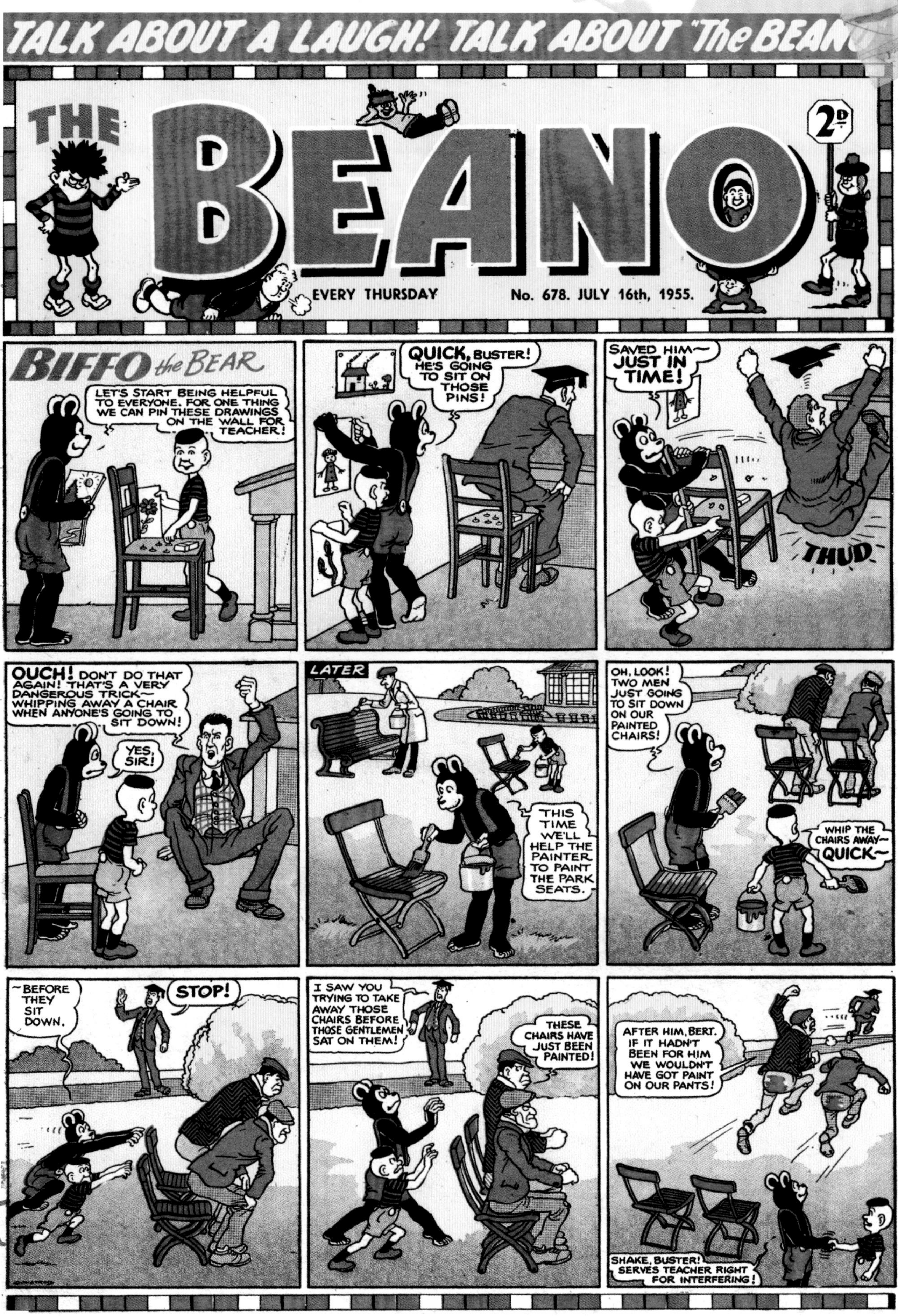

TALK ABOUT A LAUGH! TALK ABOUT "The BEAN
THE BEANO
2d
EVERY THURSDAY
No. 678. JULY 16th, 1955.
BIFFO the BEAR
LET'S START BEING HELPFUL TO EVERYONE. FOR ONE THING WE CAN PIN THESE DRAWINGS ON THE WALL FOR TEACHER!
QUICK, BUSTER! HE'S GOING TO SIT ON THOSE PINS!
SAVED HIM~ JUST IN TIME!
THUD
OUCH! DON'T DO THAT AGAIN! THAT'S A VERY DANGEROUS TRICK~ WHIPPING AWAY A CHAIR WHEN ANYONE'S GOING TO SIT DOWN!
YES, SIR!
LATER
THIS TIME WE'LL HELP THE PAINTER TO PAINT THE PARK SEATS.
OH, LOOK! TWO MEN JUST GOING TO SIT DOWN ON OUR PAINTED CHAIRS!
WHIP THE CHAIRS AWAY~ QUICK~
~BEFORE THEY SIT DOWN.
STOP!
I SAW YOU TRYING TO TAKE AWAY THOSE CHAIRS BEFORE THOSE GENTLEMEN SAT ON THEM!
THESE CHAIRS HAVE JUST BEEN PAINTED!
AFTER HIM, BERT. IF IT HADN'T BEEN FOR HIM WE WOULDN'T HAVE GOT PAINT ON OUR PANTS!
SHAKE, BUSTER! SERVES TEACHER RIGHT FOR INTERFERING!

THE WORLD'S WILDEST SCHOOLBOY

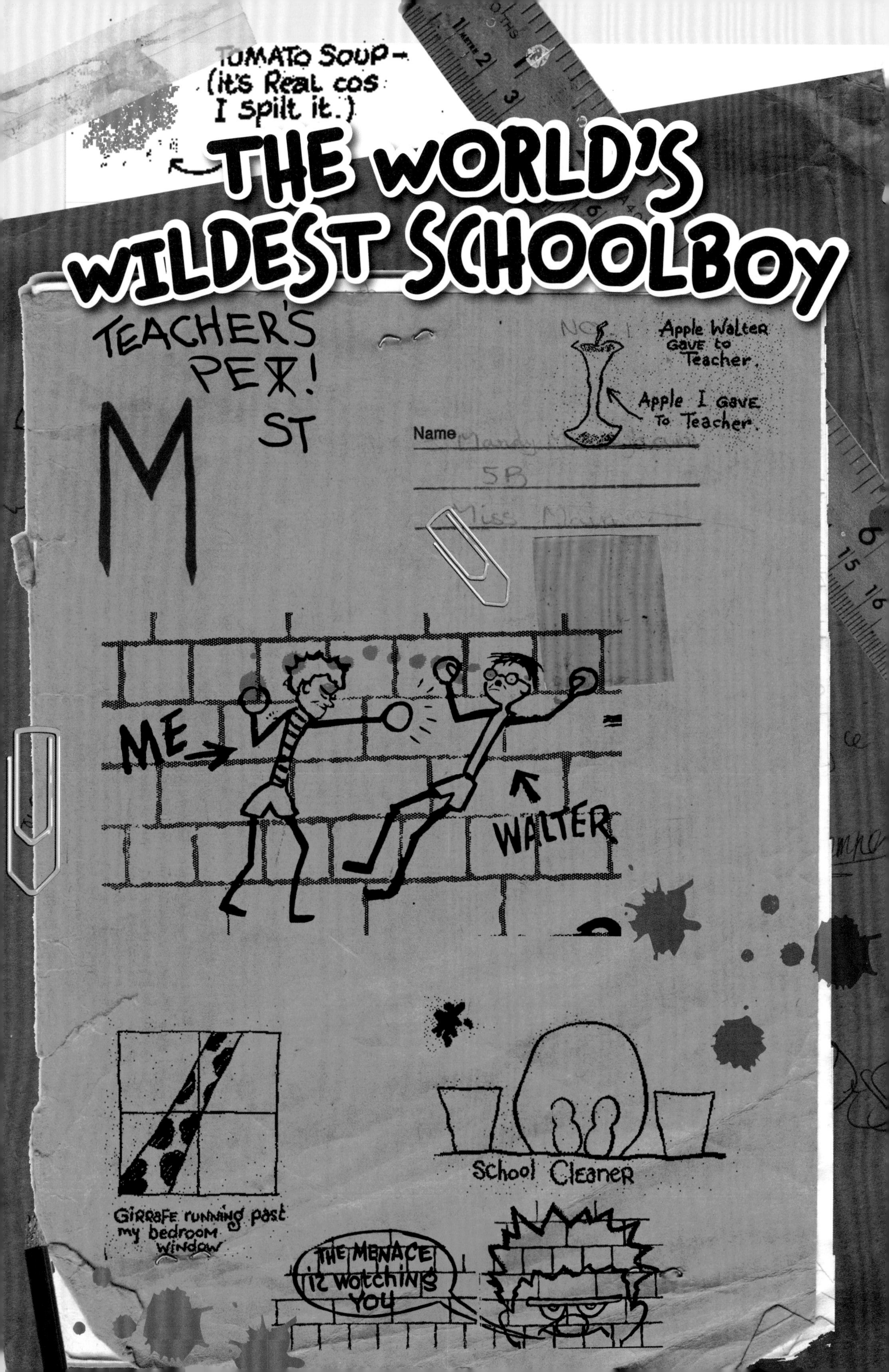
TUMATO SOUP-
(it's Real cos
I spilt it.)
TEACHER'S
PET!
ST
M
Name
5B
Apple Walter
GAVE to
Teacher.
Apple I GAVE
To Teacher.
ME
WALTER
GiRRaFE running past
my bedroom
window
School Cleaner
THE MENACE
iz wotchin9
YOU

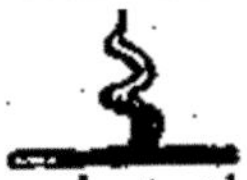
Drawing pin that Teacher sat on 15 times.

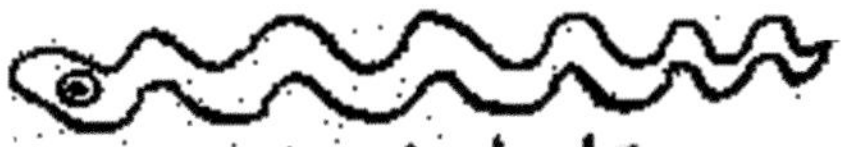
Python with the hiccups.

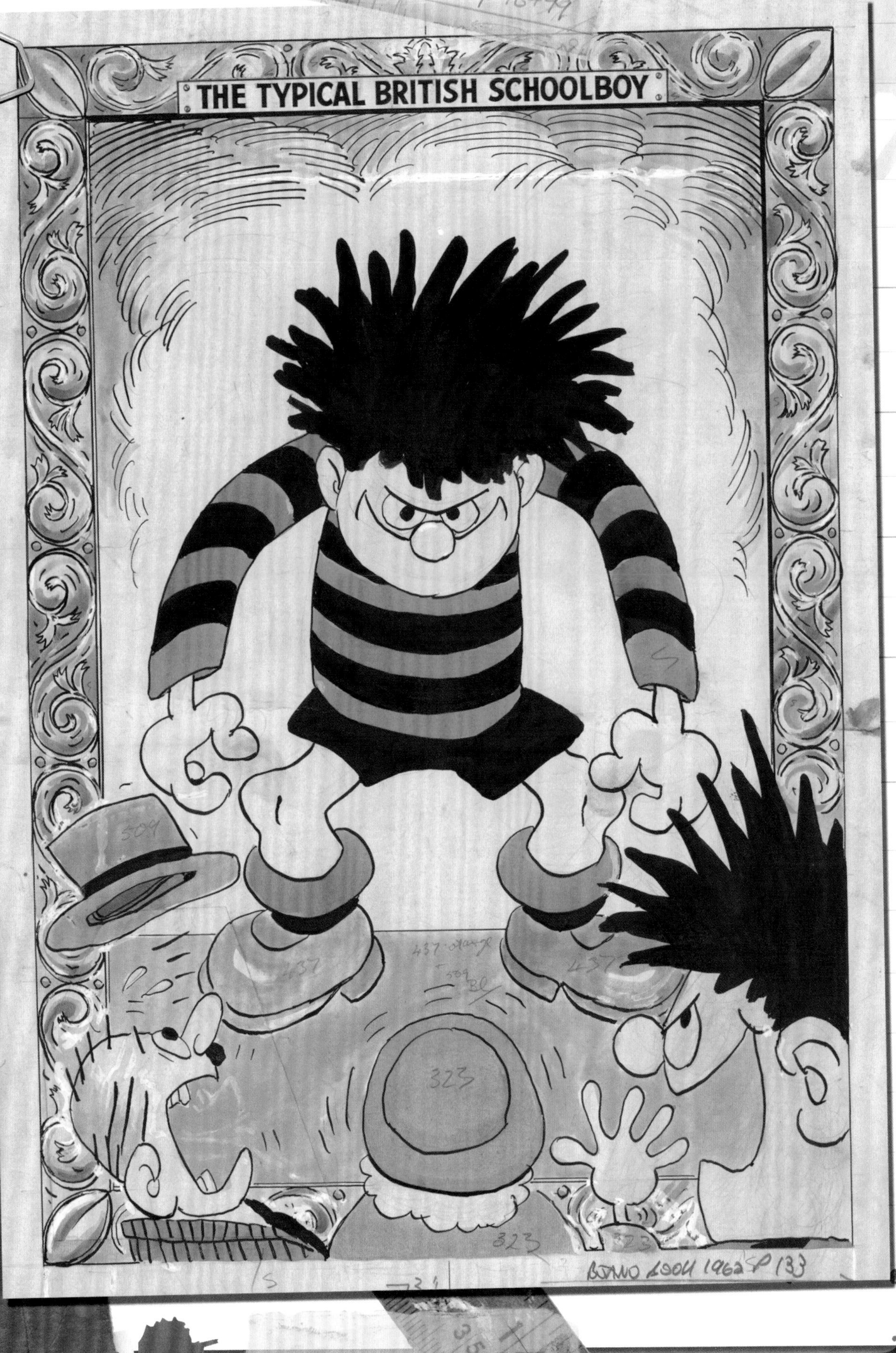
THE TYPICAL BRITISH SCHOOLBOY

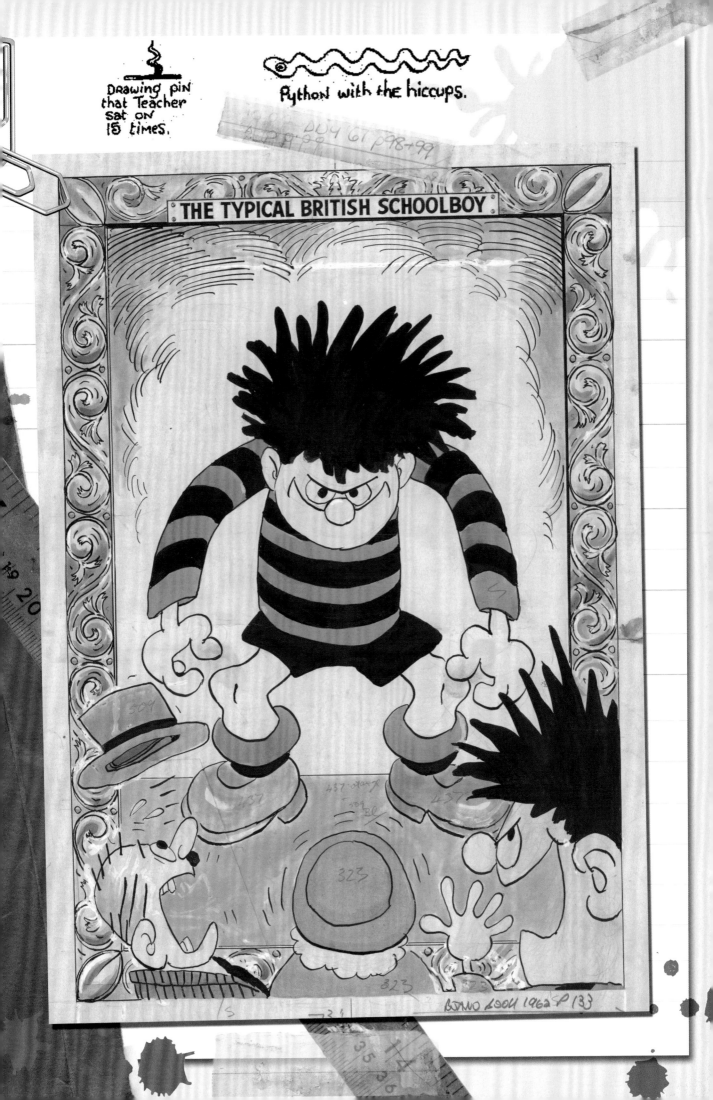

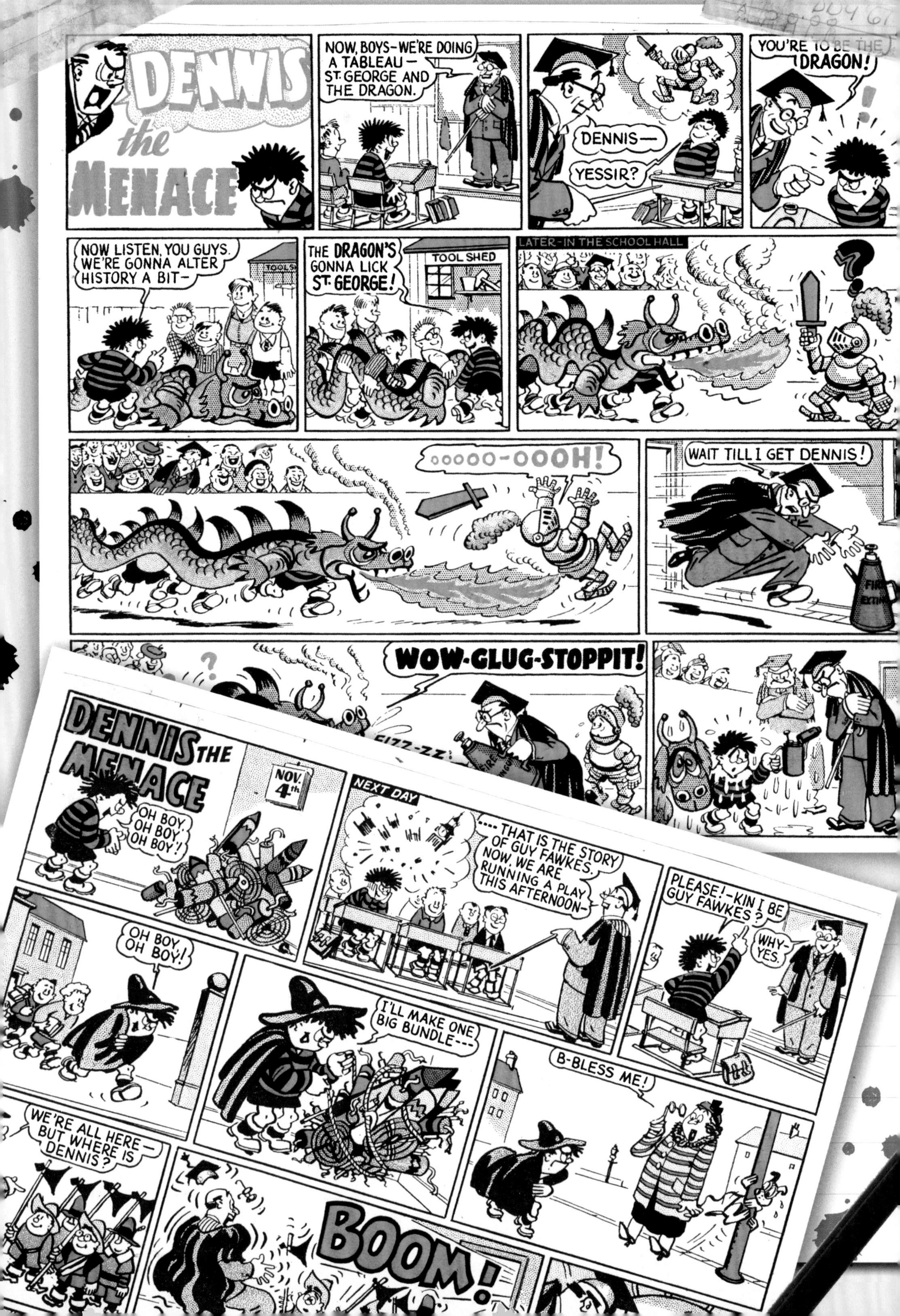
DENNIS the MENACE
NOW, BOYS—WE'RE DOING A TABLEAU— ST. GEORGE AND THE DRAGON.
DENNIS—
YESSIR?
YOU'RE TO BE THE DRAGON!
NOW LISTEN, YOU GUYS. WE'RE GONNA ALTER HISTORY A BIT—
THE DRAGON'S GONNA LICK ST. GEORGE!
TOOL SHED
LATER—IN THE SCHOOL HALL
OOOOO-OOOH!
WAIT TILL I GET DENNIS!
WOW-GLUG-STOPPIT!
FIZZ-ZZ
DENNIS THE MENACE
NOV. 4th
OH BOY, OH BOY, OH BOY!
NEXT DAY
----THAT IS THE STORY OF GUY FAWKES. NOW, WE ARE RUNNING A PLAY THIS AFTERNOON—
PLEASE!—KIN I BE GUY FAWKES?
WHY—YES.
OH BOY, OH BOY!
I'LL MAKE ONE BIG BUNDLE---
B-BLESS ME!
WE'RE ALL HERE—BUT WHERE IS DENNIS?
BOOM!

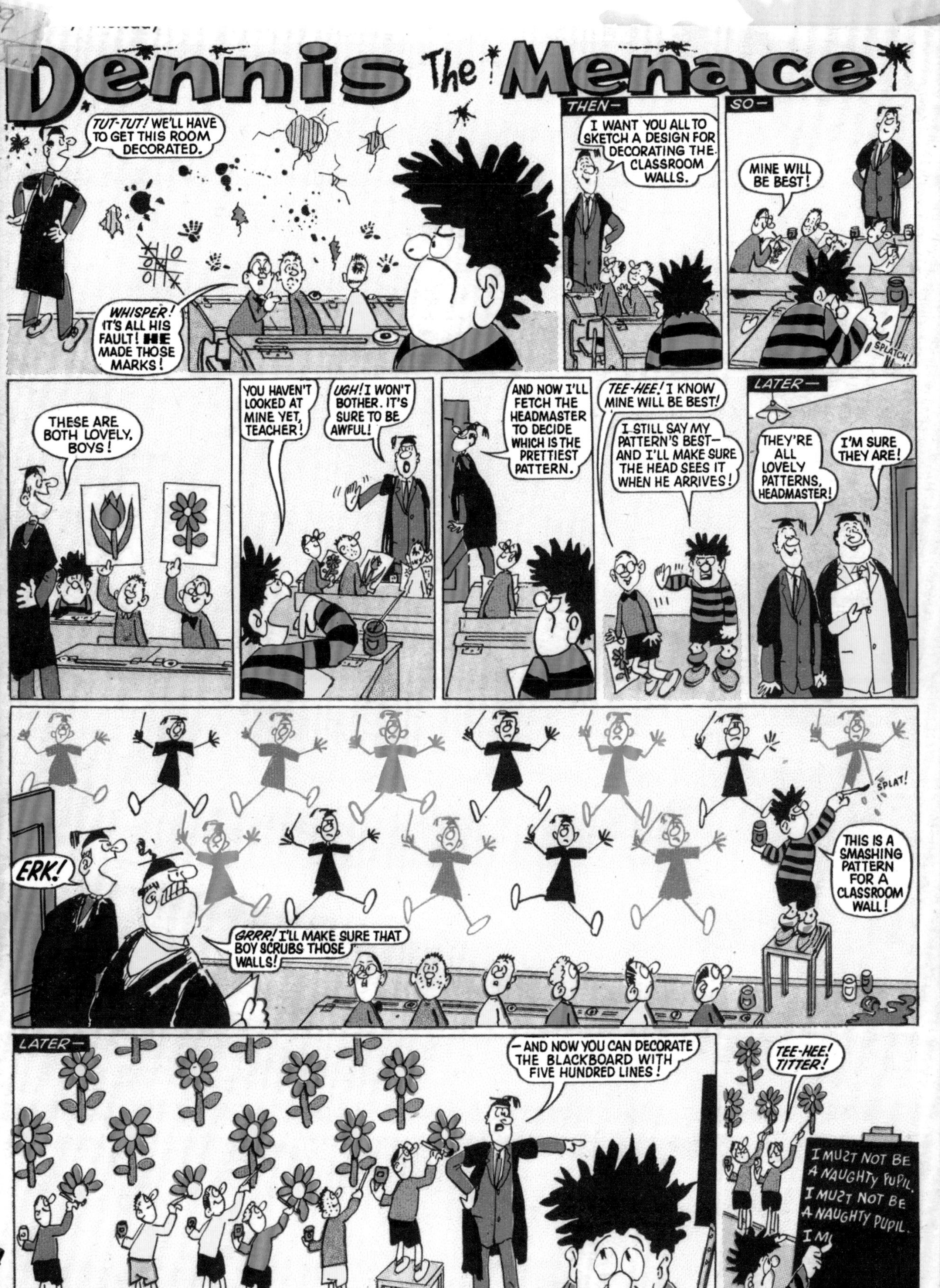
Dennis The Menace
TUT-TUT! WE'LL HAVE TO GET THIS ROOM DECORATED.
WHISPER! IT'S ALL HIS FAULT! HE MADE THOSE MARKS!
THEN—
I WANT YOU ALL TO SKETCH A DESIGN FOR DECORATING THE CLASSROOM WALLS.
SO—
MINE WILL BE BEST!
SPLATCH!
THESE ARE BOTH LOVELY, BOYS!
YOU HAVEN'T LOOKED AT MINE YET, TEACHER!
UGH! I WON'T BOTHER. IT'S SURE TO BE AWFUL!
AND NOW I'LL FETCH THE HEADMASTER TO DECIDE WHICH IS THE PRETTIEST PATTERN.
TEE-HEE! I KNOW MINE WILL BE BEST!
I STILL SAY MY PATTERN'S BEST— AND I'LL MAKE SURE THE HEAD SEES IT WHEN HE ARRIVES!
LATER—
THEY'RE ALL LOVELY PATTERNS, HEADMASTER!
I'M SURE THEY ARE!
SPLAT!
THIS IS A SMASHING PATTERN FOR A CLASSROOM WALL!
ERK!
GRRR! I'LL MAKE SURE THAT BOY SCRUBS THOSE WALLS!
LATER—
—AND NOW YOU CAN DECORATE THE BLACKBOARD WITH FIVE HUNDRED LINES!
TEE-HEE! TITTER!
I MUST NOT BE A NAUGHTY PUPIL.
I MUST NOT BE A NAUGHTY PUPIL.
I M

Printed and Published in Great Britain by D. C. THOMSON & Co., Ltd., ... Co. Ltd., 12 Fetter Lane, Fleet Street, London, E.C.4.

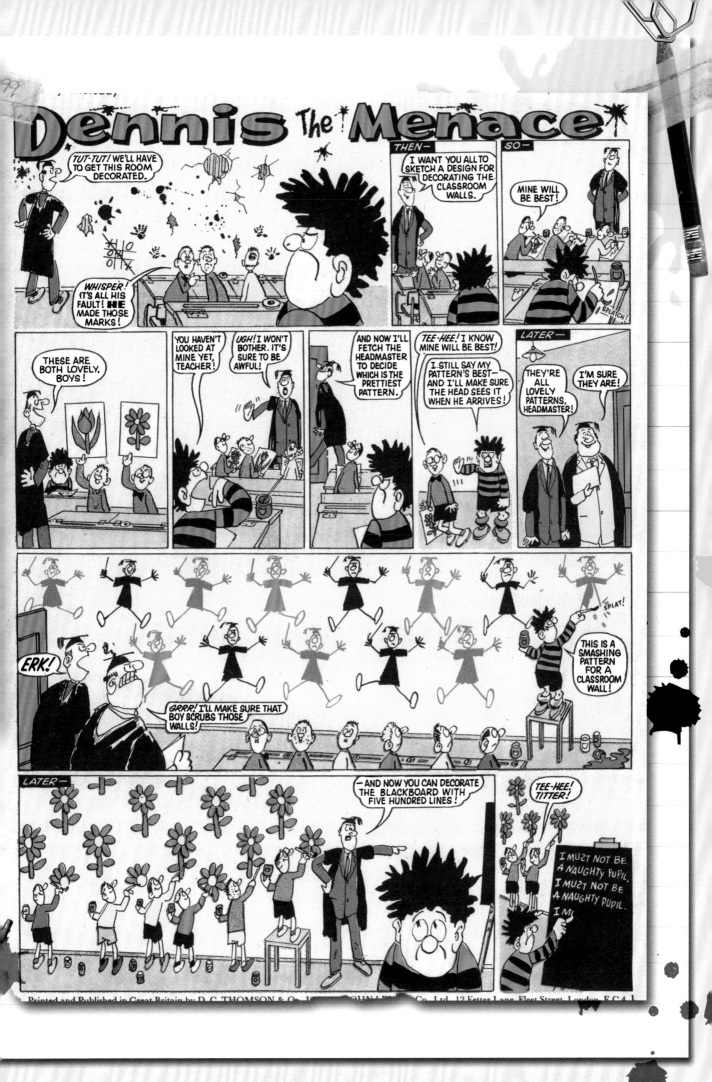

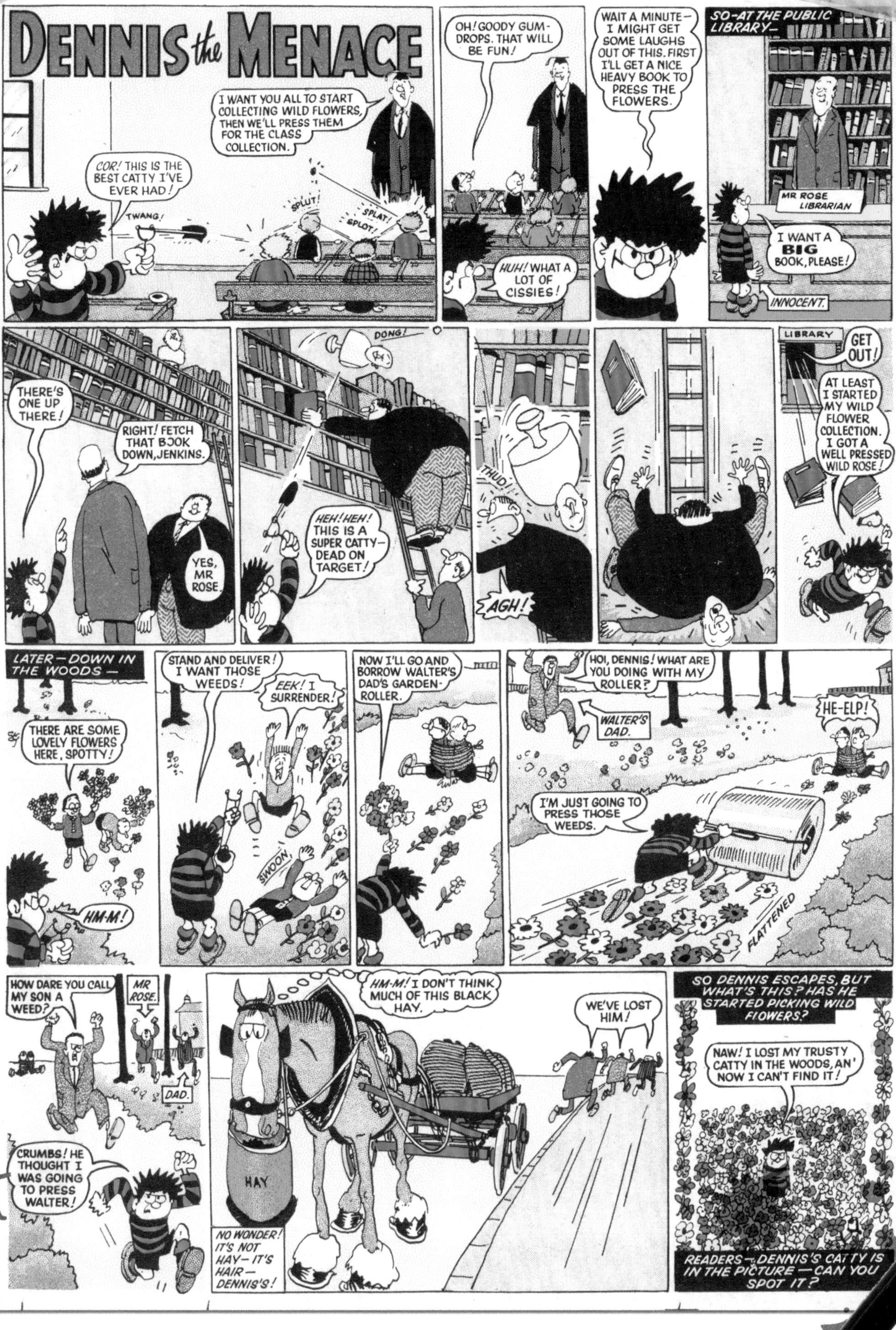

DENNIS the MENACE
I WANT YOU ALL TO START COLLECTING WILD FLOWERS, THEN WE'LL PRESS THEM FOR THE CLASS COLLECTION.
COR! THIS IS THE BEST CATTY I'VE EVER HAD!
TWANG!
SPLUT!
SPLAT!
SPLOT!
OH! GOODY GUM-DROPS. THAT WILL BE FUN!
HUH! WHAT A LOT OF CISSIES!
WAIT A MINUTE— I MIGHT GET SOME LAUGHS OUT OF THIS. FIRST I'LL GET A NICE HEAVY BOOK TO PRESS THE FLOWERS.
SO—AT THE PUBLIC LIBRARY—
MR ROSE LIBRARIAN
I WANT A BIG BOOK, PLEASE!
INNOCENT.
THERE'S ONE UP THERE!
RIGHT! FETCH THAT BOOK DOWN, JENKINS.
YES, MR ROSE.
DONG!
HEH! HEH! THIS IS A SUPER CATTY— DEAD ON TARGET!
THUD!
AGH!
LIBRARY
GET OUT!
AT LEAST I STARTED MY WILD FLOWER COLLECTION. I GOT A WELL PRESSED WILD ROSE!
LATER—DOWN IN THE WOODS—
THERE ARE SOME LOVELY FLOWERS HERE, SPOTTY!
HM-M!
STAND AND DELIVER! I WANT THOSE WEEDS!
EEK! I SURRENDER!
SWOON
NOW I'LL GO AND BORROW WALTER'S DAD'S GARDEN-ROLLER.
HOI, DENNIS! WHAT ARE YOU DOING WITH MY ROLLER?
WALTER'S DAD.
HE-ELP!
I'M JUST GOING TO PRESS THOSE WEEDS.
FLATTENED
HOW DARE YOU CALL MY SON A WEED?
MR ROSE.
DAD.
CRUMBS! HE THOUGHT I WAS GOING TO PRESS WALTER!
HM-M! I DON'T THINK MUCH OF THIS BLACK HAY.
WE'VE LOST HIM!
HAY
NO WONDER! IT'S NOT HAY— IT'S HAIR— DENNIS'S!
SO DENNIS ESCAPES, BUT WHAT'S THIS? HAS HE STARTED PICKING WILD FLOWERS?
NAW! I LOST MY TRUSTY CATTY IN THE WOODS, AN' NOW I CAN'T FIND IT!
READERS—DENNIS'S CATTY IS IN THE PICTURE—CAN YOU SPOT IT?

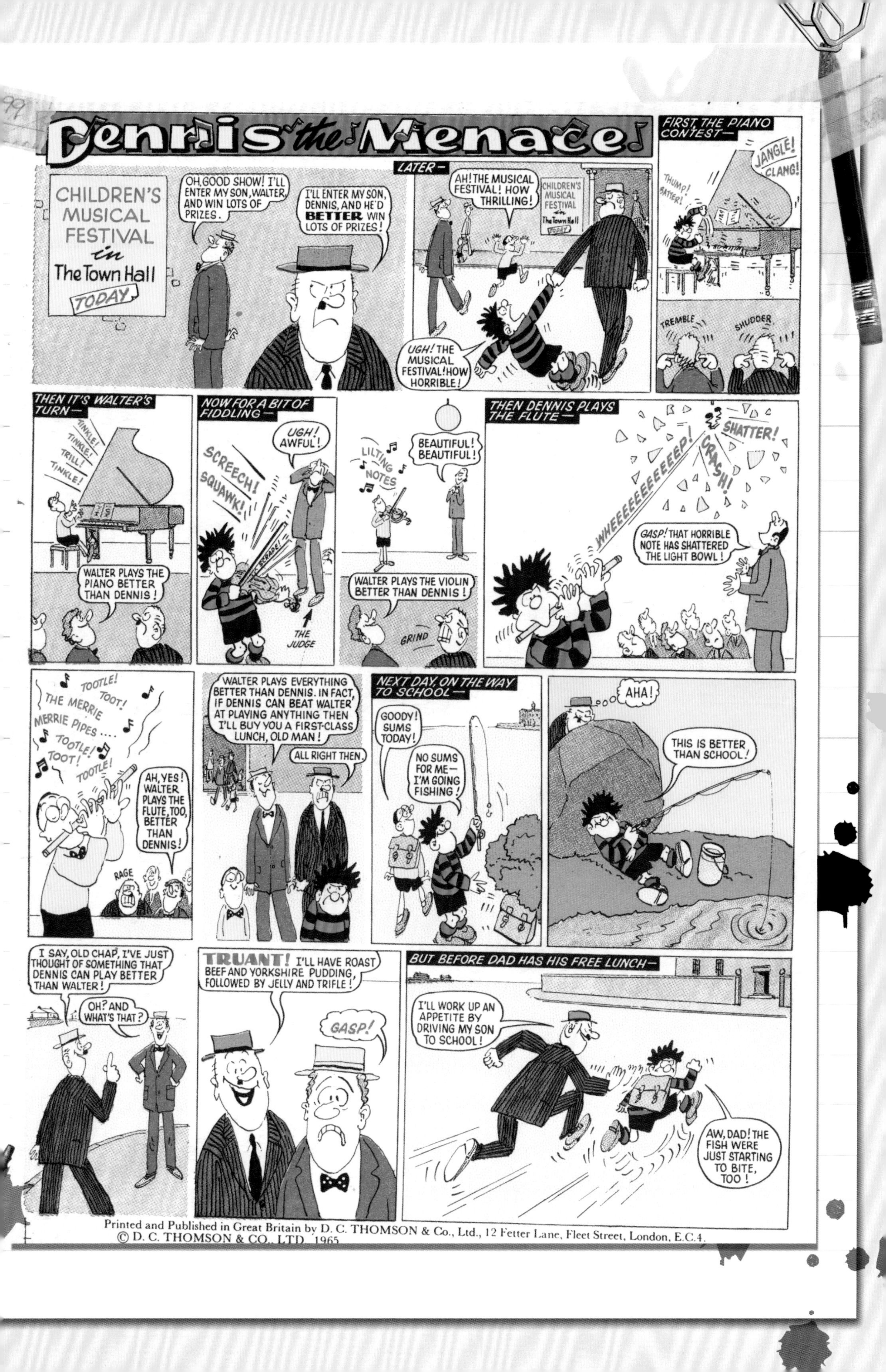
Dennis the Menace
CHILDREN'S MUSICAL FESTIVAL in The Town Hall TODAY
OH, GOOD SHOW! I'LL ENTER MY SON, WALTER, AND WIN LOTS OF PRIZES.
I'LL ENTER MY SON, DENNIS, AND HE'D BETTER WIN LOTS OF PRIZES!
LATER—
AH! THE MUSICAL FESTIVAL! HOW THRILLING!
CHILDREN'S MUSICAL FESTIVAL in The Town Hall TODAY
UGH! THE MUSICAL FESTIVAL! HOW HORRIBLE!
FIRST, THE PIANO CONTEST—
JANGLE! CLANG!
THUMP! BATTER!
TREMBLE
SHUDDER
THEN IT'S WALTER'S TURN—
TINKLE! TINKLE! TRILL! TINKLE!
WALTER PLAYS THE PIANO BETTER THAN DENNIS!
NOW FOR A BIT OF FIDDLING—
UGH! AWFUL!
SCREECH! SQUAWK!
SCRAPE!
THE JUDGE
LILTING NOTES
BEAUTIFUL! BEAUTIFUL!
WALTER PLAYS THE VIOLIN BETTER THAN DENNIS!
GRIND
THEN DENNIS PLAYS THE FLUTE—
WHEEEEEEEEEEEEP!
SHATTER!
CRASH!
GASP! THAT HORRIBLE NOTE HAS SHATTERED THE LIGHT BOWL!
TOOTLE! TOOT! THE MERRIE MERRIE PIPES.... TOOTLE! TOOT! TOOTLE!
AH, YES! WALTER PLAYS THE FLUTE, TOO, BETTER THAN DENNIS!
RAGE
WALTER PLAYS EVERYTHING BETTER THAN DENNIS. IN FACT, IF DENNIS CAN BEAT WALTER AT PLAYING ANYTHING THEN I'LL BUY YOU A FIRST-CLASS LUNCH, OLD MAN!
ALL RIGHT THEN.
NEXT DAY, ON THE WAY TO SCHOOL—
GOODY! SUMS TODAY!
NO SUMS FOR ME— I'M GOING FISHING!
AHA!
THIS IS BETTER THAN SCHOOL!
I SAY, OLD CHAP, I'VE JUST THOUGHT OF SOMETHING THAT DENNIS CAN PLAY BETTER THAN WALTER!
OH? AND WHAT'S THAT?
TRUANT! I'LL HAVE ROAST BEEF AND YORKSHIRE PUDDING, FOLLOWED BY JELLY AND TRIFLE!
GASP!
BUT BEFORE DAD HAS HIS FREE LUNCH—
I'LL WORK UP AN APPETITE BY DRIVING MY SON TO SCHOOL!
AW, DAD! THE FISH WERE JUST STARTING TO BITE, TOO!

Printed and Published in Great Britain by D. C. THOMSON & Co., Ltd., 12 Fetter Lane, Fleet Street, London, E.C.4.

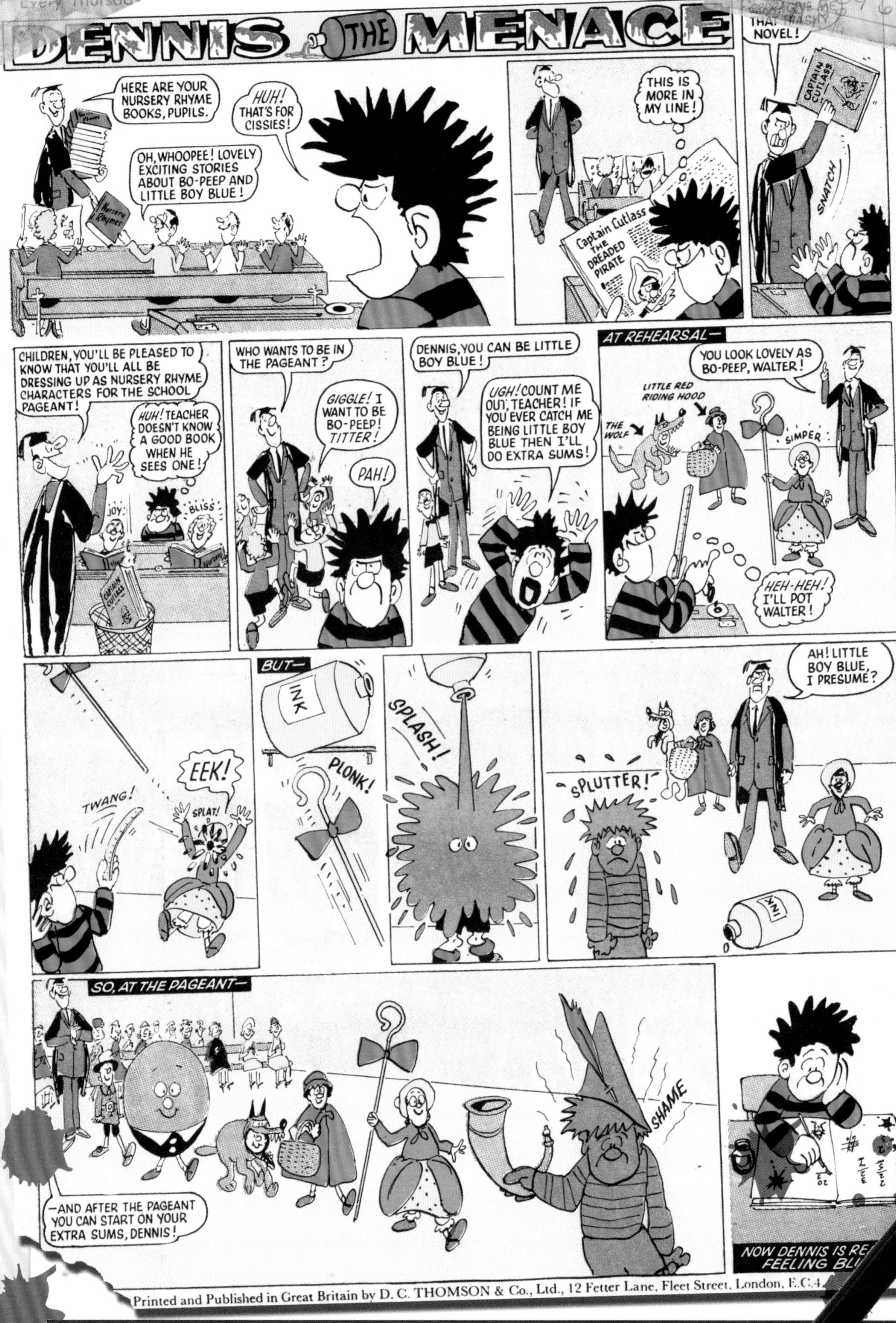
DENNIS THE MENACE
HERE ARE YOUR NURSERY RHYME BOOKS, PUPILS.
HUH! THAT'S FOR CISSIES!
OH, WHOOPEE! LOVELY EXCITING STORIES ABOUT BO-PEEP AND LITTLE BOY BLUE!
Nursery Rhymes
THIS IS MORE IN MY LINE!
Captain Cutlass THE DREADED PIRATE
GRRR! GIVE ME THAT TRASHY NOVEL!
CAPTAIN CUTLASS
SNATCH
CHILDREN, YOU'LL BE PLEASED TO KNOW THAT YOU'LL ALL BE DRESSING UP AS NURSERY RHYME CHARACTERS FOR THE SCHOOL PAGEANT!
HUH! TEACHER DOESN'T KNOW A GOOD BOOK WHEN HE SEES ONE!
JOY!
BLISS
CAPTAIN CUTLASS
WHO WANTS TO BE IN THE PAGEANT?
GIGGLE! I WANT TO BE BO-PEEP! TITTER!
PAH!
DENNIS, YOU CAN BE LITTLE BOY BLUE!
UGH! COUNT ME OUT, TEACHER! IF YOU EVER CATCH ME BEING LITTLE BOY BLUE THEN I'LL DO EXTRA SUMS!
AT REHEARSAL—
YOU LOOK LOVELY AS BO-PEEP, WALTER!
LITTLE RED RIDING HOOD
THE WOLF
SIMPER
HEH-HEH! I'LL POT WALTER!
EEK!
TWANG!
SPLAT!
BUT—
INK
PLONK!
SPLASH!
AH! LITTLE BOY BLUE, I PRESUME?
SPLUTTER!
INK
SO, AT THE PAGEANT—
SHAME
—AND AFTER THE PAGEANT YOU CAN START ON YOUR EXTRA SUMS, DENNIS!
NOW DENNIS IS RE
FEELING BL

Printed and Published in Great Britain by D. C. THOMSON & Co., Ltd., 12 Fetter Lane, Fleet Street, London, E.C.4.

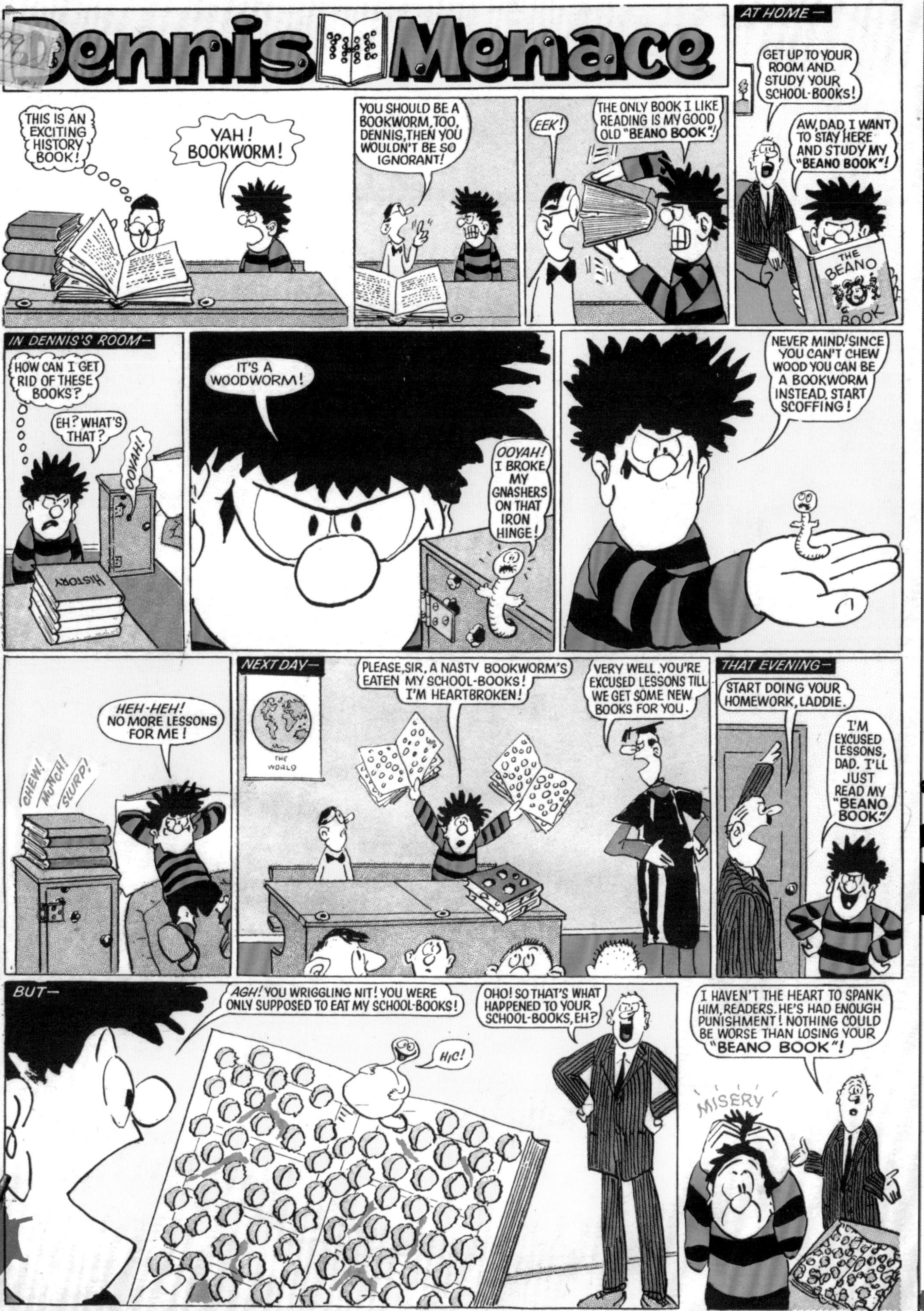
Dennis the Menace
AT HOME—
THIS IS AN EXCITING HISTORY BOOK!
YAH! BOOKWORM!
YOU SHOULD BE A BOOKWORM, TOO, DENNIS, THEN YOU WOULDN'T BE SO IGNORANT!
EEK!
THE ONLY BOOK I LIKE READING IS MY GOOD OLD "BEANO BOOK"!
GET UP TO YOUR ROOM AND STUDY YOUR SCHOOL-BOOKS!
AW, DAD, I WANT TO STAY HERE AND STUDY MY "BEANO BOOK"!
THE BEANO BOOK
IN DENNIS'S ROOM—
HOW CAN I GET RID OF THESE BOOKS?
EH? WHAT'S THAT?
OOYAH!
HISTORY
IT'S A WOODWORM!
OOYAH! I BROKE MY GNASHERS ON THAT IRON HINGE!
NEVER MIND! SINCE YOU CAN'T CHEW WOOD YOU CAN BE A BOOKWORM INSTEAD. START SCOFFING!
CHEW! MUNCH! SLURP!
HEH-HEH! NO MORE LESSONS FOR ME!
NEXT DAY—
THE WORLD
PLEASE, SIR, A NASTY BOOKWORM'S EATEN MY SCHOOL-BOOKS! I'M HEARTBROKEN!
VERY WELL. YOU'RE EXCUSED LESSONS TILL WE GET SOME NEW BOOKS FOR YOU.
THAT EVENING—
START DOING YOUR HOMEWORK, LADDIE.
I'M EXCUSED LESSONS, DAD. I'LL JUST READ MY "BEANO BOOK."
BUT—
AGH! YOU WRIGGLING NIT! YOU WERE ONLY SUPPOSED TO EAT MY SCHOOL-BOOKS!
HIC!
OHO! SO THAT'S WHAT HAPPENED TO YOUR SCHOOL-BOOKS, EH?
I HAVEN'T THE HEART TO SPANK HIM, READERS. HE'S HAD ENOUGH PUNISHMENT! NOTHING COULD BE WORSE THAN LOSING YOUR "BEANO BOOK"!
MISERY

Printed and Published in Great Britain by D. C. THOMSON & Co., Ltd., and JOHN LENG & Co., Ltd., 12 Fetter Lane, Fleet Street, London, E.C.4.

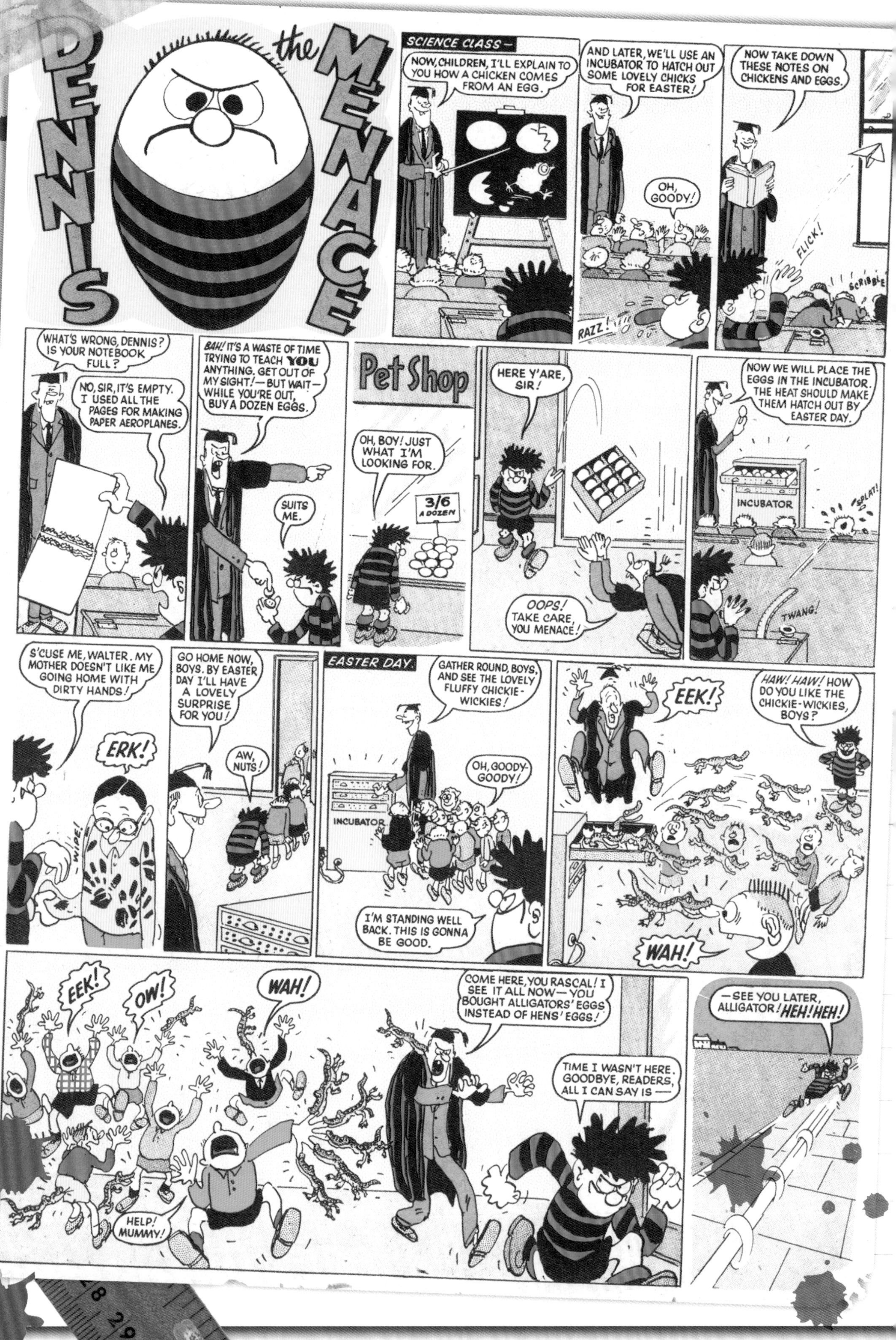
DENNIS the MENACE
SCIENCE CLASS—
NOW, CHILDREN, I'LL EXPLAIN TO YOU HOW A CHICKEN COMES FROM AN EGG.
AND LATER, WE'LL USE AN INCUBATOR TO HATCH OUT SOME LOVELY CHICKS FOR EASTER!
OH, GOODY!
RAZZ!
NOW TAKE DOWN THESE NOTES ON CHICKENS AND EGGS.
FLICK!
SCRIBBLE
WHAT'S WRONG, DENNIS? IS YOUR NOTEBOOK FULL?
NO, SIR, IT'S EMPTY. I USED ALL THE PAGES FOR MAKING PAPER AEROPLANES.
BAH! IT'S A WASTE OF TIME TRYING TO TEACH YOU ANYTHING. GET OUT OF MY SIGHT!—BUT WAIT—WHILE YOU'RE OUT, BUY A DOZEN EGGS.
SUITS ME.
Pet Shop
OH, BOY! JUST WHAT I'M LOOKING FOR.
3/6 A DOZEN
HERE Y'ARE, SIR!
OOPS! TAKE CARE, YOU MENACE!
NOW WE WILL PLACE THE EGGS IN THE INCUBATOR. THE HEAT SHOULD MAKE THEM HATCH OUT BY EASTER DAY.
INCUBATOR
SPLAT!
TWANG!
S'CUSE ME, WALTER. MY MOTHER DOESN'T LIKE ME GOING HOME WITH DIRTY HANDS!
ERK!
WIPE!
GO HOME NOW, BOYS. BY EASTER DAY I'LL HAVE A LOVELY SURPRISE FOR YOU!
AW, NUTS!
EASTER DAY.
GATHER ROUND, BOYS, AND SEE THE LOVELY FLUFFY CHICKIE-WICKIES!
OH, GOODY-GOODY!
INCUBATOR
I'M STANDING WELL BACK. THIS IS GONNA BE GOOD.
EEK!
HAW! HAW! HOW DO YOU LIKE THE CHICKIE-WICKIES, BOYS?
WAH!
EEK!
OW!
WAH!
COME HERE, YOU RASCAL! I SEE IT ALL NOW—YOU BOUGHT ALLIGATORS' EGGS INSTEAD OF HENS' EGGS!
TIME I WASN'T HERE. GOODBYE, READERS, ALL I CAN SAY IS —
HELP! MUMMY!
—SEE YOU LATER, ALLIGATOR! HEH! HEH!

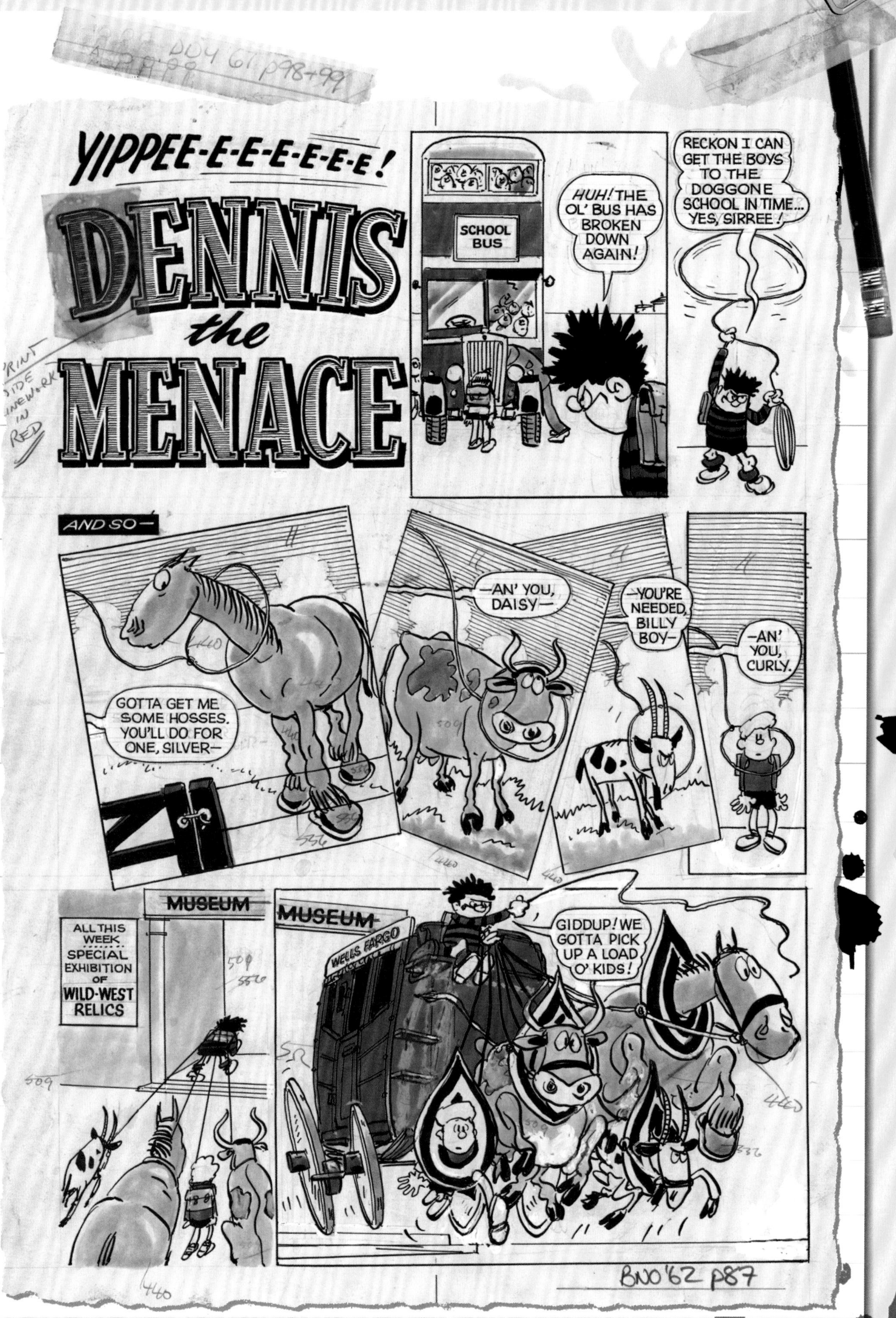
DOY 61 p98+99
YIPPEE-E-E-E-E-E-E-E!
DENNIS the MENACE
PRINT SIDE LINEWORK IN RED
SCHOOL BUS
HUH! THE OL' BUS HAS BROKEN DOWN AGAIN!
RECKON I CAN GET THE BOYS TO THE DOGGONE SCHOOL IN TIME... YES, SIRREE!
AND SO—
GOTTA GET ME SOME HOSSES. YOU'LL DO FOR ONE, SILVER—
—AN' YOU, DAISY—
—YOU'RE NEEDED, BILLY BOY—
—AN' YOU, CURLY.
MUSEUM
ALL THIS WEEK SPECIAL EXHIBITION OF WILD-WEST RELICS
MUSEUM
WELLS FARGO
GIDDUP! WE GOTTA PICK UP A LOAD O' KIDS!
BNO '62 p87

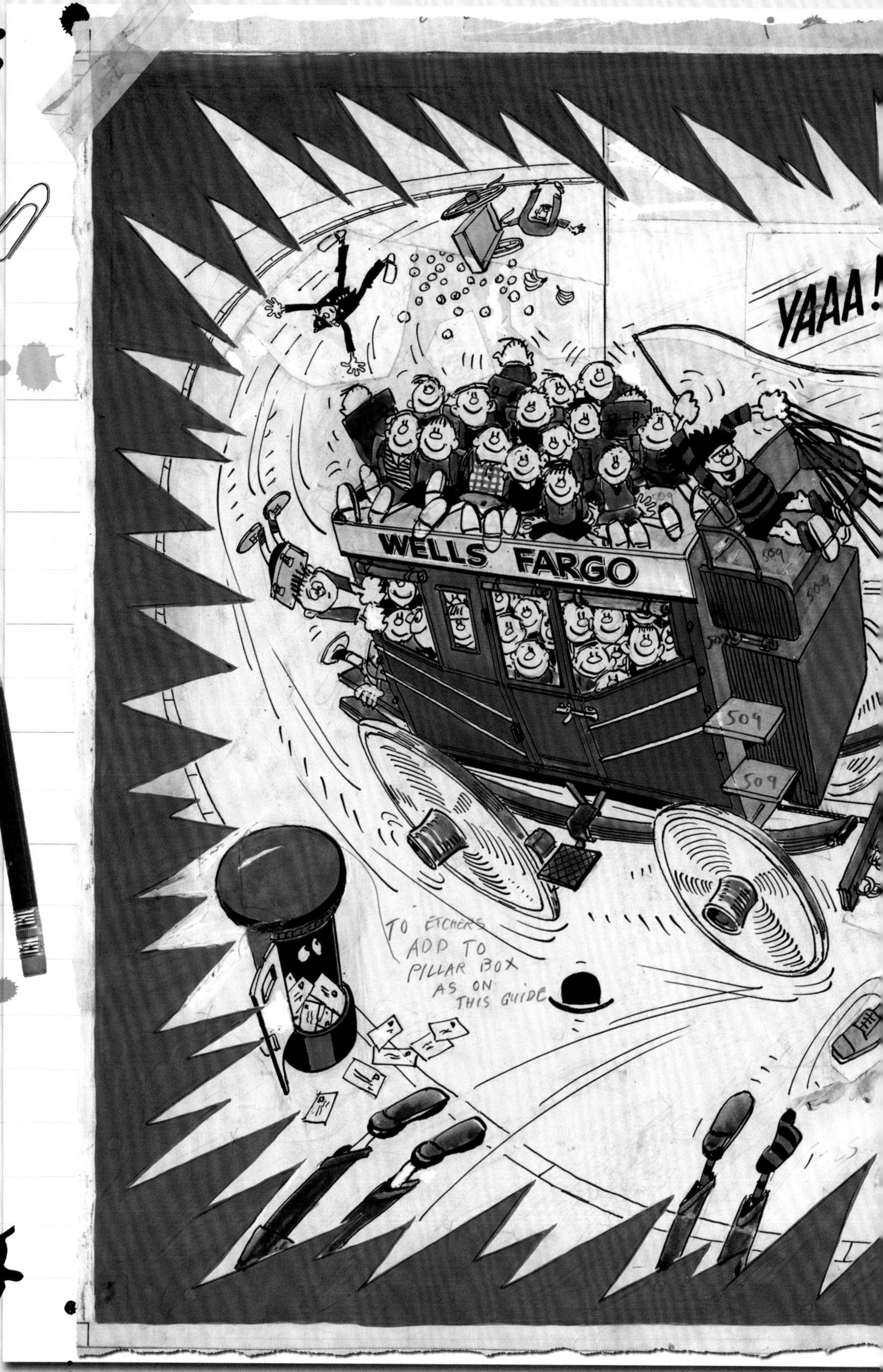
YAAA!
WELLS FARGO
509
TO ETCHER'S
ADD TO
PILLAR BOX
AS ON
THIS GUIDE

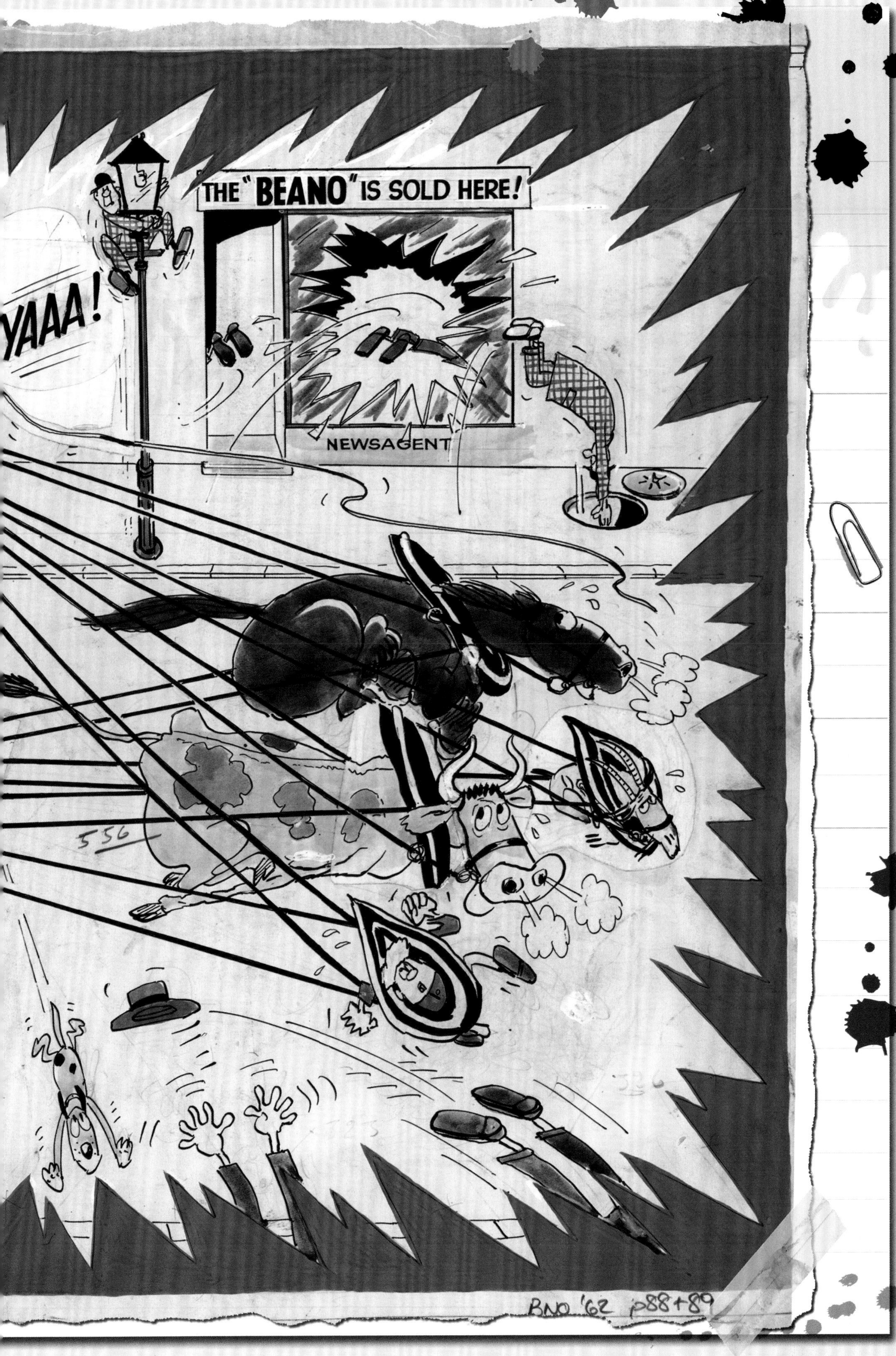
YAAA!
THE "BEANO" IS SOLD HERE!
NEWSAGENT
556
BNO '62 p88+89

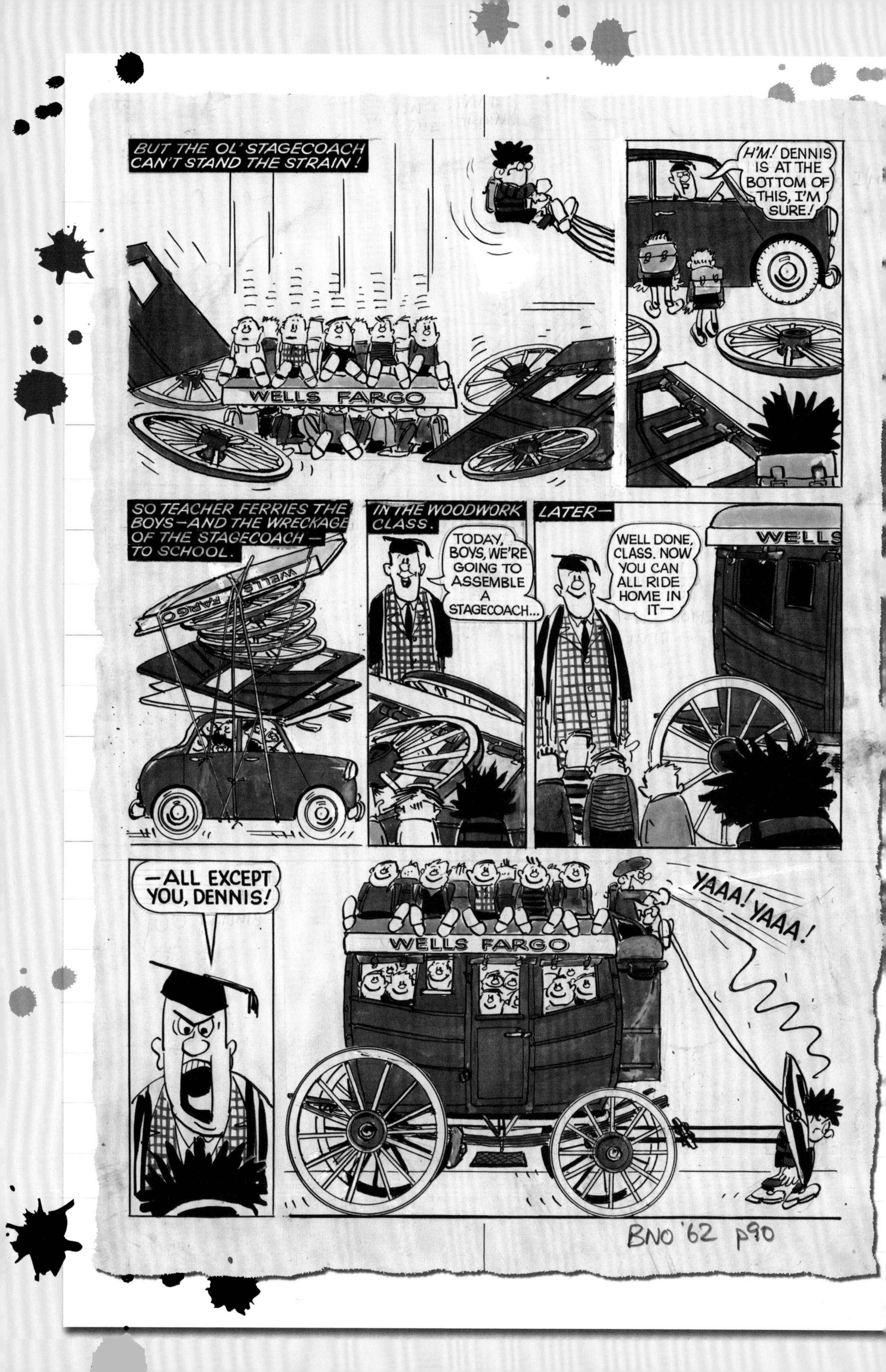

BUT THE OL' STAGECOACH CAN'T STAND THE STRAIN!
WELLS FARGO
H'M! DENNIS IS AT THE BOTTOM OF THIS, I'M SURE!
SO TEACHER FERRIES THE BOYS—AND THE WRECKAGE OF THE STAGECOACH—TO SCHOOL.
WELLS FARGO
IN THE WOODWORK CLASS.
TODAY, BOYS, WE'RE GOING TO ASSEMBLE A STAGECOACH...
LATER—
WELL DONE, CLASS. NOW YOU CAN ALL RIDE HOME IN IT—
WELLS
—ALL EXCEPT YOU, DENNIS!
WELLS FARGO
YAAA! YAAA!
BNO '62 p90

Our Teacher's a Walrus was so popular a story it appeared first in text then as a picture strip drawn by the amazing Dudley D Watkins.

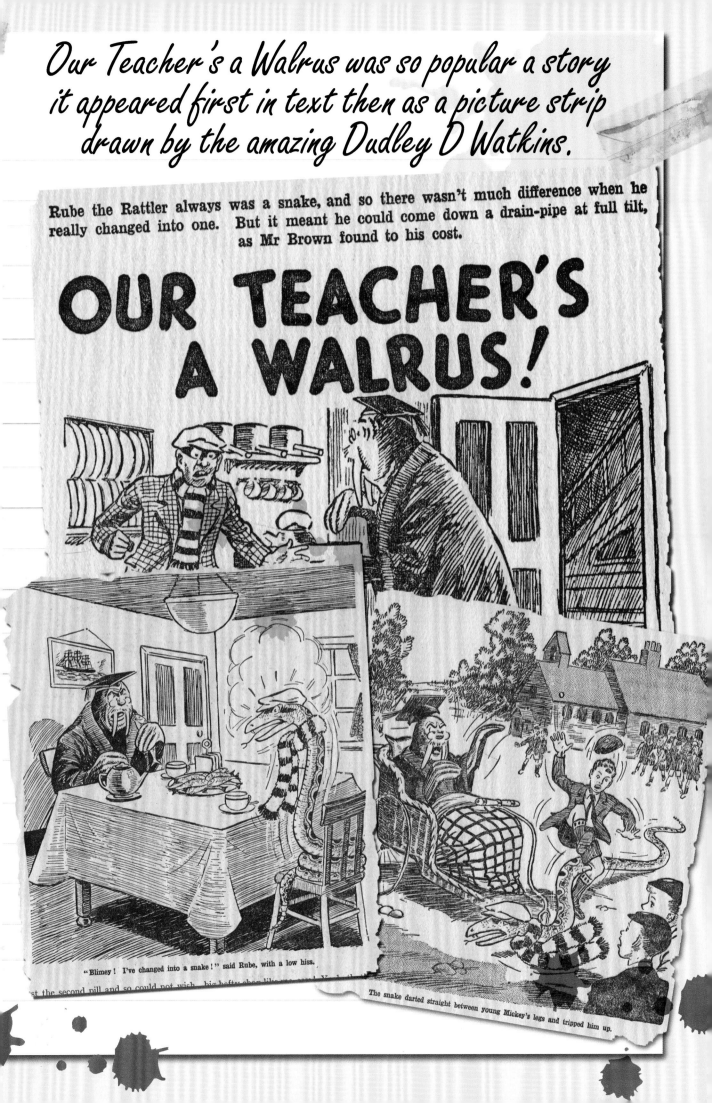

Rube the Rattler always was a snake, and so there wasn't much difference when he really changed into one. But it meant he could come down a drain-pipe at full tilt, as Mr Brown found to his cost.

OUR TEACHER'S A WALRUS!

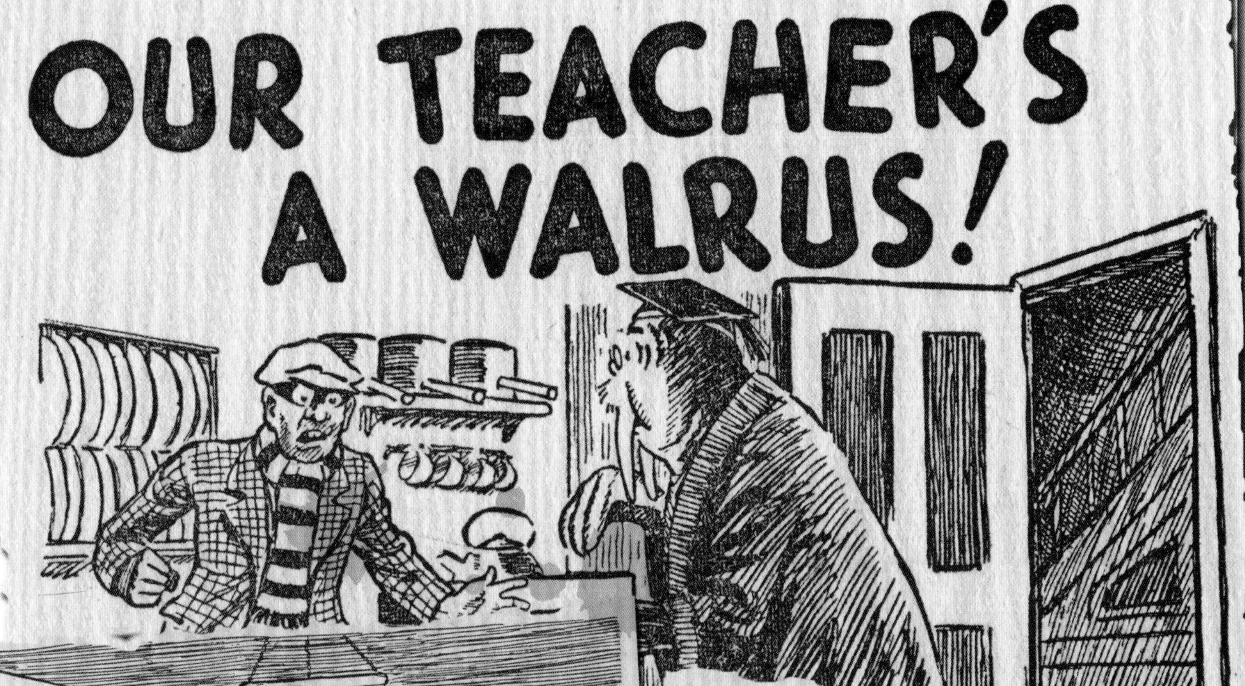

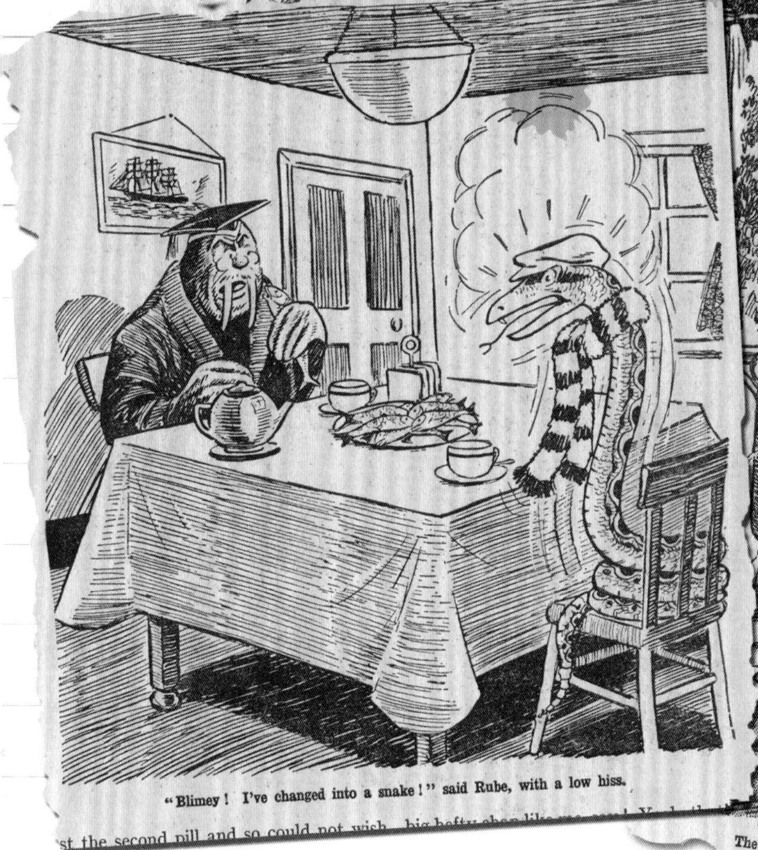

"Blimey! I've changed into a snake!" said Rube, with a low hiss.

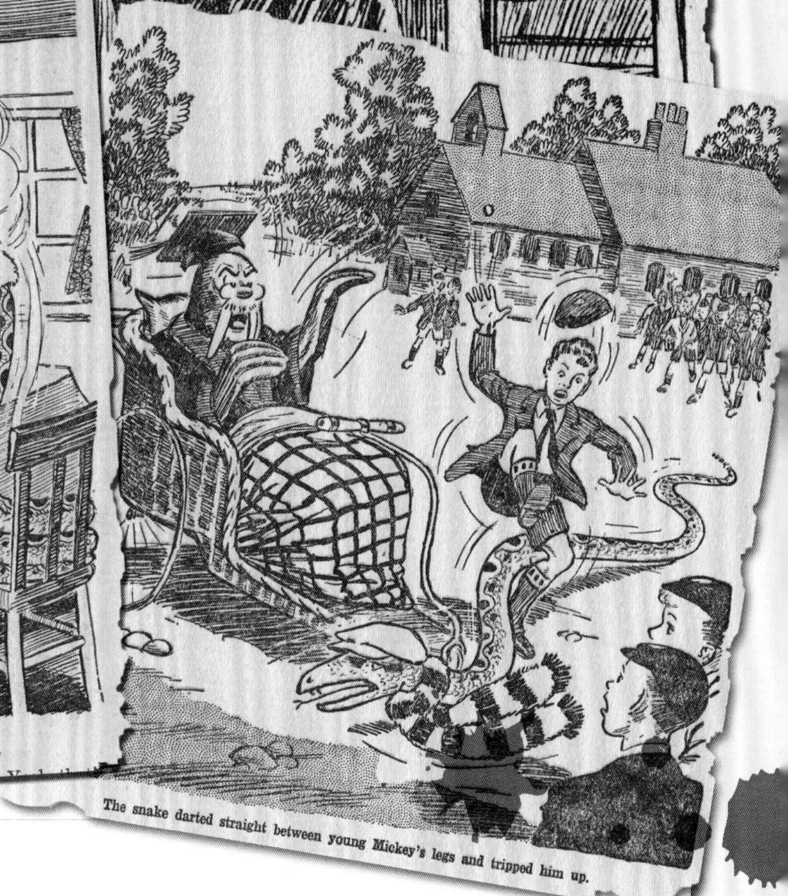

The snake darted straight between young Mickey's legs and tripped him up.

This is the first episode of what was a 16 week run.

Here's something New! Starting to-day—

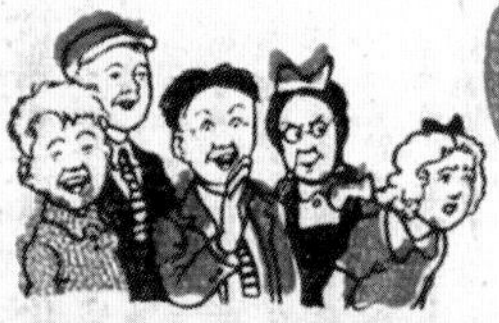

OUR TEACHER'S A WALRUS!

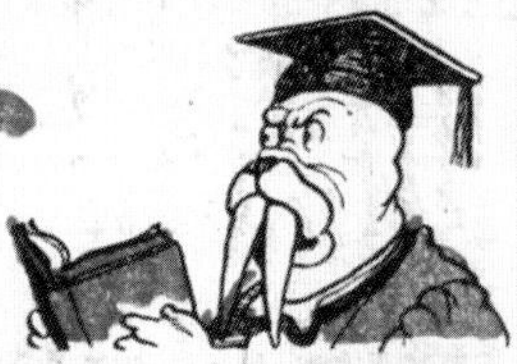

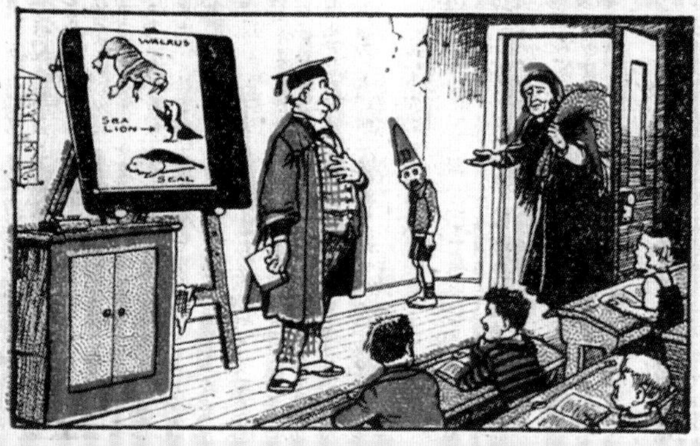

WALRUS
SEA LION
SEAL

Mr Brown has been our teacher at Burford School for many years. A funny-looking chap he is. "Old Walrus Face" we call him, because of his big walrus moustache. But he's a good sport, and we all like him very much. We're not quite so fond of lessons, of course, but we get a lot of fun at school. Well, one day a very strange thing happened at our school. It was the day Johnny Mack was standing in the corner wearing the dunce's cap. (He didn't know the capital of France, the chump!)

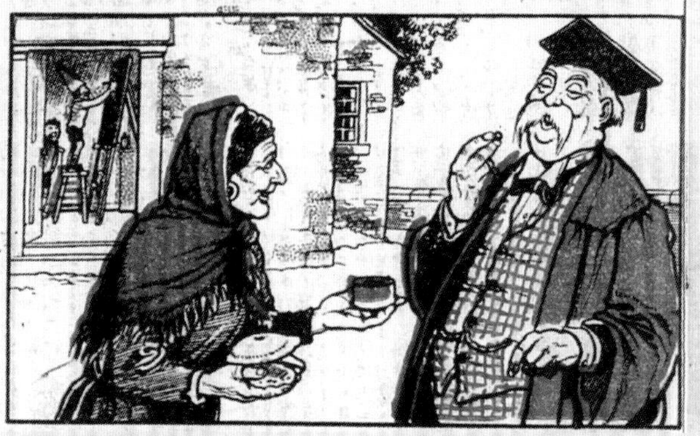

A strange-looking gipsy woman came to the door and begged something from Mr Brown. He's a good-hearted chap, is our teacher, so he gave the gipsy some food. "Your generosity will be repaid," the gipsy said. "Look, these are magic pills! Take one, make a wish – and your wish will come true!" That made Mr Brown chuckle, for he doesn't believe in magic. But we saw him take a pill and swallow it. He never guessed the trouble that pill would cause him. Poor Old Walrus Face!

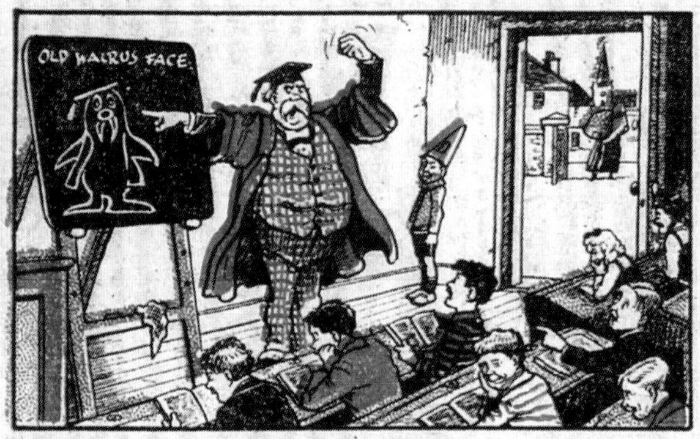

OLD WALRUS FACE.

Now, as usual, our class had been kicking up a row while Mr Brown was out. Johnny Mack drew a funny picture on the blackboard. It was meant to be our teacher, but he was drawn like an old walrus. When Mr Brown caught sight of that drawing he went off the deep end. And it was funny to see how really like an angry old walrus he looked, with his big whiskers and all. "So!" he cried. "We have an artist in the class – a comic artist!" You know the way angry teachers talk.

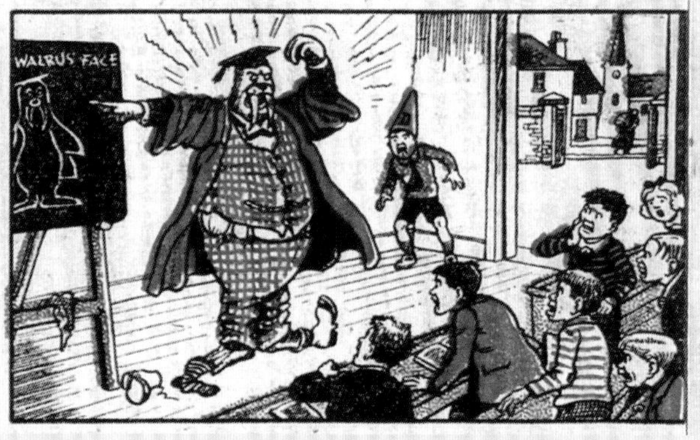

WALRUS FACE

Presently we heard him say something like this – "I wish I WERE a walrus! I'd give you all a proper fright, I would!" And that's when the awful thing happened! One moment Mr Brown was standing there. And next moment it was a real live walrus that was stamping on the classroom floor! A walrus dressed up in Mr Brown's clothes! We don't know how it happened, but Mr Brown's hands and feet suddenly turned into flippers – and two great big shiny tusks grew out from his mouth!

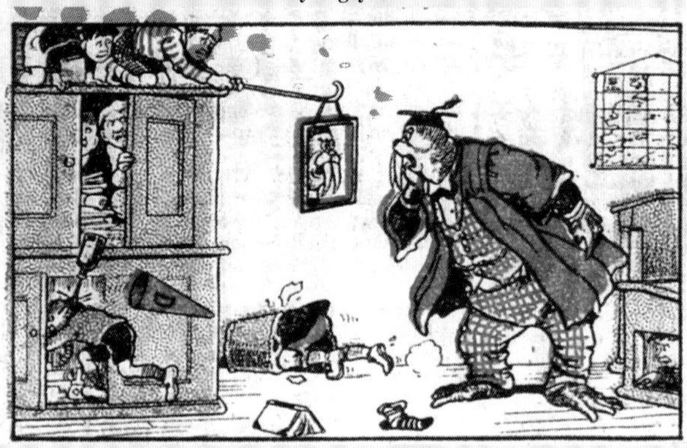

We all thought this ferocious-looking beast would tear us into little pieces. We hid under the desks, inside the cupboards, anywhere. "What's going on here?" the walrus cried. And the voice we heard was still our teacher's voice, though it had gone hoarse and croaky. "I feel funny. What's happened to me?" "Y–you don't look f–funny, sir," quavered Dickie Moore. He held up a mirror to let the walrus see its face.

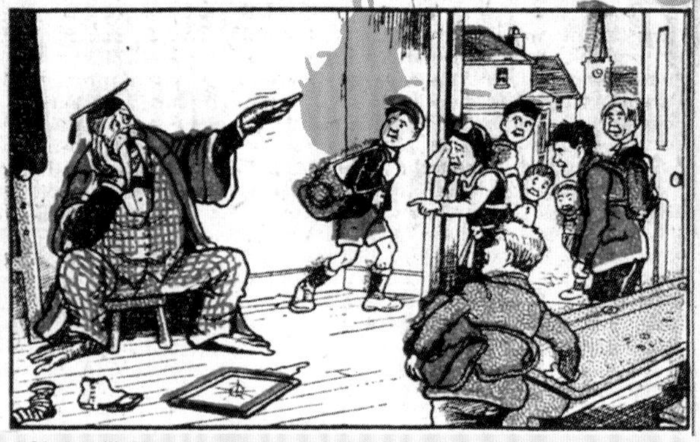

"Oh dear!" The walrus groaned. "Oh dear, oh dear! What on earth has happened to me? It must have been that gipsy's magic pill! This is terrible!" Poor old Mr Brown! We began to see that the walrus really was Mr Brown, although he had changed so much. He had taken on the shape and looks of a real walrus, but he could still speak and think like a man. Our teacher sat down on a stool. He seemed to be dazed.

The story of our teacher's magic wish—It made him think forever of nothing but fish!

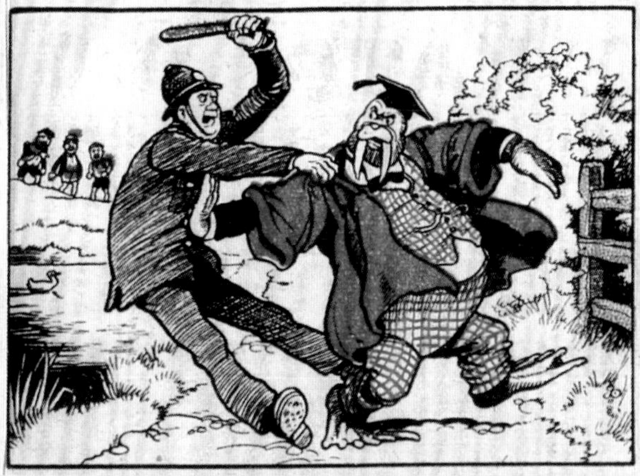

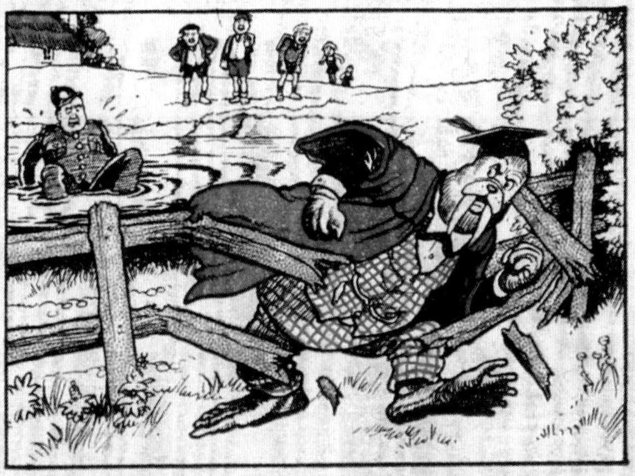

"Go home, children," Mr Brown told us in his croaky walrus voice. "Don't say a word about this. I'll have to think it over." Well, we all went home, and the funny thing was we weren't glad. We were really sorry for poor Mr Brown. He went home, too, but on the way he was nearly arrested. PC Gobbins, the village flatfoot, met up with him and thought he must have escaped from a circus. But when he tried to take this fancy-dressed walrus in charge, he got shoved into a duck-pond!

After that, Mr Brown burst clean through the fence and sneaked off home by a roundabout way. He was worrying all the time, worrying about what Miss Primrose, his housekeeper, would say; and worrying about the police, whether they would lock him up in a zoo like a real walrus. A few of us youngsters were worried, too. We didn't want our old teacher to be taken away, and maybe get a nasty school mistress in his place. So we hurried up to Mr Brown's house just after tea.

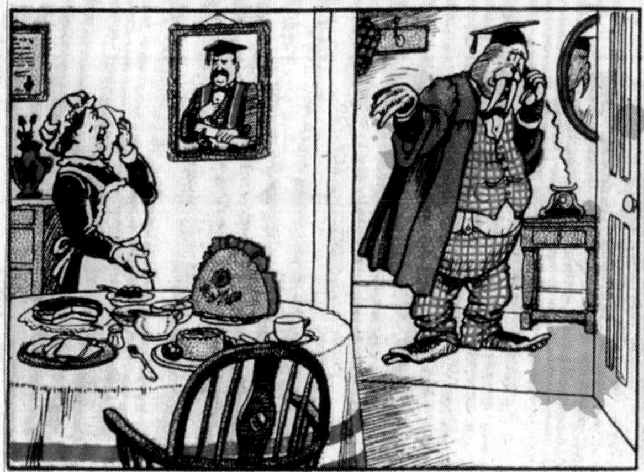

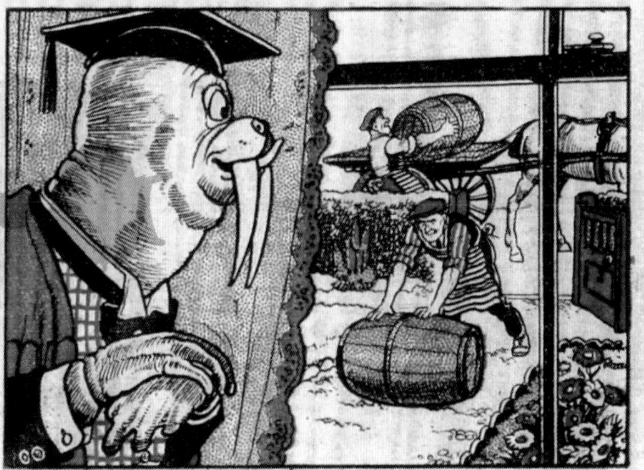

What goings-on there had been! First of all, when Miss Primrose opened the door she screamed with fright. And our teacher said, "Please don't be alarmed, Miss Primrose. There's been a strange accident, and I have turned into a w–walrus." That was enough. Miss Primrose didn't say a word. She just flopped down in a faint, and Mr Brown had to pull her inside the house and pour cold water over her. He must have had a tough job explaining things to her when she got her senses back.

Anyway, she said – "I don't understand, Mr Brown. But tea's ready." "Tea!" Mr Brown growled. "Bah! I don't want tea! I want fish – a lot of fish!" He seized the phone and called up the Burford fishmonger. "This is Mr Brown speaking," he said. "I have a tame walrus at home just now. Could you let me have two barrels of fish to feed it with?" I'll bet that fishmonger got a shock! Still, he sent the fish up, and Mr Brown fairly rubbed his flippers as he watched them being delivered.

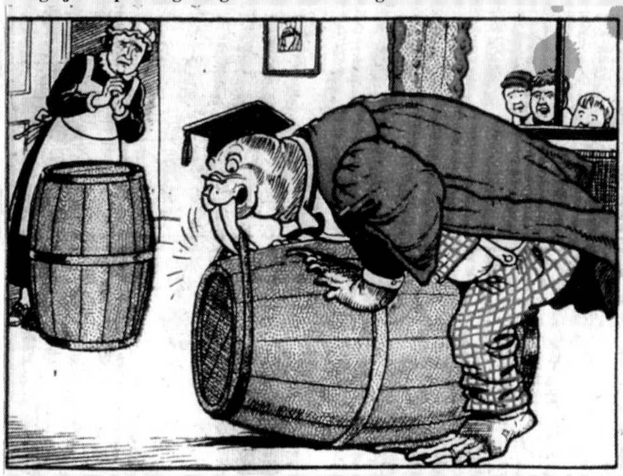

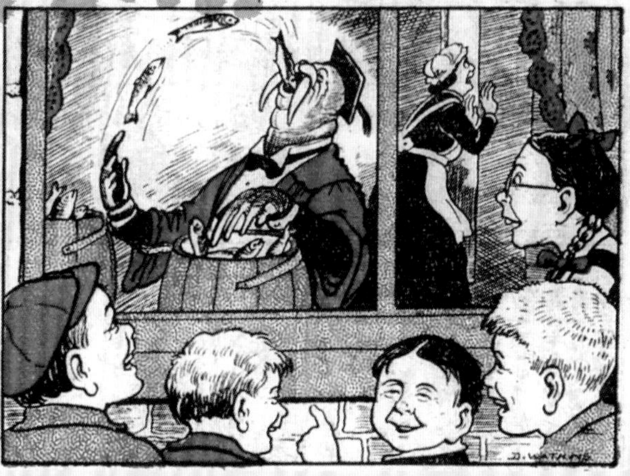

Our teacher was hungry, of course – hungry as a walrus! When those barrels of fish arrived we watched him using his walrus tusks to tear off the metal hoops and burst the barrels open. Then he started eating. What a sight that was! Those fish were tossed into his big mouth in a never-ending stream. It was funny. At least, we thought it was funny, till Dickie Moore said – "Listen, you chaps, this is a bad business."

He went on talking quietly. "Our teacher's in danger. What do you think will happen when people find out he's been changed into a walrus? They'll lock him up somewhere – old Brown, the best teacher in the world. We'll have to save him – somehow!" But it looked as though Mr Brown enjoyed being a walrus by now, the way he was scoffing those fish. It was going to be a big job, getting him turned back into a man again.

So as not to disappoint you — here is the last episode.

Tons of walrus trouble, heaps of walrus strife—
OUR TEACHER'S A WALRUS!

Education Office, Wellgrove 2/12/47
Dear Mr Brown, This is to inform you that Mr Lawson, school inspector, will arrive at Burford School to-morrow.
Yours sincerely, J. Hatton Education Officer.

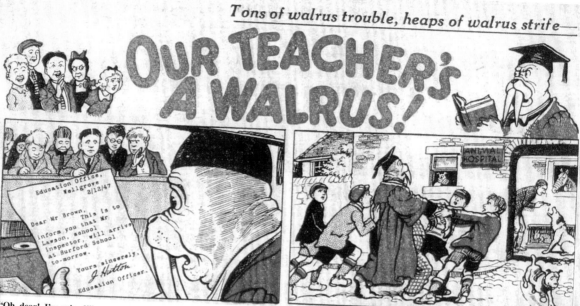

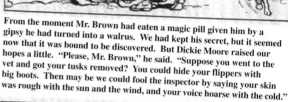

"Oh, dear! I'm ruined!" gasped our teacher in his hoarse voice. We wondered what was wrong, but he soon told us, his big walrus eyes blinking as he spoke. "Children," he rambled, "I'm afraid you'll soon have a new teacher. This letter that has just arrived says he will be discovered." His voice broke. "They – they'll s-sack me!" Poor old Walrus Face. We were all sorry for him, for he was a very kind old chap.

ANIMAL HOSPITAL

From the moment Mr. Brown had eaten a magic pill given him by a gipsy he had turned into a walrus. We had kept his secret, but it seemed now that it was bound to be discovered. But Dickie Moore raised our hopes a little. "Please, Mr. Brown," he said. "Suppose you went to the vet and got your tusks removed? You could hide your flippers with big boots. Then may be we could fool the inspector by saying your skin was rough with the sun and the wind, and your voice hoarse with the cold."

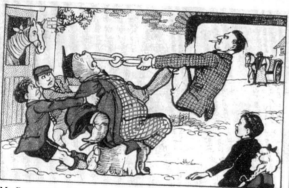

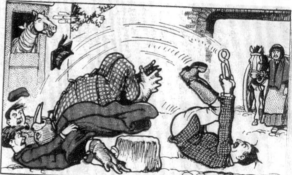

Mr. Brown didn't like the idea at all, but in the end he agreed to try it. So we took him along to the animal hospital in the village. Poor Mr. Brown! He behaved just like one of us going to the dentist's! His courage deserted him, and he we finished up by dragging him inside. "Don't be a big cissy, Mr. Brown," cried Dickie. "You want to be a man again, don't you? Come on." Just the same, when we saw the et try to pull our teacher's tusks – well, we didn't blame our teacher for being scared"

The vet placed Mr. Brown on an old tree stump in the yard. He told us to keep a tight grip on his shoulders, then grabbed a tusk with his very biggest pair of pliers. He yanked and grunted and yanked again, then braced his feet on our teacher's tummy and yanked like billyo. Did the tusk come out? It did not! But the pliers slipped off the tusk. The vet went flying in one direction and Mr. Brown toppled over the opposite way – right on top of us. It was too late. The tusks wouldn't come out.

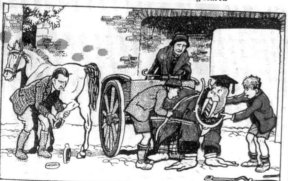

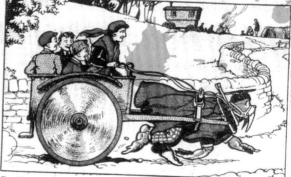

But just then someone appeared on the scene – the person Mr. Brown had been seeking for weeks and weeks – the very gipsy woman who had given him the magic pill! Walrus Face groaned out his story to the gipsy and she was very sorry to hear about his misfortune in turning into a walrus! "I can help you, sir," she said. "I can get you one more magic wishing pill. But my pony is lame. He won't be able to take us to my camp."

But Mr. Brown couldn't wait. He was desperate. And Dickie Moore came to the rescue with another idea. "If you draw the little trap, Mr. Brown," he suggested, "we – er – some of us could go to the gipsy camp with you. We wouldn't use the whip, of course." He hurriedly added that bit when he saw our teacher's face. But he needn't have worried. Walrus face was anxious to become a man again. He wouldn't need any whipping!

Till a pill puts an end to our teacher's walrus life!

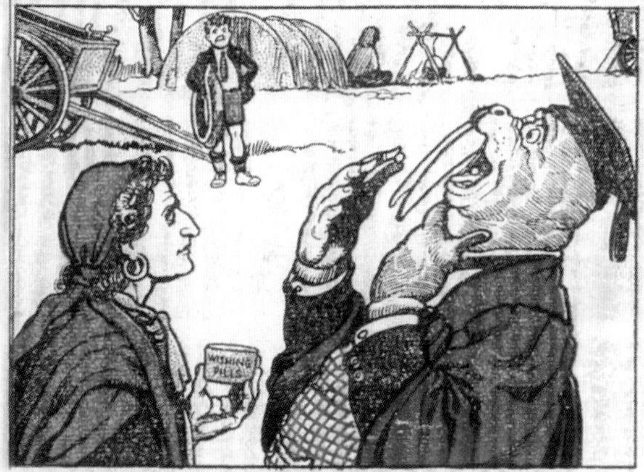
WISHING PILLS

Soon he was harnessed into the shafts of the trap, and off he pranced on all fours, much faster than he ever could get along on two legs. In half an hour we reached the gipsy camp, which was just off the main road. The gipsy woman kept her word. She brought out her special box with a single magic wishing pill in it, and she gave it to Walrus Face. "Remember you have only one chance, sir. You must make the wish after you swallow the pill. Don't make a mistake this time."

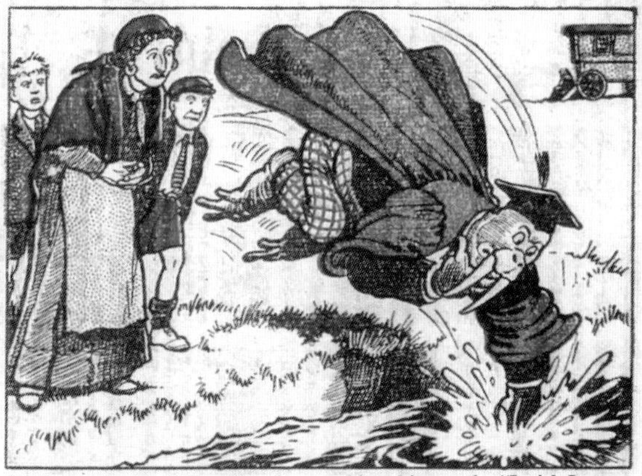

M. Brown grabbed the pill and popped into his mouth. "I wish I were myself again! I wish I were myself again!" he muttered, repeating his dearest wish over and over again to make certain he wouldn't make a bloomer this time. But something went wrong! His throat was so dry he couldn't swallow!" "Take a drink of water," urged the gipsy. And Walrus Face was so eager that he leapt right into the stream that ran at the foot of the meadow. He remained under the surface for a long time.

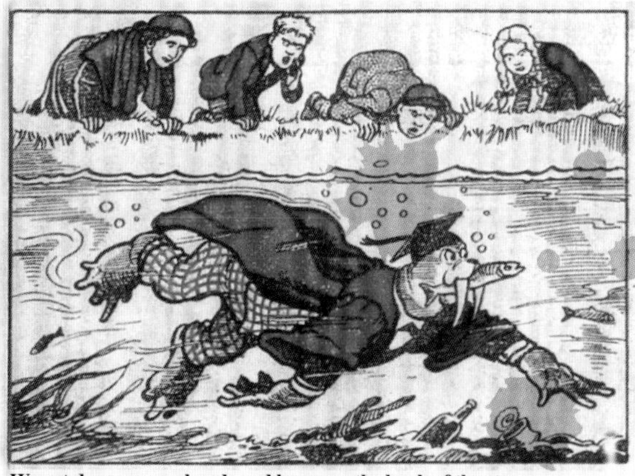

We got down on our hands and knees on the bank of the stream. "Remember to wish, Mr. Brown!" yelled Dickie. Of course, Walrus Face couldn't hear him. He was under water. To our horror we saw him swim after a fish and grab it in his great mouth. "Oh, dear! He's still a walrus! He's forgotten to wish!" cried Winnie Moffat. But Winnie was wrong. For just then we saw the most amazing change come over Walrus Face!

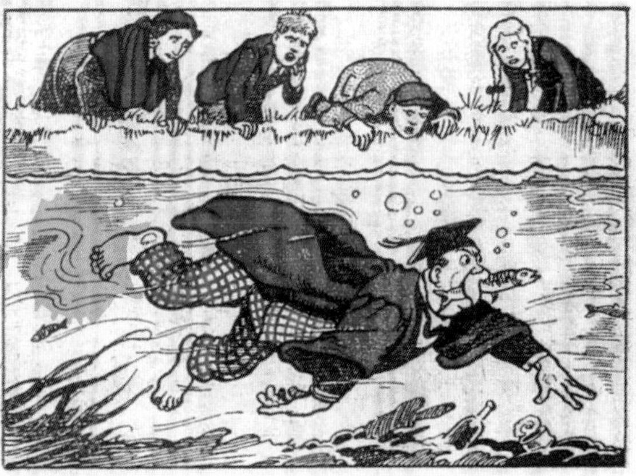

He was on his way up from his dive, with the fish in his mouth. But in spite of his walrus hunting instincts he must have remember his wish. For as we watched we saw his leather skin turn pale pink. His tusks vanished and were replaced by our teacher's familiar moustache. His big walrus snout grew smaller. His huge flippers turned into ordinary human hands and feet. Our teacher was a man again!

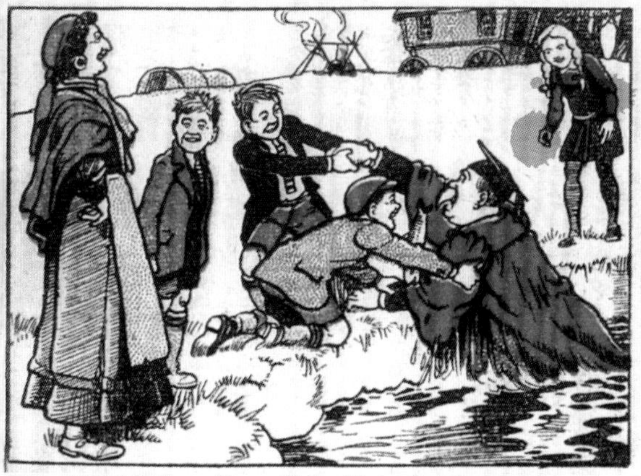

"Hurrah for Mr. Brown!" we yelled as his head came out of the water. Our teacher was so flummoxed by the change in his appearance that he still had the fish in his mouth. He spat it out. "Phew! I hate fish!" he growled – but his voice wasn't hoarse any longer"! He spoke exactly as he had done before he became a walrus. "It's cold – let's go home!" he said then. After thanking the gipsy, we scooted home as fast as we could.

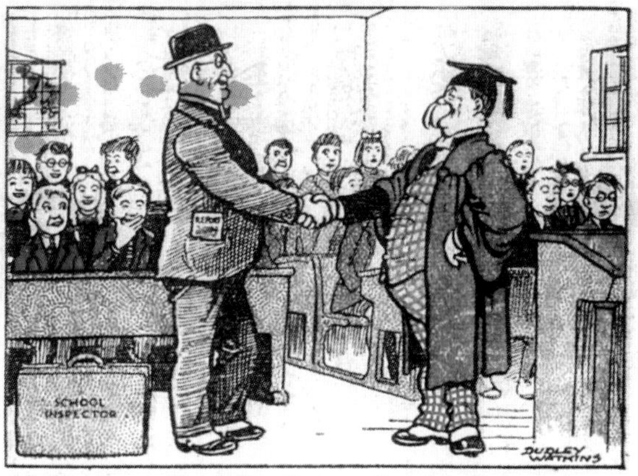
SCHOOL INSPECTOR
DUDLEY WATKINS

Mr. Brown was cold and shivery but very pleased that he was a man once again. We tucked him snugly into bed. But next day at school, our teacher turned up just as he always had been before he ate the magic pill. It was grand to hear the inspector congratulate him. Mr. Brown was very proud. It was good to have him back again – but afterwards we often thought longingly of the fun we had when our teacher was a walrus."

LORD SNOOTY

Lord Snooty dressed for top public school Eton but actually attended the Bunkerton village school with his pals. These early strips are from Beano Books and drawn by Dudley D Watkins.

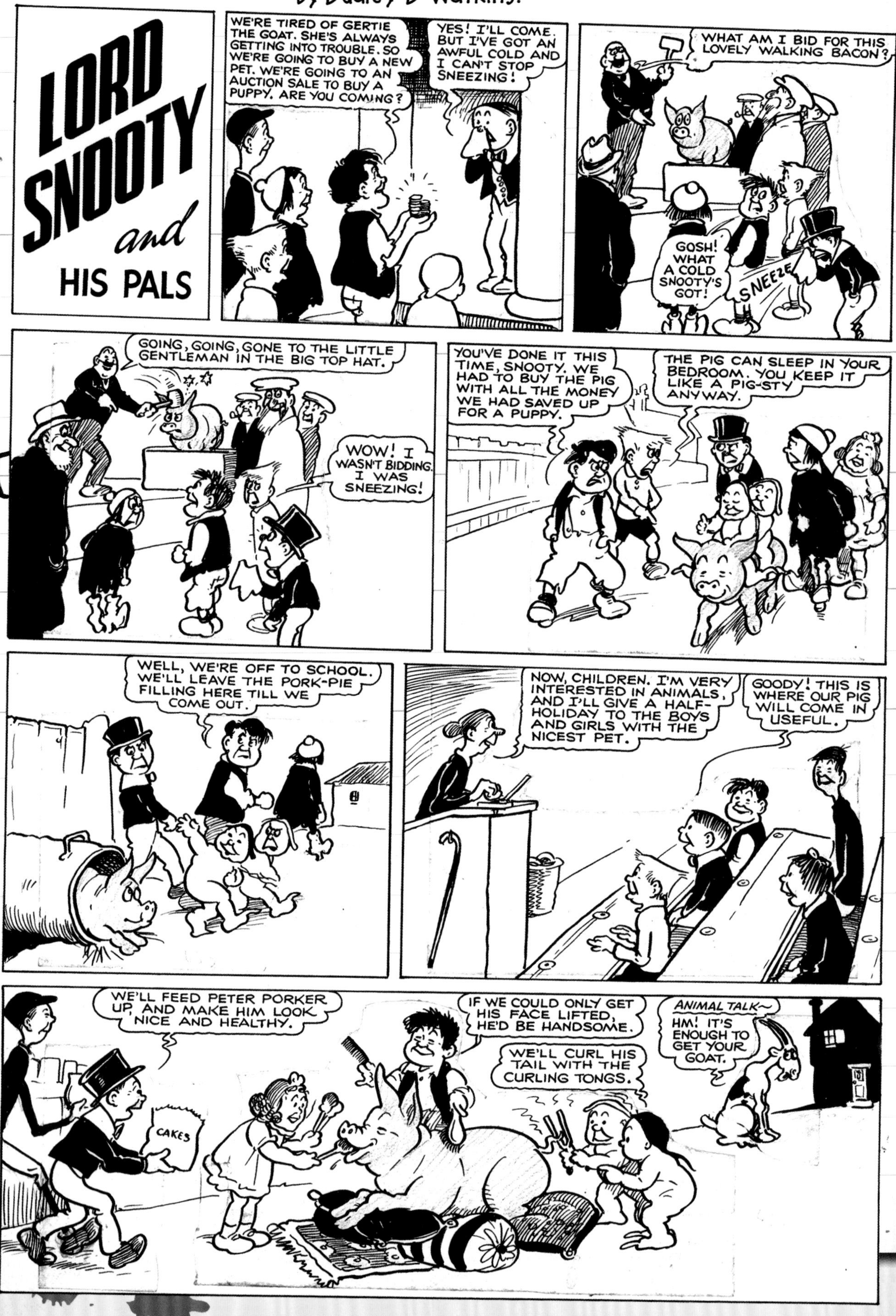
LORD SNOOTY and HIS PALS
WE'RE TIRED OF GERTIE THE GOAT. SHE'S ALWAYS GETTING INTO TROUBLE. SO WE'RE GOING TO BUY A NEW PET. WE'RE GOING TO AN AUCTION SALE TO BUY A PUPPY. ARE YOU COMING?
YES! I'LL COME. BUT I'VE GOT AN AWFUL COLD AND I CAN'T STOP SNEEZING!
WHAT AM I BID FOR THIS LOVELY WALKING BACON?
GOSH! WHAT A COLD SNOOTY'S GOT!
SNEEZE
GOING, GOING, GONE TO THE LITTLE GENTLEMAN IN THE BIG TOP HAT.
WOW! I WASN'T BIDDING. I WAS SNEEZING!
YOU'VE DONE IT THIS TIME, SNOOTY. WE HAD TO BUY THE PIG WITH ALL THE MONEY WE HAD SAVED UP FOR A PUPPY.
THE PIG CAN SLEEP IN YOUR BEDROOM. YOU KEEP IT LIKE A PIG-STY ANYWAY.
WELL, WE'RE OFF TO SCHOOL. WE'LL LEAVE THE PORK-PIE FILLING HERE TILL WE COME OUT.
NOW, CHILDREN. I'M VERY INTERESTED IN ANIMALS, AND I'LL GIVE A HALF-HOLIDAY TO THE BOYS AND GIRLS WITH THE NICEST PET.
GOODY! THIS IS WHERE OUR PIG WILL COME IN USEFUL.
WE'LL FEED PETER PORKER UP, AND MAKE HIM LOOK NICE AND HEALTHY.
CAKES
IF WE COULD ONLY GET HIS FACE LIFTED, HE'D BE HANDSOME.
WE'LL CURL HIS TAIL WITH THE CURLING TONGS.
ANIMAL TALK~
HM! IT'S ENOUGH TO GET YOUR GOAT.

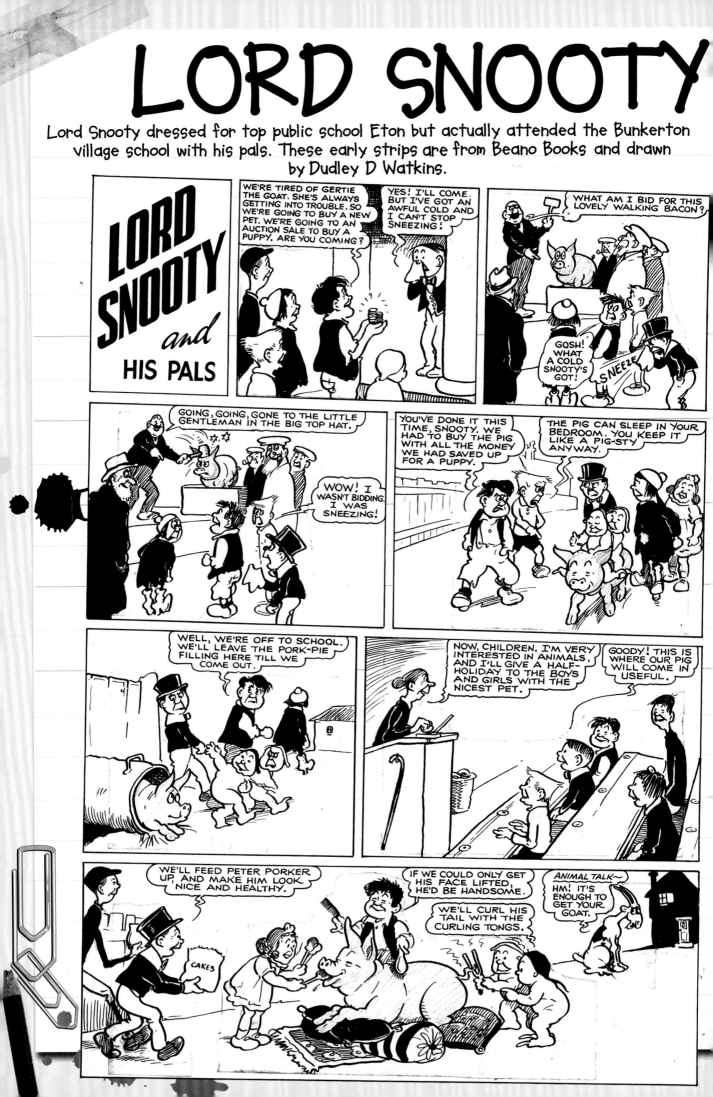

AT SCHOOL

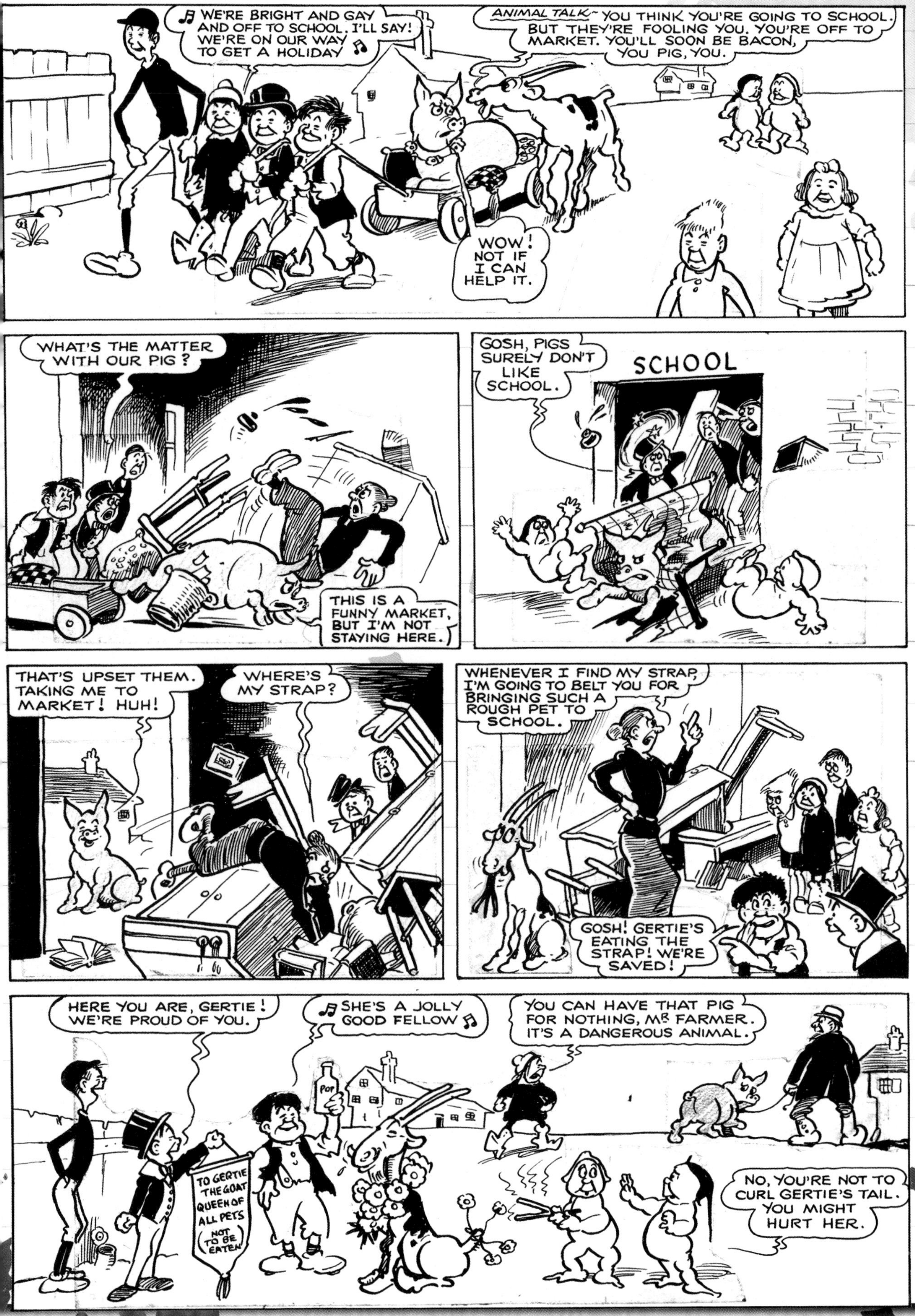
WE'RE BRIGHT AND GAY AND OFF TO SCHOOL. I'LL SAY! WE'RE ON OUR WAY TO GET A HOLIDAY
ANIMAL TALK ~ YOU THINK YOU'RE GOING TO SCHOOL. BUT THEY'RE FOOLING YOU. YOU'RE OFF TO MARKET. YOU'LL SOON BE BACON, YOU PIG, YOU.
WOW! NOT IF I CAN HELP IT.
WHAT'S THE MATTER WITH OUR PIG?
THIS IS A FUNNY MARKET, BUT I'M NOT STAYING HERE.
GOSH, PIGS SURELY DON'T LIKE SCHOOL.
SCHOOL
THAT'S UPSET THEM. TAKING ME TO MARKET! HUH!
WHERE'S MY STRAP?
WHENEVER I FIND MY STRAP, I'M GOING TO BELT YOU FOR BRINGING SUCH A ROUGH PET TO SCHOOL.
GOSH! GERTIE'S EATING THE STRAP! WE'RE SAVED!
HERE YOU ARE, GERTIE! WE'RE PROUD OF YOU.
TO GERTIE THE GOAT QUEEN OF ALL PETS (NOT TO BE EATEN)
SHE'S A JOLLY GOOD FELLOW
POP
YOU CAN HAVE THAT PIG FOR NOTHING, MR FARMER. IT'S A DANGEROUS ANIMAL.
NO, YOU'RE NOT TO CURL GERTIE'S TAIL. YOU MIGHT HURT HER.

1950 P54

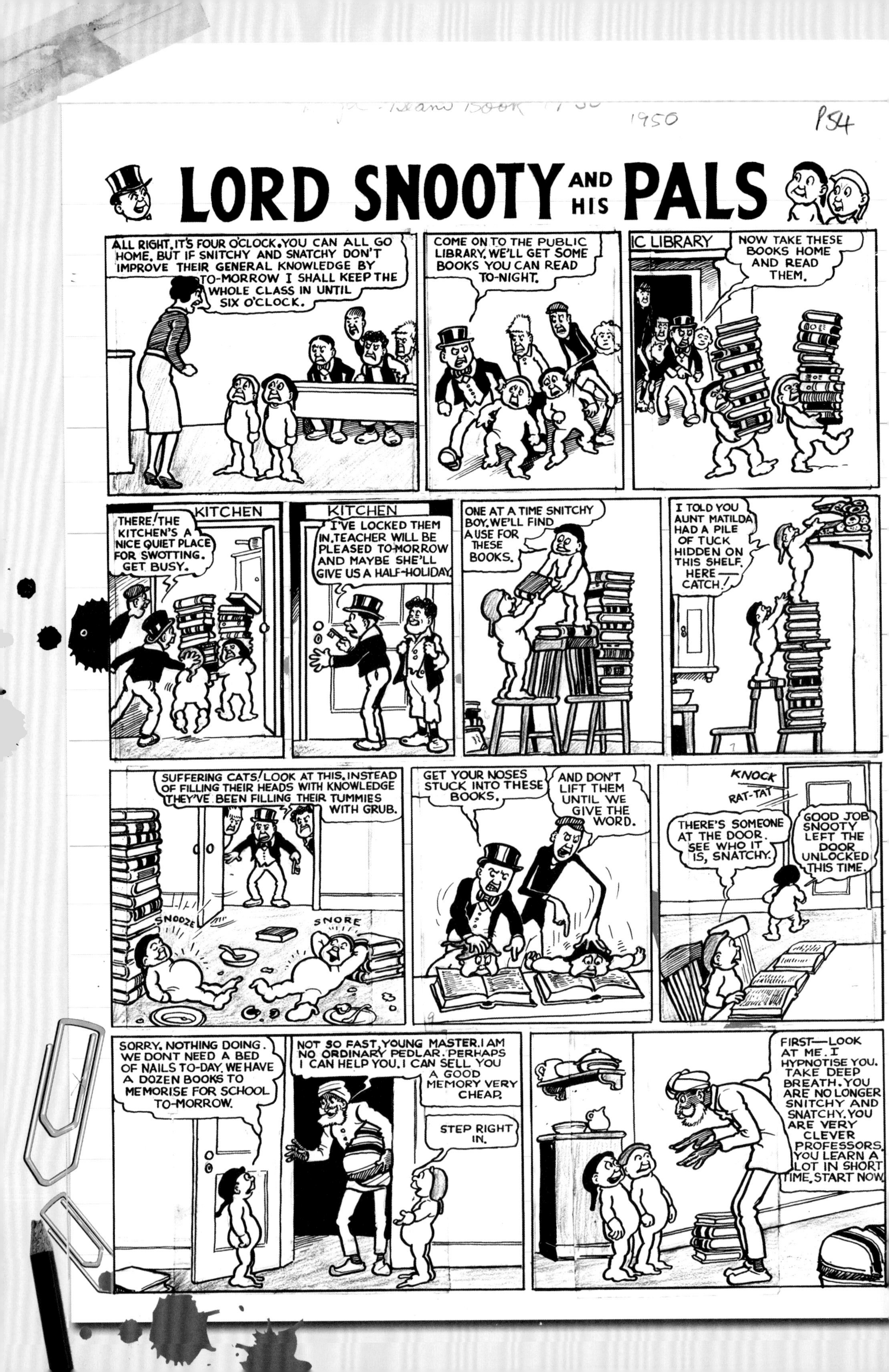

LORD SNOOTY AND HIS PALS
ALL RIGHT, IT'S FOUR O'CLOCK. YOU CAN ALL GO HOME, BUT IF SNITCHY AND SNATCHY DON'T IMPROVE THEIR GENERAL KNOWLEDGE BY TO-MORROW I SHALL KEEP THE WHOLE CLASS IN UNTIL SIX O'CLOCK.
COME ON TO THE PUBLIC LIBRARY, WE'LL GET SOME BOOKS YOU CAN READ TO-NIGHT.
IC LIBRARY
NOW TAKE THESE BOOKS HOME AND READ THEM.
KITCHEN
THERE! THE KITCHEN'S A NICE QUIET PLACE FOR SWOTTING. GET BUSY.
KITCHEN
I'VE LOCKED THEM IN. TEACHER WILL BE PLEASED TO-MORROW AND MAYBE SHE'LL GIVE US A HALF-HOLIDAY.
ONE AT A TIME SNITCHY BOY. WE'LL FIND A USE FOR THESE BOOKS.
I TOLD YOU AUNT MATILDA HAD A PILE OF TUCK HIDDEN ON THIS SHELF. HERE — CATCH!
SUFFERING CATS! LOOK AT THIS. INSTEAD OF FILLING THEIR HEADS WITH KNOWLEDGE THEY'VE BEEN FILLING THEIR TUMMIES WITH GRUB.
SNOOZE
SNORE
GET YOUR NOSES STUCK INTO THESE BOOKS.
AND DON'T LIFT THEM UNTIL WE GIVE THE WORD.
KNOCK
RAT-TAT
THERE'S SOMEONE AT THE DOOR. SEE WHO IT IS, SNATCHY.
GOOD JOB SNOOTY LEFT THE DOOR UNLOCKED THIS TIME.
SORRY, NOTHING DOING. WE DONT NEED A BED OF NAILS TO-DAY. WE HAVE A DOZEN BOOKS TO MEMORISE FOR SCHOOL TO-MORROW.
NOT SO FAST, YOUNG MASTER. I AM NO ORDINARY PEDLAR. PERHAPS I CAN HELP YOU. I CAN SELL YOU A GOOD MEMORY VERY CHEAP.
STEP RIGHT IN.
FIRST — LOOK AT ME. I HYPNOTISE YOU. TAKE DEEP BREATH. YOU ARE NO LONGER SNITCHY AND SNATCHY. YOU ARE VERY CLEVER PROFESSORS. YOU LEARN A LOT IN SHORT TIME. START NOW.

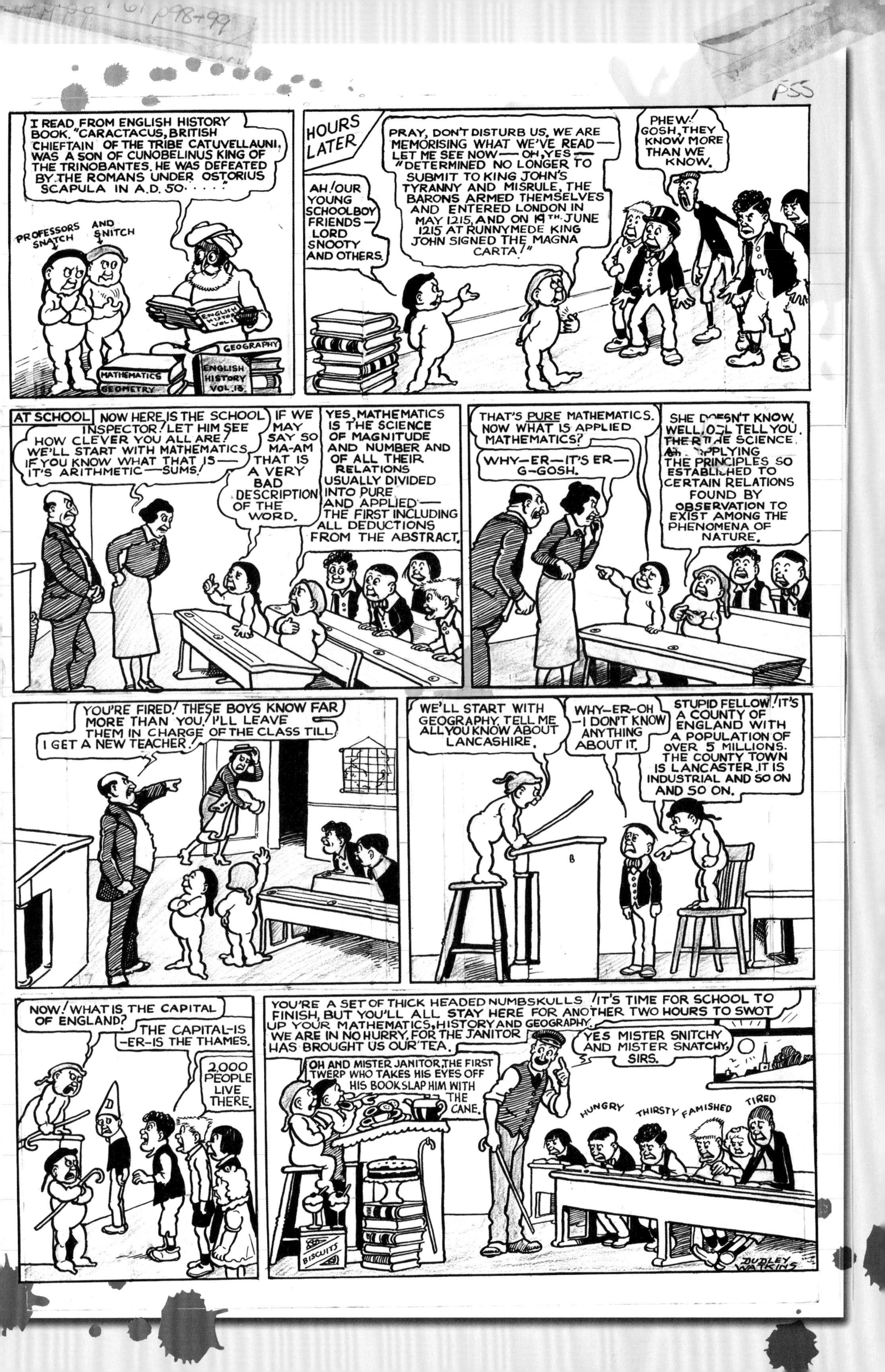

I READ FROM ENGLISH HISTORY BOOK. "CARACTACUS, BRITISH CHIEFTAIN OF THE TRIBE CATUVELLAUNI, WAS A SON OF CUNOBELINUS KING OF THE TRINOBANTES. HE WAS DEFEATED BY THE ROMANS UNDER OSTORIUS SCAPULA IN A.D. 50 . . . ."
PROFESSORS SNATCH
AND SNITCH
ENGLISH HISTORY VOL. 1
GEOGRAPHY
MATHEMATICS
GEOMETRY
ENGLISH HISTORY VOL. 15
HOURS LATER
AH! OUR YOUNG SCHOOLBOY FRIENDS — LORD SNOOTY AND OTHERS.
PRAY, DON'T DISTURB US, WE ARE MEMORISING WHAT WE'VE READ — LET ME SEE NOW — OH, YES — "DETERMINED NO LONGER TO SUBMIT TO KING JOHN'S TYRANNY AND MISRULE, THE BARONS ARMED THEMSELVES AND ENTERED LONDON IN MAY 1215, AND ON 19TH JUNE 1215 AT RUNNYMEDE KING JOHN SIGNED THE MAGNA CARTA!"
PHEW! GOSH, THEY KNOW MORE THAN WE KNOW.
AT SCHOOL
NOW HERE IS THE SCHOOL INSPECTOR! LET HIM SEE HOW CLEVER YOU ALL ARE! WE'LL START WITH MATHEMATICS IF YOU KNOW WHAT THAT IS — IT'S ARITHMETIC — SUMS!
IF WE MAY SAY SO MA-AM THAT IS A VERY BAD DESCRIPTION OF THE WORD.
YES, MATHEMATICS IS THE SCIENCE OF MAGNITUDE AND NUMBER AND OF ALL THEIR RELATIONS USUALLY DIVIDED INTO PURE AND APPLIED — THE FIRST INCLUDING ALL DEDUCTIONS FROM THE ABSTRACT.
THAT'S PURE MATHEMATICS. NOW WHAT IS APPLIED MATHEMATICS?
WHY—ER—IT'S ER— G-GOSH.
SHE DOESN'T KNOW. WELL, TELL YOU. THE SCIENCE PLYING THE PRINCIPLES SO ESTABLISHED TO CERTAIN RELATIONS FOUND BY OBSERVATION TO EXIST AMONG THE PHENOMENA OF NATURE.
YOU'RE FIRED! THESE BOYS KNOW FAR MORE THAN YOU! I'LL LEAVE THEM IN CHARGE OF THE CLASS TILL I GET A NEW TEACHER.
WE'LL START WITH GEOGRAPHY. TELL ME ALL YOU KNOW ABOUT LANCASHIRE.
WHY-ER-OH —I DON'T KNOW ANYTHING ABOUT IT.
STUPID FELLOW! IT'S A COUNTY OF ENGLAND WITH A POPULATION OF OVER 5 MILLIONS. THE COUNTY TOWN IS LANCASTER. IT IS INDUSTRIAL AND SO ON AND SO ON.
NOW! WHAT IS THE CAPITAL OF ENGLAND?
THE CAPITAL-IS -ER-IS THE THAMES.
2,000 PEOPLE LIVE THERE.
YOU'RE A SET OF THICK HEADED NUMBSKULLS! IT'S TIME FOR SCHOOL TO FINISH, BUT YOU'LL ALL STAY HERE FOR ANOTHER TWO HOURS TO SWOT UP YOUR MATHEMATICS, HISTORY AND GEOGRAPHY. WE ARE IN NO HURRY, FOR THE JANITOR HAS BROUGHT US OUR TEA.
YES MISTER SNITCHY AND MISTER SNATCHY, SIRS.
OH AND MISTER JANITOR, THE FIRST TWERP WHO TAKES HIS EYES OFF HIS BOOK SLAP HIM WITH THE CANE.
HUNGRY
THIRSTY
FAMISHED
TIRED
BISCUITS
DUDLEY WATKINS

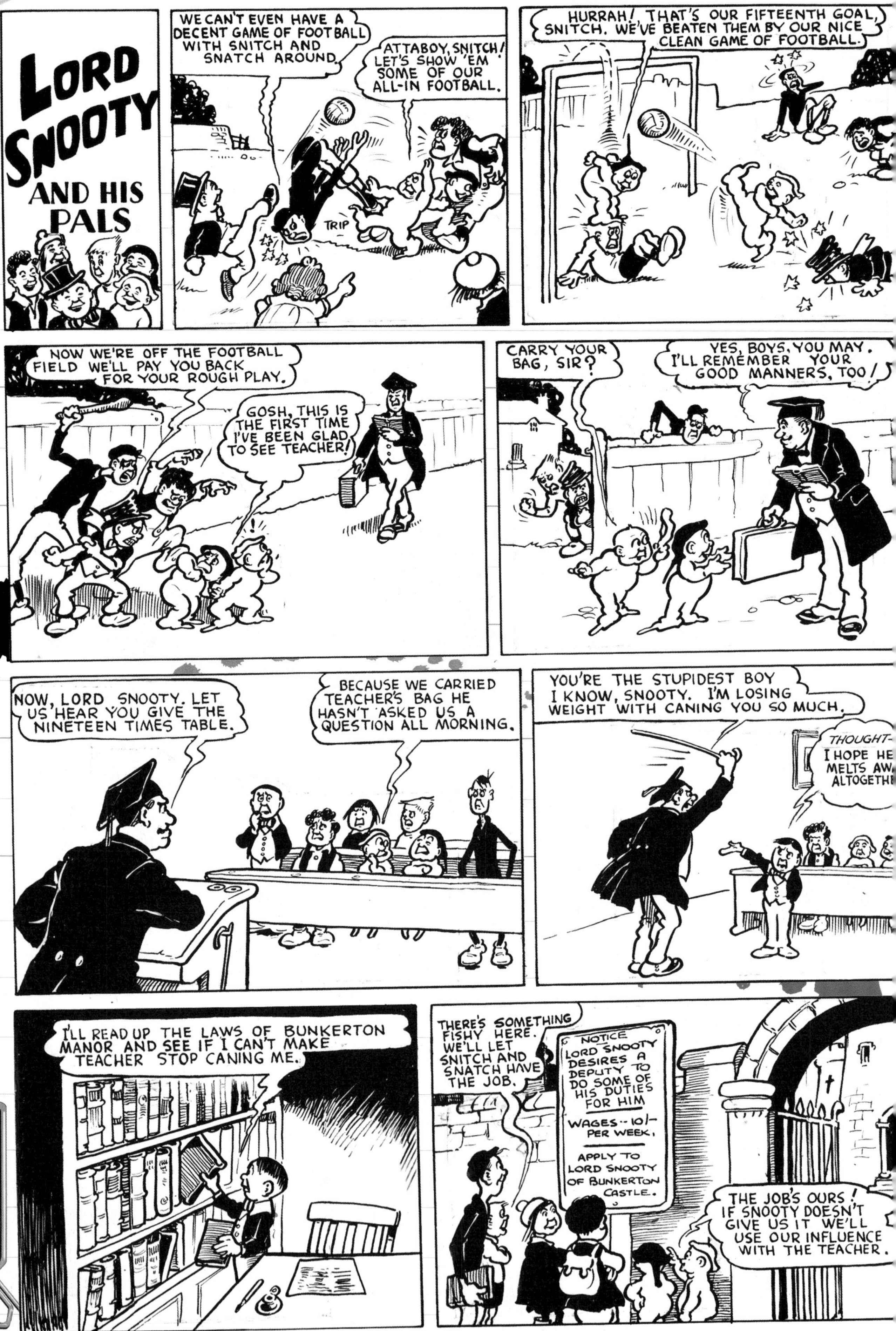
LORD SNOOTY AND HIS PALS
WE CAN'T EVEN HAVE A DECENT GAME OF FOOTBALL WITH SNITCH AND SNATCH AROUND.
ATTABOY, SNITCH! LET'S SHOW 'EM SOME OF OUR ALL-IN FOOTBALL.
TRIP
HURRAH! THAT'S OUR FIFTEENTH GOAL, SNITCH. WE'VE BEATEN THEM BY OUR NICE CLEAN GAME OF FOOTBALL.
NOW WE'RE OFF THE FOOTBALL FIELD WE'LL PAY YOU BACK FOR YOUR ROUGH PLAY.
GOSH, THIS IS THE FIRST TIME I'VE BEEN GLAD TO SEE TEACHER!
CARRY YOUR BAG, SIR?
YES, BOYS, YOU MAY. I'LL REMEMBER YOUR GOOD MANNERS, TOO!
NOW, LORD SNOOTY, LET US HEAR YOU GIVE THE NINETEEN TIMES TABLE.
BECAUSE WE CARRIED TEACHER'S BAG HE HASN'T ASKED US A QUESTION ALL MORNING.
YOU'RE THE STUPIDEST BOY I KNOW, SNOOTY. I'M LOSING WEIGHT WITH CANING YOU SO MUCH.
THOUGHT-
I HOPE HE MELTS AW
ALTOGETH
I'LL READ UP THE LAWS OF BUNKERTON MANOR AND SEE IF I CAN'T MAKE TEACHER STOP CANING ME.
THERE'S SOMETHING FISHY HERE. WE'LL LET SNITCH AND SNATCH HAVE THE JOB.
NOTICE
LORD SNOOTY DESIRES A DEPUTY TO DO SOME OF HIS DUTIES FOR HIM
WAGES -- 10/- PER WEEK.
APPLY TO LORD SNOOTY OF BUNKERTON CASTLE.
THE JOB'S OURS! IF SNOOTY DOESN'T GIVE US IT WE'LL USE OUR INFLUENCE WITH THE TEACHER.

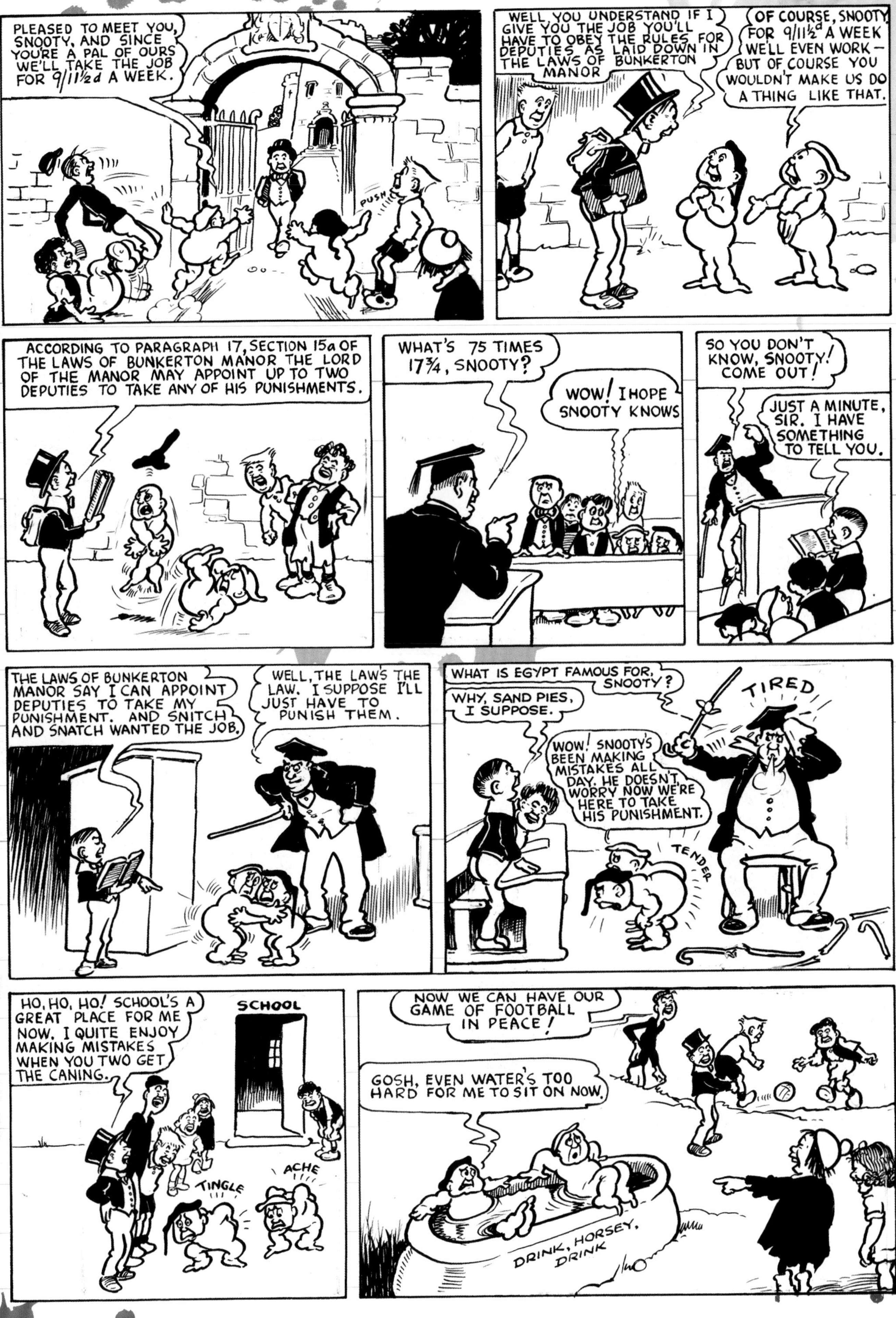
PLEASED TO MEET YOU, SNOOTY, AND SINCE YOU'RE A PAL OF OURS WE'LL TAKE THE JOB FOR 9/11½d A WEEK.
PUSH
WELL YOU UNDERSTAND IF I GIVE YOU THE JOB YOU'LL HAVE TO OBEY THE RULES FOR DEPUTIES AS LAID DOWN IN THE LAWS OF BUNKERTON MANOR
OF COURSE, SNOOTY, FOR 9/11½d A WEEK WE'LL EVEN WORK — BUT OF COURSE YOU WOULDN'T MAKE US DO A THING LIKE THAT.
ACCORDING TO PARAGRAPH 17, SECTION 15a OF THE LAWS OF BUNKERTON MANOR THE LORD OF THE MANOR MAY APPOINT UP TO TWO DEPUTIES TO TAKE ANY OF HIS PUNISHMENTS.
WHAT'S 75 TIMES 17¾, SNOOTY?
WOW! I HOPE SNOOTY KNOWS
SO YOU DON'T KNOW, SNOOTY! COME OUT!
JUST A MINUTE, SIR. I HAVE SOMETHING TO TELL YOU.
THE LAWS OF BUNKERTON MANOR SAY I CAN APPOINT DEPUTIES TO TAKE MY PUNISHMENT. AND SNITCH AND SNATCH WANTED THE JOB.
WELL, THE LAW'S THE LAW. I SUPPOSE I'LL JUST HAVE TO PUNISH THEM.
WHAT IS EGYPT FAMOUS FOR, SNOOTY?
WHY, SAND PIES, I SUPPOSE.
TIRED
WOW! SNOOTY'S BEEN MAKING MISTAKES ALL DAY. HE DOESN'T WORRY NOW WE'RE HERE TO TAKE HIS PUNISHMENT.
TENDER
HO, HO, HO! SCHOOL'S A GREAT PLACE FOR ME NOW. I QUITE ENJOY MAKING MISTAKES WHEN YOU TWO GET THE CANING.
SCHOOL
TINGLE
ACHE
NOW WE CAN HAVE OUR GAME OF FOOTBALL IN PEACE!
GOSH, EVEN WATER'S TOO HARD FOR ME TO SIT ON NOW.
DRINK, HORSEY, DRINK

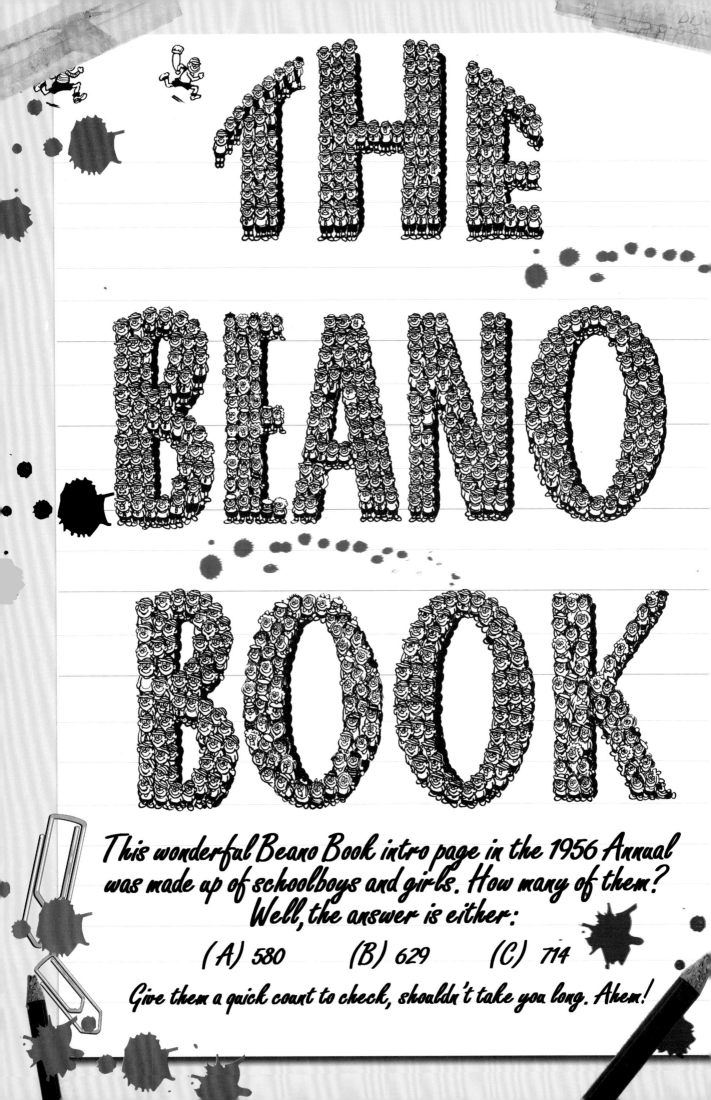

THE BEANO BOOK

This wonderful Beano Book intro page in the 1956 Annual
was made up of schoolboys and girls. How many of them?
Well, the answer is either:

(A) 580   (B) 629   (C) 714

Give them a quick count to check, shouldn't take you long. Ahem!

Winker WATSON

One of the best known schoolboys in Britain, Winker was billed as the champion schoolboy wangler. His life as a pupil at Greytowers School was full of prep classes, boring old history lessons, cricket and wonderful midnight feasts with a tuck hamper in the dorm.

In the many series of this story Winker worked his wangles against bullies, rich rotters and stuffy school rules. His main opponent was his nasty form master Clarence Creep.

The classic series were drawn by the inimitable Eric Roberts and during the sixties and seventies Winker was the only strip ever to better Desperate Dan in the Dandy readers popularity polls.

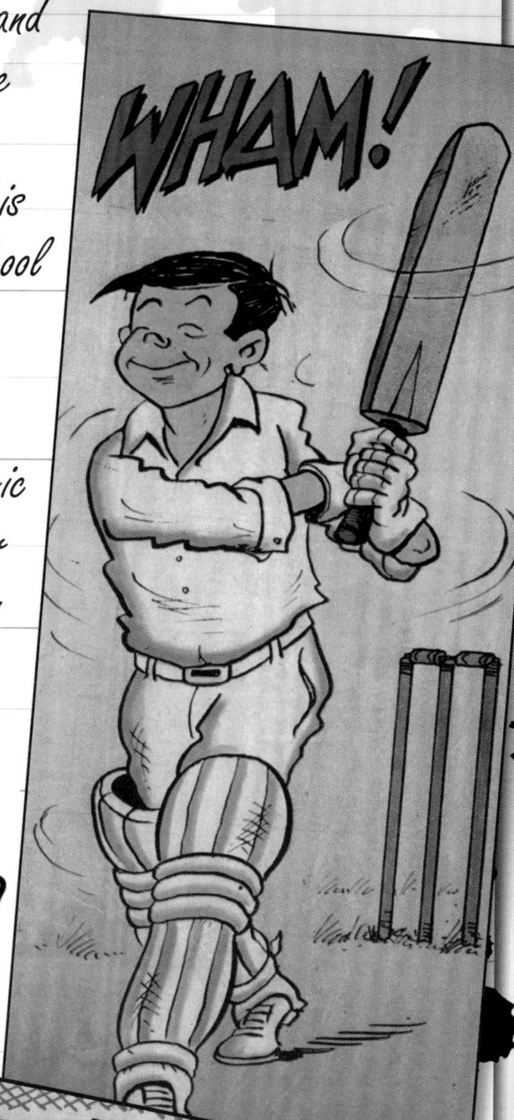
WHAM!

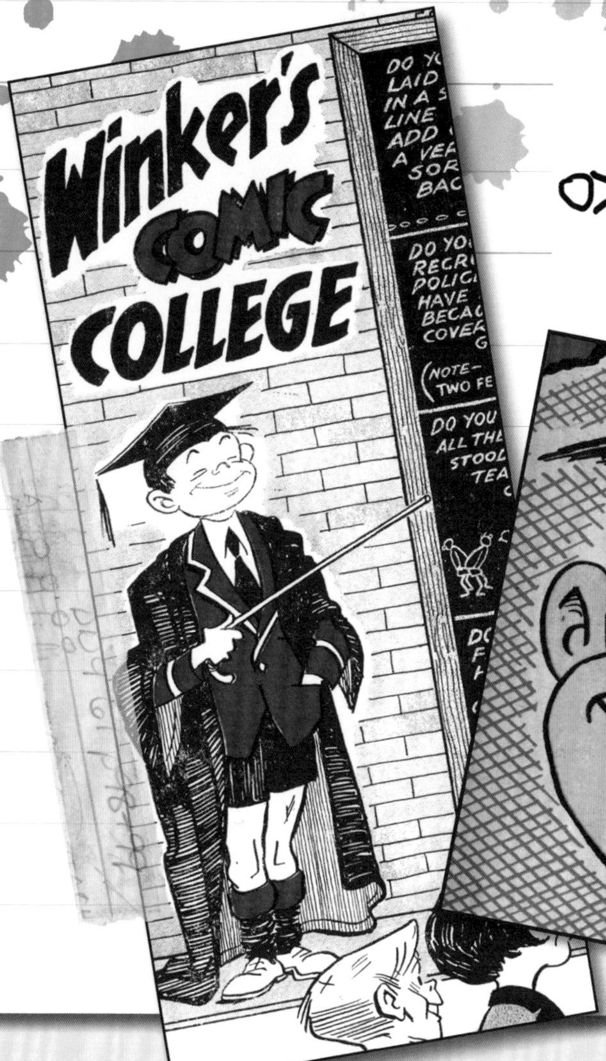
Winker's
COMIC
COLLEGE

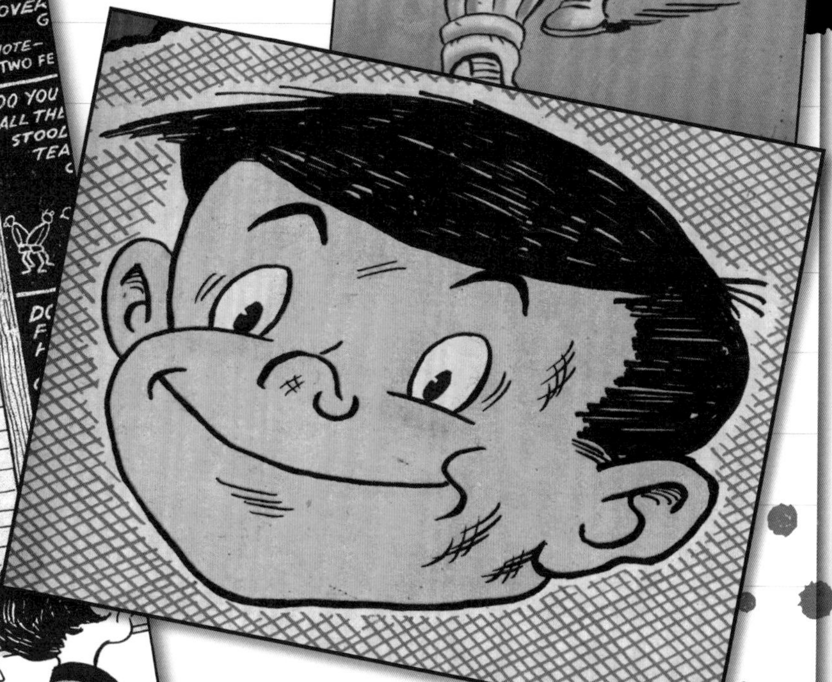

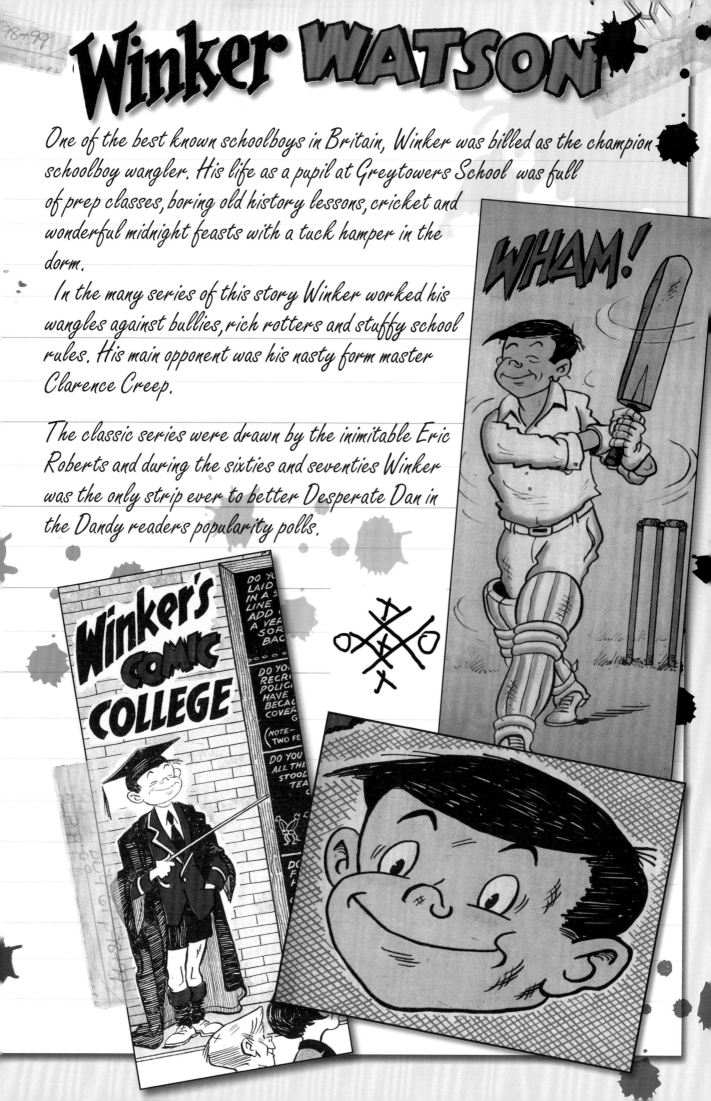

A taster of Winker from The Dandy Annual on sale winter 1960.

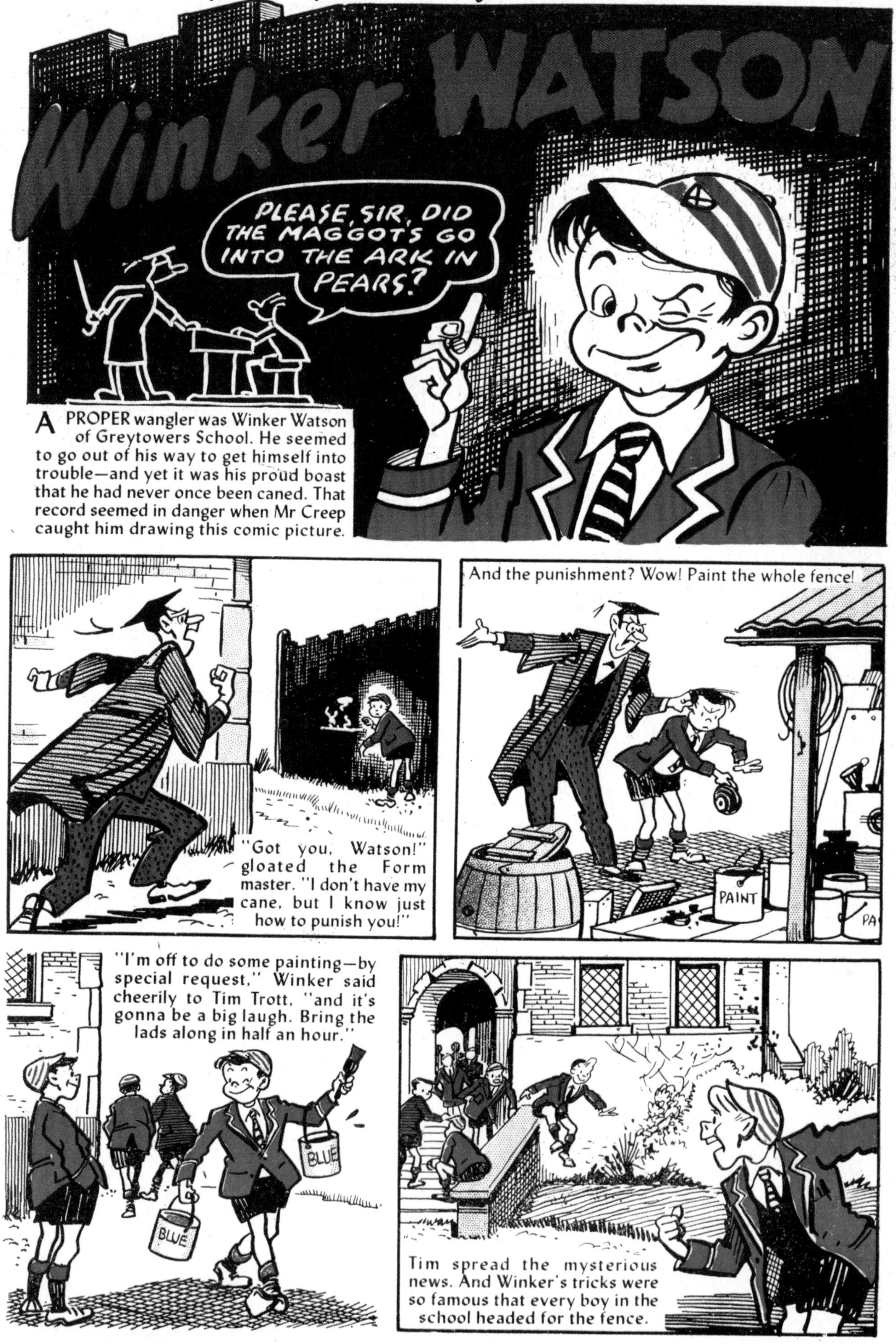

Winker WATSON
PLEASE, SIR, DID THE MAGGOT'S GO INTO THE ARK IN PEARS?
A PROPER wangler was Winker Watson of Greytowers School. He seemed to go out of his way to get himself into trouble—and yet it was his proud boast that he had never once been caned. That record seemed in danger when Mr Creep caught him drawing this comic picture.
"Got you, Watson!" gloated the Form master. "I don't have my cane, but I know just how to punish you!"
And the punishment? Wow! Paint the whole fence!
PAINT
"I'm off to do some painting—by special request," Winker said cheerily to Tim Trott, "and it's gonna be a big laugh. Bring the lads along in half an hour."
BLUE
BLUE
Tim spread the mysterious news. And Winker's tricks were so famous that every boy in the school headed for the fence.

He did not appear in the weekly until springtime.

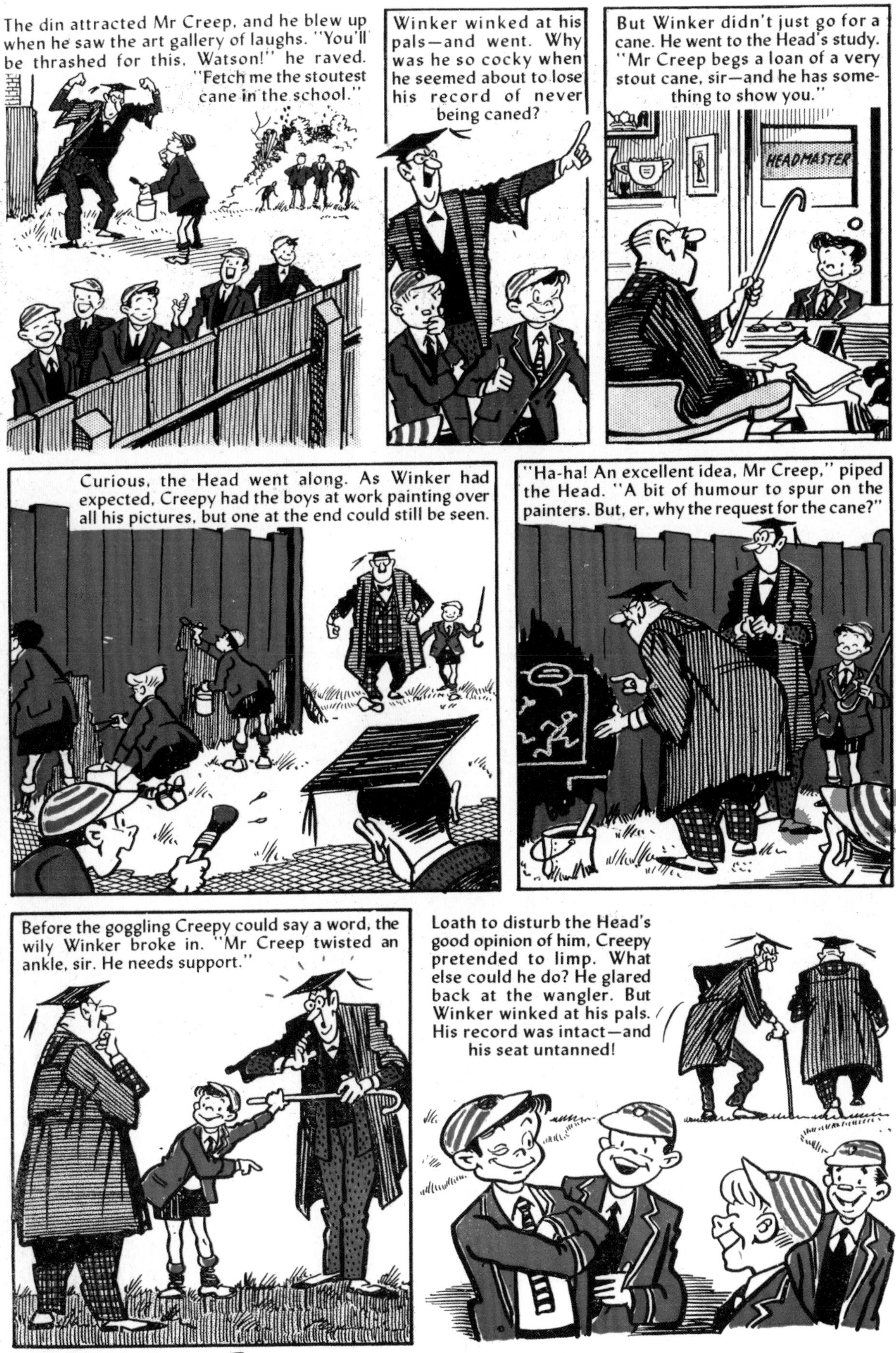
The din attracted Mr Creep, and he blew up when he saw the art gallery of laughs. "You'll be thrashed for this, Watson!" he raved. "Fetch me the stoutest cane in the school."
Winker winked at his pals—and went. Why was he so cocky when he seemed about to lose his record of never being caned?
But Winker didn't just go for a cane. He went to the Head's study. "Mr Creep begs a loan of a very stout cane, sir—and he has something to show you."
HEADMASTER
Curious, the Head went along. As Winker had expected, Creepy had the boys at work painting over all his pictures, but one at the end could still be seen.
"Ha-ha! An excellent idea, Mr Creep," piped the Head. "A bit of humour to spur on the painters. But, er, why the request for the cane?"
Before the goggling Creepy could say a word, the wily Winker broke in. "Mr Creep twisted an ankle, sir. He needs support."
Loath to disturb the Head's good opinion of him, Creepy pretended to limp. What else could he do? He glared back at the wangler. But Winker winked at his pals. His record was intact—and his seat untanned!

Turn the page to see what Winker drew.

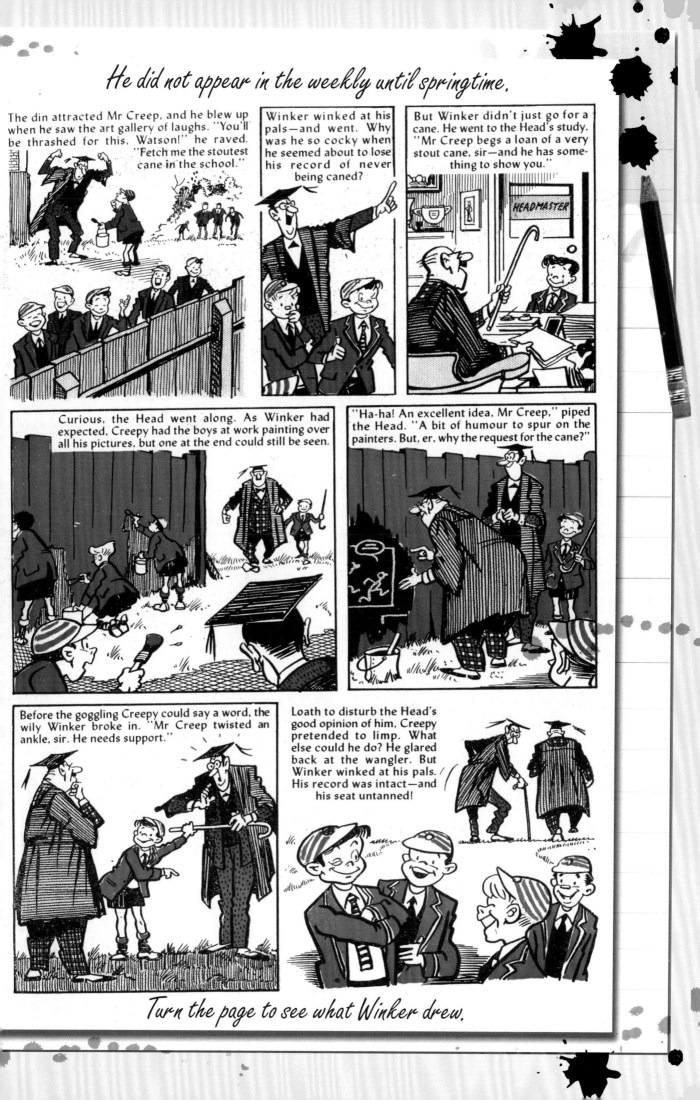

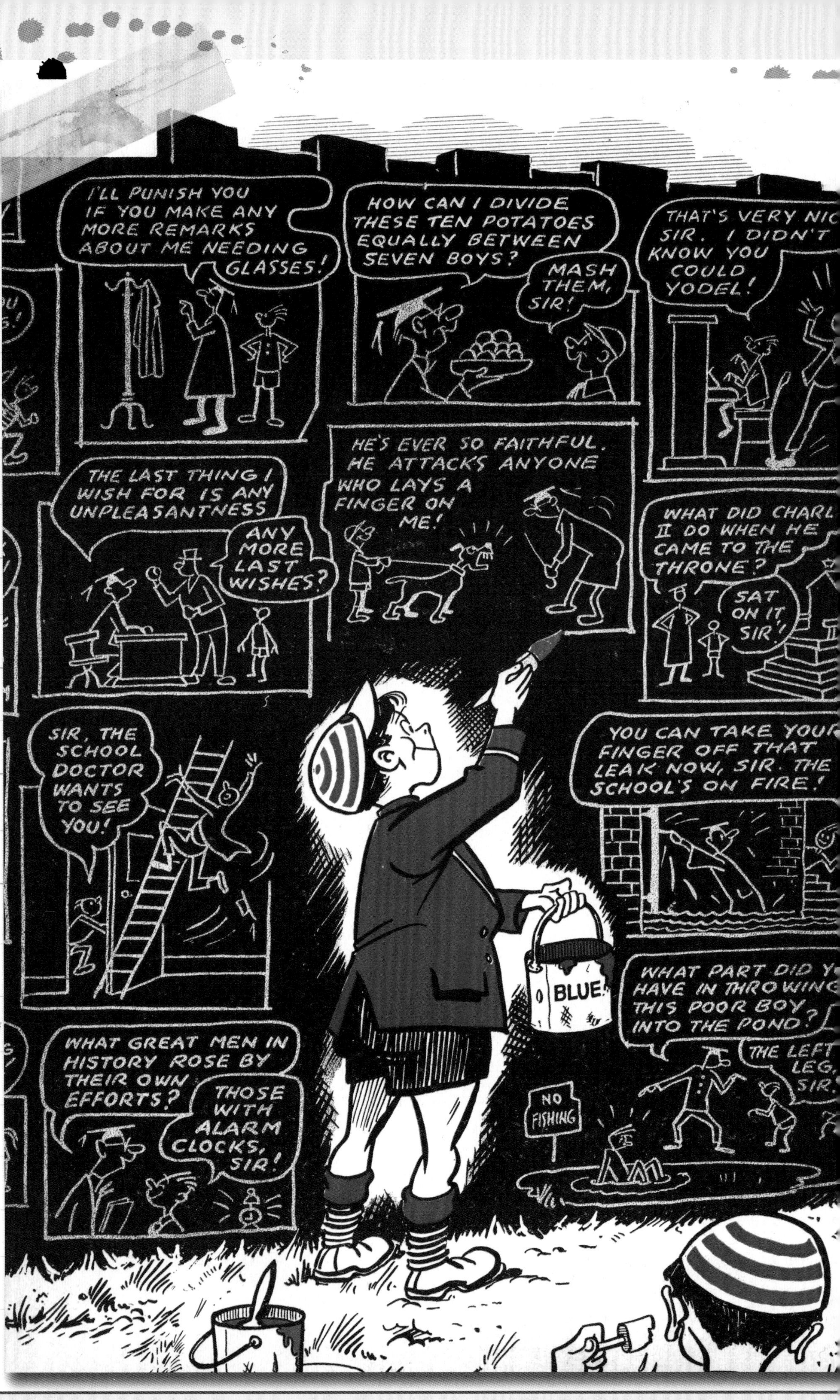
I'LL PUNISH YOU IF YOU MAKE ANY MORE REMARKS ABOUT ME NEEDING GLASSES!
HOW CAN I DIVIDE THESE TEN POTATOES EQUALLY BETWEEN SEVEN BOYS?
MASH THEM, SIR!
THAT'S VERY NIC SIR. I DIDN'T KNOW YOU COULD YODEL!
THE LAST THING I WISH FOR IS ANY UNPLEASANTNESS
ANY MORE LAST WISHES?
HE'S EVER SO FAITHFUL. HE ATTACKS ANYONE WHO LAYS A FINGER ON ME!
WHAT DID CHARL II DO WHEN HE CAME TO THE THRONE?
SAT ON IT, SIR!
SIR, THE SCHOOL DOCTOR WANTS TO SEE YOU!
YOU CAN TAKE YOUR FINGER OFF THAT LEAK NOW, SIR. THE SCHOOL'S ON FIRE!
BLUE
WHAT PART DID Y HAVE IN THROWING THIS POOR BOY INTO THE POND?
THE LEFT LEG, SIR.
NO FISHING
WHAT GREAT MEN IN HISTORY ROSE BY THEIR OWN EFFORTS?
THOSE WITH ALARM CLOCKS, SIR!

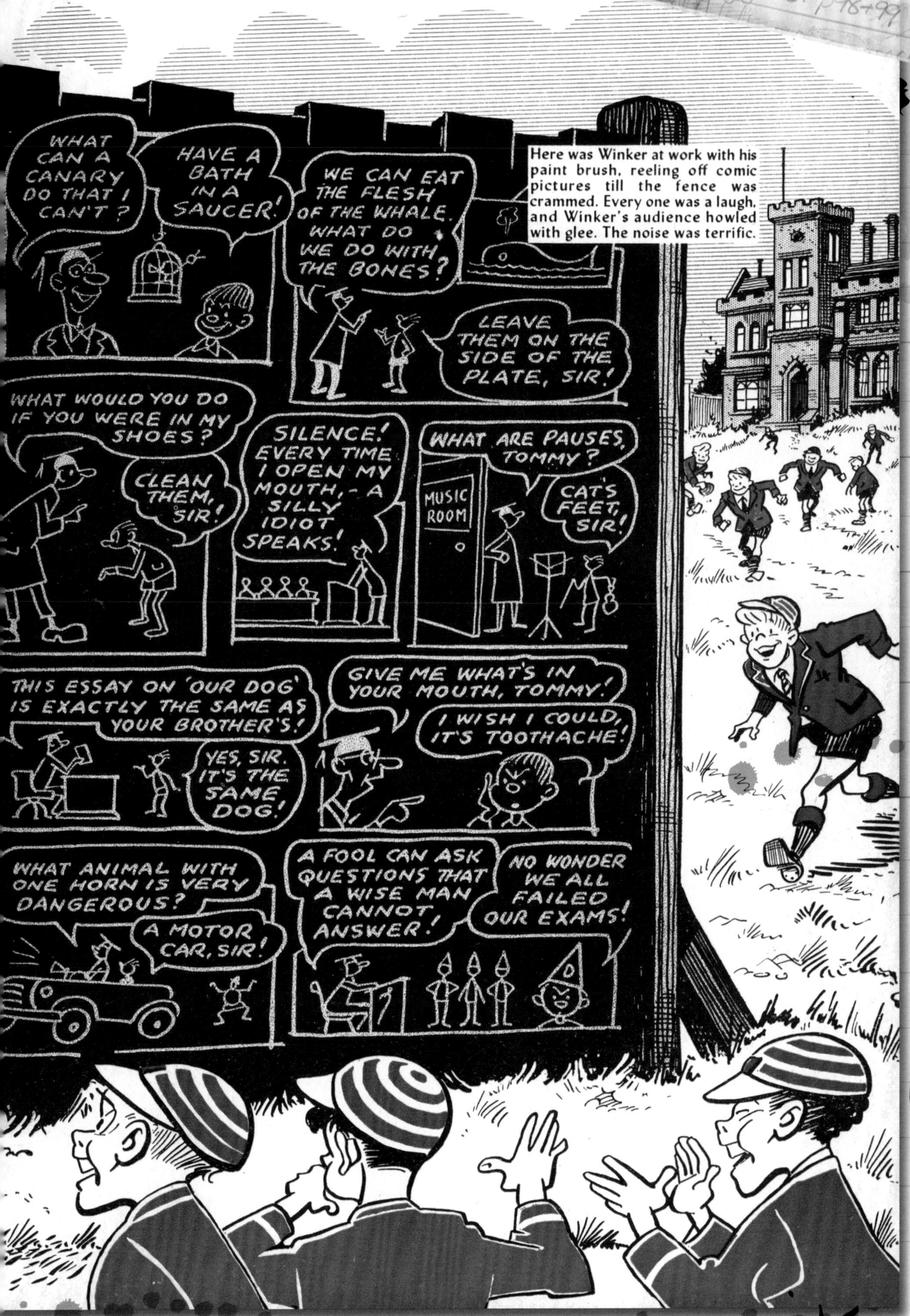
Here was Winker at work with his paint brush, reeling off comic pictures till the fence was crammed. Every one was a laugh, and Winker's audience howled with glee. The noise was terrific.
WHAT CAN A CANARY DO THAT I CAN'T?
HAVE A BATH IN A SAUCER!
WE CAN EAT THE FLESH OF THE WHALE. WHAT DO WE DO WITH THE BONES?
LEAVE THEM ON THE SIDE OF THE PLATE, SIR!
WHAT WOULD YOU DO IF YOU WERE IN MY SHOES?
CLEAN THEM, SIR!
SILENCE! EVERY TIME I OPEN MY MOUTH, - A SILLY IDIOT SPEAKS!
WHAT ARE PAUSES, TOMMY?
MUSIC ROOM
CAT'S FEET, SIR!
THIS ESSAY ON 'OUR DOG' IS EXACTLY THE SAME AS YOUR BROTHER'S!
YES, SIR. IT'S THE SAME DOG!
GIVE ME WHAT'S IN YOUR MOUTH, TOMMY!
I WISH I COULD, IT'S TOOTHACHE!
WHAT ANIMAL WITH ONE HORN IS VERY DANGEROUS?
A MOTOR CAR, SIR!
A FOOL CAN ASK QUESTIONS THAT A WISE MAN CANNOT ANSWER!
NO WONDER WE ALL FAILED OUR EXAMS!
D

HIP-HOORAY! No. 1 TODAY

About the boy who gets into scrapes — By working lots of crafty japes!

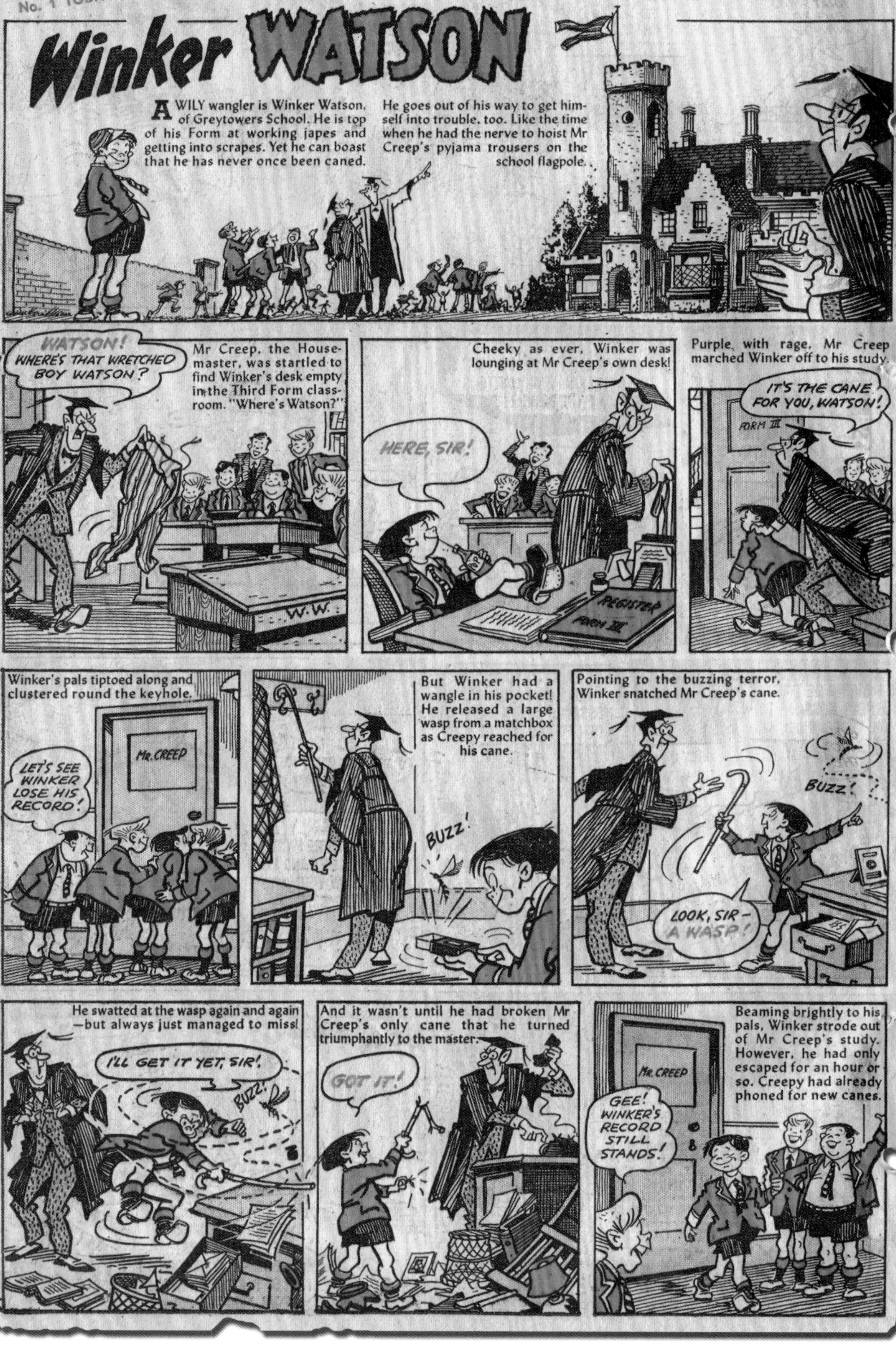

Winker WATSON
A WILY wangler is Winker Watson, of Greytowers School. He is top of his Form at working japes and getting into scrapes. Yet he can boast that he has never once been caned.
He goes out of his way to get himself into trouble, too. Like the time when he had the nerve to hoist Mr Creep's pyjama trousers on the school flagpole.
WATSON! WHERE'S THAT WRETCHED BOY WATSON?
Mr Creep, the Housemaster, was startled to find Winker's desk empty in the Third Form classroom. "Where's Watson?"
W. W.
Cheeky as ever, Winker was lounging at Mr Creep's own desk!
HERE, SIR!
REGISTER FORM III
Purple with rage, Mr Creep marched Winker off to his study.
IT'S THE CANE FOR YOU, WATSON!
FORM III
Winker's pals tiptoed along and clustered round the keyhole.
MR. CREEP
LET'S SEE WINKER LOSE HIS RECORD!
But Winker had a wangle in his pocket! He released a large wasp from a matchbox as Creepy reached for his cane.
BUZZ!
Pointing to the buzzing terror, Winker snatched Mr Creep's cane.
BUZZ!
LOOK, SIR — A WASP!
He swatted at the wasp again and again — but always just managed to miss!
I'LL GET IT YET, SIR!
BUZZ!
And it wasn't until he had broken Mr Creep's only cane that he turned triumphantly to the master.
GOT IT!
Beaming brightly to his pals, Winker strode out of Mr Creep's study. However, he had only escaped for an hour or so. Creepy had already phoned for new canes.
MR. CREEP
GEE! WINKER'S RECORD STILL STANDS!

'Twas the wrong parcel Winker bumped—But still he got old Creepy "stumped"!

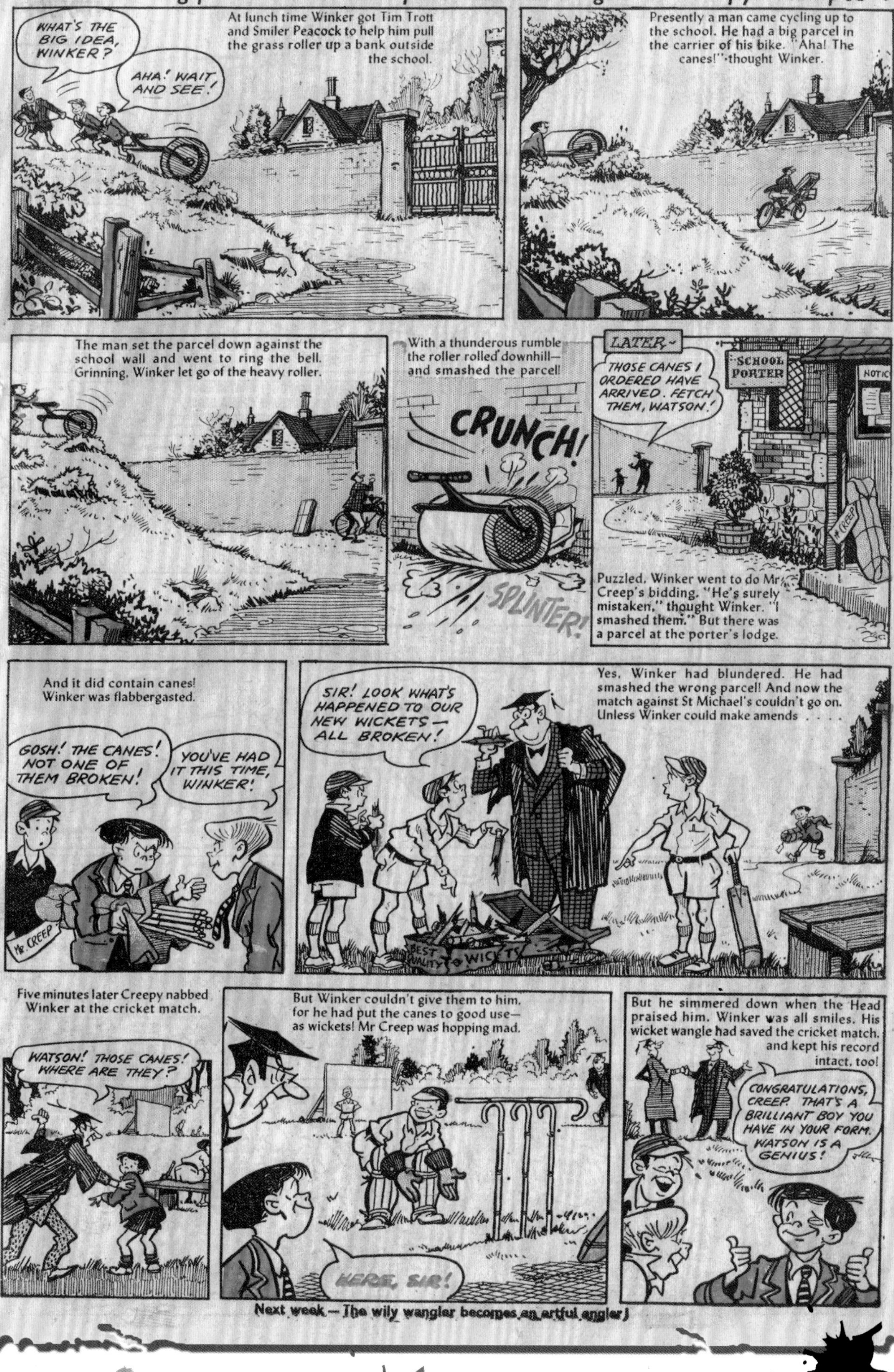

At lunch time Winker got Tim Trott and Smiler Peacock to help him pull the grass roller up a bank outside the school.
WHAT'S THE BIG IDEA, WINKER?
AHA! WAIT AND SEE!
Presently a man came cycling up to the school. He had a big parcel in the carrier of his bike. "Aha! The canes!" thought Winker.
The man set the parcel down against the school wall and went to ring the bell. Grinning, Winker let go of the heavy roller.
With a thunderous rumble the roller rolled downhill—and smashed the parcel!
CRUNCH!
SPLINTER!
LATER
THOSE CANES I ORDERED HAVE ARRIVED. FETCH THEM, WATSON.
SCHOOL PORTER
Puzzled, Winker went to do Mr Creep's bidding. "He's surely mistaken," thought Winker. "I smashed them." But there was a parcel at the porter's lodge.
And it did contain canes! Winker was flabbergasted.
GOSH! THE CANES! NOT ONE OF THEM BROKEN!
YOU'VE HAD IT THIS TIME, WINKER!
MR. CREEP
SIR! LOOK WHAT'S HAPPENED TO OUR NEW WICKETS—ALL BROKEN!
Yes, Winker had blundered. He had smashed the wrong parcel! And now the match against St Michael's couldn't go on. Unless Winker could make amends . . . .
BEST QUALITY WICKETS
Five minutes later Creepy nabbed Winker at the cricket match.
WATSON! THOSE CANES! WHERE ARE THEY?
But Winker couldn't give them to him, for he had put the canes to good use—as wickets! Mr Creep was hopping mad.
HERE, SIR!
But he simmered down when the Head praised him. Winker was all smiles. His wicket wangle had saved the cricket match, and kept his record intact, too!
CONGRATULATIONS, CREEP. THAT'S A BRILLIANT BOY YOU HAVE IN YOUR FORM. WATSON IS A GENIUS!

Next week—The wily wangler becomes an artful angler!

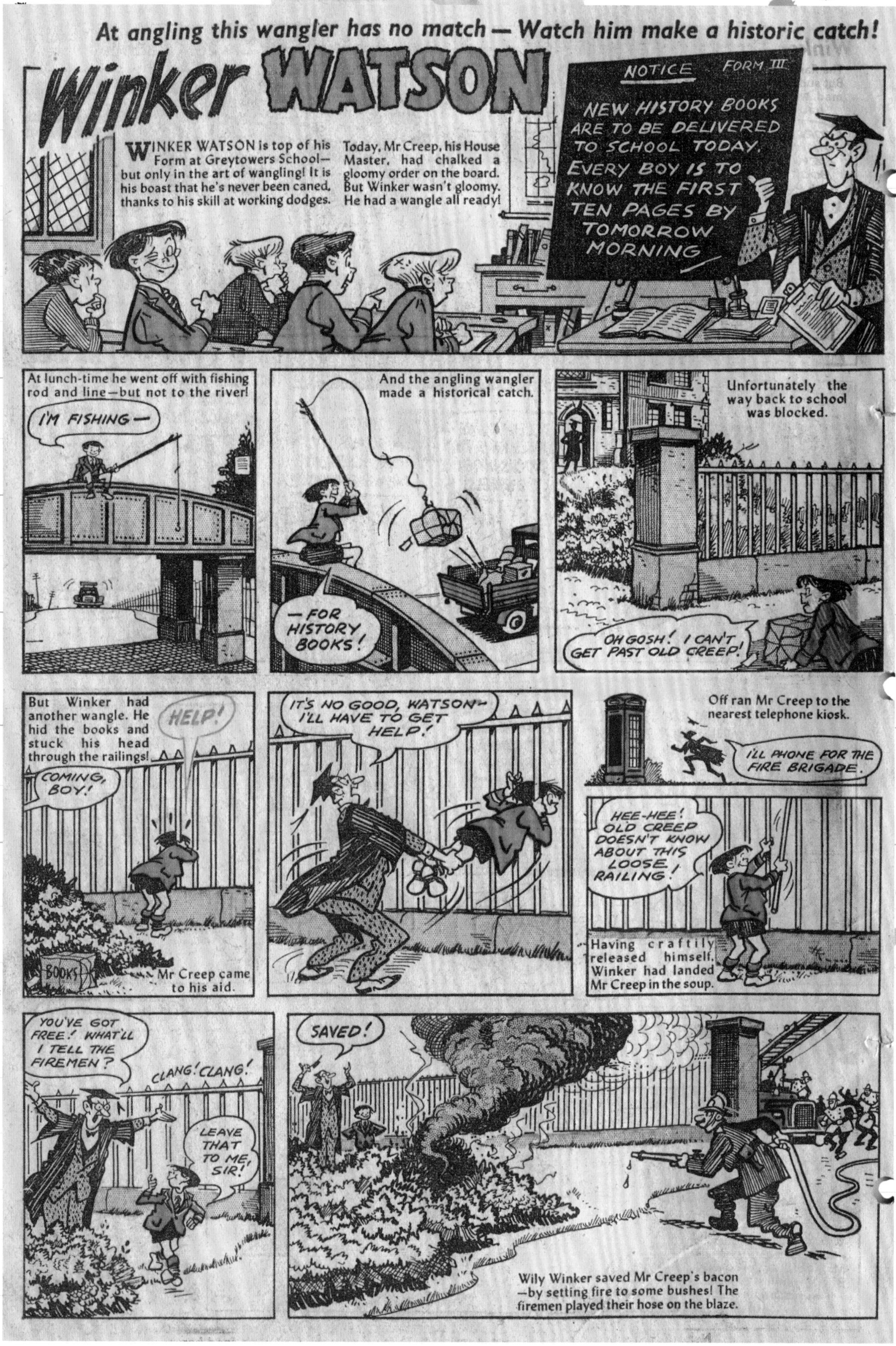

At angling this wangler has no match — Watch him make a historic catch!
Winker WATSON
NOTICE FORM III
NEW HISTORY BOOKS ARE TO BE DELIVERED TO SCHOOL TODAY. EVERY BOY IS TO KNOW THE FIRST TEN PAGES BY TOMORROW MORNING
WINKER WATSON is top of his Form at Greytowers School—but only in the art of wangling! It is his boast that he's never been caned, thanks to his skill at working dodges.
Today, Mr Creep, his House Master, had chalked a gloomy order on the board. But Winker wasn't gloomy. He had a wangle all ready!
At lunch-time he went off with fishing rod and line—but not to the river!
I'M FISHING—
And the angling wangler made a historical catch.
—FOR HISTORY BOOKS!
Unfortunately the way back to school was blocked.
OH GOSH! I CAN'T GET PAST OLD CREEP!
But Winker had another wangle. He hid the books and stuck his head through the railings!
HELP!
COMING, BOY!
BOOKS
Mr Creep came to his aid.
IT'S NO GOOD, WATSON—I'LL HAVE TO GET HELP!
Off ran Mr Creep to the nearest telephone kiosk.
I'LL PHONE FOR THE FIRE BRIGADE.
HEE-HEE! OLD CREEP DOESN'T KNOW ABOUT THIS LOOSE RAILING!
Having craftily released himself, Winker had landed Mr Creep in the soup.
YOU'VE GOT FREE! WHAT'LL I TELL THE FIREMEN?
CLANG! CLANG!
LEAVE THAT TO ME, SIR!
SAVED!
Wily Winker saved Mr Creep's bacon—by setting fire to some bushes! The firemen played their hose on the blaze.

Winker Watson takes great pains — And up in smoke go Creepy's canes.

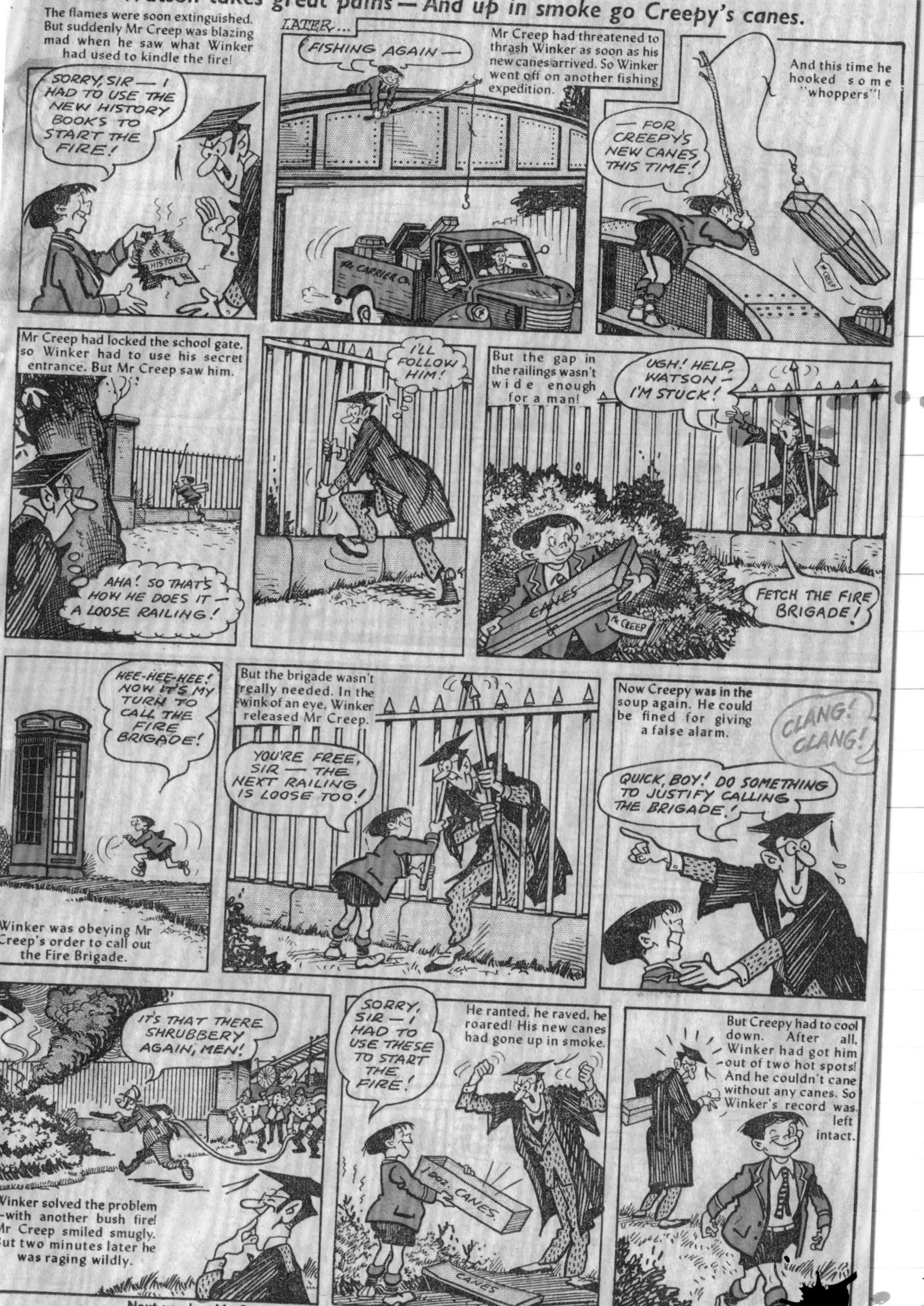
The flames were soon extinguished. But suddenly Mr Creep was blazing mad when he saw what Winker had used to kindle the fire!
SORRY, SIR — I HAD TO USE THE NEW HISTORY BOOKS TO START THE FIRE!
HISTORY
LATER...
FISHING AGAIN —
Mr Creep had threatened to thrash Winker as soon as his new canes arrived. So Winker went off on another fishing expedition.
THE CARRIER CO.
And this time he hooked some "whoppers"!
— FOR CREEPY'S NEW CANES THIS TIME!
Mr CREEP
Mr Creep had locked the school gate, so Winker had to use his secret entrance. But Mr Creep saw him.
AHA! SO THAT'S HOW HE DOES IT — A LOOSE RAILING!
I'LL FOLLOW HIM!
But the gap in the railings wasn't wide enough for a man!
UGH! HELP, WATSON — I'M STUCK!
FETCH THE FIRE BRIGADE!
CANES
Mr CREEP
HEE-HEE-HEE! NOW IT'S MY TURN TO CALL THE FIRE BRIGADE!
Winker was obeying Mr Creep's order to call out the Fire Brigade.
But the brigade wasn't really needed. In the wink of an eye, Winker released Mr Creep.
YOU'RE FREE, SIR — THE NEXT RAILING IS LOOSE TOO!
Now Creepy was in the soup again. He could be fined for giving a false alarm.
CLANG! CLANG!
QUICK, BOY! DO SOMETHING TO JUSTIFY CALLING THE BRIGADE!
IT'S THAT THERE SHRUBBERY AGAIN, MEN!
Winker solved the problem —with another bush fire! Mr Creep smiled smugly. But two minutes later he was raging wildly.
SORRY, SIR — I HAD TO USE THESE TO START THE FIRE!
He ranted, he raved, he roared! His new canes had gone up in smoke.
1 DOZ. CANES
CANES
But Creepy had to cool down. After all, Winker had got him out of two hot spots! And he couldn't cane without any canes. So Winker's record was left intact.

Next week — Mr Creep the furious stamper — Does a dance on the Head's food hamper!

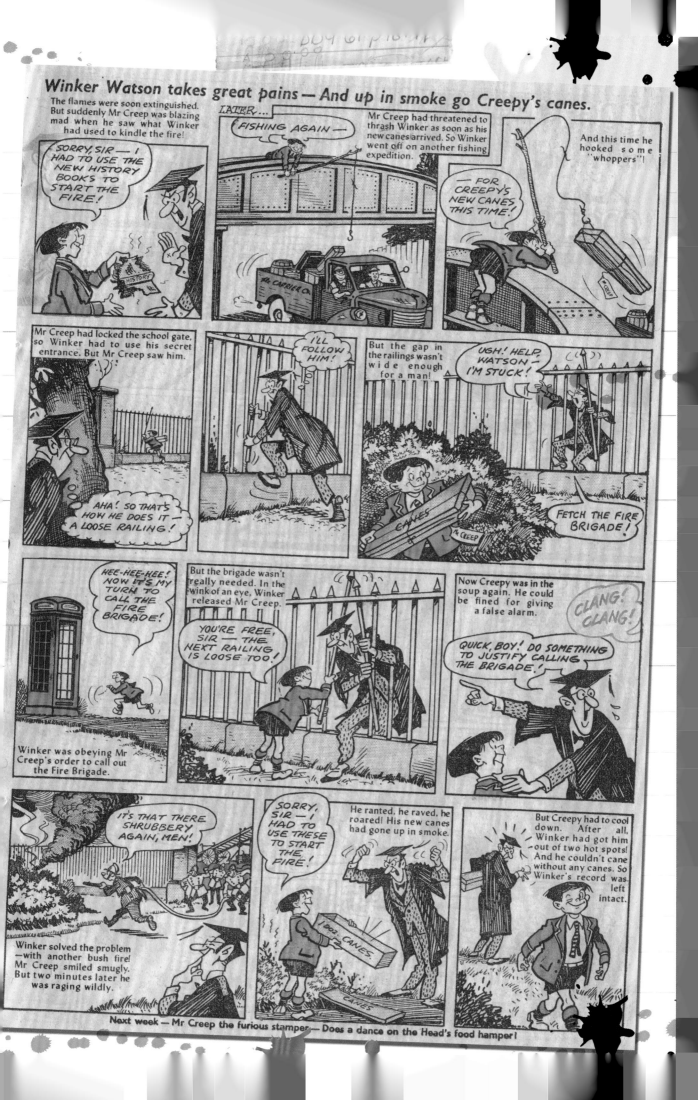

TWO TRICKY CATCHES by

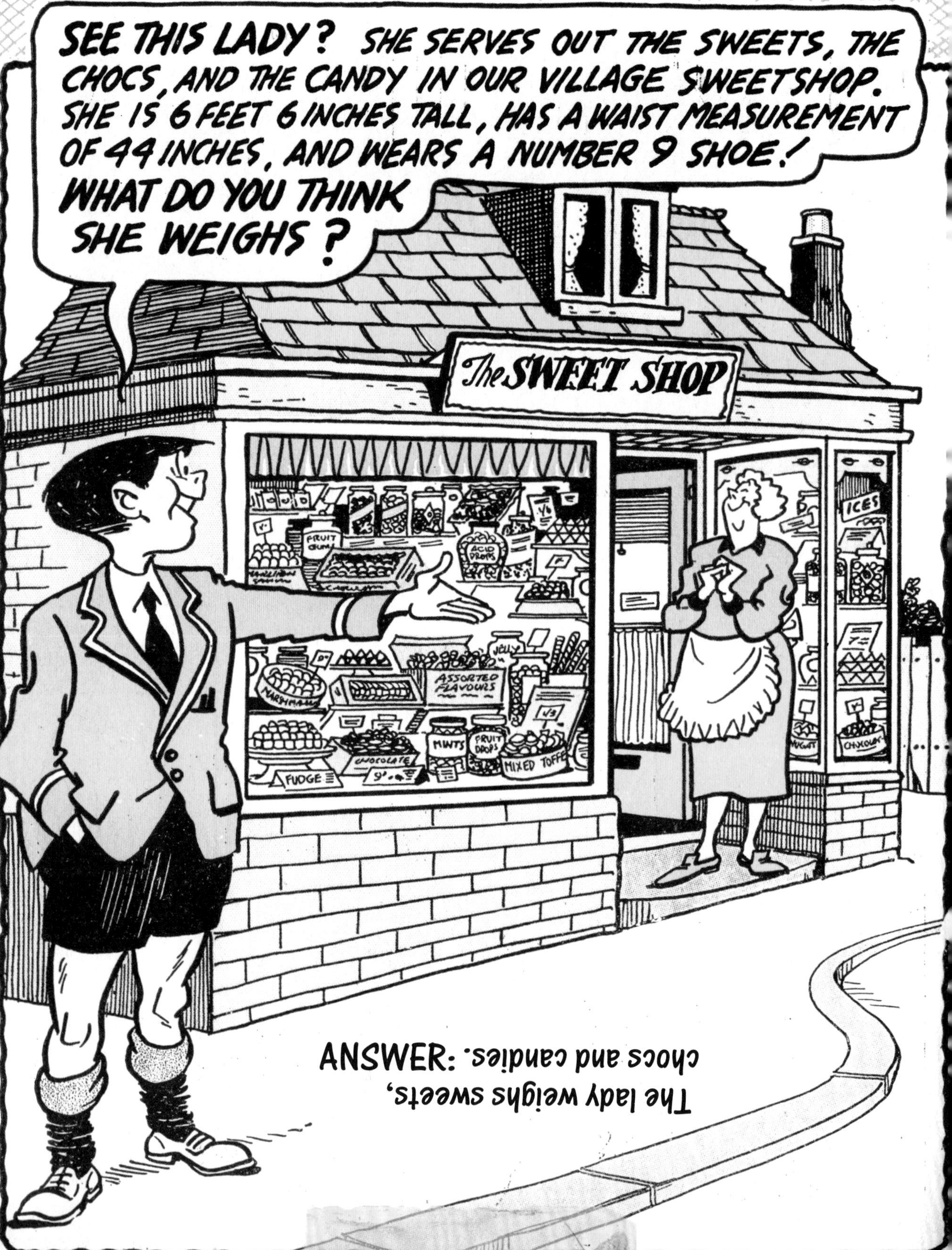
SEE THIS LADY? SHE SERVES OUT THE SWEETS, THE CHOCS, AND THE CANDY IN OUR VILLAGE SWEETSHOP. SHE IS 6 FEET 6 INCHES TALL, HAS A WAIST MEASUREMENT OF 44 INCHES, AND WEARS A NUMBER 9 SHOE! WHAT DO YOU THINK SHE WEIGHS?
The SWEET SHOP
FRUIT GUMS
ACID DROPS
ICES
ASSORTED FLAVOURS
JELLY
MINTS
FRUIT DROPS
MIXED TOFFEE
CHOCOLATE
FUDGE
ANSWER:
The lady weighs sweets, chocs and candies.

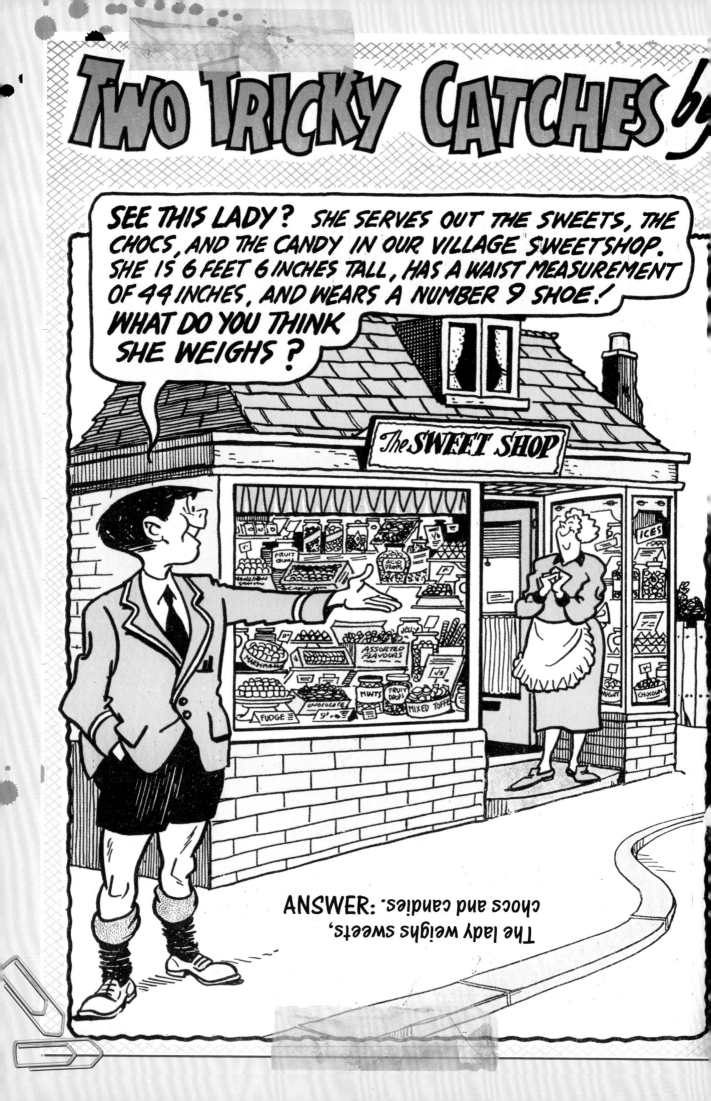

Two Catchy Tricksters

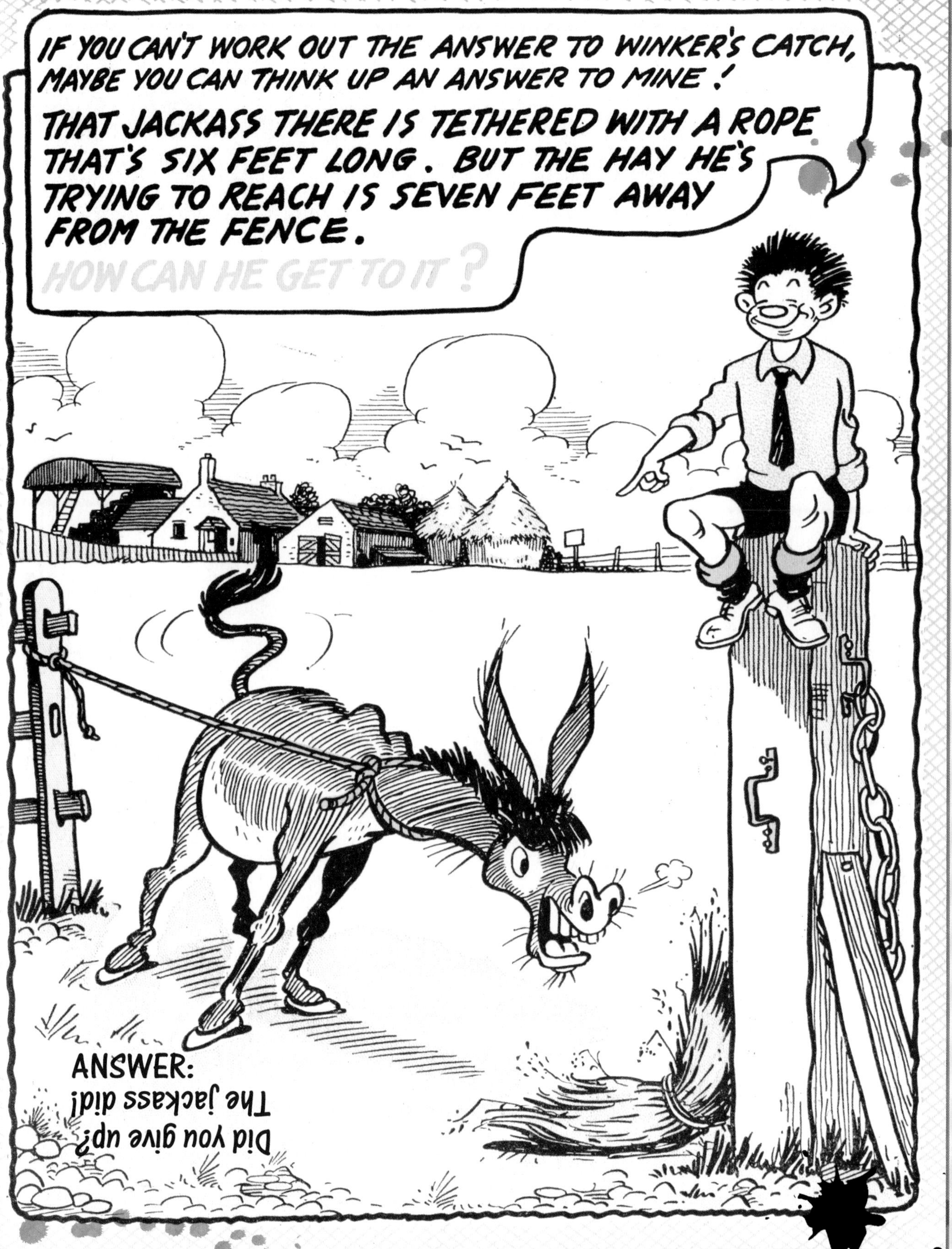
IF YOU CAN'T WORK OUT THE ANSWER TO WINKER'S CATCH, MAYBE YOU CAN THINK UP AN ANSWER TO MINE!
THAT JACKASS THERE IS TETHERED WITH A ROPE THAT'S SIX FEET LONG. BUT THE HAY HE'S TRYING TO REACH IS SEVEN FEET AWAY FROM THE FENCE.
HOW CAN HE GET TO IT?
ANSWER:
Did you give up?
The jackass did!

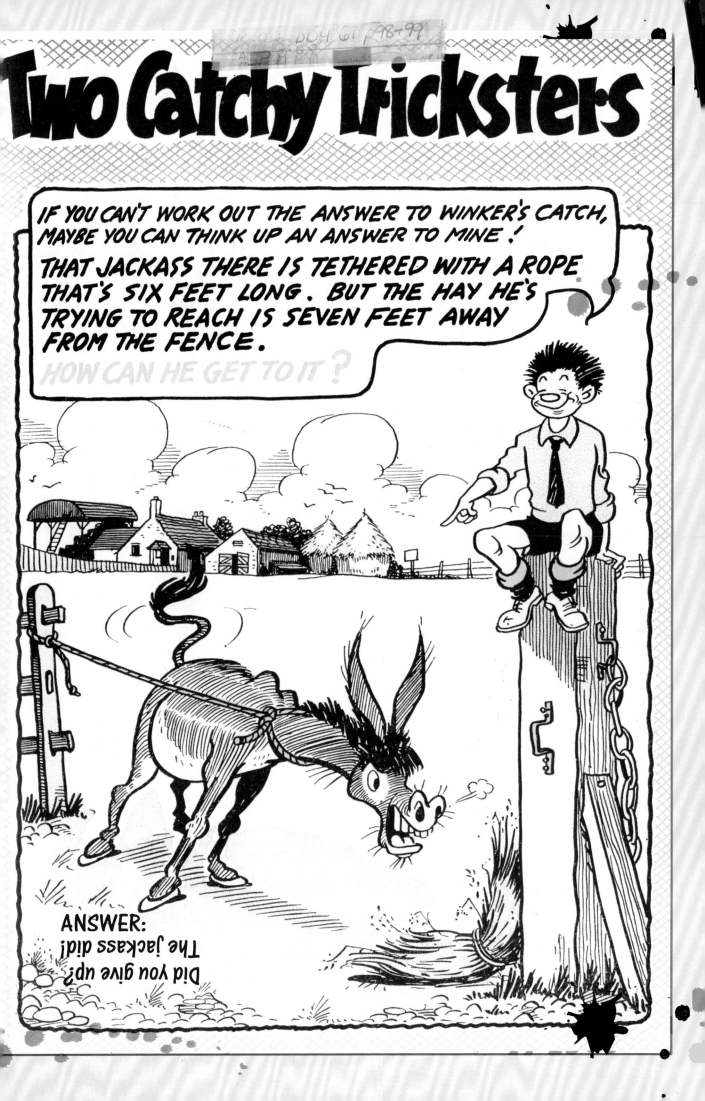

6 months before Winker appeared, artist Eric Roberts had started drawing the Dirty Dick sets for Dandy.

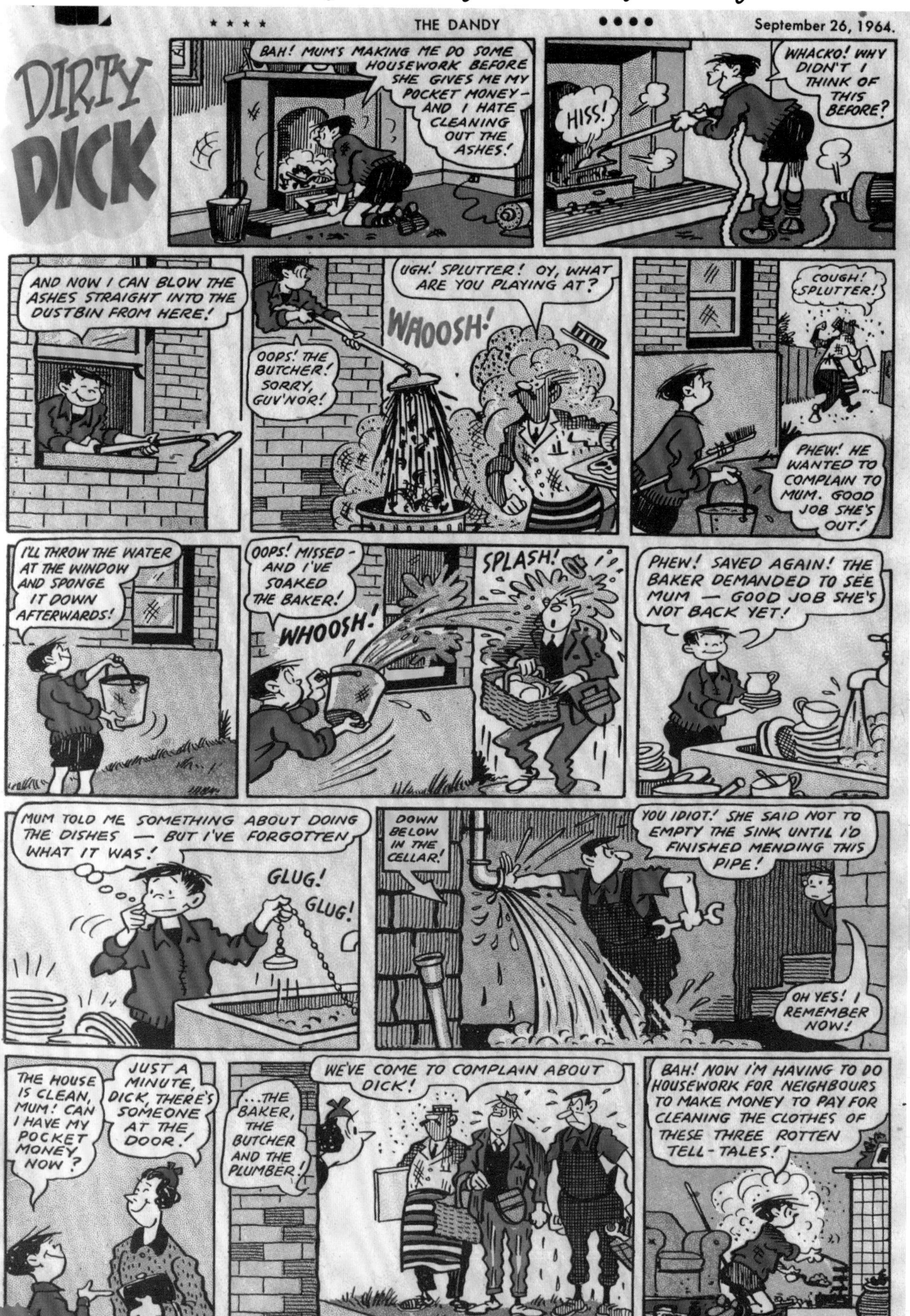
★ ★ ★ ★ THE DANDY ● ● ● ● September 26, 1964.
DIRTY DICK
BAH! MUM'S MAKING ME DO SOME HOUSEWORK BEFORE SHE GIVES ME MY POCKET MONEY — AND I HATE CLEANING OUT THE ASHES!
HISS!
WHACKO! WHY DIDN'T I THINK OF THIS BEFORE?
AND NOW I CAN BLOW THE ASHES STRAIGHT INTO THE DUSTBIN FROM HERE!
UGH! SPLUTTER! OY, WHAT ARE YOU PLAYING AT?
WHOOSH!
OOPS! THE BUTCHER! SORRY, GUV'NOR!
COUGH! SPLUTTER!
PHEW! HE WANTED TO COMPLAIN TO MUM. GOOD JOB SHE'S OUT!
I'LL THROW THE WATER AT THE WINDOW AND SPONGE IT DOWN AFTERWARDS!
OOPS! MISSED — AND I'VE SOAKED THE BAKER!
WHOOSH!
SPLASH!
PHEW! SAVED AGAIN! THE BAKER DEMANDED TO SEE MUM — GOOD JOB SHE'S NOT BACK YET!
MUM TOLD ME SOMETHING ABOUT DOING THE DISHES — BUT I'VE FORGOTTEN WHAT IT WAS!
GLUG! GLUG!
DOWN BELOW IN THE CELLAR!
YOU IDIOT! SHE SAID NOT TO EMPTY THE SINK UNTIL I'D FINISHED MENDING THIS PIPE!
OH YES! I REMEMBER NOW!
THE HOUSE IS CLEAN, MUM! CAN I HAVE MY POCKET MONEY NOW?
JUST A MINUTE, DICK, THERE'S SOMEONE AT THE DOOR!
...THE BAKER, THE BUTCHER AND THE PLUMBER!
WE'VE COME TO COMPLAIN ABOUT DICK!
BAH! NOW I'M HAVING TO DO HOUSEWORK FOR NEIGHBOURS TO MAKE MONEY TO PAY FOR CLEANING THE CLOTHES OF THESE THREE ROTTEN TELL-TALES!
...ed and Published in Great Britain by D. C. THOMSON & Co., Ltd., and JOHN LENG & Co., Ltd., 12 Fetter Lane, Fleet Street, London, E.C.4. © D. C. THOMSON & CO., LTD., 1964.

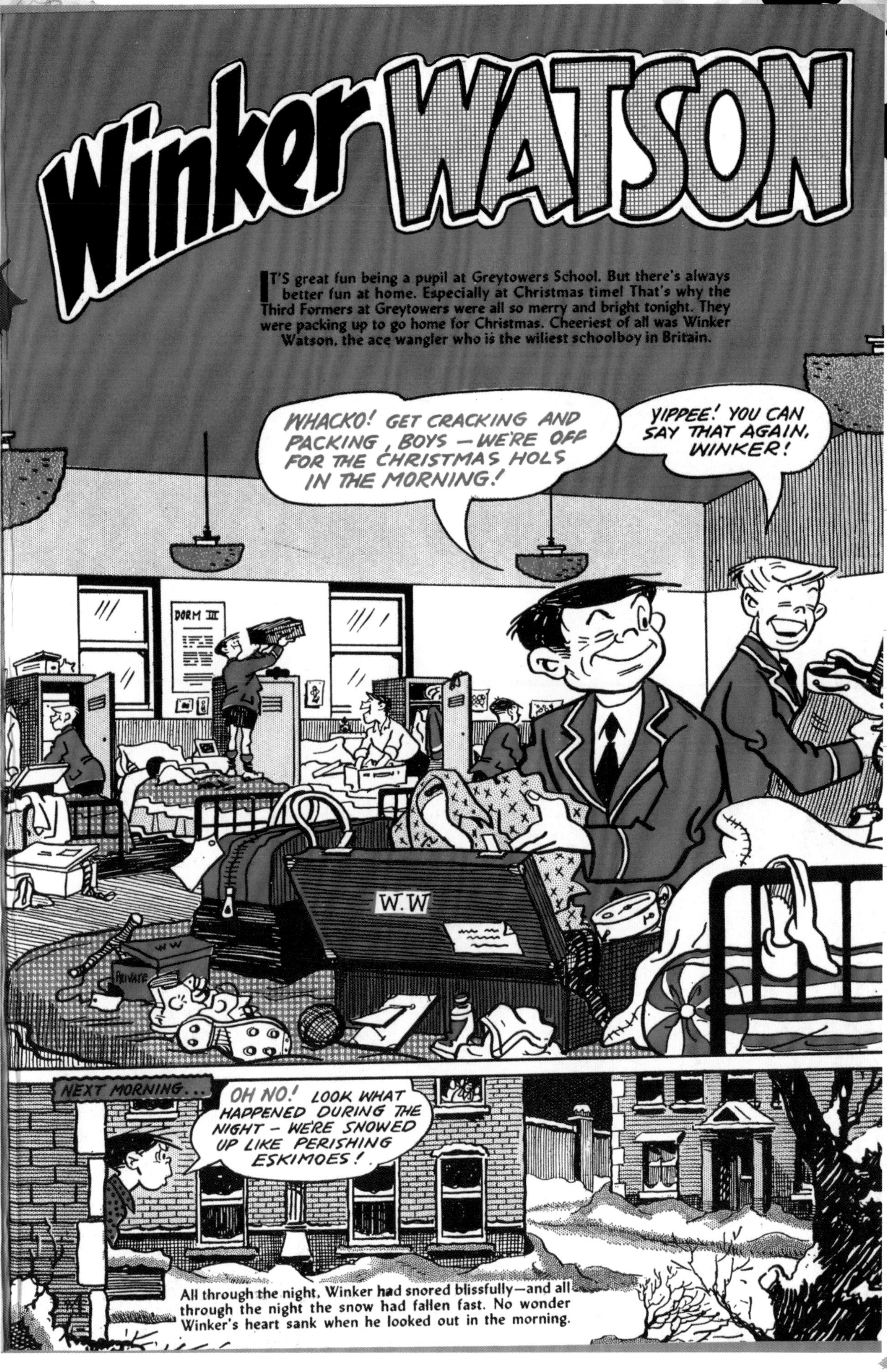
Winker WATSON
IT'S great fun being a pupil at Greytowers School. But there's always better fun at home. Especially at Christmas time! That's why the Third Formers at Greytowers were all so merry and bright tonight. They were packing up to go home for Christmas. Cheeriest of all was Winker Watson, the ace wangler who is the wiliest schoolboy in Britain.
WHACKO! GET CRACKING AND PACKING, BOYS — WE'RE OFF FOR THE CHRISTMAS HOLS IN THE MORNING!
YIPPEE! YOU CAN SAY THAT AGAIN, WINKER!
DORM III
W.W
PRIVATE
NEXT MORNING...
OH NO! LOOK WHAT HAPPENED DURING THE NIGHT — WE'RE SNOWED UP LIKE PERISHING ESKIMOES!
All through the night, Winker had snored blissfully—and all through the night the snow had fallen fast. No wonder Winker's heart sank when he looked out in the morning.

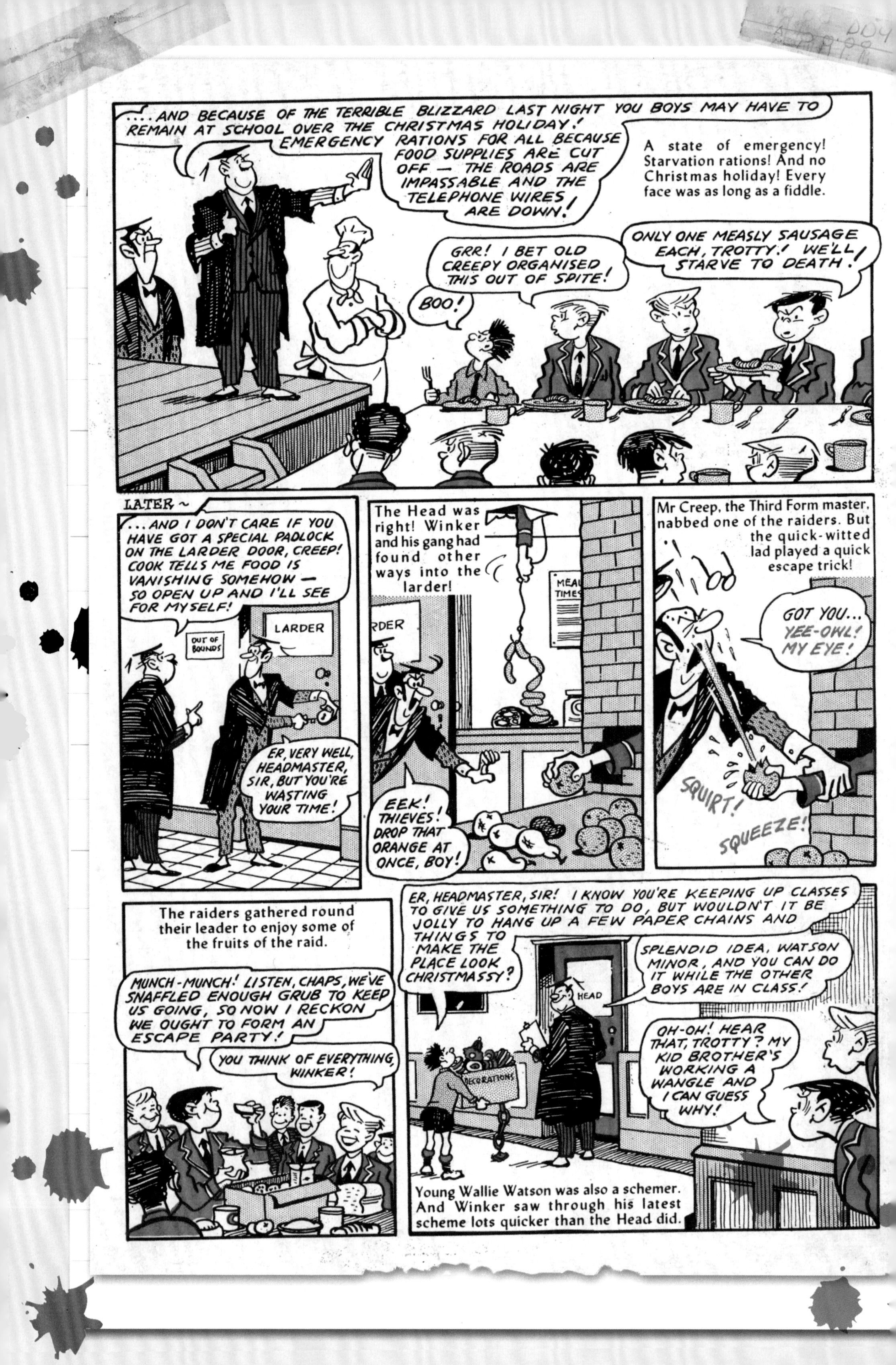
....AND BECAUSE OF THE TERRIBLE BLIZZARD LAST NIGHT YOU BOYS MAY HAVE TO REMAIN AT SCHOOL OVER THE CHRISTMAS HOLIDAY! EMERGENCY RATIONS FOR ALL BECAUSE FOOD SUPPLIES ARE CUT OFF — THE ROADS ARE IMPASSABLE AND THE TELEPHONE WIRES ARE DOWN!
A state of emergency! Starvation rations! And no Christmas holiday! Every face was as long as a fiddle.
BOO!
GRR! I BET OLD CREEPY ORGANISED THIS OUT OF SPITE!
ONLY ONE MEASLY SAUSAGE EACH, TROTTY! WE'LL STARVE TO DEATH!
LATER ~
...AND I DON'T CARE IF YOU HAVE GOT A SPECIAL PADLOCK ON THE LARDER DOOR, CREEP! COOK TELLS ME FOOD IS VANISHING SOMEHOW — SO OPEN UP AND I'LL SEE FOR MYSELF!
OUT OF BOUNDS
LARDER
ER, VERY WELL, HEADMASTER, SIR, BUT YOU'RE WASTING YOUR TIME!
The Head was right! Winker and his gang had found other ways into the larder!
RDER
MEAL TIMES
EEK! THIEVES! DROP THAT ORANGE AT ONCE, BOY!
Mr Creep, the Third Form master, nabbed one of the raiders. But the quick-witted lad played a quick escape trick!
GOT YOU... YEE-OWL! MY EYE!
SQUIRT!
SQUEEZE!
The raiders gathered round their leader to enjoy some of the fruits of the raid.
MUNCH-MUNCH! LISTEN, CHAPS, WE'VE SNAFFLED ENOUGH GRUB TO KEEP US GOING, SO NOW I RECKON WE OUGHT TO FORM AN ESCAPE PARTY!
YOU THINK OF EVERYTHING, WINKER!
ER, HEADMASTER, SIR! I KNOW YOU'RE KEEPING UP CLASSES TO GIVE US SOMETHING TO DO, BUT WOULDN'T IT BE JOLLY TO HANG UP A FEW PAPER CHAINS AND THINGS TO MAKE THE PLACE LOOK CHRISTMASSY?
SPLENDID IDEA, WATSON MINOR, AND YOU CAN DO IT WHILE THE OTHER BOYS ARE IN CLASS!
HEAD
DECORATIONS
OH-OH! HEAR THAT, TROTTY? MY KID BROTHER'S WORKING A WANGLE AND I CAN GUESS WHY!
Young Wallie Watson was also a schemer. And Winker saw through his latest scheme lots quicker than the Head did.

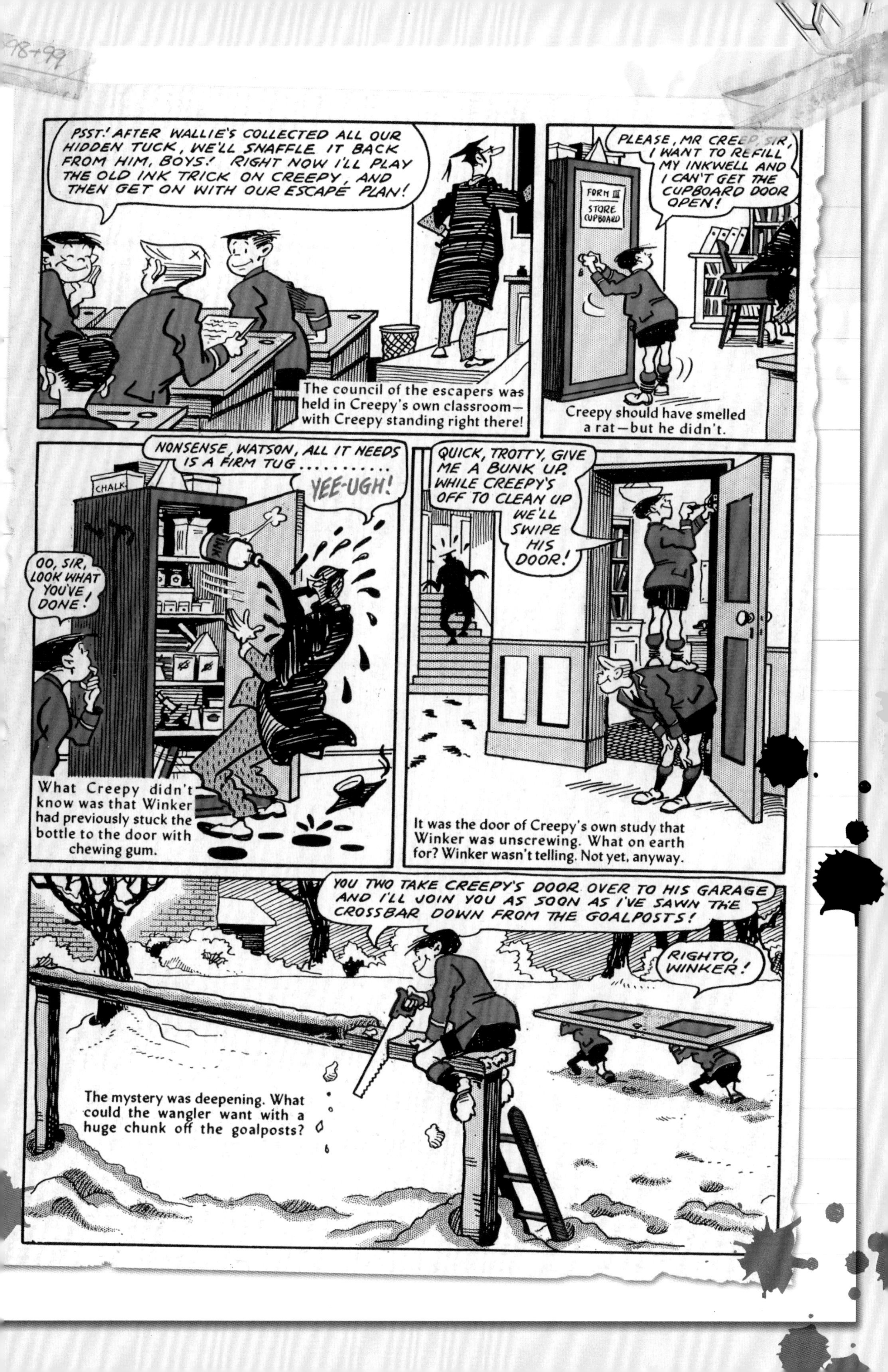
98+99
PSST! AFTER WALLIE'S COLLECTED ALL OUR HIDDEN TUCK, WE'LL SNAFFLE IT BACK FROM HIM, BOYS! RIGHT NOW I'LL PLAY THE OLD INK TRICK ON CREEPY, AND THEN GET ON WITH OUR ESCAPE PLAN!
The council of the escapers was held in Creepy's own classroom—with Creepy standing right there!
PLEASE, MR CREEP, SIR, I WANT TO REFILL MY INKWELL AND I CAN'T GET THE CUPBOARD DOOR OPEN!
FORM III STORE CUPBOARD
Creepy should have smelled a rat—but he didn't.
NONSENSE, WATSON, ALL IT NEEDS IS A FIRM TUG..........
YEE-UGH!
OO, SIR, LOOK WHAT YOU'VE DONE!
CHALK
INK
What Creepy didn't know was that Winker had previously stuck the bottle to the door with chewing gum.
QUICK, TROTTY, GIVE ME A BUNK UP. WHILE CREEPY'S OFF TO CLEAN UP WE'LL SWIPE HIS DOOR!
It was the door of Creepy's own study that Winker was unscrewing. What on earth for? Winker wasn't telling. Not yet, anyway.
YOU TWO TAKE CREEPY'S DOOR OVER TO HIS GARAGE AND I'LL JOIN YOU AS SOON AS I'VE SAWN THE CROSSBAR DOWN FROM THE GOALPOSTS!
RIGHTO, WINKER!
The mystery was deepening. What could the wangler want with a huge chunk off the goalposts?

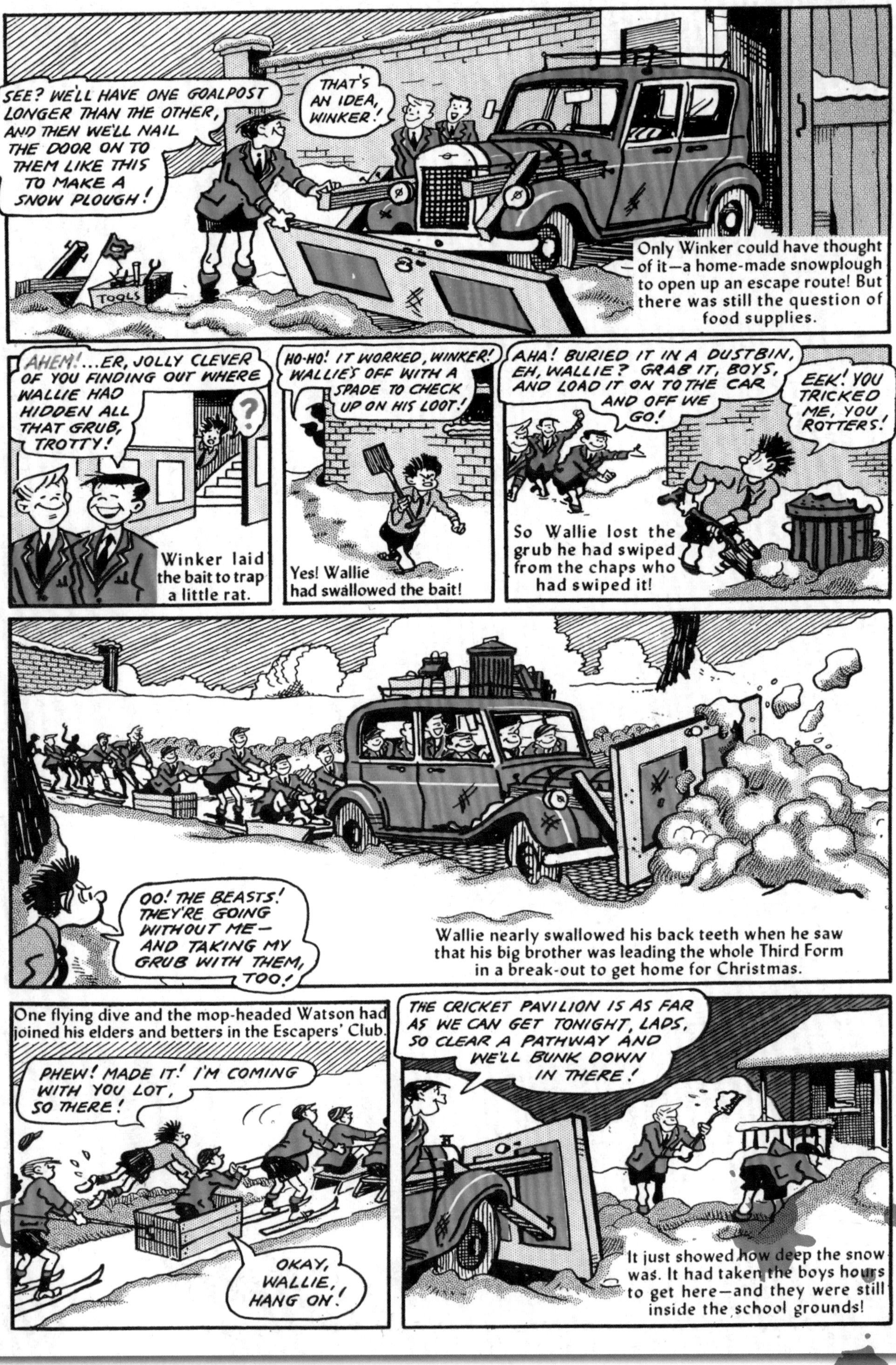
SEE? WE'LL HAVE ONE GOALPOST LONGER THAN THE OTHER, AND THEN WE'LL NAIL THE DOOR ON TO THEM LIKE THIS TO MAKE A SNOW PLOUGH!
THAT'S AN IDEA, WINKER!
TOOLS
Only Winker could have thought of it—a home-made snowplough to open up an escape route! But there was still the question of food supplies.
AHEM! ...ER, JOLLY CLEVER OF YOU FINDING OUT WHERE WALLIE HAD HIDDEN ALL THAT GRUB, TROTTY!
?
Winker laid the bait to trap a little rat.
HO-HO! IT WORKED, WINKER! WALLIE'S OFF WITH A SPADE TO CHECK UP ON HIS LOOT!
Yes! Wallie had swallowed the bait!
AHA! BURIED IT IN A DUSTBIN, EH, WALLIE? GRAB IT, BOYS, AND LOAD IT ON TO THE CAR AND OFF WE GO!
EEK! YOU TRICKED ME, YOU ROTTERS!
So Wallie lost the grub he had swiped from the chaps who had swiped it!
OO! THE BEASTS! THEY'RE GOING WITHOUT ME—AND TAKING MY GRUB WITH THEM, TOO!
Wallie nearly swallowed his back teeth when he saw that his big brother was leading the whole Third Form in a break-out to get home for Christmas.
One flying dive and the mop-headed Watson had joined his elders and betters in the Escapers' Club.
PHEW! MADE IT! I'M COMING WITH YOU LOT, SO THERE!
OKAY, WALLIE, HANG ON!
THE CRICKET PAVILION IS AS FAR AS WE CAN GET TONIGHT, LADS, SO CLEAR A PATHWAY AND WE'LL BUNK DOWN IN THERE!
It just showed how deep the snow was. It had taken the boys hours to get here—and they were still inside the school grounds!

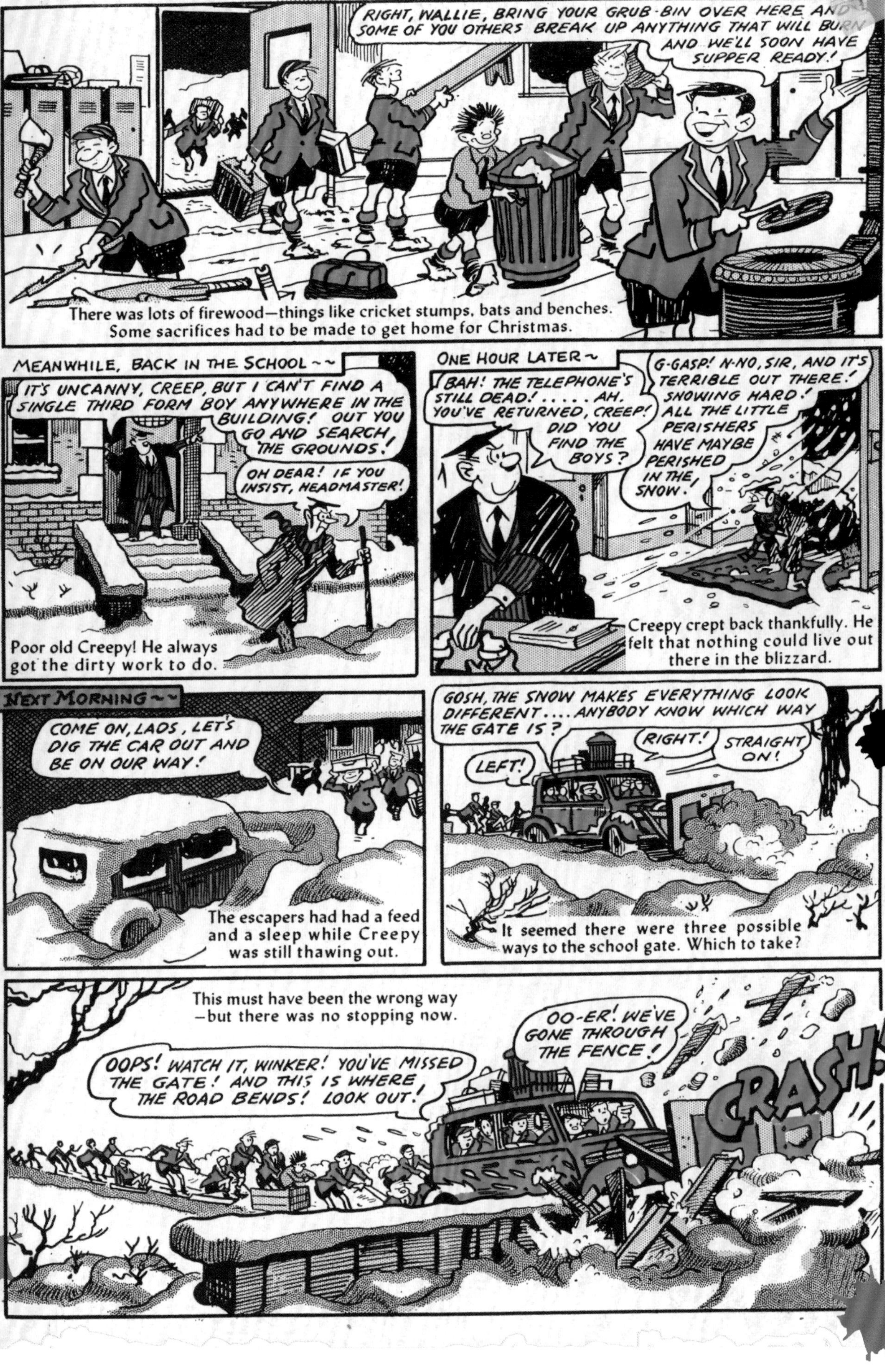
RIGHT, WALLIE, BRING YOUR GRUB-BIN OVER HERE AND SOME OF YOU OTHERS BREAK UP ANYTHING THAT WILL BURN AND WE'LL SOON HAVE SUPPER READY!
There was lots of firewood—things like cricket stumps, bats and benches. Some sacrifices had to be made to get home for Christmas.
MEANWHILE, BACK IN THE SCHOOL ~~
IT'S UNCANNY, CREEP, BUT I CAN'T FIND A SINGLE THIRD FORM BOY ANYWHERE IN THE BUILDING! OUT YOU GO AND SEARCH THE GROUNDS!
OH DEAR! IF YOU INSIST, HEADMASTER!
Poor old Creepy! He always got the dirty work to do.
ONE HOUR LATER ~
BAH! THE TELEPHONE'S STILL DEAD! ..... AH. YOU'VE RETURNED, CREEP! DID YOU FIND THE BOYS?
G-GASP! N-NO, SIR, AND IT'S TERRIBLE OUT THERE! SNOWING HARD! ALL THE LITTLE PERISHERS HAVE MAYBE PERISHED IN THE SNOW!
Creepy crept back thankfully. He felt that nothing could live out there in the blizzard.
NEXT MORNING ~~
COME ON, LADS, LET'S DIG THE CAR OUT AND BE ON OUR WAY!
The escapers had had a feed and a sleep while Creepy was still thawing out.
GOSH, THE SNOW MAKES EVERYTHING LOOK DIFFERENT.... ANYBODY KNOW WHICH WAY THE GATE IS?
LEFT!
RIGHT!
STRAIGHT ON!
It seemed there were three possible ways to the school gate. Which to take?
This must have been the wrong way —but there was no stopping now.
OOPS! WATCH IT, WINKER! YOU'VE MISSED THE GATE! AND THIS IS WHERE THE ROAD BENDS! LOOK OUT!
OO-ER! WE'VE GONE THROUGH THE FENCE!
CRASH!

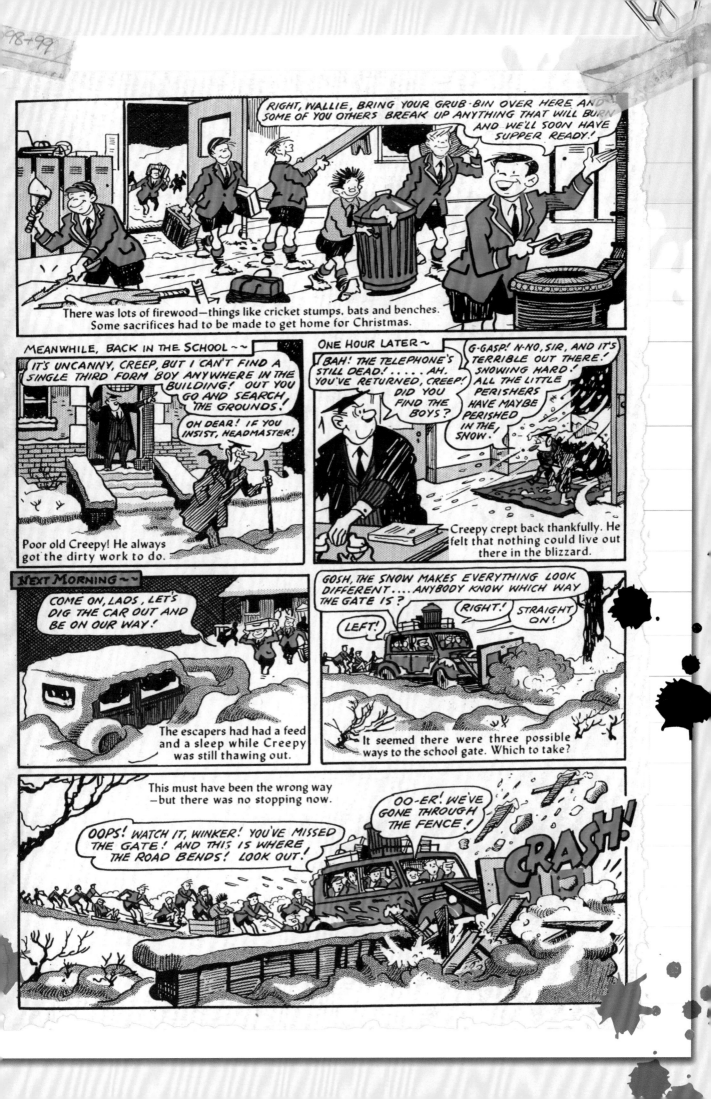

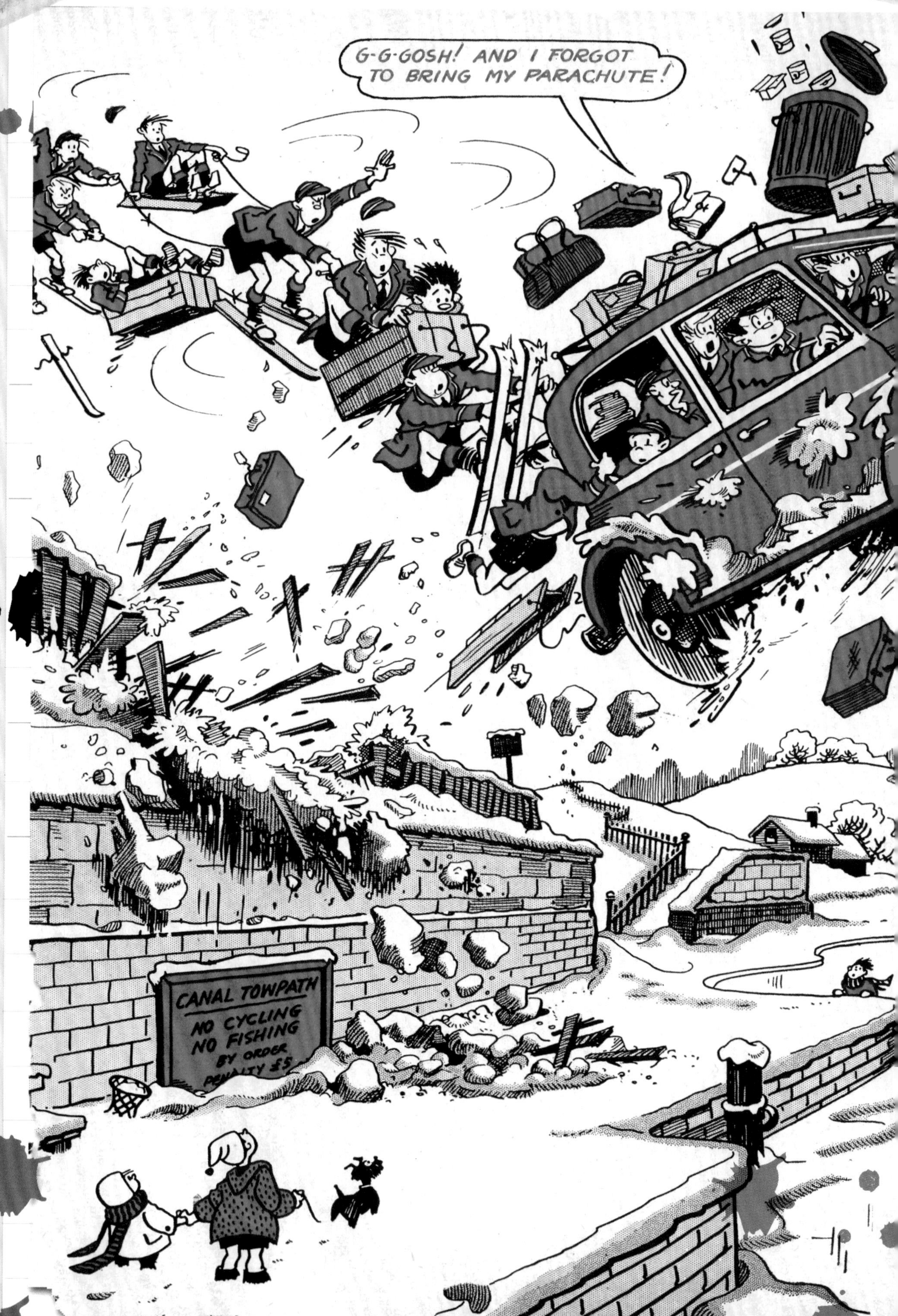
G-G-GOSH! AND I FORGOT TO BRING MY PARACHUTE!
CANAL TOWPATH
NO CYCLING
NO FISHING
BY ORDER
PENALTY £5

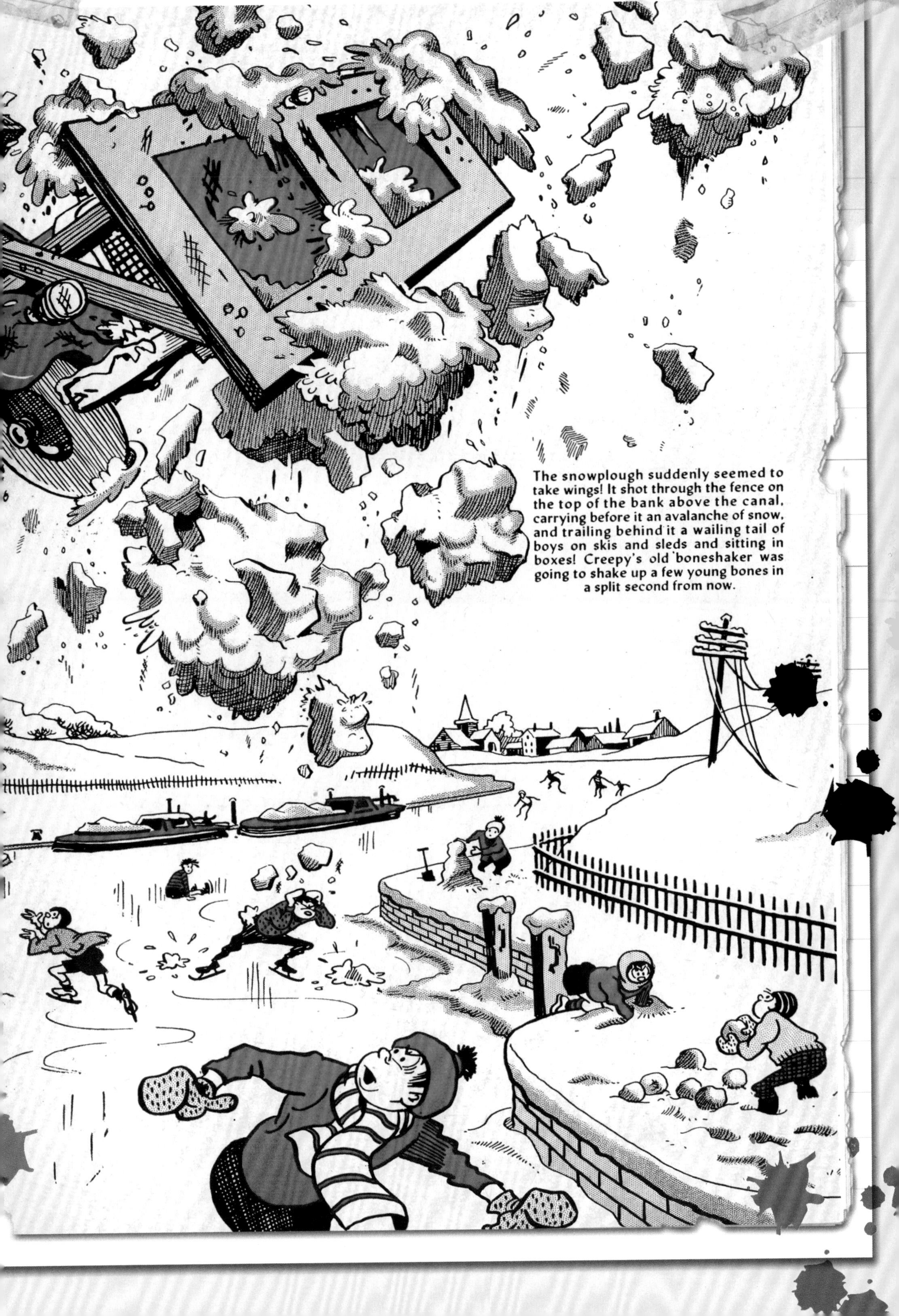
The snowplough suddenly seemed to take wings! It shot through the fence on the top of the bank above the canal, carrying before it an avalanche of snow, and trailing behind it a wailing tail of boys on skis and sleds and sitting in boxes! Creepy's old boneshaker was going to shake up a few young bones in a split second from now.

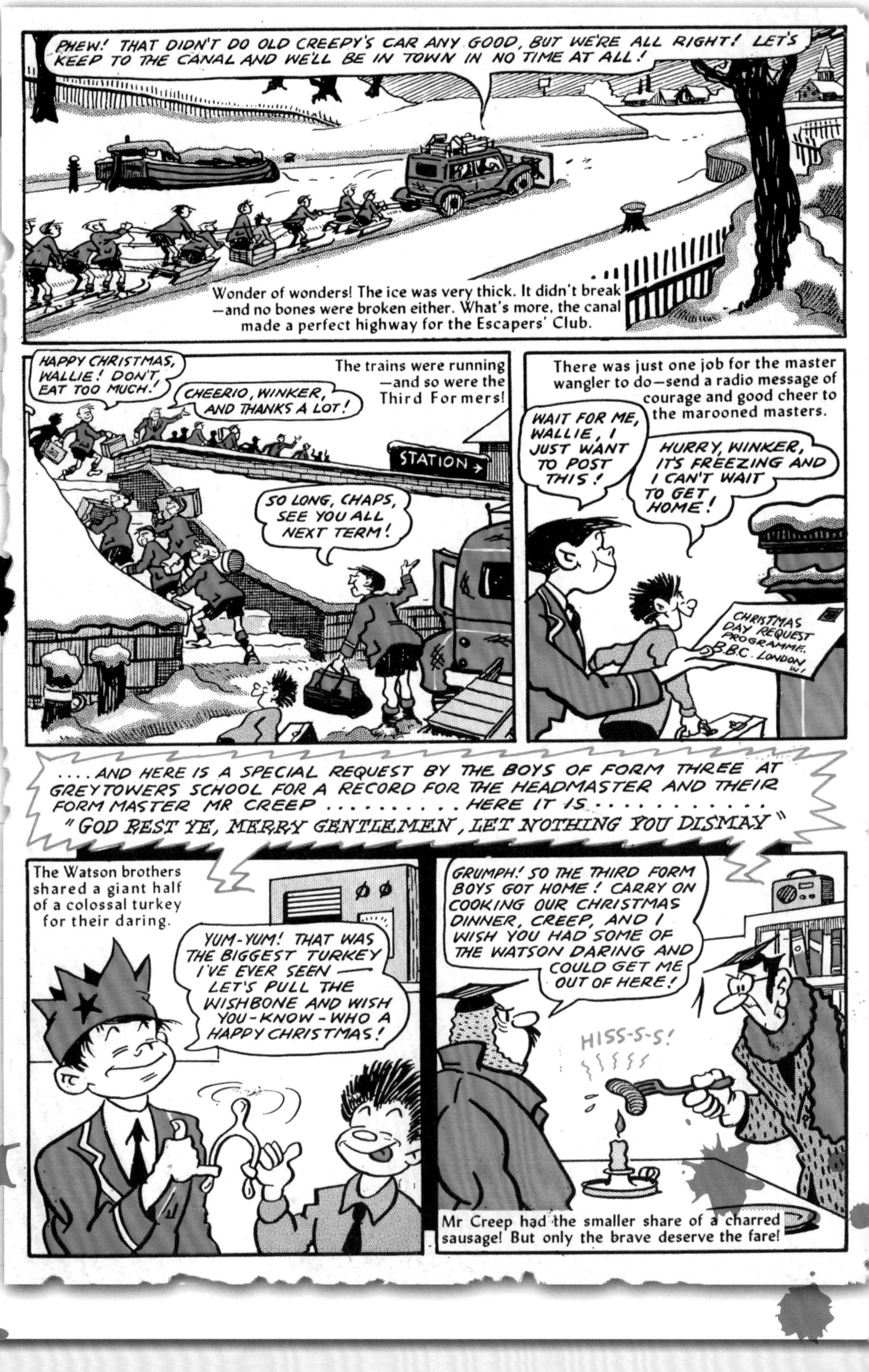
PHEW! THAT DIDN'T DO OLD CREEPY'S CAR ANY GOOD, BUT WE'RE ALL RIGHT! LET'S KEEP TO THE CANAL AND WE'LL BE IN TOWN IN NO TIME AT ALL!
Wonder of wonders! The ice was very thick. It didn't break —and no bones were broken either. What's more, the canal made a perfect highway for the Escapers' Club.
The trains were running —and so were the Third Formers!
HAPPY CHRISTMAS, WALLIE! DON'T EAT TOO MUCH!
CHEERIO, WINKER, AND THANKS A LOT!
STATION
SO LONG, CHAPS, SEE YOU ALL NEXT TERM!
There was just one job for the master wangler to do—send a radio message of courage and good cheer to the marooned masters.
WAIT FOR ME, WALLIE, I JUST WANT TO POST THIS!
HURRY, WINKER, IT'S FREEZING AND I CAN'T WAIT TO GET HOME!
CHRISTMAS DAY REQUEST PROGRAMME. B.B.C. LONDON W1
....AND HERE IS A SPECIAL REQUEST BY THE BOYS OF FORM THREE AT GREYTOWERS SCHOOL FOR A RECORD FOR THE HEADMASTER AND THEIR FORM MASTER MR CREEP ....HERE IT IS...........
"GOD REST YE, MERRY GENTLEMEN, LET NOTHING YOU DISMAY"
The Watson brothers shared a giant half of a colossal turkey for their daring.
YUM-YUM! THAT WAS THE BIGGEST TURKEY I'VE EVER SEEN — LET'S PULL THE WISHBONE AND WISH YOU-KNOW-WHO A HAPPY CHRISTMAS!
GRUMPH! SO THE THIRD FORM BOYS GOT HOME! CARRY ON COOKING OUR CHRISTMAS DINNER, CREEP, AND I WISH YOU HAD SOME OF THE WATSON DARING AND COULD GET ME OUT OF HERE!
HISS-S-S!
Mr Creep had the smaller share of a charred sausage! But only the brave deserve the fare!

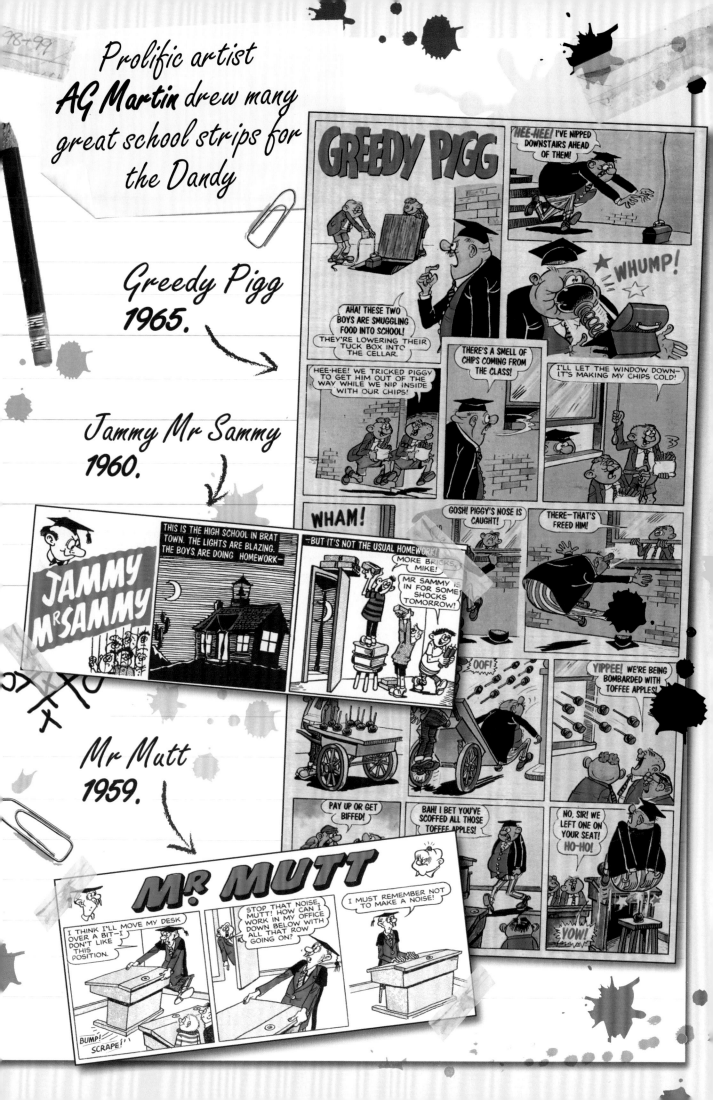

Prolific artist **AG Martin** drew many great school strips for the Dandy

Greedy Pigg 1965.

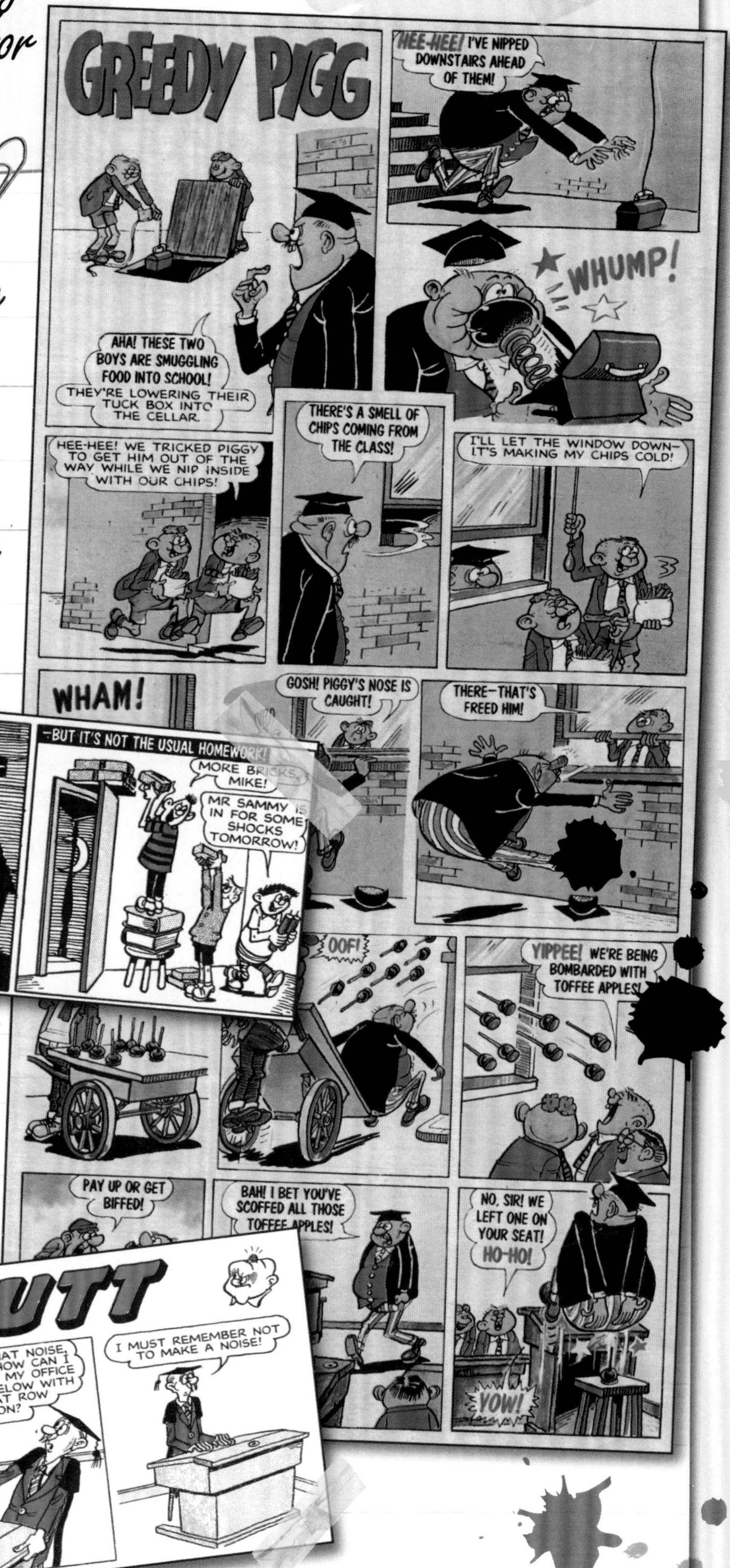
GREEDY PIGG
AHA! THESE TWO BOYS ARE SMUGGLING FOOD INTO SCHOOL!
THEY'RE LOWERING THEIR TUCK BOX INTO THE CELLAR.
HEE-HEE! I'VE NIPPED DOWNSTAIRS AHEAD OF THEM!
WHUMP!
HEE-HEE! WE TRICKED PIGGY TO GET HIM OUT OF THE WAY WHILE WE NIP INSIDE WITH OUR CHIPS!
THERE'S A SMELL OF CHIPS COMING FROM THE CLASS!
I'LL LET THE WINDOW DOWN—IT'S MAKING MY CHIPS COLD!
WHAM!
GOSH! PIGGY'S NOSE IS CAUGHT!
THERE—THAT'S FREED HIM!
OOF!
YIPPEE! WE'RE BEING BOMBARDED WITH TOFFEE APPLES!
PAY UP OR GET BIFFED!
BAH! I BET YOU'VE SCOFFED ALL THOSE TOFFEE APPLES!
NO, SIR! WE LEFT ONE ON YOUR SEAT!
HO-HO!
YOW!

Jammy Mr Sammy 1960.

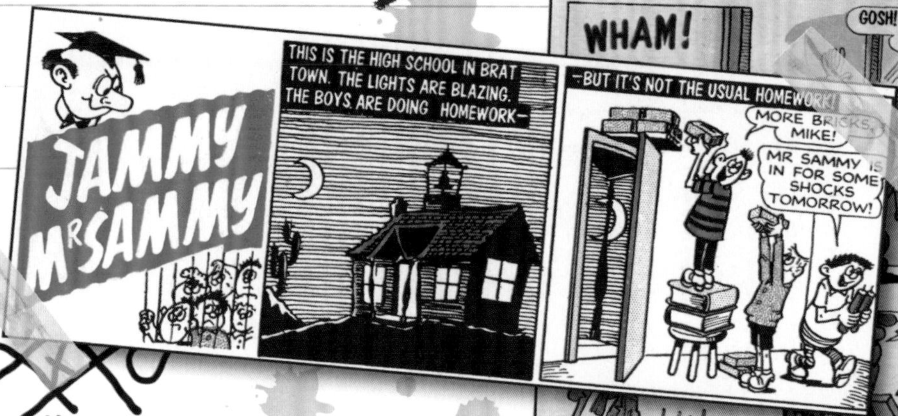
JAMMY MR SAMMY
THIS IS THE HIGH SCHOOL IN BRAT TOWN. THE LIGHTS ARE BLAZING. THE BOYS ARE DOING HOMEWORK—
—BUT IT'S NOT THE USUAL HOMEWORK!
MORE BRICKS, MIKE!
MR SAMMY IS IN FOR SOME SHOCKS TOMORROW!

Mr Mutt 1959.

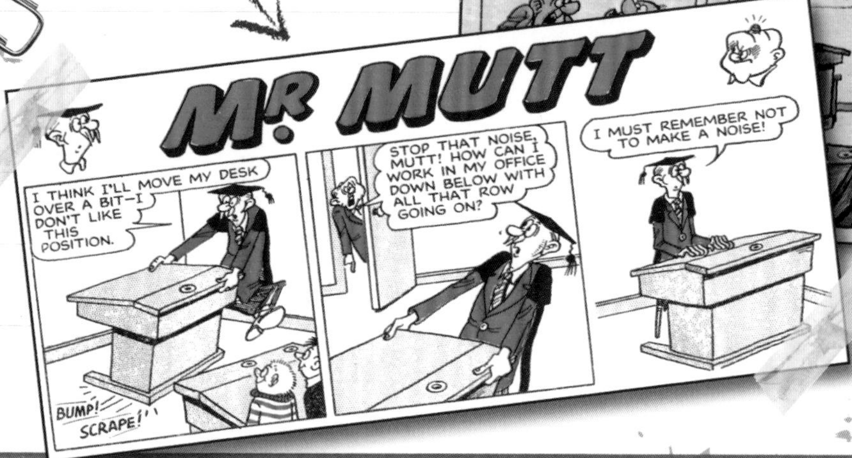
MR MUTT
I THINK I'LL MOVE MY DESK OVER A BIT—I DON'T LIKE THIS POSITION.
BUMP!
SCRAPE!
STOP THAT NOISE, MUTT! HOW CAN I WORK IN MY OFFICE DOWN BELOW WITH ALL THAT ROW GOING ON?
I MUST REMEMBER NOT TO MAKE A NOISE!

4 colourful Biffo and Buster covers from 50s Beano.

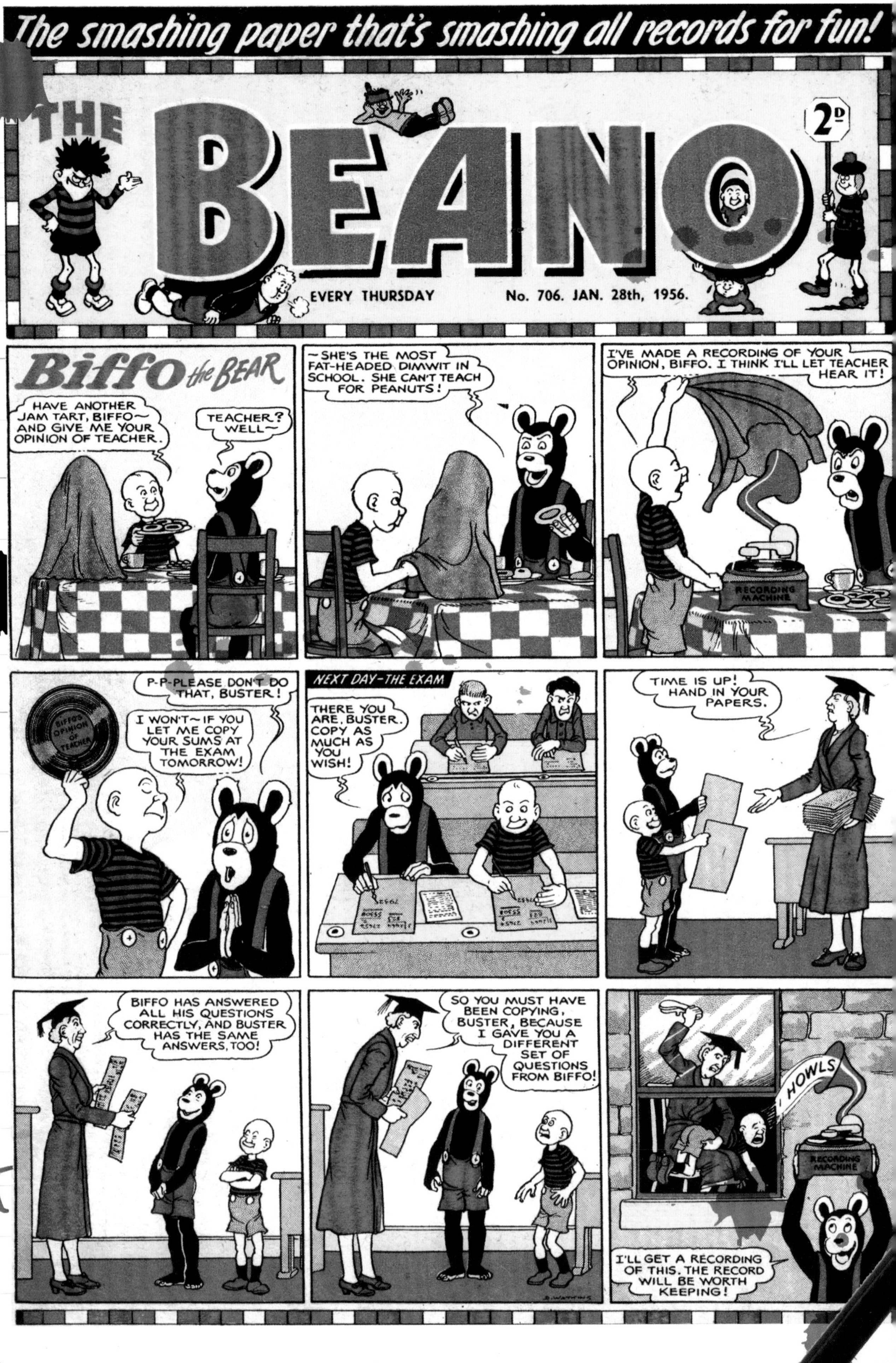
The smashing paper that's smashing all records for fun!
THE BEANO
2D
EVERY THURSDAY
No. 706. JAN. 28th, 1956.
Biffo the BEAR
HAVE ANOTHER JAM TART, BIFFO~ AND GIVE ME YOUR OPINION OF TEACHER.
TEACHER? WELL~
~SHE'S THE MOST FAT-HEADED DIMWIT IN SCHOOL. SHE CAN'T TEACH FOR PEANUTS!
I'VE MADE A RECORDING OF YOUR OPINION, BIFFO. I THINK I'LL LET TEACHER HEAR IT!
RECORDING MACHINE
BIFFO'S OPINION OF TEACHER
P-P-PLEASE DON'T DO THAT, BUSTER!
I WON'T~IF YOU LET ME COPY YOUR SUMS AT THE EXAM TOMORROW!
NEXT DAY-THE EXAM
THERE YOU ARE, BUSTER. COPY AS MUCH AS YOU WISH!
TIME IS UP! HAND IN YOUR PAPERS.
BIFFO HAS ANSWERED ALL HIS QUESTIONS CORRECTLY, AND BUSTER HAS THE SAME ANSWERS, TOO!
SO YOU MUST HAVE BEEN COPYING, BUSTER, BECAUSE I GAVE YOU A DIFFERENT SET OF QUESTIONS FROM BIFFO!
HOWLS
RECORDING MACHINE
I'LL GET A RECORDING OF THIS. THE RECORD WILL BE WORTH KEEPING!

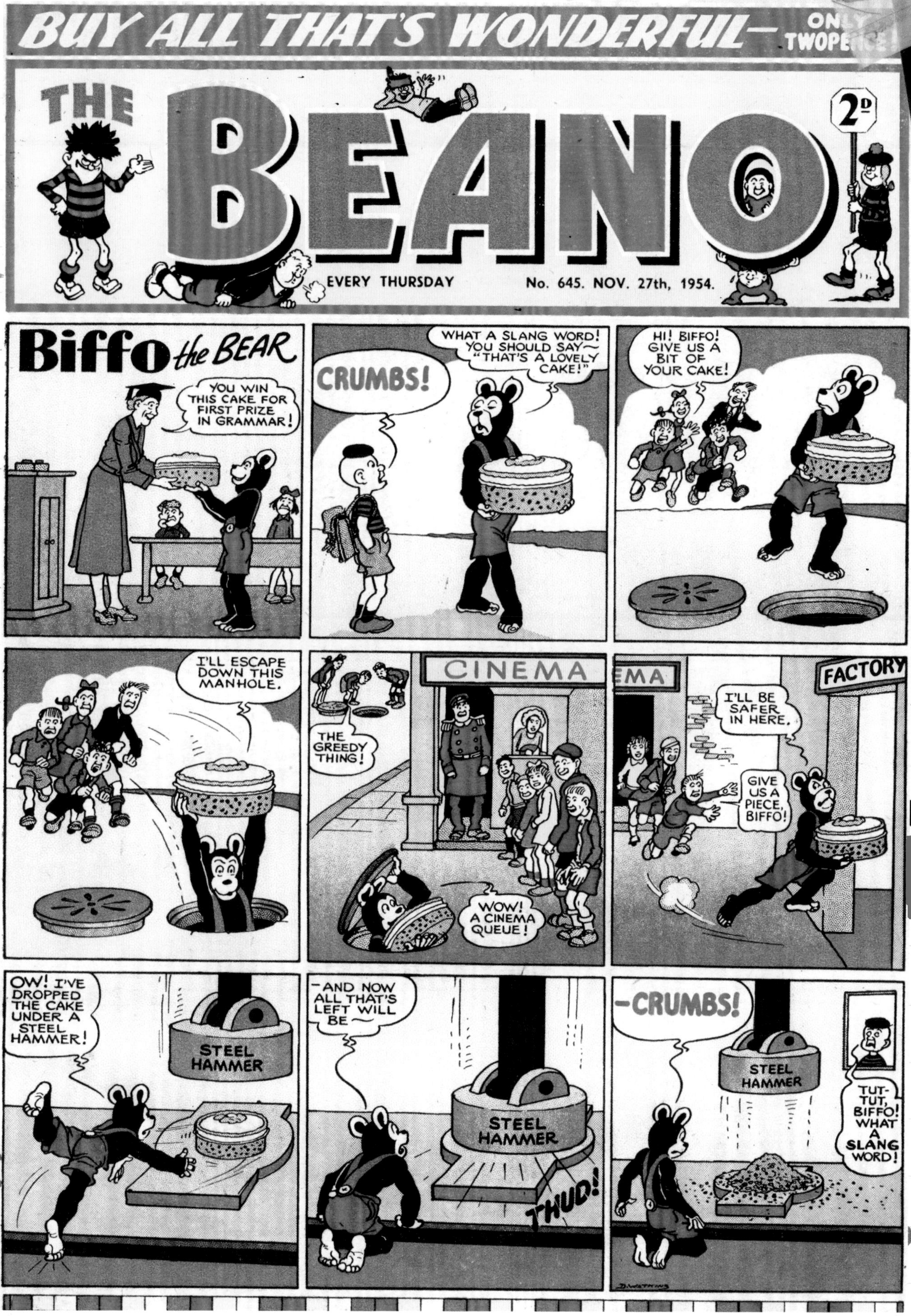
BUY ALL THAT'S WONDERFUL— ONLY TWOPENCE!
THE BEANO
2D
EVERY THURSDAY
No. 645. NOV. 27th, 1954.
Biffo the BEAR
YOU WIN THIS CAKE FOR FIRST PRIZE IN GRAMMAR!
CRUMBS!
WHAT A SLANG WORD! YOU SHOULD SAY— "THAT'S A LOVELY CAKE!"
HI! BIFFO! GIVE US A BIT OF YOUR CAKE!
I'LL ESCAPE DOWN THIS MANHOLE.
CINEMA
THE GREEDY THING!
WOW! A CINEMA QUEUE!
EMA
FACTORY
I'LL BE SAFER IN HERE.
GIVE US A PIECE, BIFFO!
OW! I'VE DROPPED THE CAKE UNDER A STEEL HAMMER!
STEEL HAMMER
—AND NOW ALL THAT'S LEFT WILL BE—
STEEL HAMMER
THUD!
—CRUMBS!
STEEL HAMMER
TUT-TUT, BIFFO! WHAT A SLANG WORD!

Beano Stars Bring A Twinkle To Your Eye!

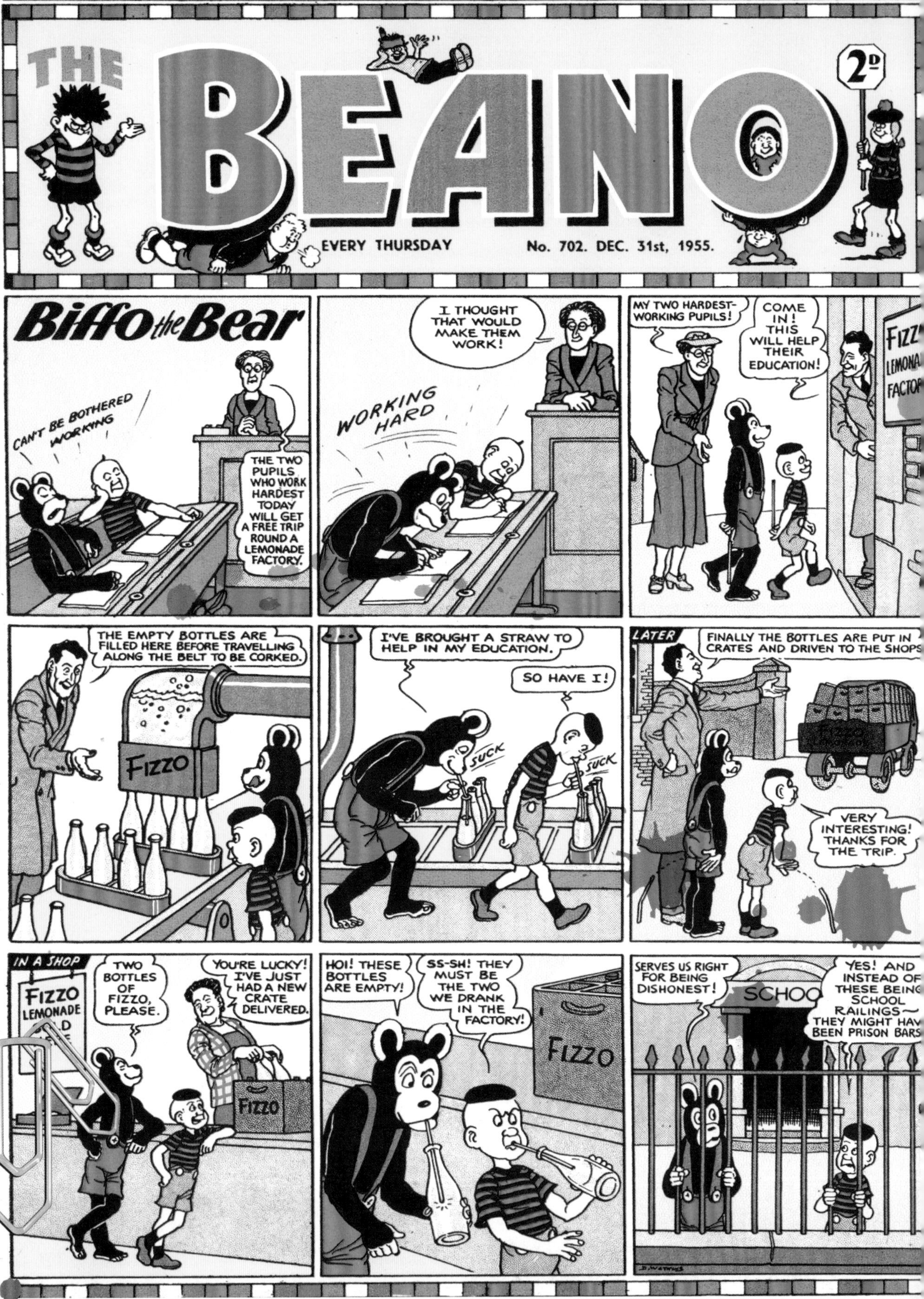

THE BEANO
2D
EVERY THURSDAY
No. 702. DEC. 31st, 1955.
Biffo the Bear
CAN'T BE BOTHERED WORKING
THE TWO PUPILS WHO WORK HARDEST TODAY WILL GET A FREE TRIP ROUND A LEMONADE FACTORY.
I THOUGHT THAT WOULD MAKE THEM WORK!
WORKING HARD
MY TWO HARDEST-WORKING PUPILS!
COME IN! THIS WILL HELP THEIR EDUCATION!
THE EMPTY BOTTLES ARE FILLED HERE BEFORE TRAVELLING ALONG THE BELT TO BE CORKED.
FIZZO
I'VE BROUGHT A STRAW TO HELP IN MY EDUCATION.
SO HAVE I!
SUCK
SUCK
LATER
FINALLY THE BOTTLES ARE PUT IN CRATES AND DRIVEN TO THE SHOPS
VERY INTERESTING! THANKS FOR THE TRIP.
IN A SHOP
FIZZO LEMONADE
TWO BOTTLES OF FIZZO, PLEASE.
YOU'RE LUCKY! I'VE JUST HAD A NEW CRATE DELIVERED.
FIZZO
HOI! THESE BOTTLES ARE EMPTY!
SS-SH! THEY MUST BE THE TWO WE DRANK IN THE FACTORY!
FIZZO
SERVES US RIGHT FOR BEING DISHONEST!
YES! AND INSTEAD OF THESE BEING SCHOOL RAILINGS— THEY MIGHT HAV BEEN PRISON BARS

This Biffo was not drawn by regular artist Dudley D Watkins.

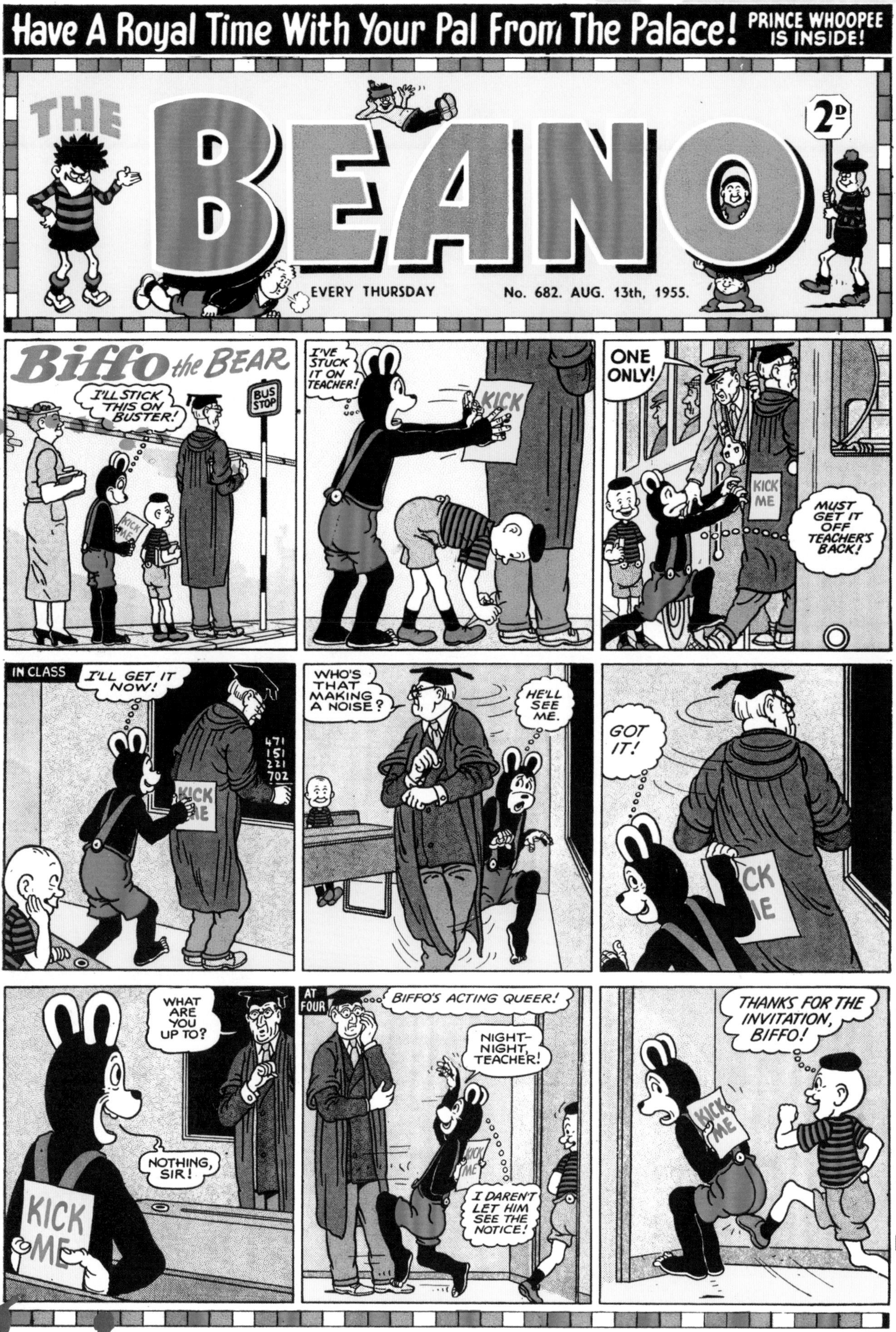
Have A Royal Time With Your Pal From The Palace! PRINCE WHOOPEE IS INSIDE!
THE BEANO
2D
EVERY THURSDAY
No. 682. AUG. 13th, 1955.
Biffo the BEAR
I'LL STICK THIS ON BUSTER!
BUS STOP
KICK ME
I'VE STUCK IT ON TEACHER!
KICK
ONE ONLY!
KICK ME
MUST GET IT OFF TEACHER'S BACK!
IN CLASS
I'LL GET IT NOW!
KICK ME
WHO'S THAT MAKING A NOISE?
HE'LL SEE ME.
GOT IT!
WHAT ARE YOU UP TO?
NOTHING, SIR!
KICK ME
AT FOUR
BIFFO'S ACTING QUEER!
NIGHT-NIGHT, TEACHER!
I DAREN'T LET HIM SEE THE NOTICE!
THANKS FOR THE INVITATION, BIFFO!
KICK ME

Leo Baxendale drew this one.

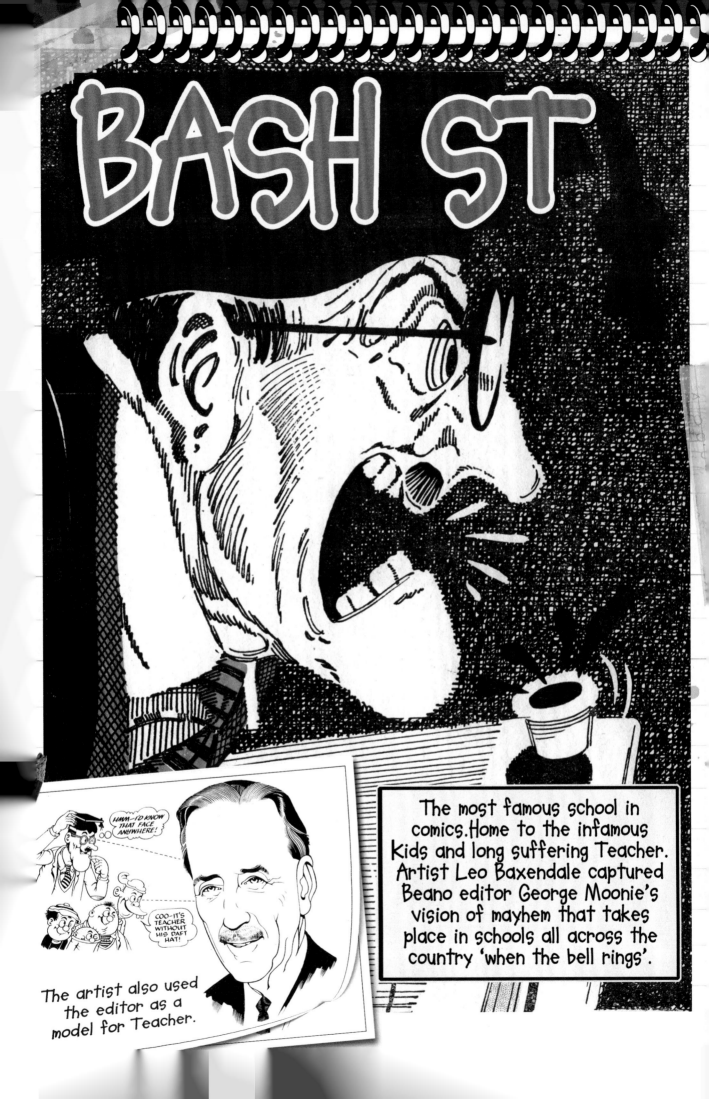

BASH ST

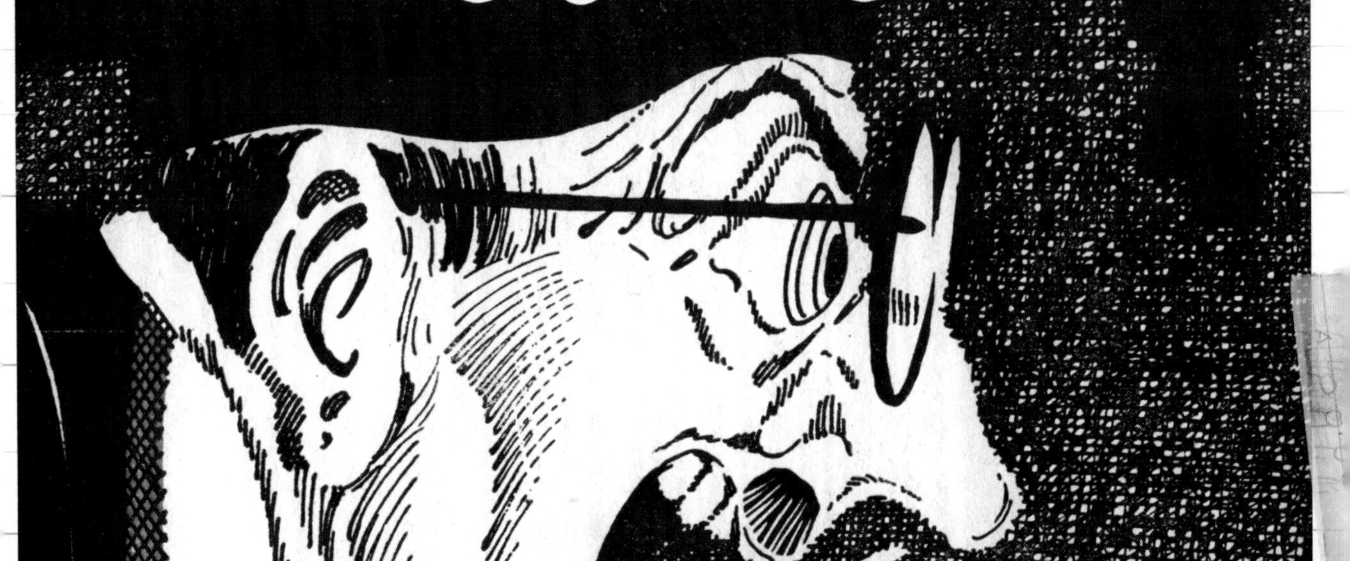

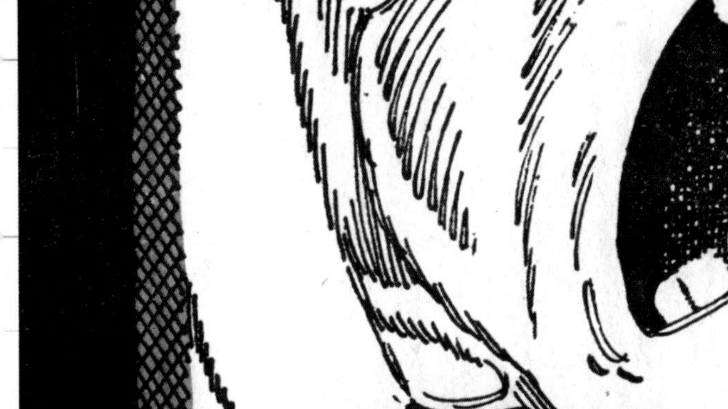
HMM—I'D KNOW THAT FACE ANYWHERE!
COO—IT'S TEACHER WITHOUT HIS DAFT HAT!

The artist also used the editor as a model for Teacher.

The most famous school in comics.Home to the infamous Kids and long suffering Teacher. Artist Leo Baxendale captured Beano editor George Moonie's vision of mayhem that takes place in schools all across the country 'when the bell rings'.

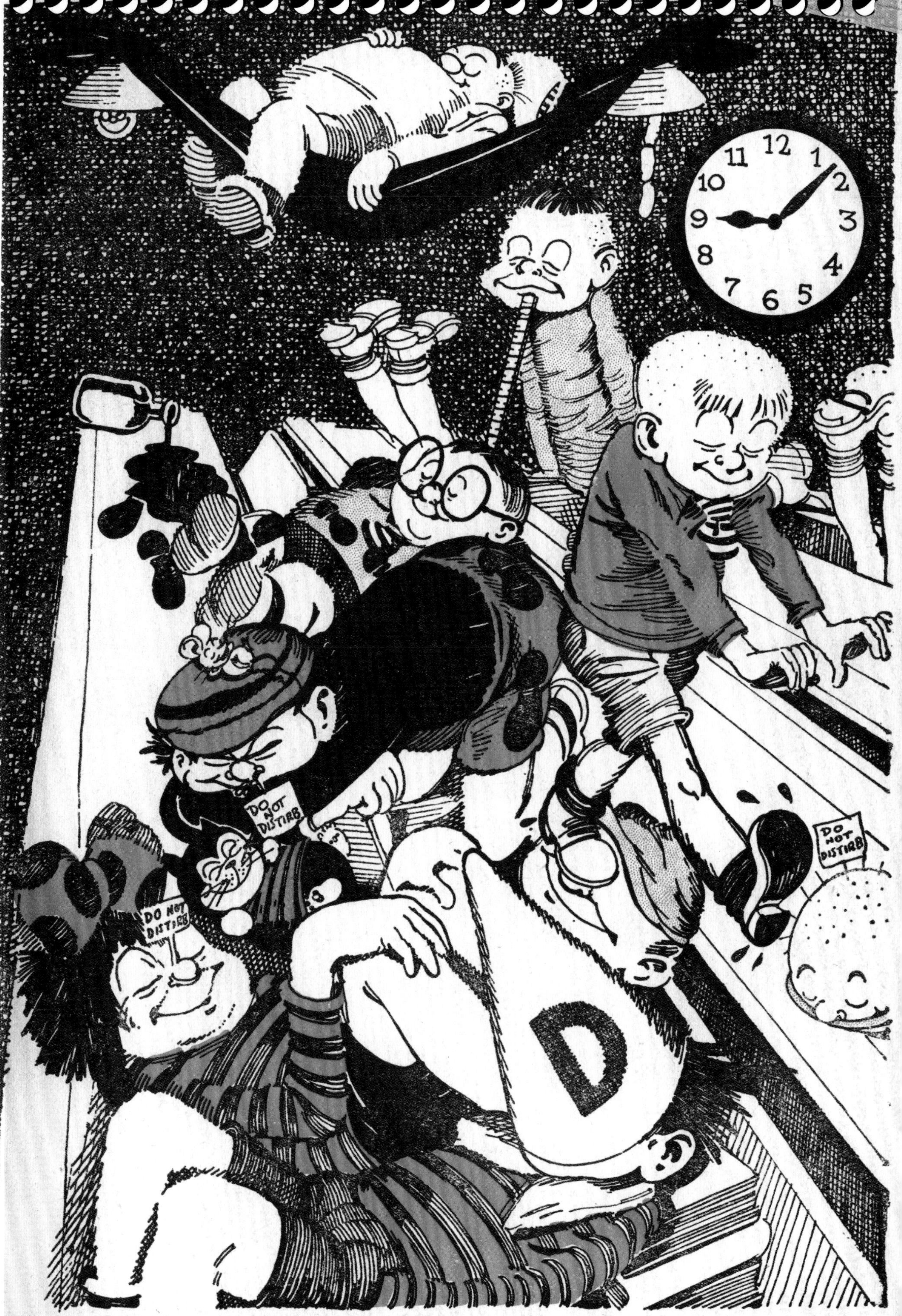
DO NOT DISTIRB
DO NOT DISTIRB
DO NOT DISTIRB

When The Bell Rings was the original title for the strip when it launched in February 1954. It would be almost three years later before they were called simply The Bash St Kids.

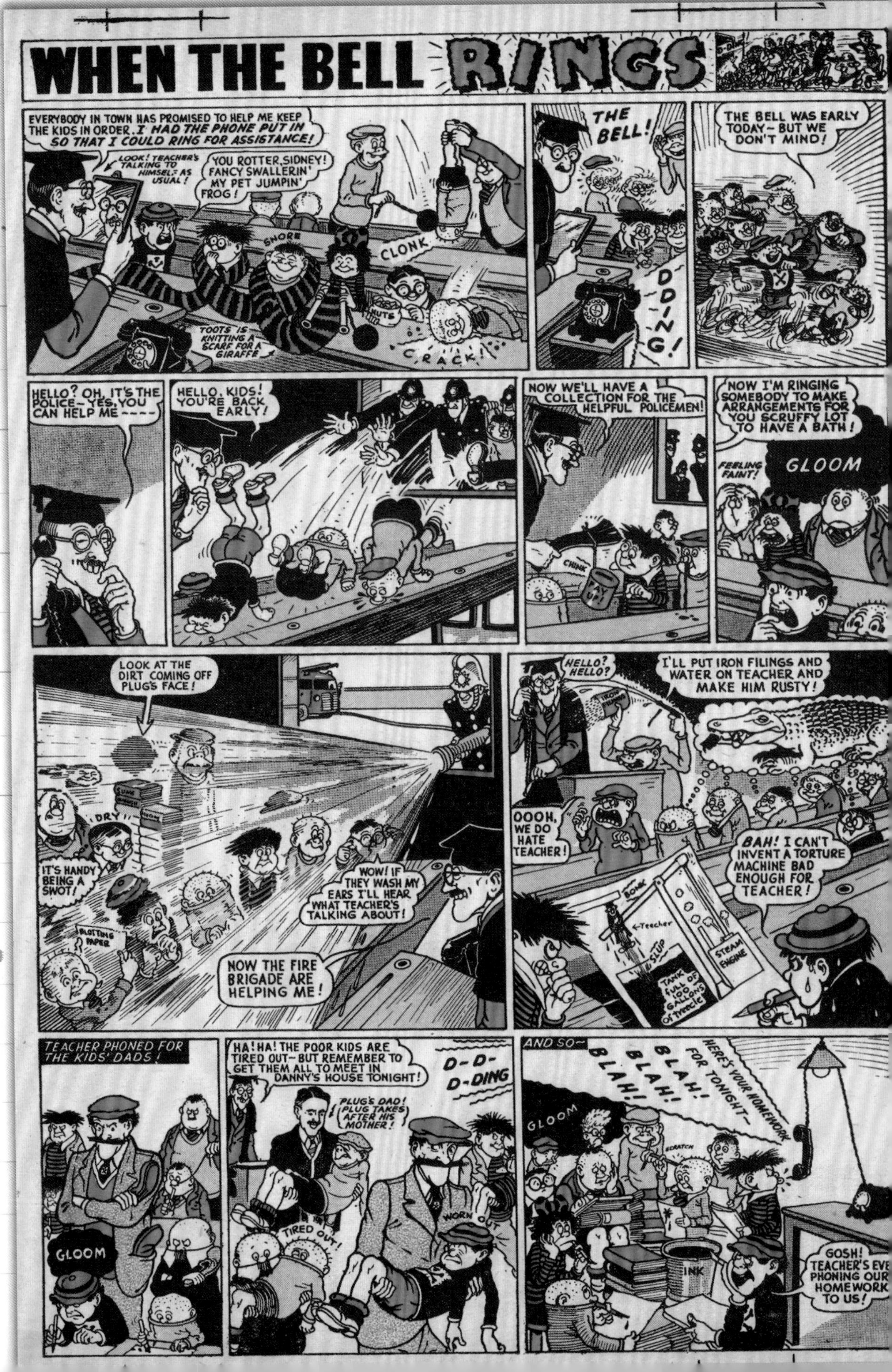

WHEN THE BELL RINGS
EVERYBODY IN TOWN HAS PROMISED TO HELP ME KEEP THE KIDS IN ORDER. I HAD THE PHONE PUT IN SO THAT I COULD RING FOR ASSISTANCE!
LOOK! TEACHER'S TALKING TO HIMSELF AS USUAL!
YOU ROTTER, SIDNEY! FANCY SWALLERIN' MY PET JUMPIN' FROG!
SNORE
CLONK
NUTS
TOOTS IS KNITTING A SCARF FOR A GIRAFFE
CRACK!
THE BELL!
D-D-DING!
THE BELL WAS EARLY TODAY— BUT WE DON'T MIND!
HELLO? OH, IT'S THE POLICE— YES, YOU CAN HELP ME ----
HELLO, KIDS! YOU'RE BACK EARLY!
NOW WE'LL HAVE A COLLECTION FOR THE HELPFUL POLICEMEN!
CHINK
PAY UP!
NOW I'M RINGING SOMEBODY TO MAKE ARRANGEMENTS FOR YOU SCRUFFY LOT TO HAVE A BATH!
FEELING FAINT!
GLOOM
LOOK AT THE DIRT COMING OFF PLUG'S FACE!
DRY
IT'S HANDY BEING A SWOT!
BLOTTING PAPER
WOW! IF THEY WASH MY EARS I'LL HEAR WHAT TEACHER'S TALKING ABOUT!
NOW THE FIRE BRIGADE ARE HELPING ME!
HELLO? HELLO?
I'LL PUT IRON FILINGS AND WATER ON TEACHER AND MAKE HIM RUSTY!
OOOH, WE DO HATE TEACHER!
BAH! I CAN'T INVENT A TORTURE MACHINE BAD ENOUGH FOR TEACHER!
Teacher
SLUP
STEAM ENGINE
TANK full of 100 GALLONS of Treacle
TEACHER PHONED FOR THE KIDS' DADS!
GLOOM
HA! HA! THE POOR KIDS ARE TIRED OUT— BUT REMEMBER TO GET THEM ALL TO MEET IN DANNY'S HOUSE TONIGHT!
D-D-D-DING
PLUG'S DAD! PLUG TAKES AFTER HIS MOTHER!
TIRED OUT!
WORN OUT
AND SO—
HERE'S YOUR HOMEWORK FOR TONIGHT— BLAH! BLAH! BLAH!
GLOOM
SCRATCH
INK
GOSH! TEACHER'S EVEN PHONING OUR HOMEWORK TO US!

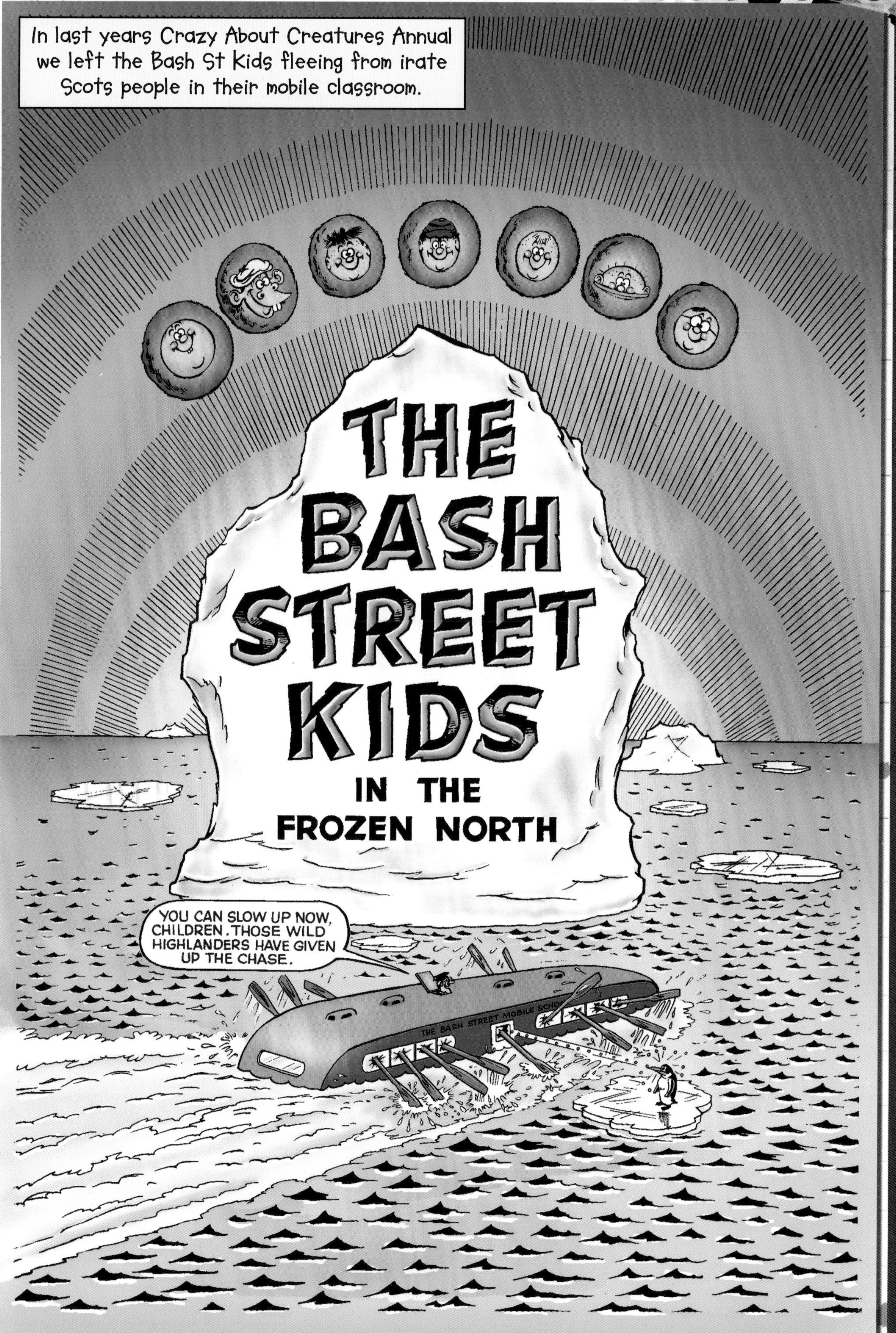
In last years Crazy About Creatures Annual we left the Bash St Kids fleeing from irate Scots people in their mobile classroom.
THE BASH STREET KIDS
IN THE FROZEN NORTH
YOU CAN SLOW UP NOW, CHILDREN. THOSE WILD HIGHLANDERS HAVE GIVEN UP THE CHASE.

The mobile school makes lovely fuel!

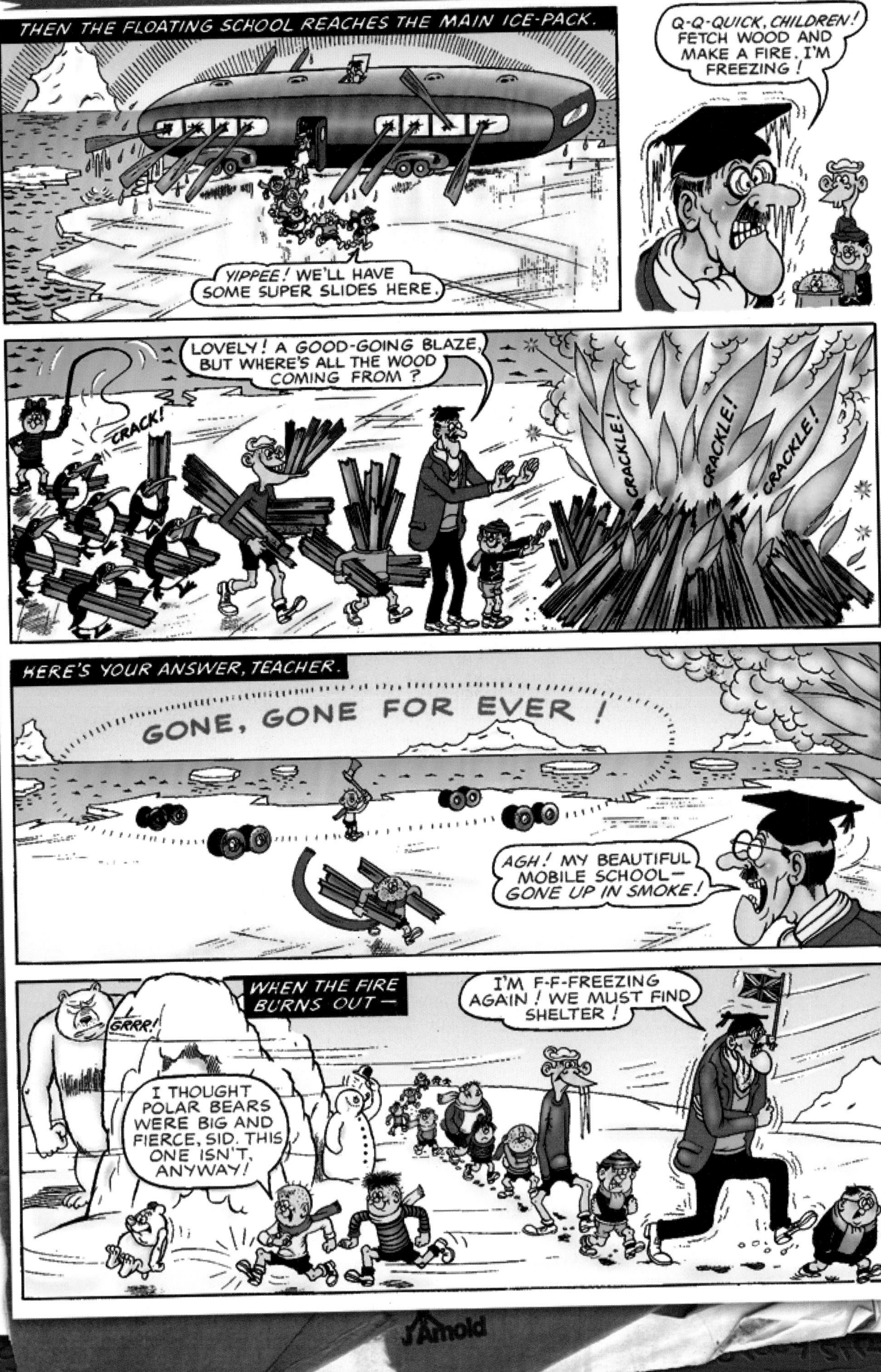

THEN THE FLOATING SCHOOL REACHES THE MAIN ICE-PACK.
YIPPEE! WE'LL HAVE SOME SUPER SLIDES HERE.
Q-Q-QUICK, CHILDREN! FETCH WOOD AND MAKE A FIRE. I'M FREEZING!
LOVELY! A GOOD-GOING BLAZE, BUT WHERE'S ALL THE WOOD COMING FROM?
CRACK!
CRACKLE!
CRACKLE!
CRACKLE!
HERE'S YOUR ANSWER, TEACHER.
GONE, GONE FOR EVER!
AGH! MY BEAUTIFUL MOBILE SCHOOL— GONE UP IN SMOKE!
WHEN THE FIRE BURNS OUT—
GRRR!
I'M F-F-FREEZING AGAIN! WE MUST FIND SHELTER!
I THOUGHT POLAR BEARS WERE BIG AND FIERCE, SID. THIS ONE ISN'T, ANYWAY!
J Arnold

Eskimo food doesn't smell good!

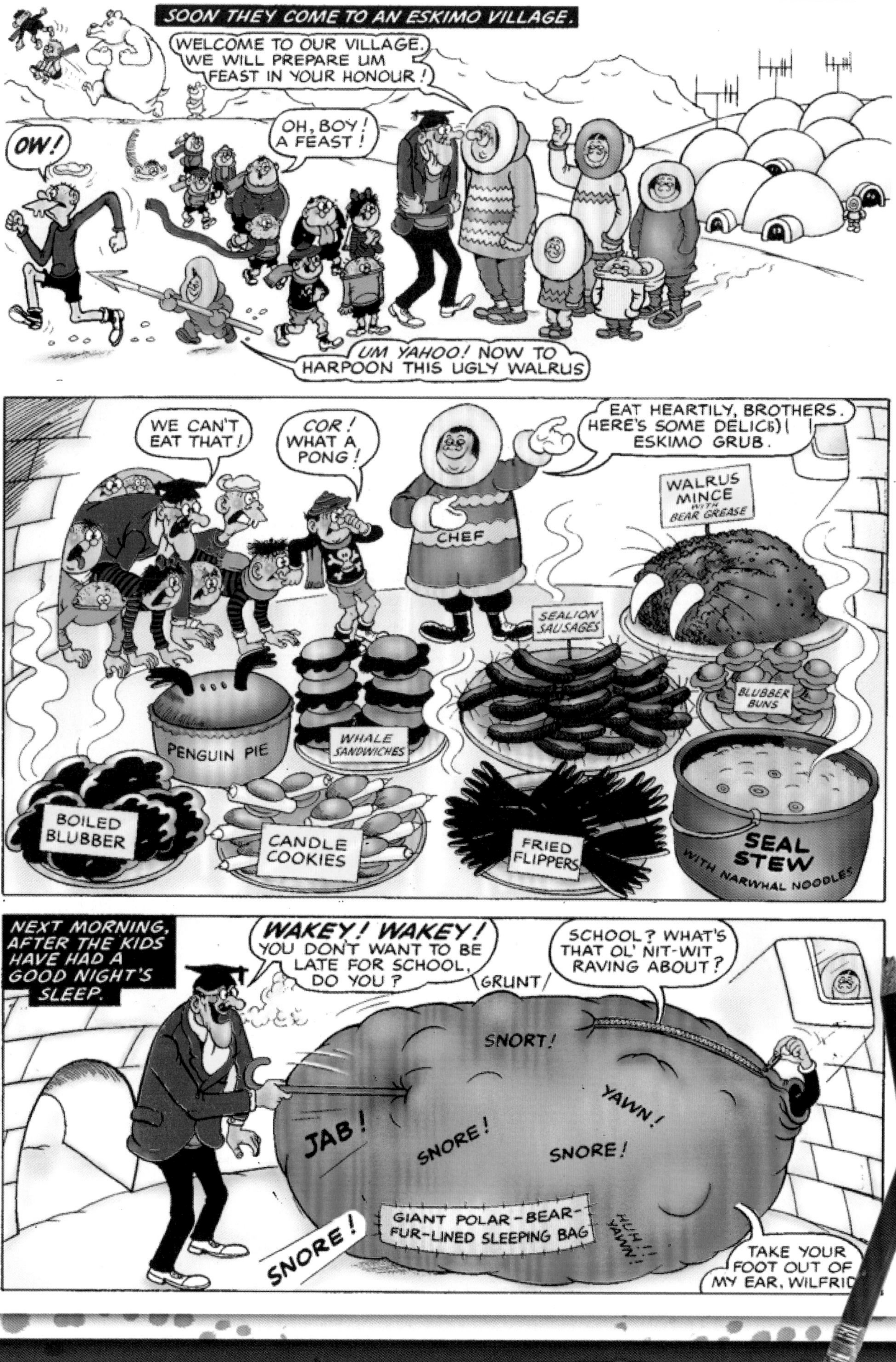

SOON THEY COME TO AN ESKIMO VILLAGE.
WELCOME TO OUR VILLAGE. WE WILL PREPARE UM FEAST IN YOUR HONOUR!
OH, BOY! A FEAST!
OW!
UM YAHOO! NOW TO HARPOON THIS UGLY WALRUS
WE CAN'T EAT THAT!
COR! WHAT A PONG!
EAT HEARTILY, BROTHERS. HERE'S SOME DELIC
ESKIMO GRUB.
CHEF
WALRUS MINCE WITH BEAR GREASE
SEALION SAUSAGES
BLUBBER BUNS
PENGUIN PIE
WHALE SANDWICHES
BOILED BLUBBER
CANDLE COOKIES
FRIED FLIPPERS
SEAL STEW WITH NARWHAL NOODLES
NEXT MORNING, AFTER THE KIDS HAVE HAD A GOOD NIGHT'S SLEEP.
WAKEY! WAKEY! YOU DON'T WANT TO BE LATE FOR SCHOOL, DO YOU?
GRUNT!
SCHOOL? WHAT'S THAT OL' NIT-WIT RAVING ABOUT?
SNORT!
YAWN!
JAB!
SNORE!
SNORE!
GIANT POLAR-BEAR-FUR-LINED SLEEPING BAG
HUH!! YAWN!
SNORE!
TAKE YOUR FOOT OUT OF MY EAR, WILFRID

An ice school is nice an' cool!

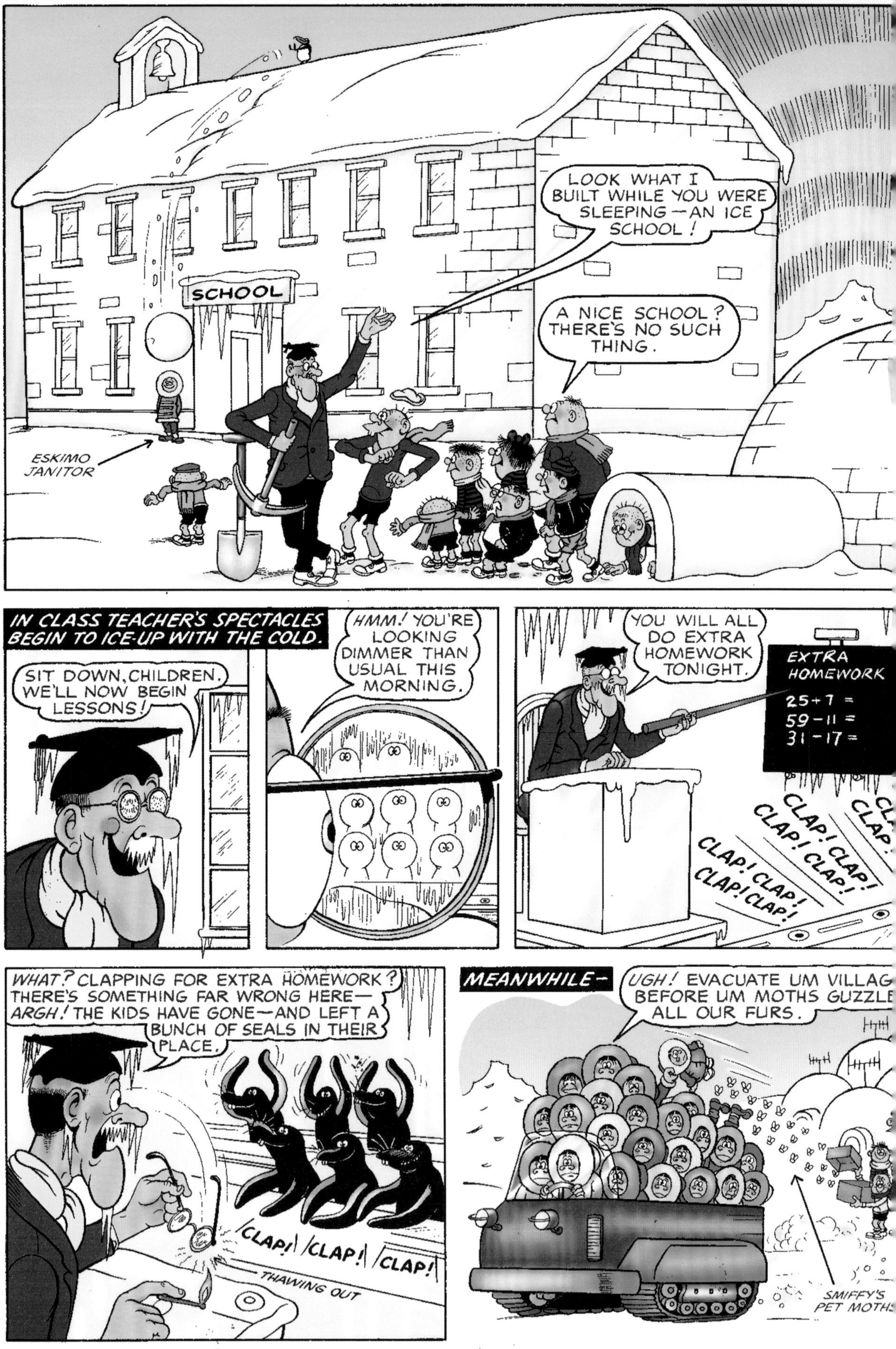

LOOK WHAT I BUILT WHILE YOU WERE SLEEPING—AN ICE SCHOOL!
A NICE SCHOOL? THERE'S NO SUCH THING.
SCHOOL
ESKIMO JANITOR
IN CLASS TEACHER'S SPECTACLES BEGIN TO ICE-UP WITH THE COLD.
SIT DOWN, CHILDREN. WE'LL NOW BEGIN LESSONS!
HMM! YOU'RE LOOKING DIMMER THAN USUAL THIS MORNING.
YOU WILL ALL DO EXTRA HOMEWORK TONIGHT.
EXTRA HOMEWORK
25+7 =
59−11 =
31−17 =
CLAP! CLAP! CLAP! CLAP! CLAP! CLAP! CLAP! CLAP!
WHAT? CLAPPING FOR EXTRA HOMEWORK? THERE'S SOMETHING FAR WRONG HERE—ARGH! THE KIDS HAVE GONE—AND LEFT A BUNCH OF SEALS IN THEIR PLACE.
CLAP! CLAP! CLAP!
THAWING OUT
MEANWHILE—
UGH! EVACUATE UM VILLAG BEFORE UM MOTHS GUZZLE ALL OUR FURS.
SMIFFY'S PET MOTHS

The ice is thin — The kids fall in!

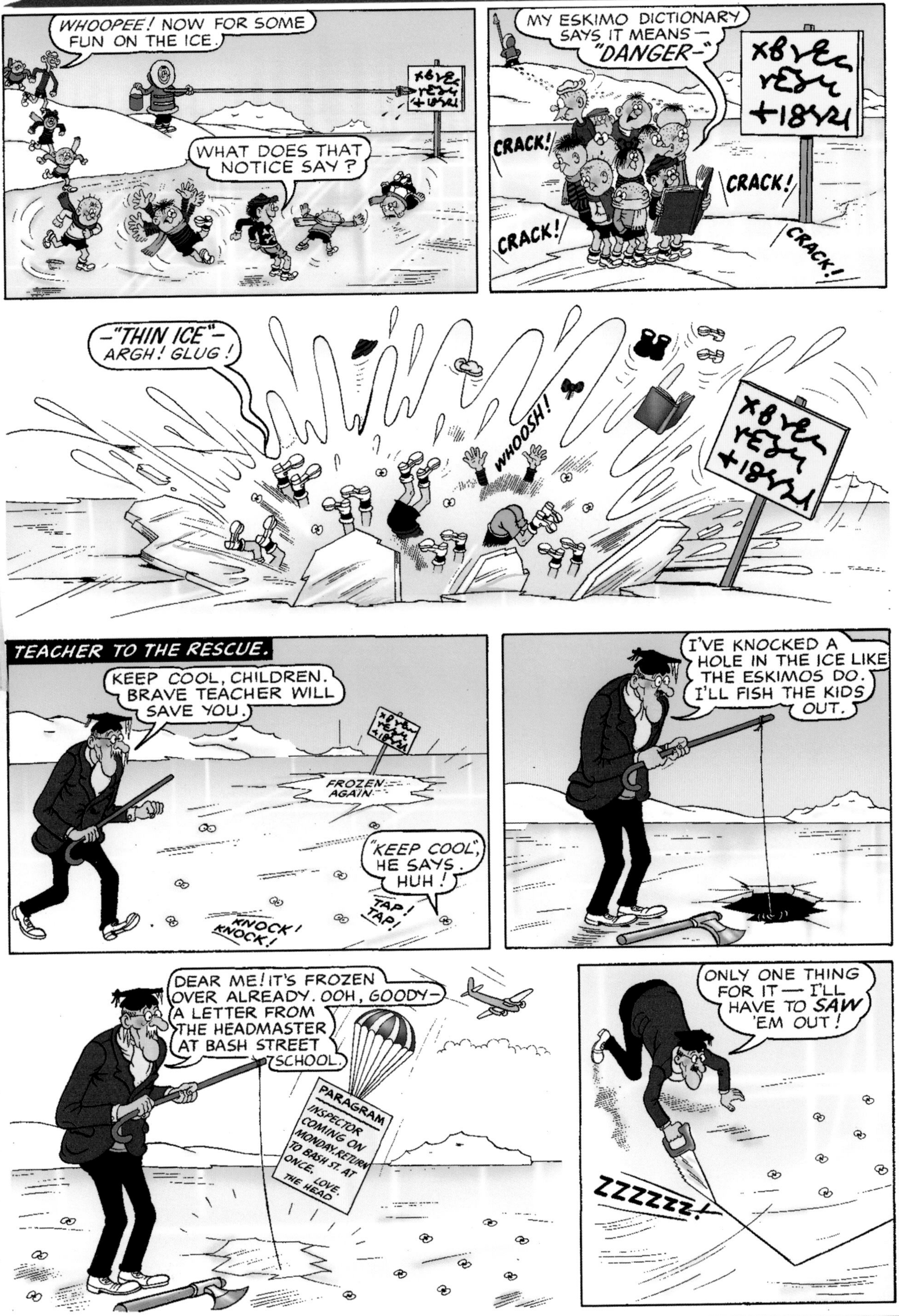
WHOOPEE! NOW FOR SOME FUN ON THE ICE.
WHAT DOES THAT NOTICE SAY?
MY ESKIMO DICTIONARY SAYS IT MEANS — "DANGER—"
CRACK!
CRACK!
CRACK!
CRACK!
—"THIN ICE"— ARGH! GLUG!
WHOOSH!
TEACHER TO THE RESCUE.
KEEP COOL, CHILDREN. BRAVE TEACHER WILL SAVE YOU.
FROZEN AGAIN
"KEEP COOL", HE SAYS. HUH!
TAP! TAP!
KNOCK! KNOCK!
I'VE KNOCKED A HOLE IN THE ICE LIKE THE ESKIMOS DO. I'LL FISH THE KIDS OUT.
DEAR ME! IT'S FROZEN OVER ALREADY. OOH, GOODY— A LETTER FROM THE HEADMASTER AT BASH STREET SCHOOL.
PARAGRAM
INSPECTOR COMING ON MONDAY. RETURN TO BASH ST. AT ONCE. LOVE, THE HEAD
ONLY ONE THING FOR IT — I'LL HAVE TO SAW 'EM OUT!
ZZZZZZ!

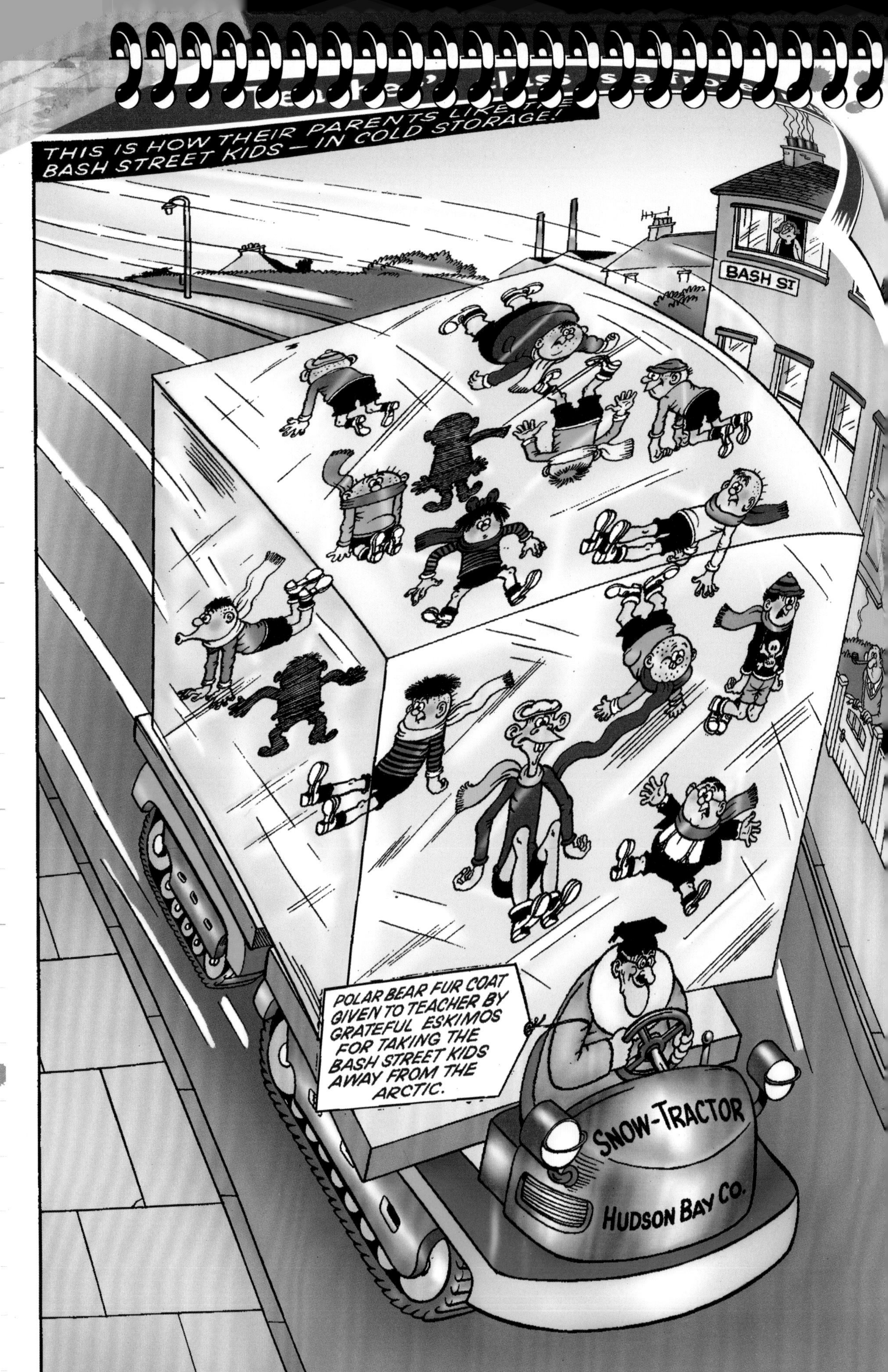
THIS IS HOW THEIR PARENTS LIKE THE BASH STREET KIDS — IN COLD STORAGE!
BASH ST
POLAR BEAR FUR COAT GIVEN TO TEACHER BY GRATEFUL ESKIMOS FOR TAKING THE BASH STREET KIDS AWAY FROM THE ARCTIC.
SNOW-TRACTOR
HUDSON BAY Co.
BUT WHEN THAT ICE-BLOC
MELTS — PARENTS BEWAR

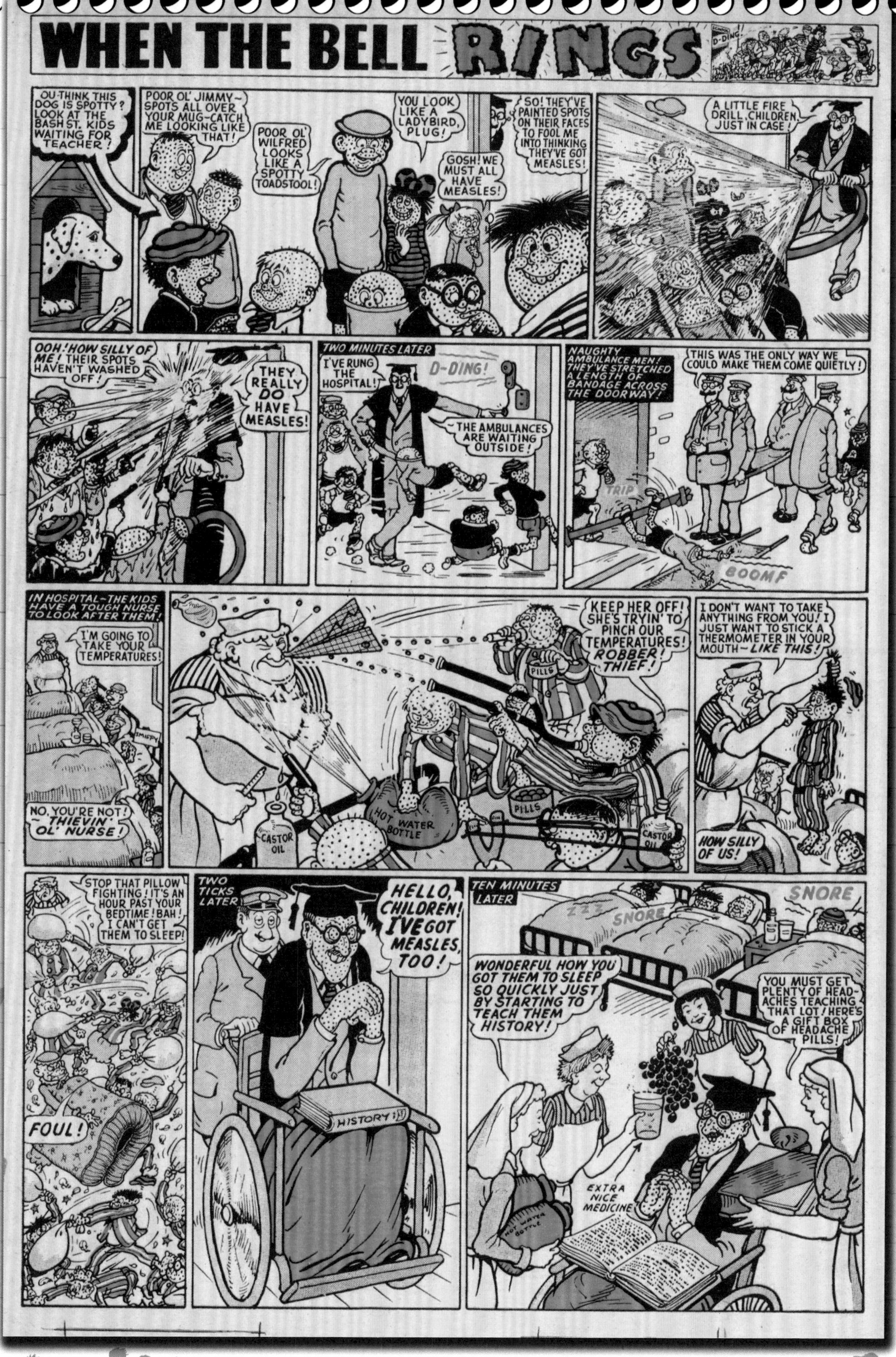
WHEN THE BELL RINGS
D-DING!
OU-THINK THIS DOG IS SPOTTY? LOOK AT THE BASH ST. KIDS WAITING FOR TEACHER!
POOR OL' JIMMY—SPOTS ALL OVER YOUR MUG—CATCH ME LOOKING LIKE THAT!
POOR OL' WILFRED LOOKS LIKE A SPOTTY TOADSTOOL!
YOU LOOK LIKE A LADYBIRD, PLUG!
GOSH! WE MUST ALL HAVE MEASLES!
SO! THEY'VE PAINTED SPOTS ON THEIR FACES TO FOOL ME INTO THINKING THEY'VE GOT MEASLES!
A LITTLE FIRE DRILL, CHILDREN, JUST IN CASE!
OOH! HOW SILLY OF ME! THEIR SPOTS HAVEN'T WASHED OFF!
THEY REALLY DO HAVE MEASLES!
TWO MINUTES LATER
I'VE RUNG THE HOSPITAL!
D-DING!
THE AMBULANCES ARE WAITING OUTSIDE!
NAUGHTY AMBULANCE MEN! THEY'VE STRETCHED A LENGTH OF BANDAGE ACROSS THE DOORWAY!
THIS WAS THE ONLY WAY WE COULD MAKE THEM COME QUIETLY!
TRIP
BOOMF
IN HOSPITAL—THE KIDS HAVE A TOUGH NURSE TO LOOK AFTER THEM!
I'M GOING TO TAKE YOUR TEMPERATURES!
NO, YOU'RE NOT! THIEVIN' OL' NURSE!
KEEP HER OFF! SHE'S TRYIN' TO PINCH OUR TEMPERATURES! ROBBER! THIEF!
PILLS
HOT WATER BOTTLE
CASTOR OIL
I DON'T WANT TO TAKE ANYTHING FROM YOU! I JUST WANT TO STICK A THERMOMETER IN YOUR MOUTH—LIKE THIS!
HOW SILLY OF US!
STOP THAT PILLOW FIGHTING! IT'S AN HOUR PAST YOUR BEDTIME! BAH! I CAN'T GET THEM TO SLEEP!
FOUL!
TWO TICKS LATER
HELLO, CHILDREN! I'VE GOT MEASLES, TOO!
HISTORY
TEN MINUTES LATER
SNORE
SNORE
WONDERFUL HOW YOU GOT THEM TO SLEEP SO QUICKLY JUST BY STARTING TO TEACH THEM HISTORY!
YOU MUST GET PLENTY OF HEADACHES TEACHING THAT LOT! HERE'S A GIFT BOX OF HEADACHE PILLS!
EXTRA NICE MEDICINE
HOT WATER BOTTLE

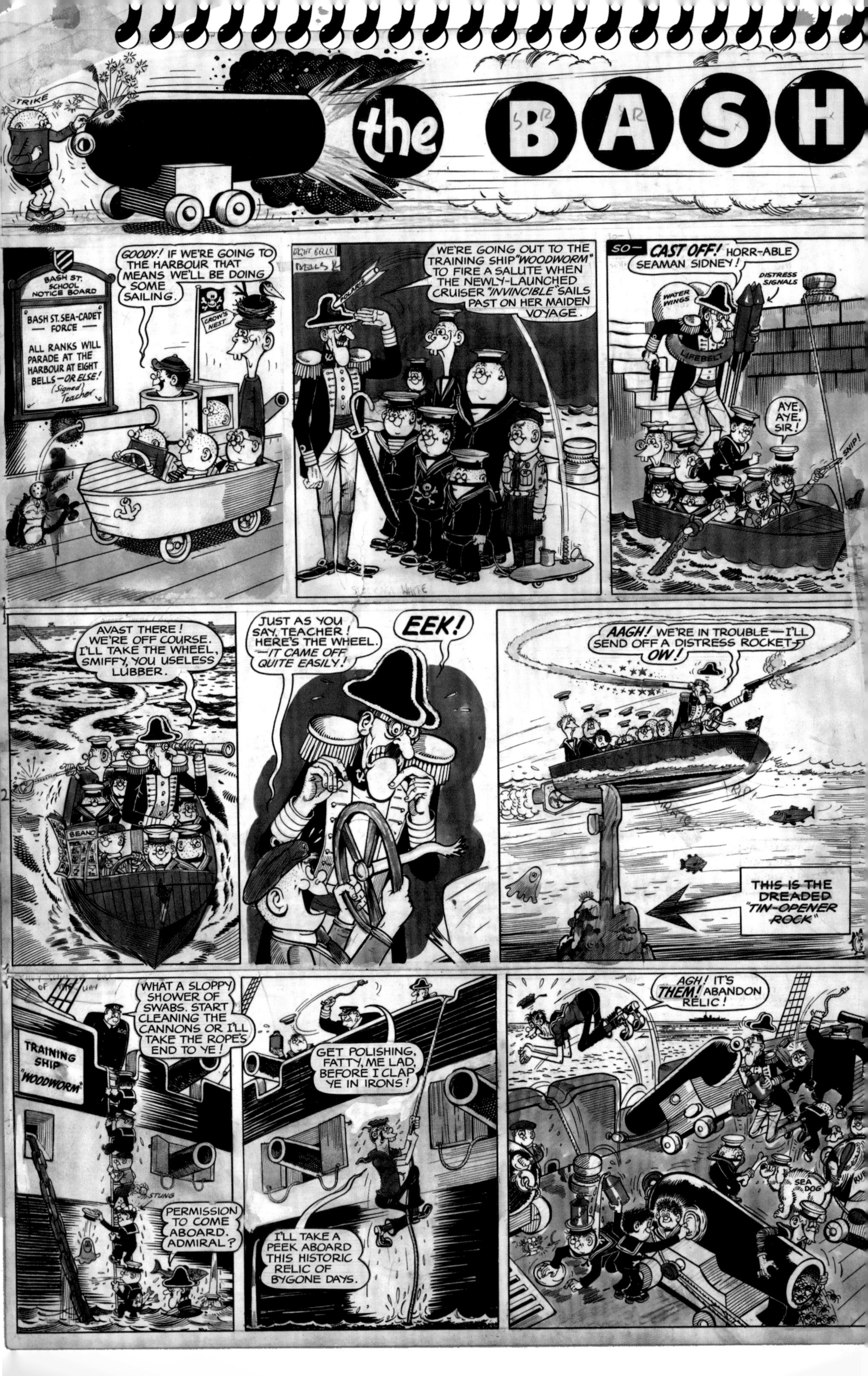
the BASH
STRIKE
BASH ST. SCHOOL NOTICE BOARD
BASH ST. SEA-CADET FORCE — ALL RANKS WILL PARADE AT THE HARBOUR AT EIGHT BELLS—OR ELSE! (Signed) Teacher
GOODY! IF WE'RE GOING TO THE HARBOUR THAT MEANS WE'LL BE DOING SOME SAILING.
CROW'S NEST
WE'RE GOING OUT TO THE TRAINING SHIP "WOODWORM" TO FIRE A SALUTE WHEN THE NEWLY-LAUNCHED CRUISER "INVINCIBLE" SAILS PAST ON HER MAIDEN VOYAGE.
SO— CAST OFF! HORR-ABLE SEAMAN SIDNEY!
WATER WINGS
DISTRESS SIGNALS
LIFEBELT
AYE, AYE, SIR!
SNIP!
AVAST THERE! WE'RE OFF COURSE. I'LL TAKE THE WHEEL, SMIFFY, YOU USELESS LUBBER.
BEANO
JUST AS YOU SAY, TEACHER! HERE'S THE WHEEL. —IT CAME OFF QUITE EASILY!
EEK!
AAGH! WE'RE IN TROUBLE—I'LL SEND OFF A DISTRESS ROCKET— OW!
THIS IS THE DREADED "TIN-OPENER ROCK"
WHAT A SLOPPY SHOWER OF SWABS. START CLEANING THE CANNONS OR I'LL TAKE THE ROPE'S END TO YE!
TRAINING SHIP "WOODWORM"
STUNG
PERMISSION TO COME ABOARD, ADMIRAL?
GET POLISHING, FATTY, ME LAD, BEFORE I CLAP YE IN IRONS!
I'LL TAKE A PEEK ABOARD THIS HISTORIC RELIC OF BYGONE DAYS.
AGH! IT'S THEM! ABANDON RELIC!
SEA DOG

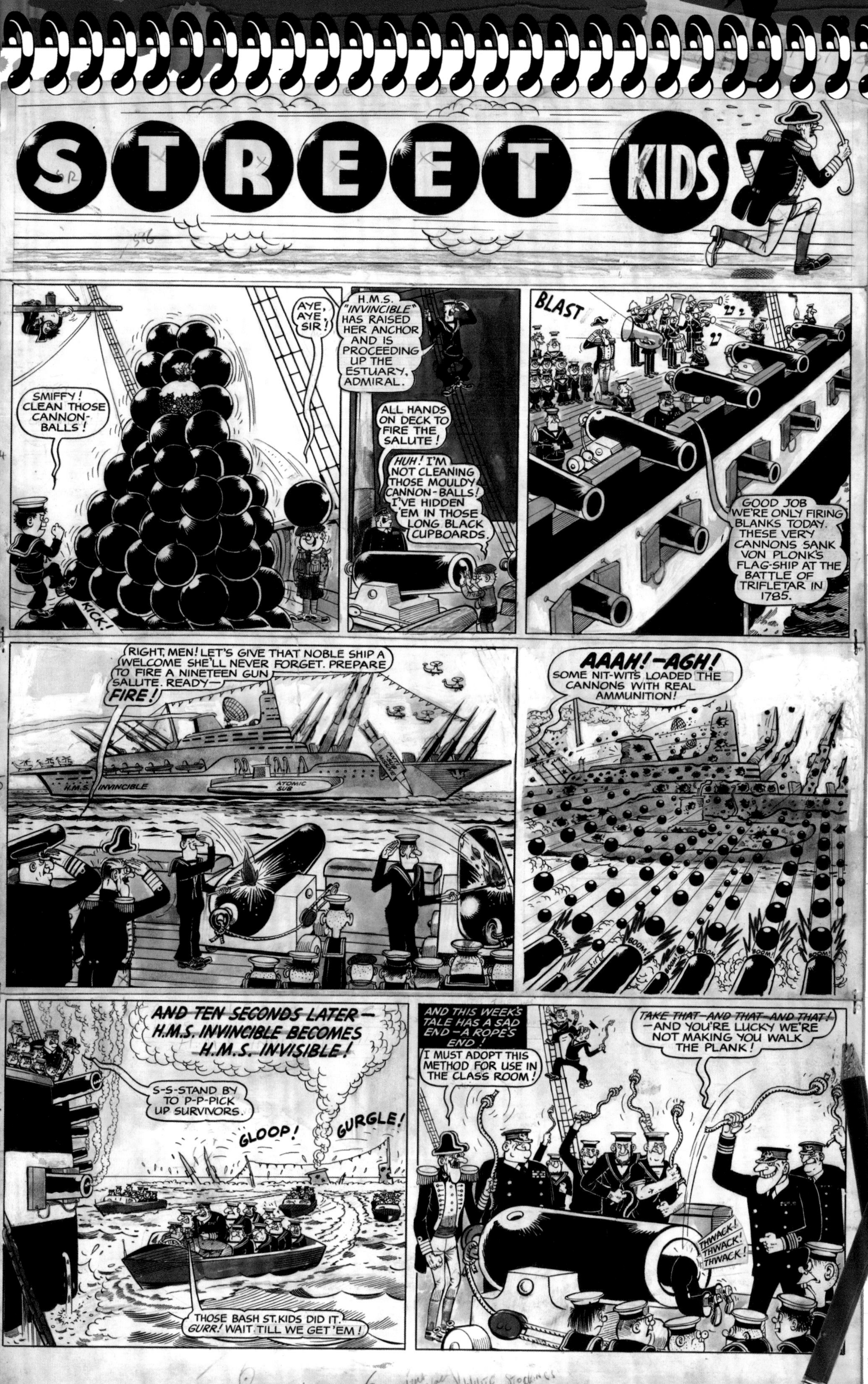
STREET KIDS
SMIFFY! CLEAN THOSE CANNON-BALLS!
AYE, AYE, SIR!
KICK!
H.M.S. "INVINCIBLE" HAS RAISED HER ANCHOR AND IS PROCEEDING UP THE ESTUARY, ADMIRAL.
ALL HANDS ON DECK TO FIRE THE SALUTE!
HUH! I'M NOT CLEANING THOSE MOULDY CANNON-BALLS! I'VE HIDDEN 'EM IN THOSE LONG BLACK CUPBOARDS.
BLAST
GOOD JOB WE'RE ONLY FIRING BLANKS TODAY. THESE VERY CANNONS SANK VON PLONK'S FLAG-SHIP AT THE BATTLE OF TRIFLETAR IN 1785.
RIGHT, MEN! LET'S GIVE THAT NOBLE SHIP A WELCOME SHE'LL NEVER FORGET. PREPARE TO FIRE A NINETEEN GUN SALUTE. READY—FIRE!
H.M.S. INVINCIBLE
ATOMIC SUB
AAAH!-AGH! SOME NIT-WITS LOADED THE CANNONS WITH REAL AMMUNITION!
BOOM!
AND TEN SECONDS LATER—H.M.S. INVINCIBLE BECOMES H.M.S. INVISIBLE!
S-S-STAND BY TO P-P-PICK UP SURVIVORS.
GLOOP!
GURGLE!
THOSE BASH ST. KIDS DID IT. GURR! WAIT TILL WE GET 'EM!
AND THIS WEEK'S TALE HAS A SAD END—A ROPE'S END!
I MUST ADOPT THIS METHOD FOR USE IN THE CLASS ROOM!
TAKE THAT—AND THAT—AND THAT! —AND YOU'RE LUCKY WE'RE NOT MAKING YOU WALK THE PLANK!
THWACK! THWACK! THWACK!

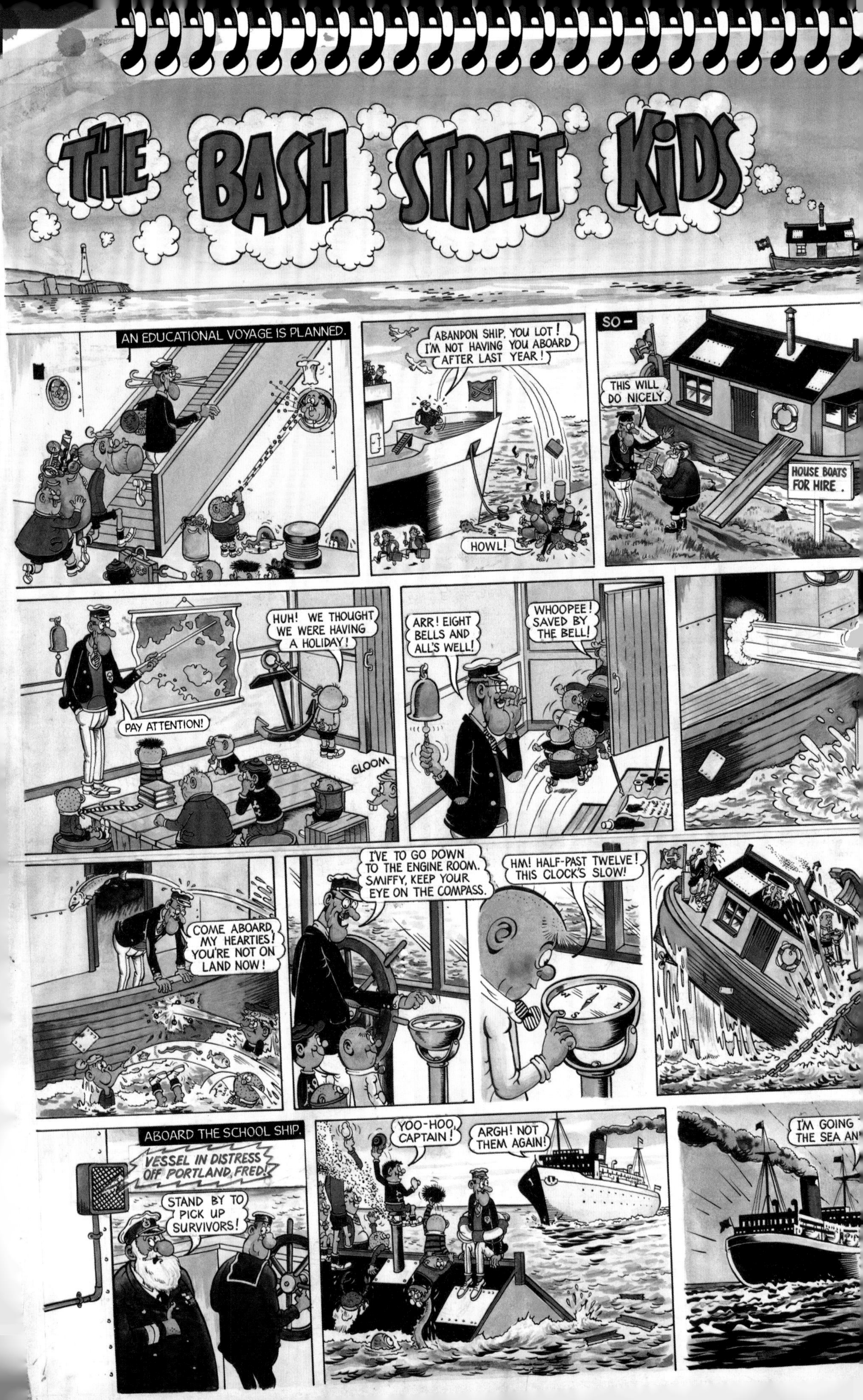
THE BASH STREET KIDS
AN EDUCATIONAL VOYAGE IS PLANNED.
ABANDON SHIP, YOU LOT! I'M NOT HAVING YOU ABOARD AFTER LAST YEAR!
HOWL!
SO—
THIS WILL DO NICELY.
HOUSE BOATS FOR HIRE.
PAY ATTENTION!
HUH! WE THOUGHT WE WERE HAVING A HOLIDAY!
GLOOM
ARR! EIGHT BELLS AND ALL'S WELL!
WHOOPEE! SAVED BY THE BELL!
COME ABOARD, MY HEARTIES! YOU'RE NOT ON LAND NOW!
I'VE TO GO DOWN TO THE ENGINE ROOM. SMIFFY, KEEP YOUR EYE ON THE COMPASS.
HM! HALF-PAST TWELVE! THIS CLOCK'S SLOW!
ABOARD THE SCHOOL SHIP.
VESSEL IN DISTRESS OFF PORTLAND, FRED!
STAND BY TO PICK UP SURVIVORS!
YOO-HOO, CAPTAIN!
ARGH! NOT THEM AGAIN!
I'M GOING THE SEA AN

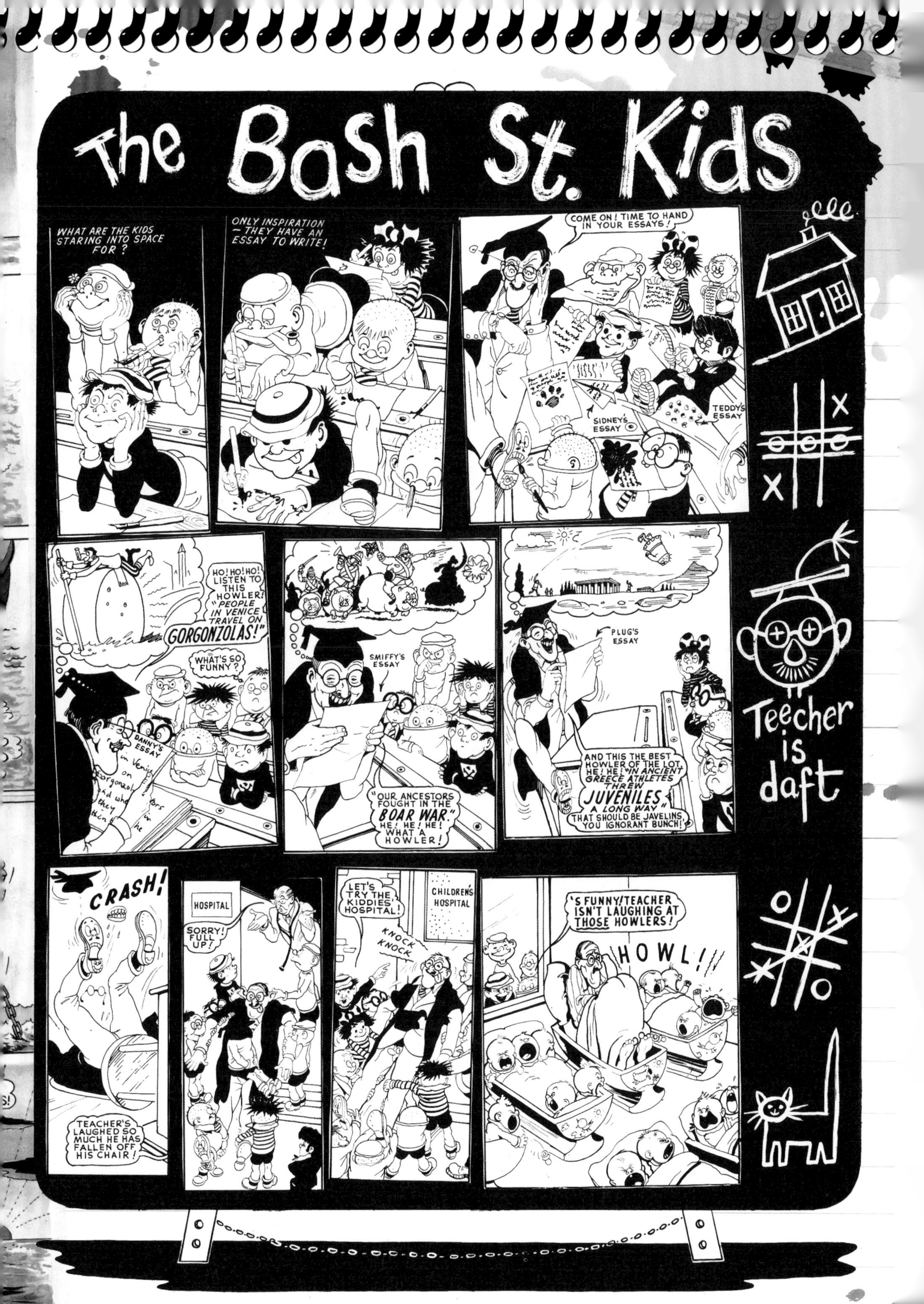
The Bash St. Kids
WHAT ARE THE KIDS STARING INTO SPACE FOR?
ONLY INSPIRATION — THEY HAVE AN ESSAY TO WRITE!
COME ON! TIME TO HAND IN YOUR ESSAYS!
FLICK
SIDNEY'S ESSAY
TEDDY'S ESSAY
HO! HO! HO! LISTEN TO THIS HOWLER! "PEOPLE IN VENICE TRAVEL ON GORGONZOLAS!"
WHAT'S SO FUNNY?
DANNY'S ESSAY
SMIFFY'S ESSAY
"OUR ANCESTORS FOUGHT IN THE BOAR WAR." HE! HE! HE! WHAT A HOWLER!
PLUG'S ESSAY
AND THIS THE BEST HOWLER OF THE LOT. HE! HE! "IN ANCIENT GREECE ATHLETES THREW JUVENILES A LONG WAY"
THAT SHOULD BE JAVELINS, YOU IGNORANT BUNCH!
Teecher is daft
CRASH!
TEACHER'S LAUGHED SO MUCH HE HAS FALLEN OFF HIS CHAIR!
HOSPITAL
SORRY! FULL UP!
LET'S TRY THE KIDDIES' HOSPITAL!
CHILDREN'S HOSPITAL
KNOCK KNOCK
'S FUNNY! TEACHER ISN'T LAUGHING AT THOSE HOWLERS!
HOWL!!!

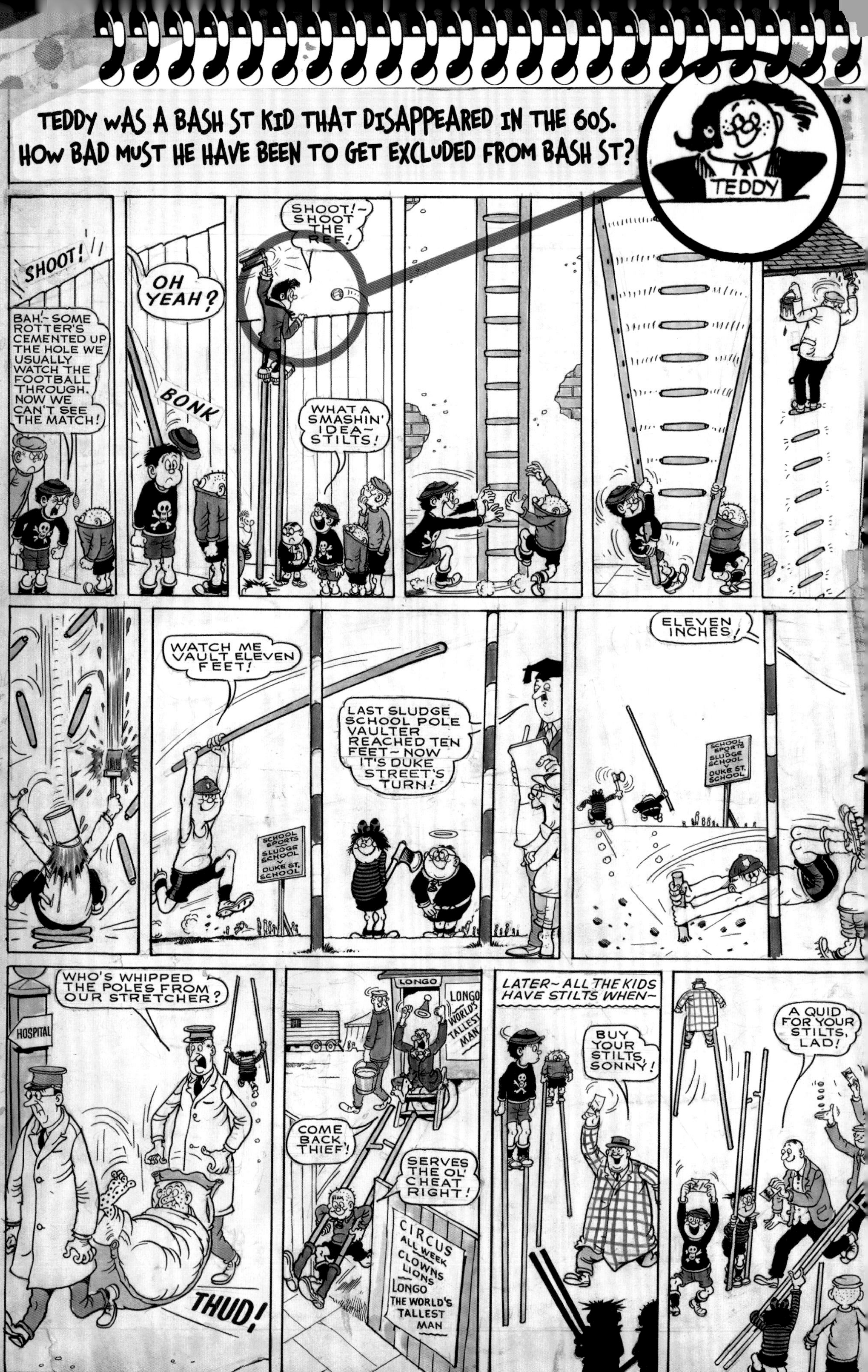

TEDDY WAS A BASH ST KID THAT DISAPPEARED IN THE 60S.
HOW BAD MUST HE HAVE BEEN TO GET EXCLUDED FROM BASH ST?
TEDDY
SHOOT!
BAH!~ SOME ROTTER'S CEMENTED UP THE HOLE WE USUALLY WATCH THE FOOTBALL THROUGH. NOW WE CAN'T SEE THE MATCH!
OH YEAH?
BONK
SHOOT!~ SHOOT THE REF!
WHAT A SMASHIN' IDEA~ STILTS!
WATCH ME VAULT ELEVEN FEET!
LAST SLUDGE SCHOOL POLE VAULTER REACHED TEN FEET~ NOW IT'S DUKE STREET'S TURN!
SCHOOL SPORTS SLUDGE SCHOOL V DUKE ST. SCHOOL
ELEVEN INCHES!
WHO'S WHIPPED THE POLES FROM OUR STRETCHER?
HOSPITAL
THUD!
LONGO
LONGO WORLD'S TALLEST MAN
COME BACK, THIEF!
SERVES THE OL' CHEAT RIGHT!
CIRCUS ALL WEEK CLOWNS LIONS LONGO THE WORLD'S TALLEST MAN
LATER~ ALL THE KIDS HAVE STILTS WHEN~
BUY YOUR STILTS, SONNY!
A QUID FOR YOUR STILTS, LAD!
BNO '60 P22

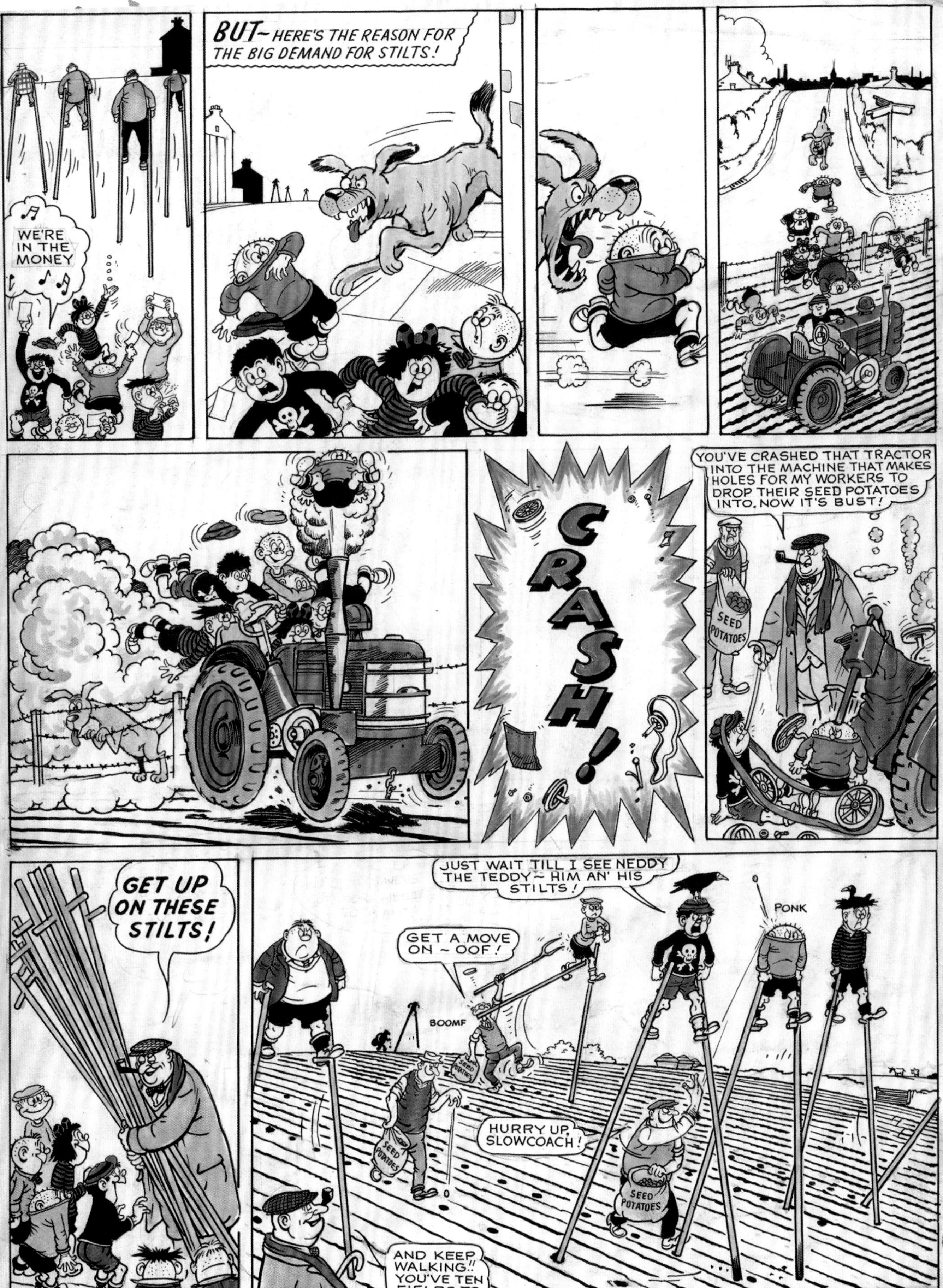

WE'RE IN THE MONEY
BUT~ HERE'S THE REASON FOR THE BIG DEMAND FOR STILTS!
YOU'VE CRASHED THAT TRACTOR INTO THE MACHINE THAT MAKES HOLES FOR MY WORKERS TO DROP THEIR SEED POTATOES INTO. NOW IT'S BUST!
CRASH!
SEED POTATOES
GET UP ON THESE STILTS!
JUST WAIT TILL I SEE NEDDY THE TEDDY~ HIM AN' HIS STILTS!
PONK
GET A MOVE ON ~ OOF!
BOOMF
SEED POTATOES
HURRY UP, SLOWCOACH!
SEED POTATOES
SEED POTATOES
AND KEEP WALKING!! YOU'VE TEN FIELDS TO PLANT!

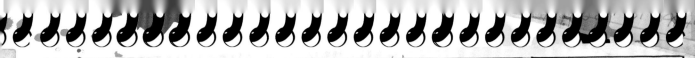

Ever with children's welfare in mind Dan helps out his old school. Check out the extremely busy spread that ended this tale. The numbers marked on the artwork are instructions to the printers.

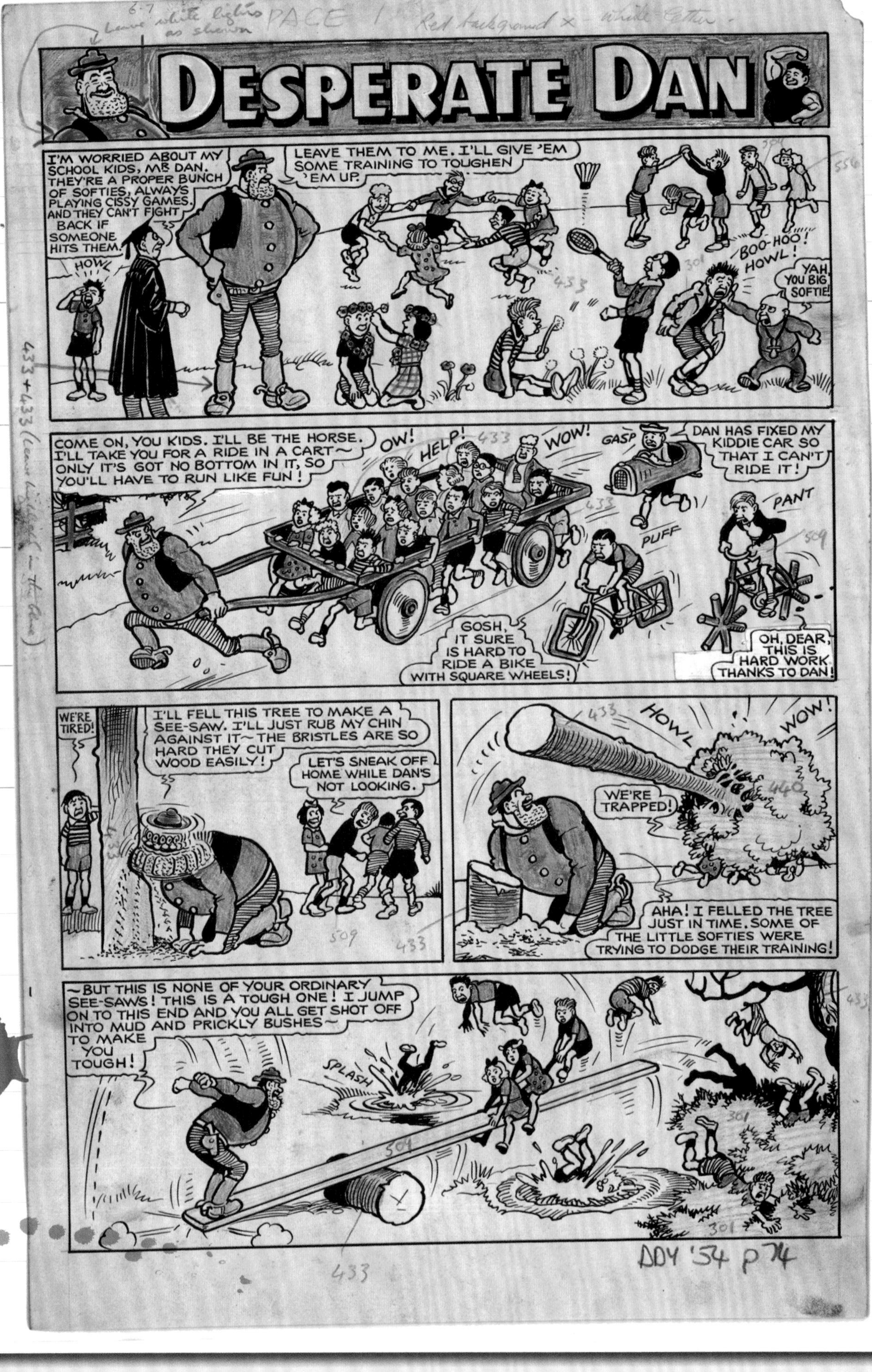
PAGE 1
DESPERATE DAN
I'M WORRIED ABOUT MY SCHOOL KIDS, MR DAN. THEY'RE A PROPER BUNCH OF SOFTIES, ALWAYS PLAYING CISSY GAMES, AND THEY CAN'T FIGHT BACK IF SOMEONE HITS THEM.
LEAVE THEM TO ME. I'LL GIVE 'EM SOME TRAINING TO TOUGHEN 'EM UP.
HOWL
BOO-HOO! HOWL!
YAH, YOU BIG SOFTIE!
COME ON, YOU KIDS. I'LL BE THE HORSE. I'LL TAKE YOU FOR A RIDE IN A CART~ ONLY IT'S GOT NO BOTTOM IN IT, SO YOU'LL HAVE TO RUN LIKE FUN!
OW!
HELP!
WOW!
GASP
DAN HAS FIXED MY KIDDIE CAR SO THAT I CAN'T RIDE IT!
PANT
PUFF
GOSH, IT SURE IS HARD TO RIDE A BIKE WITH SQUARE WHEELS!
OH, DEAR, THIS IS HARD WORK. THANKS TO DAN!
WE'RE TIRED!
I'LL FELL THIS TREE TO MAKE A SEE-SAW. I'LL JUST RUB MY CHIN AGAINST IT~ THE BRISTLES ARE SO HARD THEY CUT WOOD EASILY!
LET'S SNEAK OFF HOME WHILE DAN'S NOT LOOKING.
HOWL
WOW!
WE'RE TRAPPED!
AHA! I FELLED THE TREE JUST IN TIME. SOME OF THE LITTLE SOFTIES WERE TRYING TO DODGE THEIR TRAINING!
~BUT THIS IS NONE OF YOUR ORDINARY SEE-SAWS! THIS IS A TOUGH ONE! I JUMP ON TO THIS END AND YOU ALL GET SHOT OFF INTO MUD AND PRICKLY BUSHES~ TO MAKE YOU TOUGH!
SPLASH
DDY '54 p 74

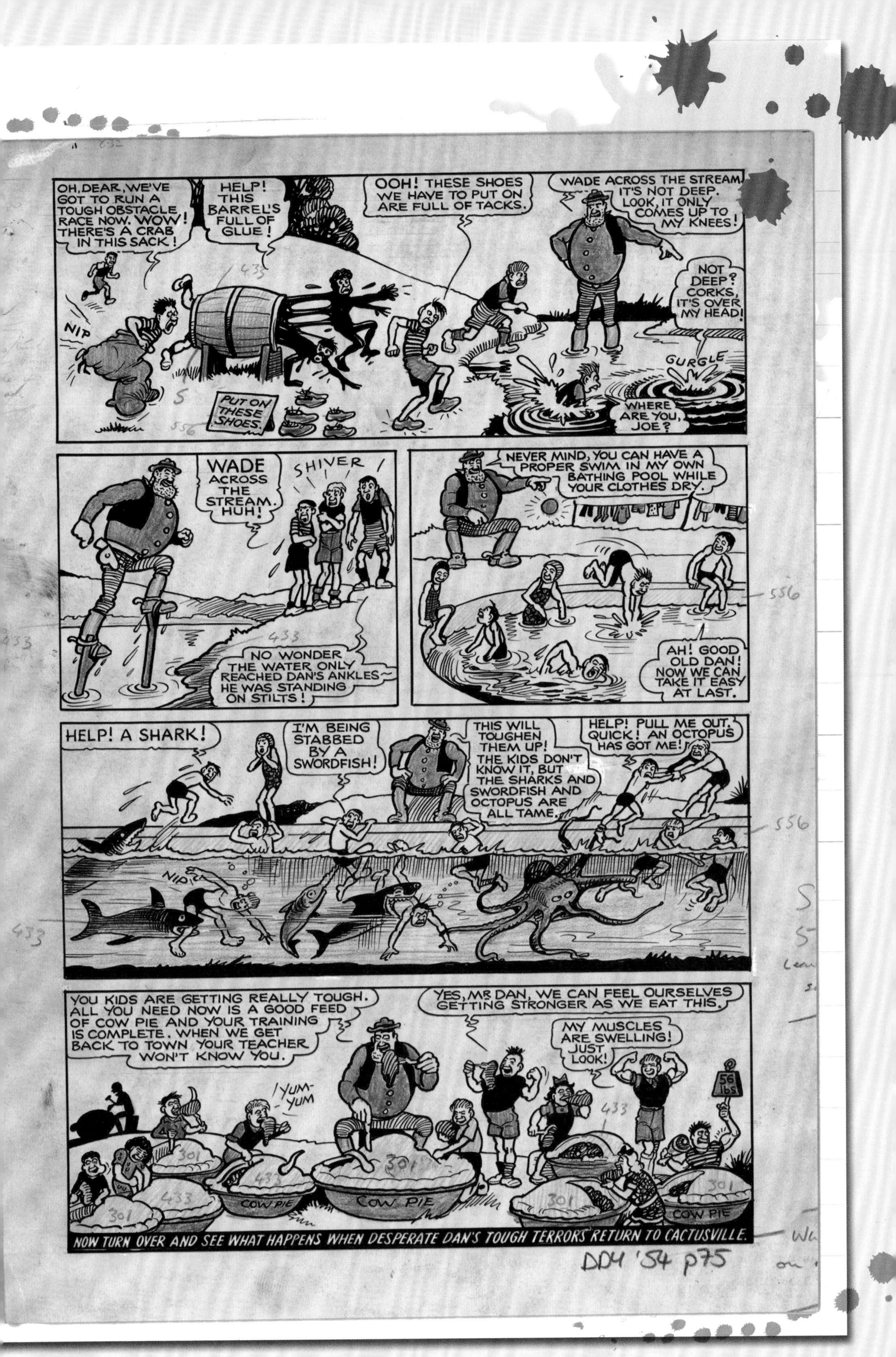
OH, DEAR, WE'VE GOT TO RUN A TOUGH OBSTACLE RACE NOW. WOW! THERE'S A CRAB IN THIS SACK!
HELP! THIS BARREL'S FULL OF GLUE!
OOH! THESE SHOES WE HAVE TO PUT ON ARE FULL OF TACKS.
WADE ACROSS THE STREAM. IT'S NOT DEEP. LOOK, IT ONLY COMES UP TO MY KNEES!
NOT DEEP? CORKS, IT'S OVER MY HEAD!
NIP
PUT ON THESE SHOES.
GURGLE
WHERE ARE YOU, JOE?
WADE ACROSS THE STREAM. HUH!
SHIVER
NO WONDER THE WATER ONLY REACHED DAN'S ANKLES— HE WAS STANDING ON STILTS!
NEVER MIND, YOU CAN HAVE A PROPER SWIM IN MY OWN BATHING POOL WHILE YOUR CLOTHES DRY.
AH! GOOD OLD DAN! NOW WE CAN TAKE IT EASY AT LAST.
HELP! A SHARK!
I'M BEING STABBED BY A SWORDFISH!
THIS WILL TOUGHEN THEM UP! THE KIDS DON'T KNOW IT, BUT THE SHARKS AND SWORDFISH AND OCTOPUS ARE ALL TAME.
HELP! PULL ME OUT, QUICK! AN OCTOPUS HAS GOT ME!
NIP!
YOU KIDS ARE GETTING REALLY TOUGH. ALL YOU NEED NOW IS A GOOD FEED OF COW PIE AND YOUR TRAINING IS COMPLETE. WHEN WE GET BACK TO TOWN YOUR TEACHER WON'T KNOW YOU.
YES, MR DAN, WE CAN FEEL OURSELVES GETTING STRONGER AS WE EAT THIS.
MY MUSCLES ARE SWELLING! JUST LOOK!
YUM-YUM
56 lbs
COW PIE
COW PIE
COW PIE
NOW TURN OVER AND SEE WHAT HAPPENS WHEN DESPERATE DAN'S TOUGH TERRORS RETURN TO CACTUSVILLE.
DD4 '54 p75

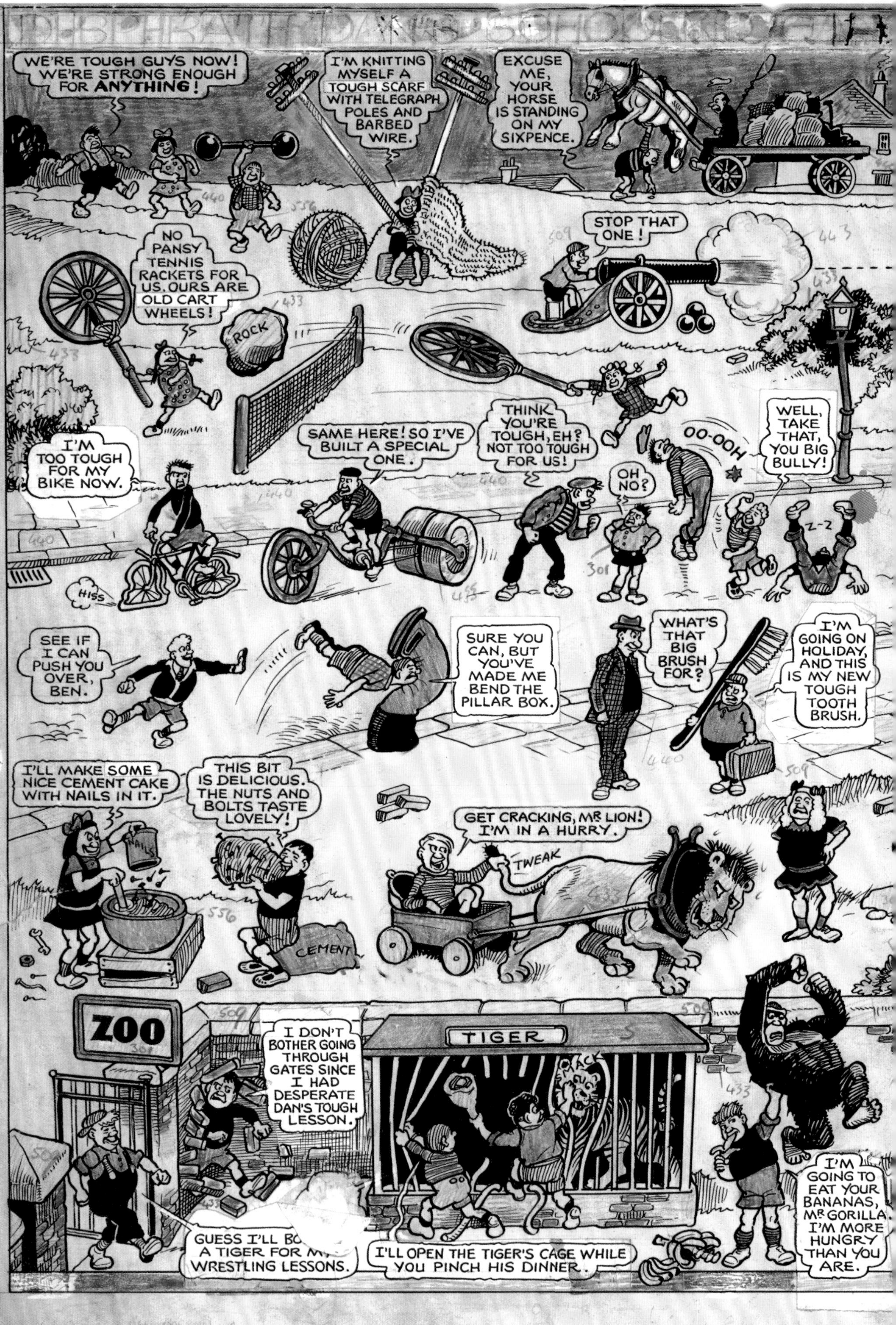
WE'RE TOUGH GUYS NOW! WE'RE STRONG ENOUGH FOR ANYTHING!
I'M KNITTING MYSELF A TOUGH SCARF WITH TELEGRAPH POLES AND BARBED WIRE.
EXCUSE ME, YOUR HORSE IS STANDING ON MY SIXPENCE.
NO PANSY TENNIS RACKETS FOR US. OURS ARE OLD CART WHEELS!
ROCK
STOP THAT ONE!
I'M TOO TOUGH FOR MY BIKE NOW.
HISS
SAME HERE! SO I'VE BUILT A SPECIAL ONE.
THINK YOU'RE TOUGH, EH? NOT TOO TOUGH FOR US!
OH NO?
OO-OOH
WELL, TAKE THAT, YOU BIG BULLY!
Z-Z
SEE IF I CAN PUSH YOU OVER, BEN.
SURE YOU CAN, BUT YOU'VE MADE ME BEND THE PILLAR BOX.
WHAT'S THAT BIG BRUSH FOR?
I'M GOING ON HOLIDAY, AND THIS IS MY NEW TOUGH TOOTH BRUSH.
I'LL MAKE SOME NICE CEMENT CAKE WITH NAILS IN IT.
NAILS
THIS BIT IS DELICIOUS. THE NUTS AND BOLTS TASTE LOVELY!
CEMENT
GET CRACKING, MR LION! I'M IN A HURRY.
TWEAK
ZOO
I DON'T BOTHER GOING THROUGH GATES SINCE I HAD DESPERATE DAN'S TOUGH LESSON.
TIGER
GUESS I'LL BO A TIGER FOR M WRESTLING LESSONS.
I'LL OPEN THE TIGER'S CAGE WHILE YOU PINCH HIS DINNER.
I'M GOING TO EAT YOUR BANANAS, MR GORILLA. I'M MORE HUNGRY THAN YOU ARE.

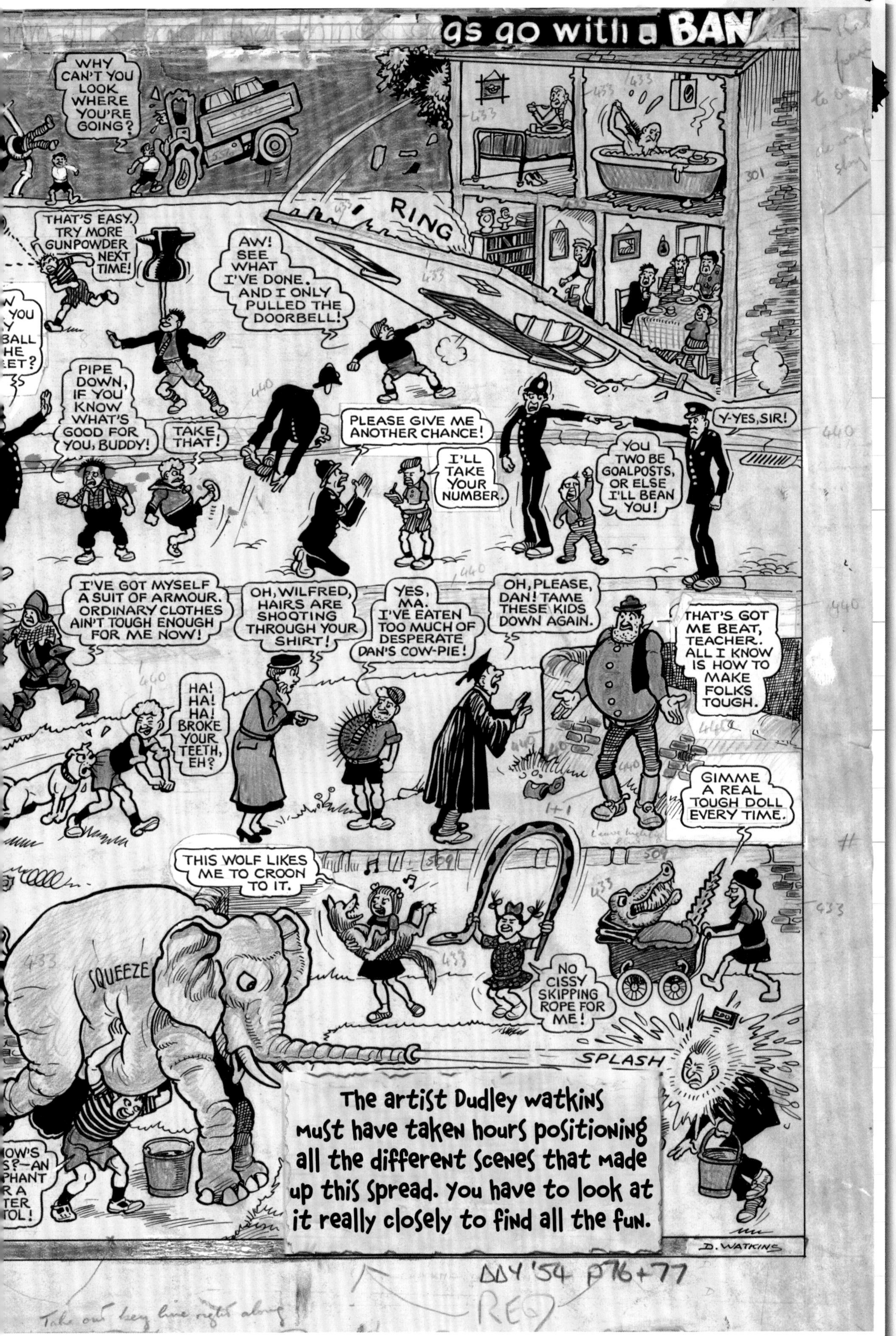
gs go with a BAN
WHY CAN'T YOU LOOK WHERE YOU'RE GOING?
THAT'S EASY. TRY MORE GUNPOWDER NEXT TIME!
AW! SEE WHAT I'VE DONE. AND I ONLY PULLED THE DOORBELL!
RING
PIPE DOWN, IF YOU KNOW WHAT'S GOOD FOR YOU, BUDDY!
TAKE THAT!
PLEASE GIVE ME ANOTHER CHANCE!
I'LL TAKE YOUR NUMBER.
Y-YES, SIR!
YOU TWO BE GOALPOSTS, OR ELSE I'LL BEAN YOU!
I'VE GOT MYSELF A SUIT OF ARMOUR. ORDINARY CLOTHES AIN'T TOUGH ENOUGH FOR ME NOW!
OH, WILFRED, HAIRS ARE SHOOTING THROUGH YOUR SHIRT!
YES, MA. I'VE EATEN TOO MUCH OF DESPERATE DAN'S COW-PIE!
OH, PLEASE, DAN! TAME THESE KIDS DOWN AGAIN.
THAT'S GOT ME BEAT, TEACHER. ALL I KNOW IS HOW TO MAKE FOLKS TOUGH.
HA! HA! HA! BROKE YOUR TEETH, EH?
GIMME A REAL TOUGH DOLL EVERY TIME.
THIS WOLF LIKES ME TO CROON TO IT.
NO CISSY SKIPPING ROPE FOR ME!
SQUEEZE
SPLASH
D. WATKINS
DAY '54 p76+77

The artist Dudley watkins must have taken hours positioning all the different scenes that made up this spread. You have to look at it really closely to find all the fun.

From early sixties onwards Ron Spencer illustrated many Dandy and Beano stories. For Dandy editor Albert Barnes he pulled out all the stops drawing the multi-characters in the school stories Whacko! and Robin Hood's Schooldays.

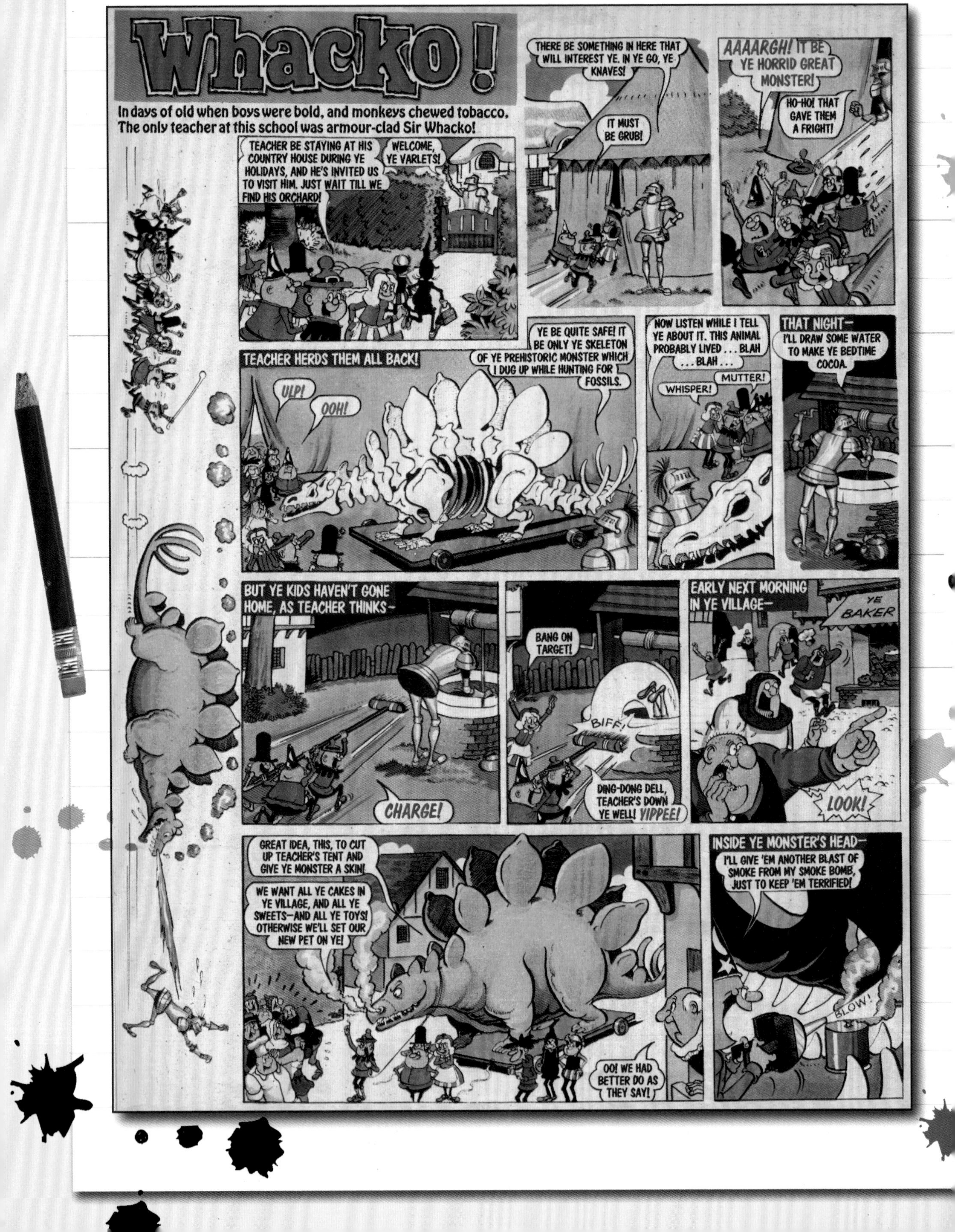
Whacko!
In days of old when boys were bold, and monkeys chewed tobacco. The only teacher at this school was armour-clad Sir Whacko!
TEACHER BE STAYING AT HIS COUNTRY HOUSE DURING YE HOLIDAYS, AND HE'S INVITED US TO VISIT HIM. JUST WAIT TILL WE FIND HIS ORCHARD!
WELCOME, YE VARLETS!
THERE BE SOMETHING IN HERE THAT WILL INTEREST YE. IN YE GO, YE KNAVES!
IT MUST BE GRUB!
AAAARGH! IT BE YE HORRID GREAT MONSTER!
HO-HO! THAT GAVE THEM A FRIGHT!
TEACHER HERDS THEM ALL BACK!
YE BE QUITE SAFE! IT BE ONLY YE SKELETON OF YE PREHISTORIC MONSTER WHICH I DUG UP WHILE HUNTING FOR FOSSILS.
ULP!
OOH!
NOW LISTEN WHILE I TELL YE ABOUT IT. THIS ANIMAL PROBABLY LIVED . . . BLAH . . . BLAH . . .
MUTTER!
WHISPER!
THAT NIGHT—
I'LL DRAW SOME WATER TO MAKE YE BEDTIME COCOA.
BUT YE KIDS HAVEN'T GONE HOME, AS TEACHER THINKS—
CHARGE!
BANG ON TARGET!
BIFF!
DING-DONG DELL, TEACHER'S DOWN YE WELL! YIPPEE!
EARLY NEXT MORNING IN YE VILLAGE—
YE BAKER
LOOK!
GREAT IDEA, THIS, TO CUT UP TEACHER'S TENT AND GIVE YE MONSTER A SKIN!
WE WANT ALL YE CAKES IN YE VILLAGE, AND ALL YE SWEETS—AND ALL YE TOYS! OTHERWISE WE'LL SET OUR NEW PET ON YE!
OO! WE HAD BETTER DO AS THEY SAY!
INSIDE YE MONSTER'S HEAD—
I'LL GIVE 'EM ANOTHER BLAST OF SMOKE FROM MY SMOKE BOMB, JUST TO KEEP 'EM TERRIFIED!
BLOW!

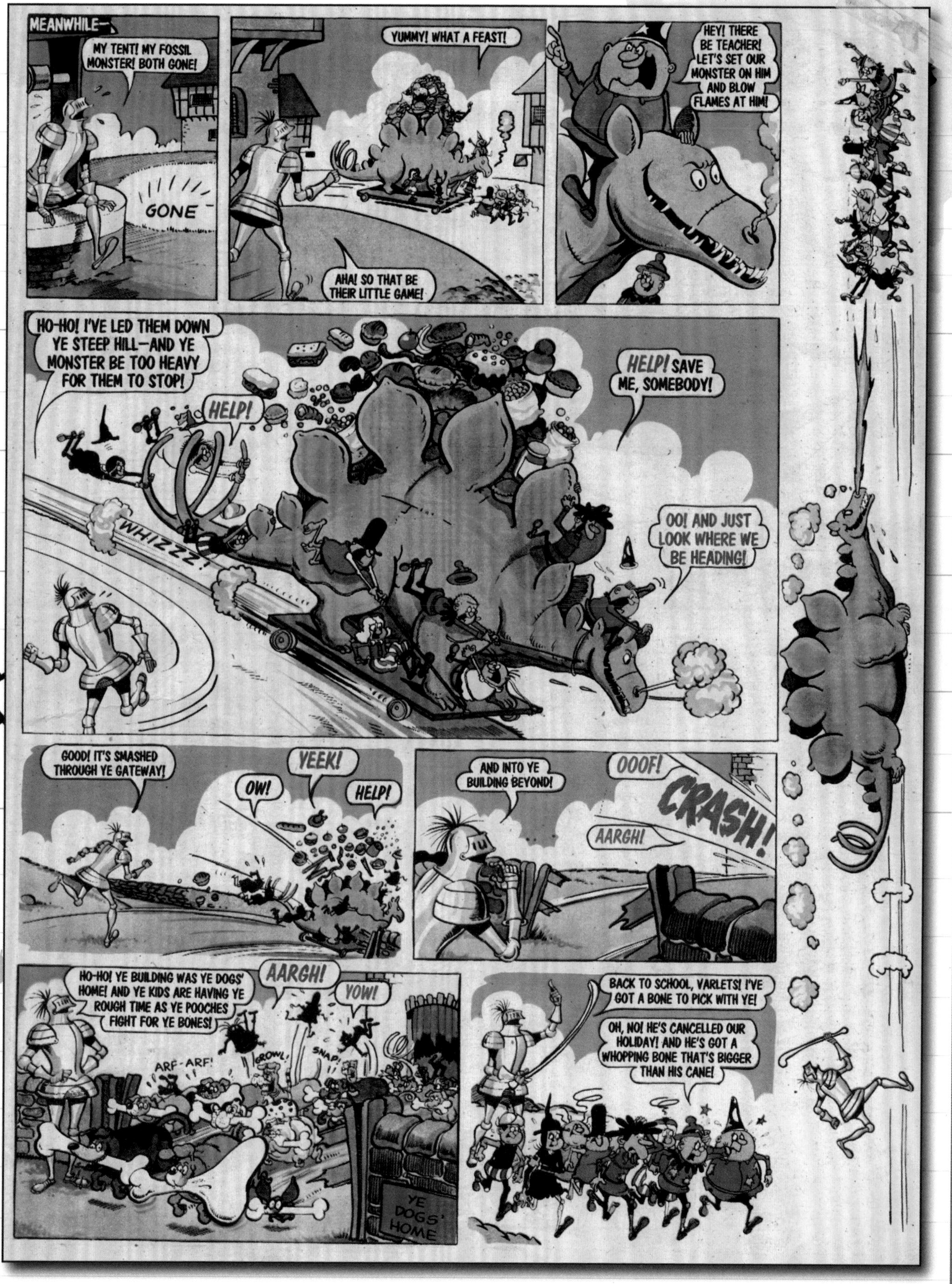

MEANWHILE—
MY TENT! MY FOSSIL MONSTER! BOTH GONE!
GONE
YUMMY! WHAT A FEAST!
AHA! SO THAT BE THEIR LITTLE GAME!
HEY! THERE BE TEACHER! LET'S SET OUR MONSTER ON HIM AND BLOW FLAMES AT HIM!
HO-HO! I'VE LED THEM DOWN YE STEEP HILL—AND YE MONSTER BE TOO HEAVY FOR THEM TO STOP!
HELP!
HELP! SAVE ME, SOMEBODY!
OO! AND JUST LOOK WHERE WE BE HEADING!
WHIZZZ!
GOOD! IT'S SMASHED THROUGH YE GATEWAY!
OW!
YEEK!
HELP!
AND INTO YE BUILDING BEYOND!
OOOF!
CRASH!
AARGHI!
HO-HO! YE BUILDING WAS YE DOGS' HOME! AND YE KIDS ARE HAVING YE ROUGH TIME AS YE POOCHES FIGHT FOR YE BONES!
AARGH!
YOW!
ARF-ARF!
GROWL!
SNAP!
ARF-ARF!
YE DOGS' HOME
BACK TO SCHOOL, VARLETS! I'VE GOT A BONE TO PICK WITH YE!
OH, NO! HE'S CANCELLED OUR HOLIDAY! AND HE'S GOT A WHOPPING BONE THAT'S BIGGER THAN HIS CANE!

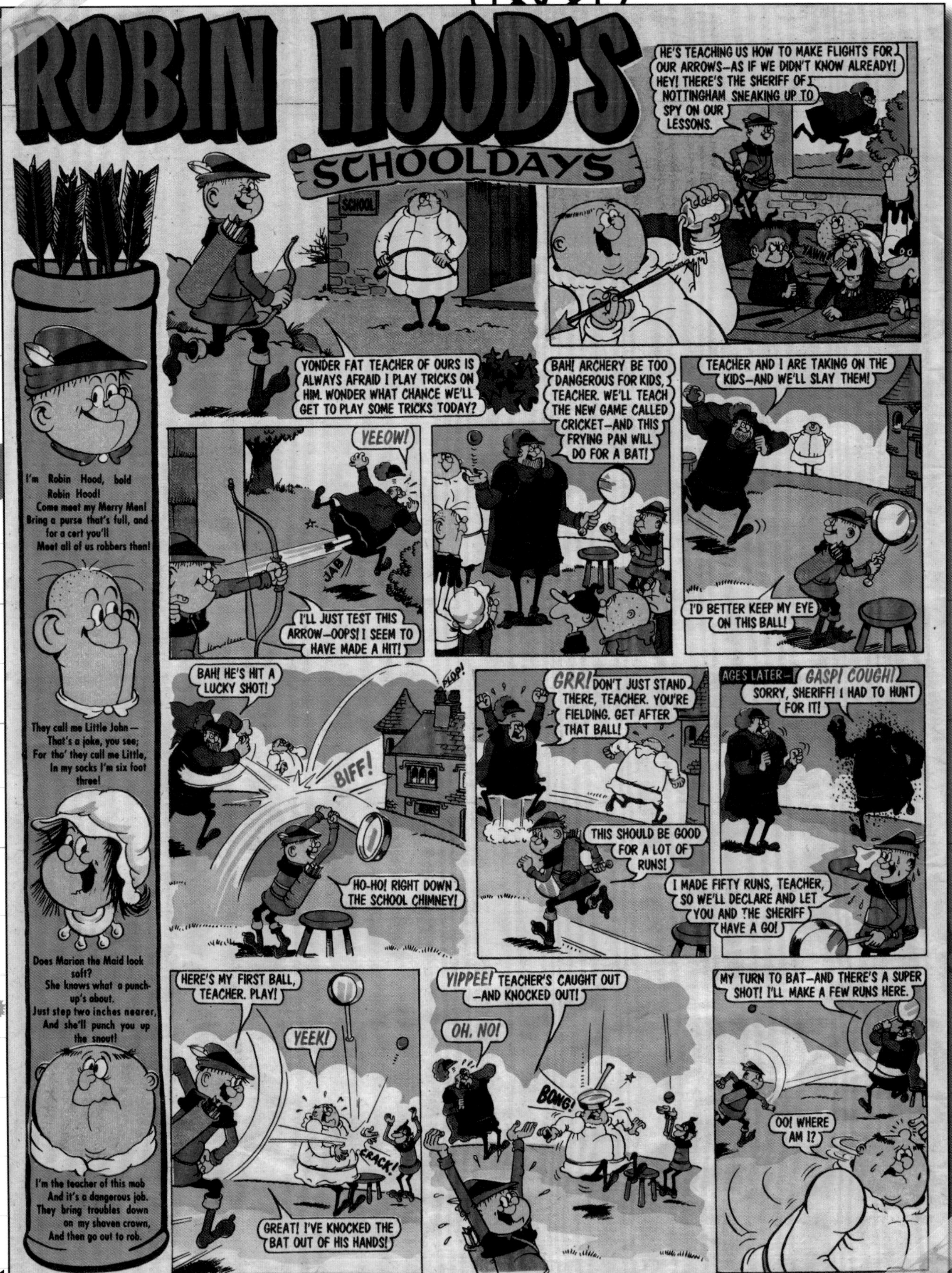
ROBIN HOOD'S
SCHOOLDAYS
I'm Robin Hood, bold Robin Hood! Come meet my Merry Men! Bring a purse that's full, and for a cert you'll Meet all of us robbers then!
They call me Little John — That's a joke, you see; For tho' they call me Little, In my socks I'm six foot three!
Does Marion the Maid look soft? She knows what a punch-up's about. Just step two inches nearer, And she'll punch you up the snout!
I'm the teacher of this mob And it's a dangerous job. They bring troubles down on my shaven crown, And then go out to rob.
SCHOOL
YONDER FAT TEACHER OF OURS IS ALWAYS AFRAID I PLAY TRICKS ON HIM. WONDER WHAT CHANCE WE'LL GET TO PLAY SOME TRICKS TODAY?
HE'S TEACHING US HOW TO MAKE FLIGHTS FOR OUR ARROWS—AS IF WE DIDN'T KNOW ALREADY! HEY! THERE'S THE SHERIFF OF NOTTINGHAM SNEAKING UP TO SPY ON OUR LESSONS.
YAWN!
YEEOW!
JAB
I'LL JUST TEST THIS ARROW—OOPS! I SEEM TO HAVE MADE A HIT!
BAH! ARCHERY BE TOO DANGEROUS FOR KIDS, TEACHER. WE'LL TEACH THE NEW GAME CALLED CRICKET—AND THIS FRYING PAN WILL DO FOR A BAT!
TEACHER AND I ARE TAKING ON THE KIDS—AND WE'LL SLAY THEM!
I'D BETTER KEEP MY EYE ON THIS BALL!
BAH! HE'S HIT A LUCKY SHOT!
PLOP!
BIFF!
HO-HO! RIGHT DOWN THE SCHOOL CHIMNEY!
GRR! DON'T JUST STAND THERE, TEACHER. YOU'RE FIELDING. GET AFTER THAT BALL!
THIS SHOULD BE GOOD FOR A LOT OF RUNS!
AGES LATER—
GASP! COUGH!
SORRY, SHERIFF! I HAD TO HUNT FOR IT!
I MADE FIFTY RUNS, TEACHER, SO WE'LL DECLARE AND LET YOU AND THE SHERIFF HAVE A GO!
HERE'S MY FIRST BALL, TEACHER. PLAY!
YEEK!
CRACK!
GREAT! I'VE KNOCKED THE BAT OUT OF HIS HANDS!
YIPPEE! TEACHER'S CAUGHT OUT —AND KNOCKED OUT!
OH, NO!
BONG!
MY TURN TO BAT—AND THERE'S A SUPER SHOT! I'LL MAKE A FEW RUNS HERE.
OO! WHERE AM I?

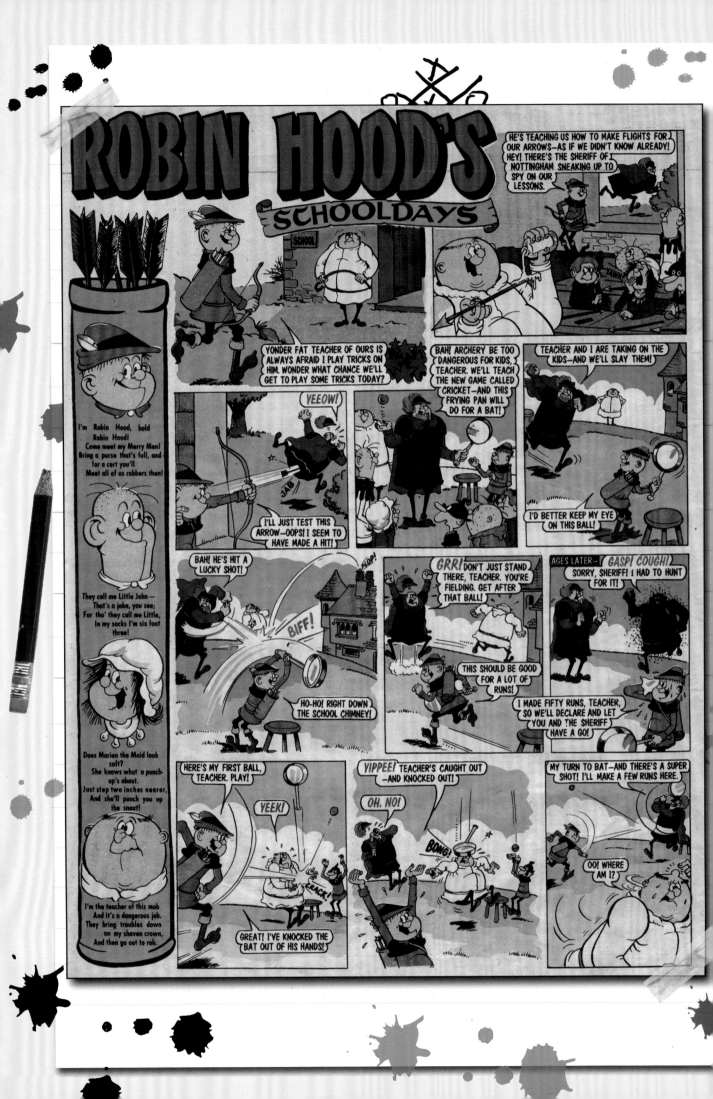

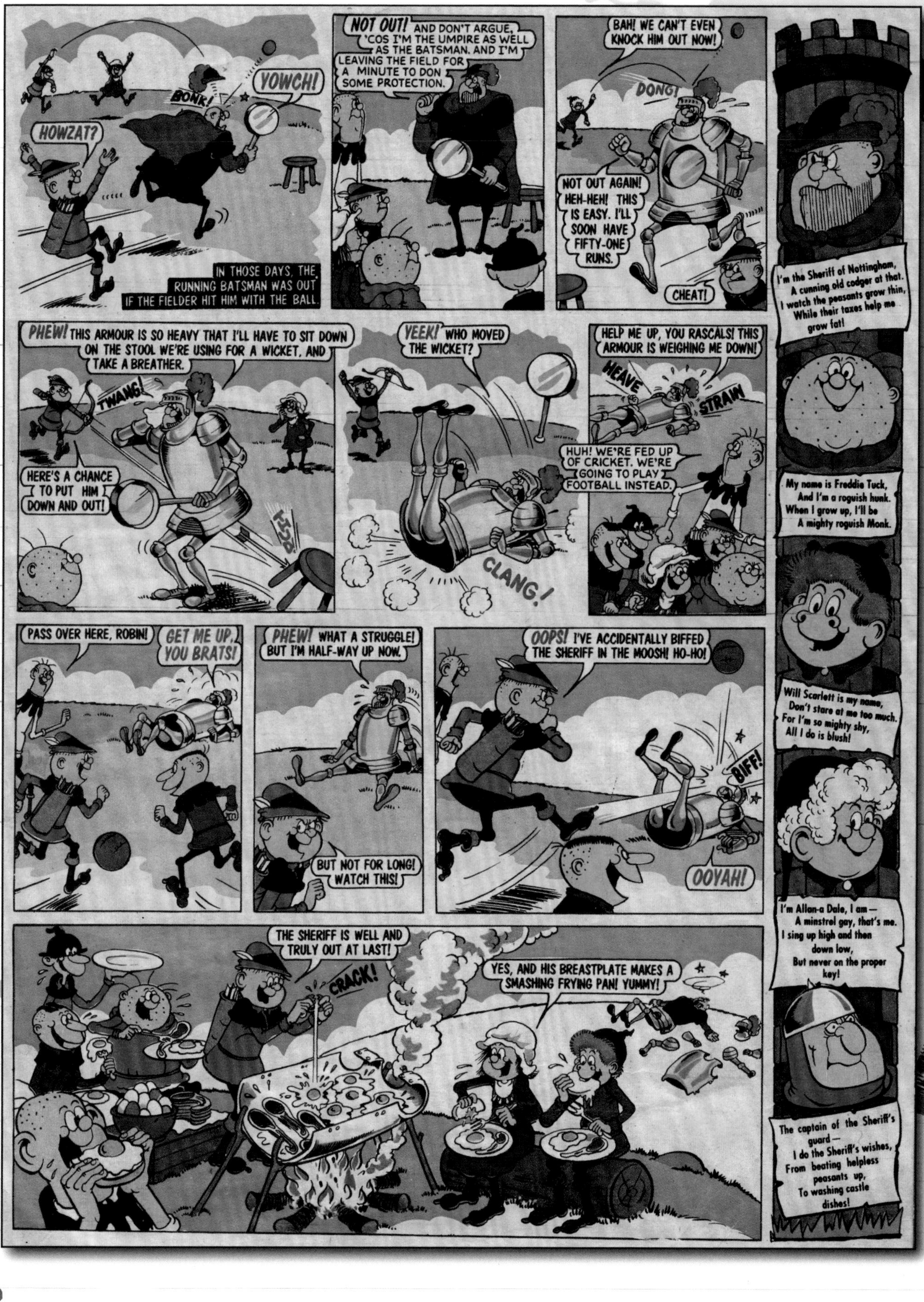
HOWZAT?
BONK!
YOWCH!
IN THOSE DAYS, THE RUNNING BATSMAN WAS OUT IF THE FIELDER HIT HIM WITH THE BALL.
NOT OUT! AND DON'T ARGUE, 'COS I'M THE UMPIRE AS WELL AS THE BATSMAN. AND I'M LEAVING THE FIELD FOR A MINUTE TO DON SOME PROTECTION.
BAH! WE CAN'T EVEN KNOCK HIM OUT NOW!
DONG!
NOT OUT AGAIN! HEH-HEH! THIS IS EASY. I'LL SOON HAVE FIFTY-ONE RUNS.
CHEAT!
I'm the Sheriff of Nottingham, A cunning old codger at that. I watch the peasants grow thin, While their taxes help me grow fat!
PHEW! THIS ARMOUR IS SO HEAVY THAT I'LL HAVE TO SIT DOWN ON THE STOOL WE'RE USING FOR A WICKET, AND TAKE A BREATHER.
TWANG!
HERE'S A CHANCE TO PUT HIM DOWN AND OUT!
YEEK! WHO MOVED THE WICKET?
CLANG!
HELP ME UP, YOU RASCALS! THIS ARMOUR IS WEIGHING ME DOWN!
HEAVE
STRAIN
HUH! WE'RE FED UP OF CRICKET. WE'RE GOING TO PLAY FOOTBALL INSTEAD.
My name is Freddie Tuck, And I'm a roguish hunk. When I grow up, I'll be A mighty roguish Monk.
PASS OVER HERE, ROBIN!
GET ME UP, YOU BRATS!
PHEW! WHAT A STRUGGLE! BUT I'M HALF-WAY UP NOW.
BUT NOT FOR LONG! WATCH THIS!
OOPS! I'VE ACCIDENTALLY BIFFED THE SHERIFF IN THE MOOSH! HO-HO!
BIFF!
OOYAH!
Will Scarlett is my name, Don't stare at me too much. For I'm so mighty shy, All I do is blush!
THE SHERIFF IS WELL AND TRULY OUT AT LAST!
CRACK!
YES, AND HIS BREASTPLATE MAKES A SMASHING FRYING PAN! YUMMY!
I'm Allan-a Dale, I am — A minstrel gay, that's me. I sing up high and then down low, But never on the proper key!
The captain of the Sheriff's guard — I do the Sheriff's wishes, From beating helpless peasants up, To washing castle dishes!

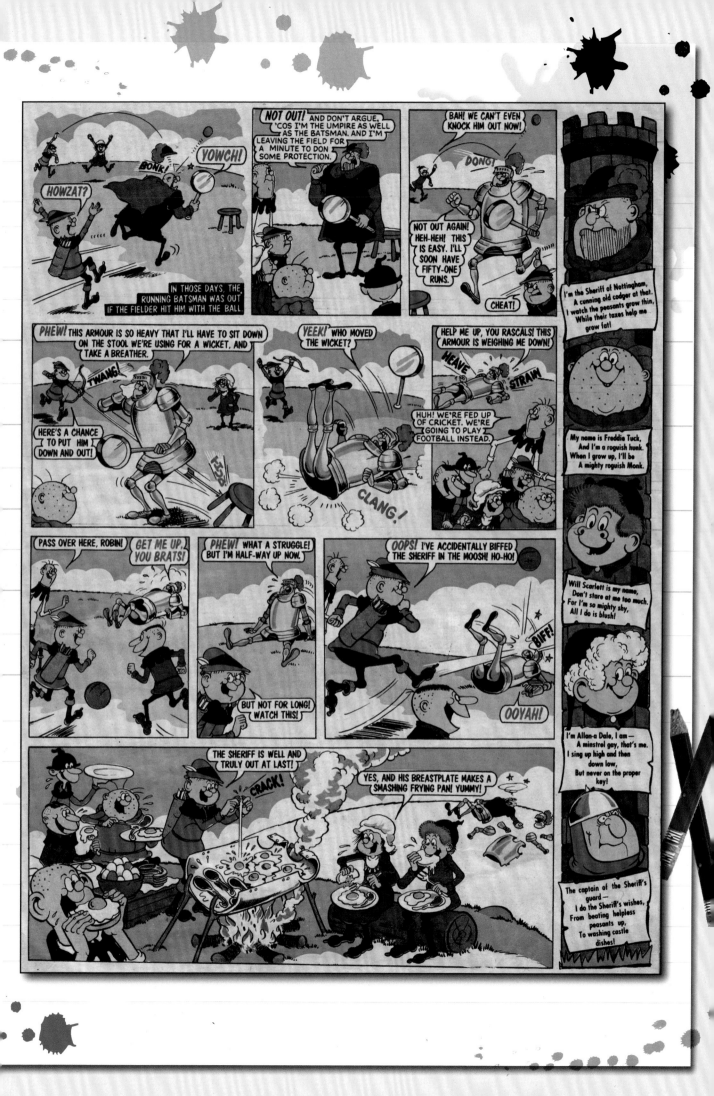

*A bizarre storyline in this Biffo school strip.
Just how easily fooled are those Beano teachers?*

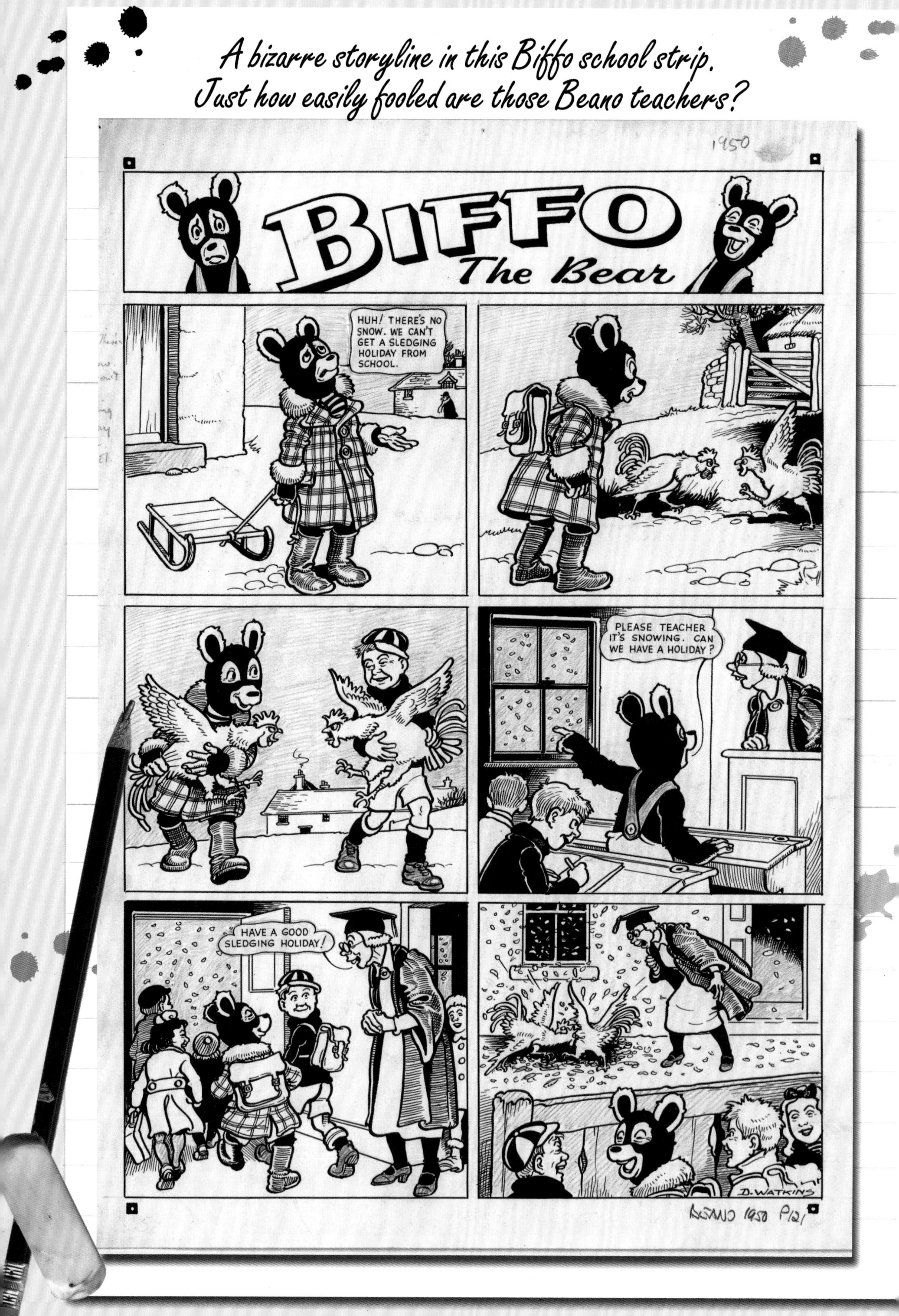
1950
BIFFO
The Bear
HUH! THERE'S NO SNOW. WE CAN'T GET A SLEDGING HOLIDAY FROM SCHOOL.
PLEASE TEACHER IT'S SNOWING. CAN WE HAVE A HOLIDAY?
HAVE A GOOD SLEDGING HOLIDAY!
D. WATKINS
BEANO 1950 P121

Another from the pen of Leo Baxendale.

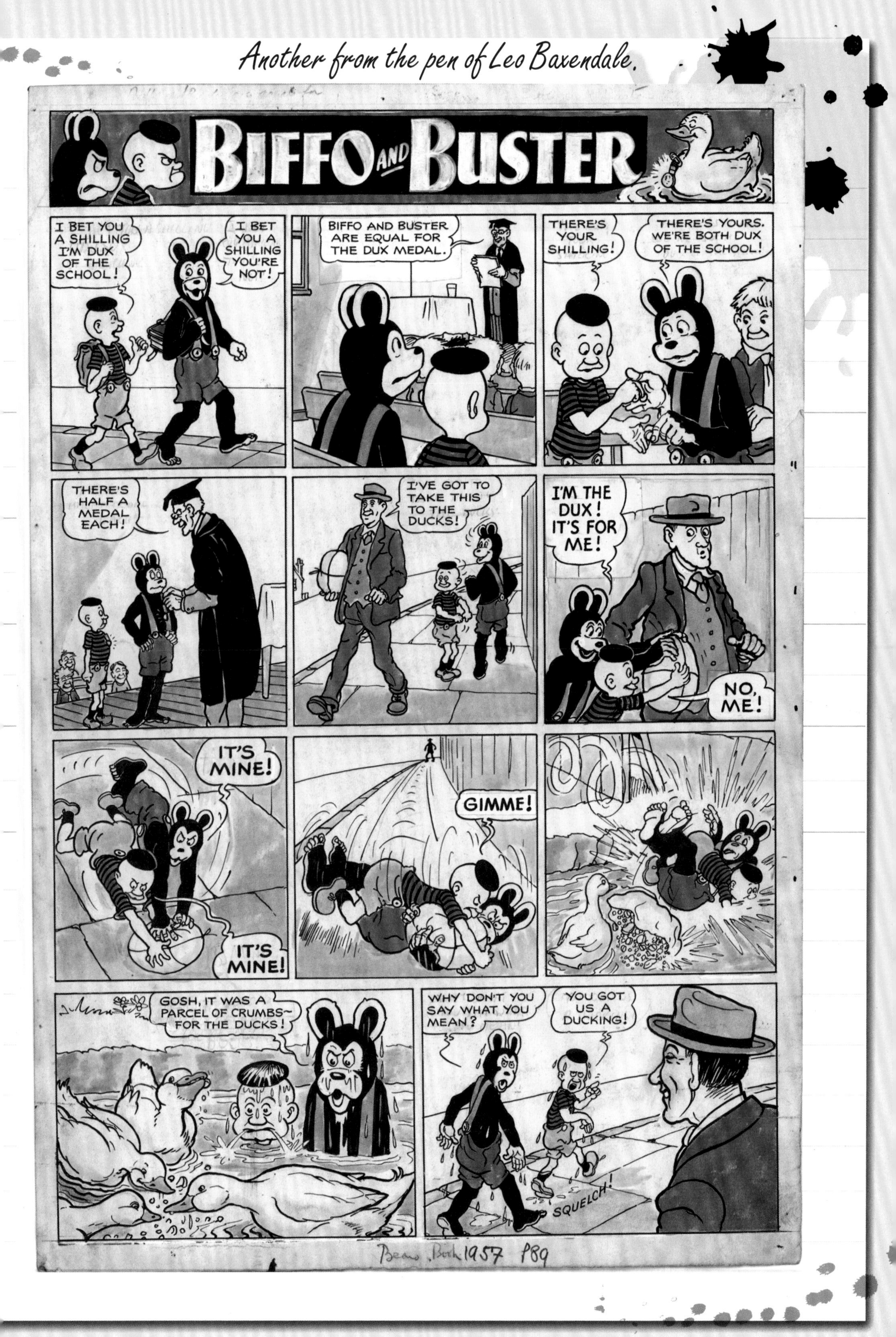
BIFFO AND BUSTER
I BET YOU A SHILLING I'M DUX OF THE SCHOOL!
I BET YOU A SHILLING YOU'RE NOT!
BIFFO AND BUSTER ARE EQUAL FOR THE DUX MEDAL.
THERE'S YOUR SHILLING!
THERE'S YOURS. WE'RE BOTH DUX OF THE SCHOOL!
THERE'S HALF A MEDAL EACH!
I'VE GOT TO TAKE THIS TO THE DUCKS!
I'M THE DUX! IT'S FOR ME!
NO, ME!
IT'S MINE!
IT'S MINE!
GIMME!
GOSH, IT WAS A PARCEL OF CRUMBS~ FOR THE DUCKS!
WHY DON'T YOU SAY WHAT YOU MEAN?
YOU GOT US A DUCKING!
SQUELCH!
Beano Book 1957 P89

BONUS FEATURES

This 8 page sponsered comic starring Bananaman was produced around 1985. It was done to promote healthy eating and dental awareness, and given out free to schools. The story was written by The Dandy scriptwriters and drawn by the original Bananaman artist John K Geering.

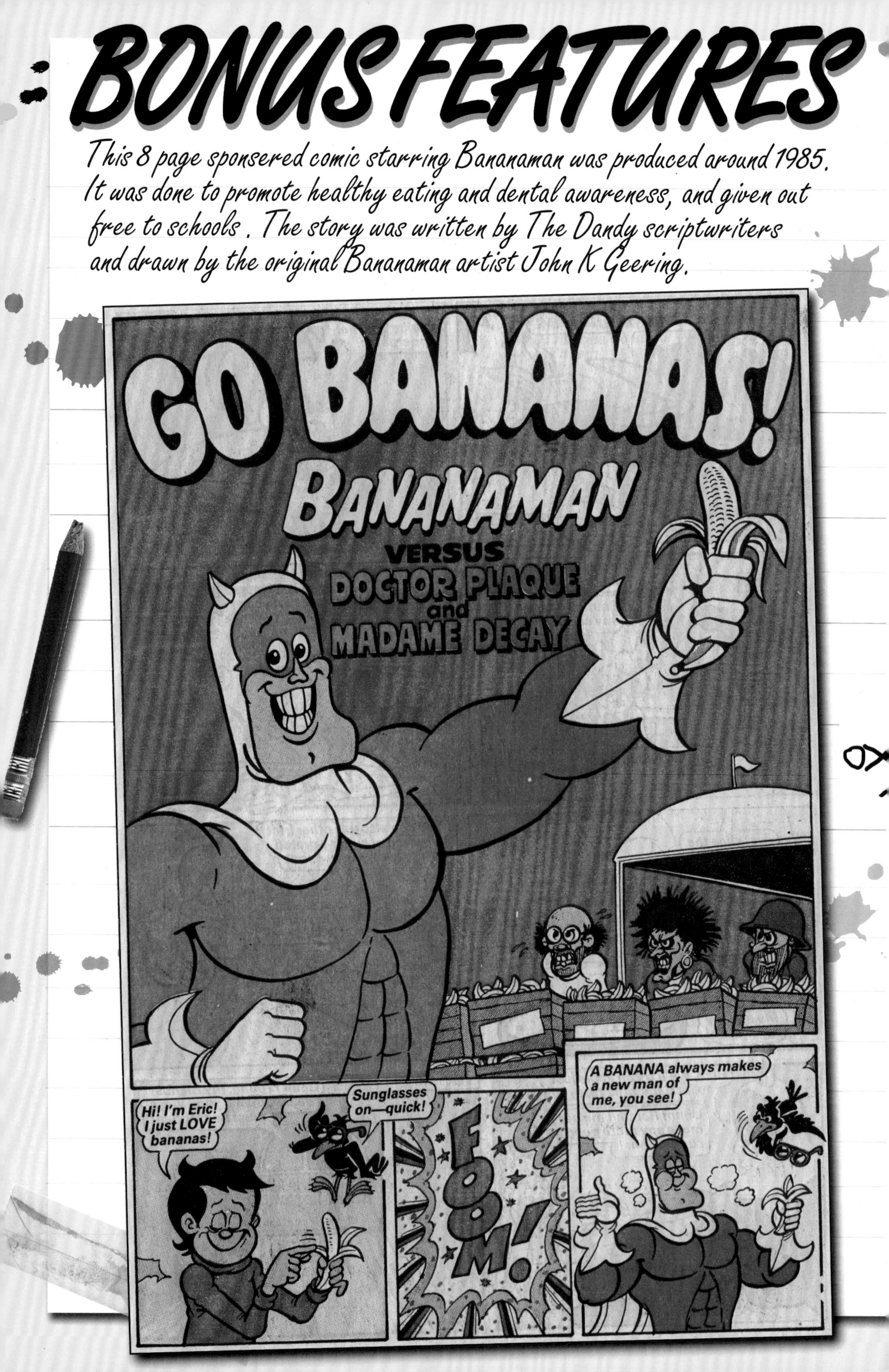
GO BANANAS!
BANANAMAN
VERSUS
DOCTOR PLAQUE
and
MADAME DECAY
Hi! I'm Eric! I just LOVE bananas!
Sunglasses on—quick!
FOOM!
A BANANA always makes a new man of me, you see!

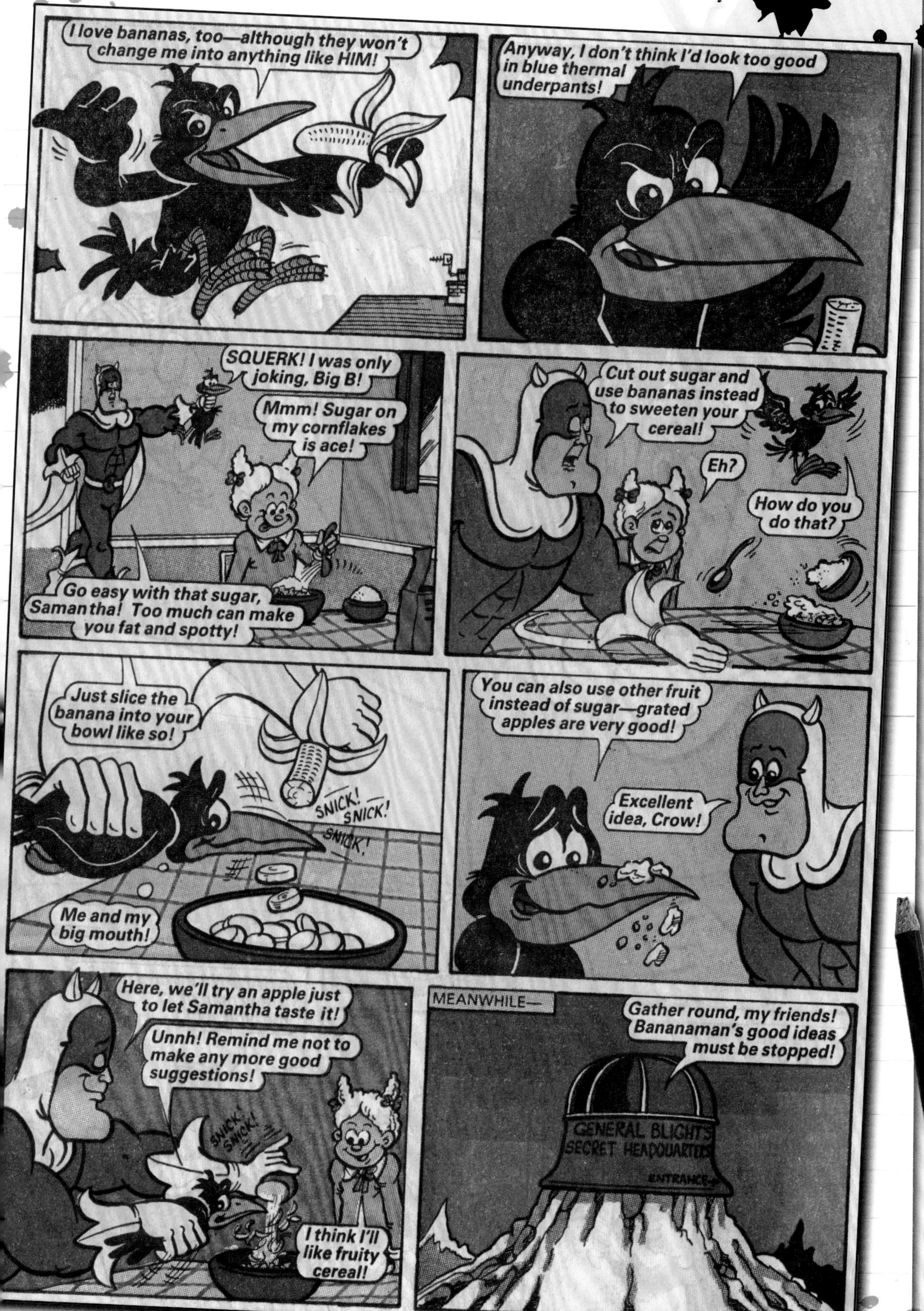
I love bananas, too—although they won't change me into anything like HIM!
Anyway, I don't think I'd look too good in blue thermal underpants!
SQUERK! I was only joking, Big B!
Mmm! Sugar on my cornflakes is ace!
Go easy with that sugar, Samantha! Too much can make you fat and spotty!
Cut out sugar and use bananas instead to sweeten your cereal!
Eh?
How do you do that?
Just slice the banana into your bowl like so!
SNICK! SNICK! SNICK!
Me and my big mouth!
You can also use other fruit instead of sugar—grated apples are very good!
Excellent idea, Crow!
Here, we'll try an apple just to let Samantha taste it!
Unnh! Remind me not to make any more good suggestions!
SNICK! SNICK!
I think I'll like fruity cereal!
MEANWHILE—
Gather round, my friends! Bananaman's good ideas must be stopped!
GENERAL BLIGHT'S SECRET HEADQUARTERS
ENTRANCE

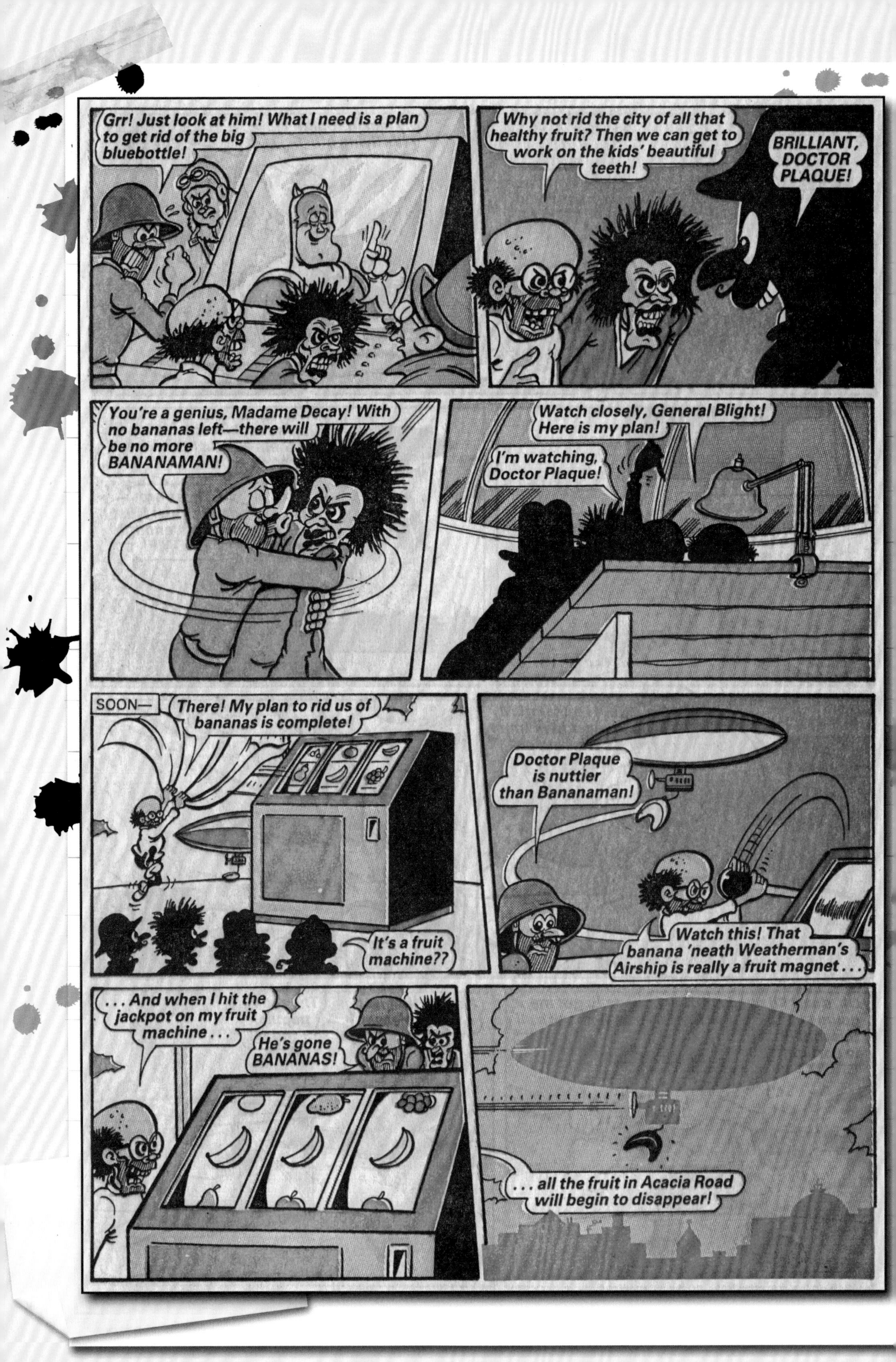

Grr! Just look at him! What I need is a plan to get rid of the big bluebottle!
Why not rid the city of all that healthy fruit? Then we can get to work on the kids' beautiful teeth!
BRILLIANT, DOCTOR PLAQUE!
You're a genius, Madame Decay! With no bananas left—there will be no more BANANAMAN!
Watch closely, General Blight! Here is my plan!
I'm watching, Doctor Plaque!
SOON—
There! My plan to rid us of bananas is complete!
It's a fruit machine??
Doctor Plaque is nuttier than Bananaman!
Watch this! That banana 'neath Weatherman's Airship is really a fruit magnet . . .
. . . And when I hit the jackpot on my fruit machine . . .
He's gone BANANAS!
. . . all the fruit in Acacia Road will begin to disappear!

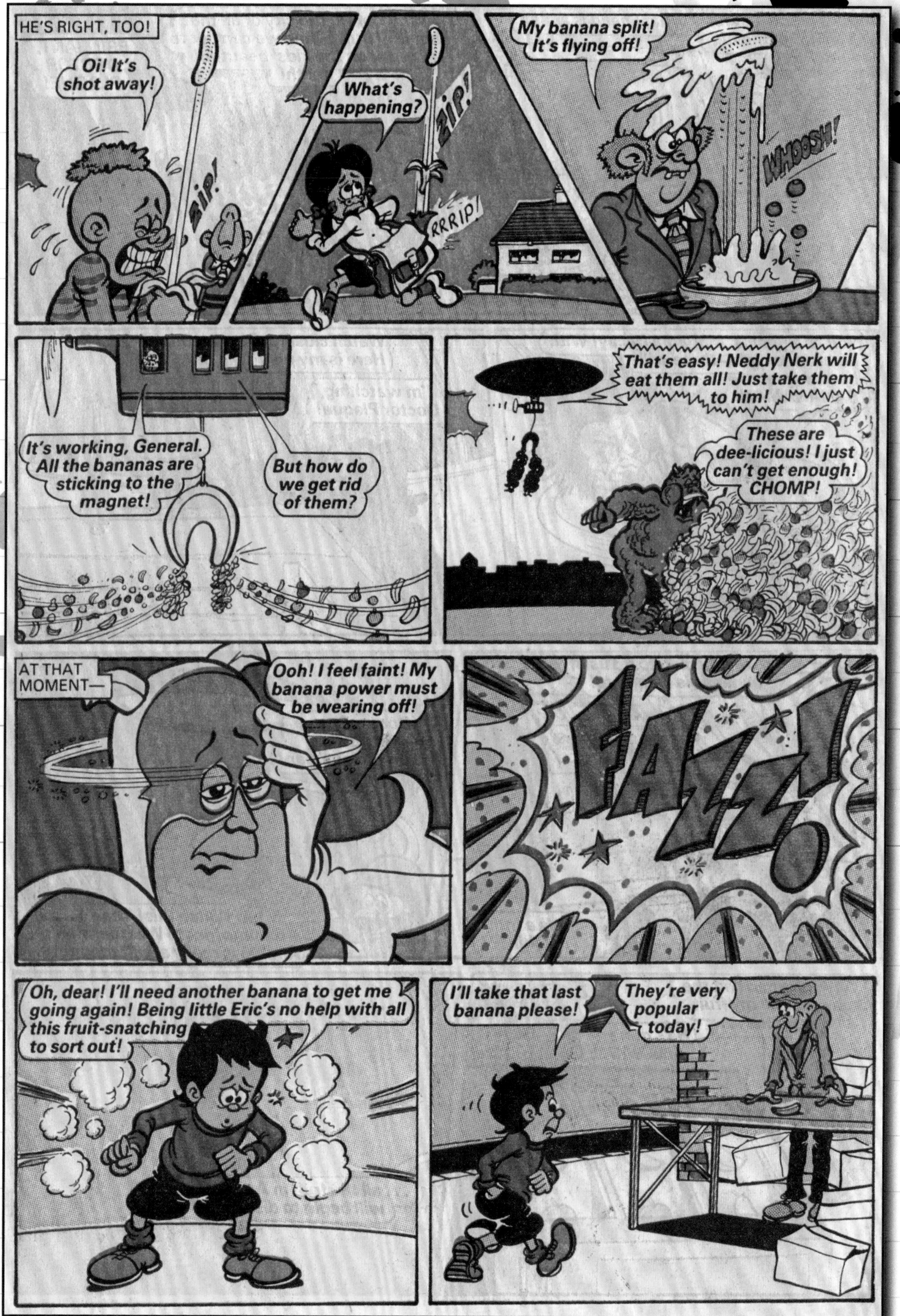
HE'S RIGHT, TOO!
Oi! It's shot away!
ZIP!
What's happening?
ZIP!
RRRIP!
My banana split! It's flying off!
WHOOSH!
It's working, General. All the bananas are sticking to the magnet!
But how do we get rid of them?
That's easy! Neddy Nerk will eat them all! Just take them to him!
These are dee-licious! I just can't get enough! CHOMP!
AT THAT MOMENT—
Ooh! I feel faint! My banana power must be wearing off!
FAZZ!
Oh, dear! I'll need another banana to get me going again! Being little Eric's no help with all this fruit-snatching to sort out!
I'll take that last banana please!
They're very popular today!

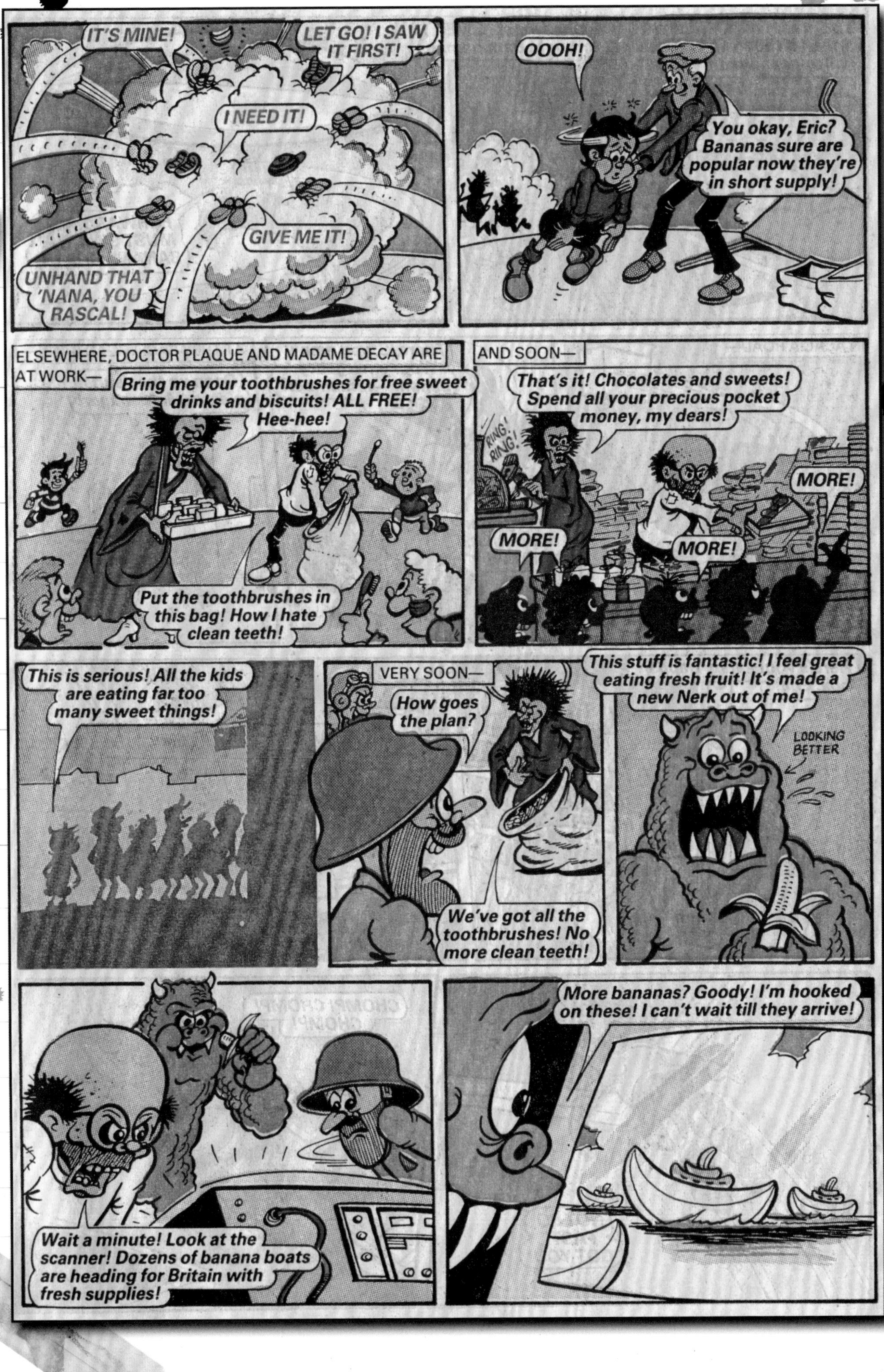

IT'S MINE!
LET GO! I SAW IT FIRST!
I NEED IT!
GIVE ME IT!
UNHAND THAT 'NANA, YOU RASCAL!
OOOH!
You okay, Eric? Bananas sure are popular now they're in short supply!
ELSEWHERE, DOCTOR PLAQUE AND MADAME DECAY ARE AT WORK—
Bring me your toothbrushes for free sweet drinks and biscuits! ALL FREE! Hee-hee!
Put the toothbrushes in this bag! How I hate clean teeth!
AND SOON—
That's it! Chocolates and sweets! Spend all your precious pocket money, my dears!
RING! RING!
MORE!
MORE!
MORE!
This is serious! All the kids are eating far too many sweet things!
VERY SOON—
How goes the plan?
We've got all the toothbrushes! No more clean teeth!
This stuff is fantastic! I feel great eating fresh fruit! It's made a new Nerk out of me!
LOOKING BETTER
Wait a minute! Look at the scanner! Dozens of banana boats are heading for Britain with fresh supplies!
More bananas? Goody! I'm hooked on these! I can't wait till they arrive!

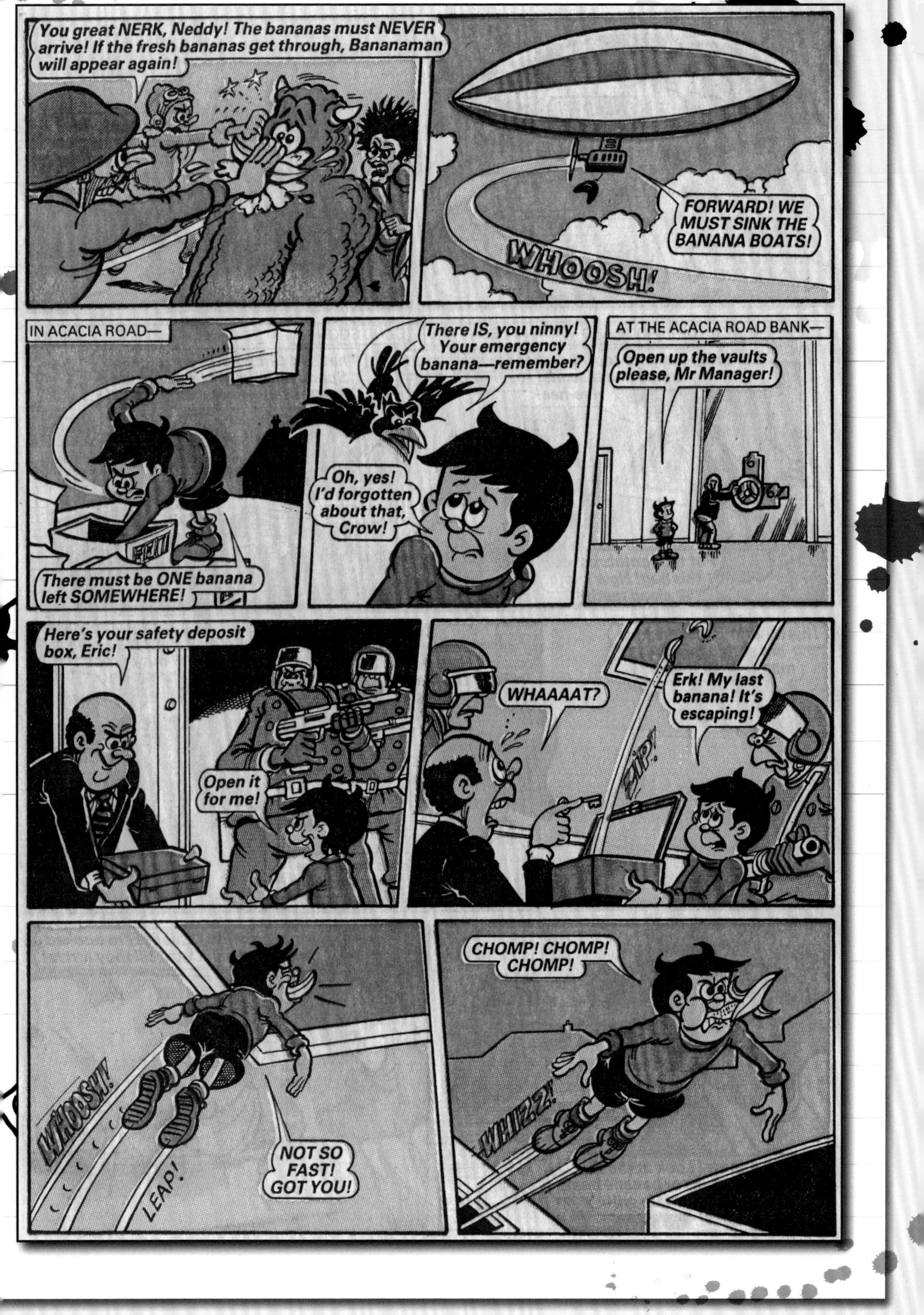
You great NERK, Neddy! The bananas must NEVER arrive! If the fresh bananas get through, Bananaman will appear again!
FORWARD! WE MUST SINK THE BANANA BOATS!
WHOOSH!
IN ACACIA ROAD—
There must be ONE banana left SOMEWHERE!
There IS, you ninny! Your emergency banana—remember?
Oh, yes! I'd forgotten about that, Crow!
AT THE ACACIA ROAD BANK—
Open up the vaults please, Mr Manager!
Here's your safety deposit box, Eric!
Open it for me!
WHAAAAT?
Erk! My last banana! It's escaping!
ZIP!
WHOOSH!
LEAP!
NOT SO FAST! GOT YOU!
CHOMP! CHOMP! CHOMP!
WHIZZ!

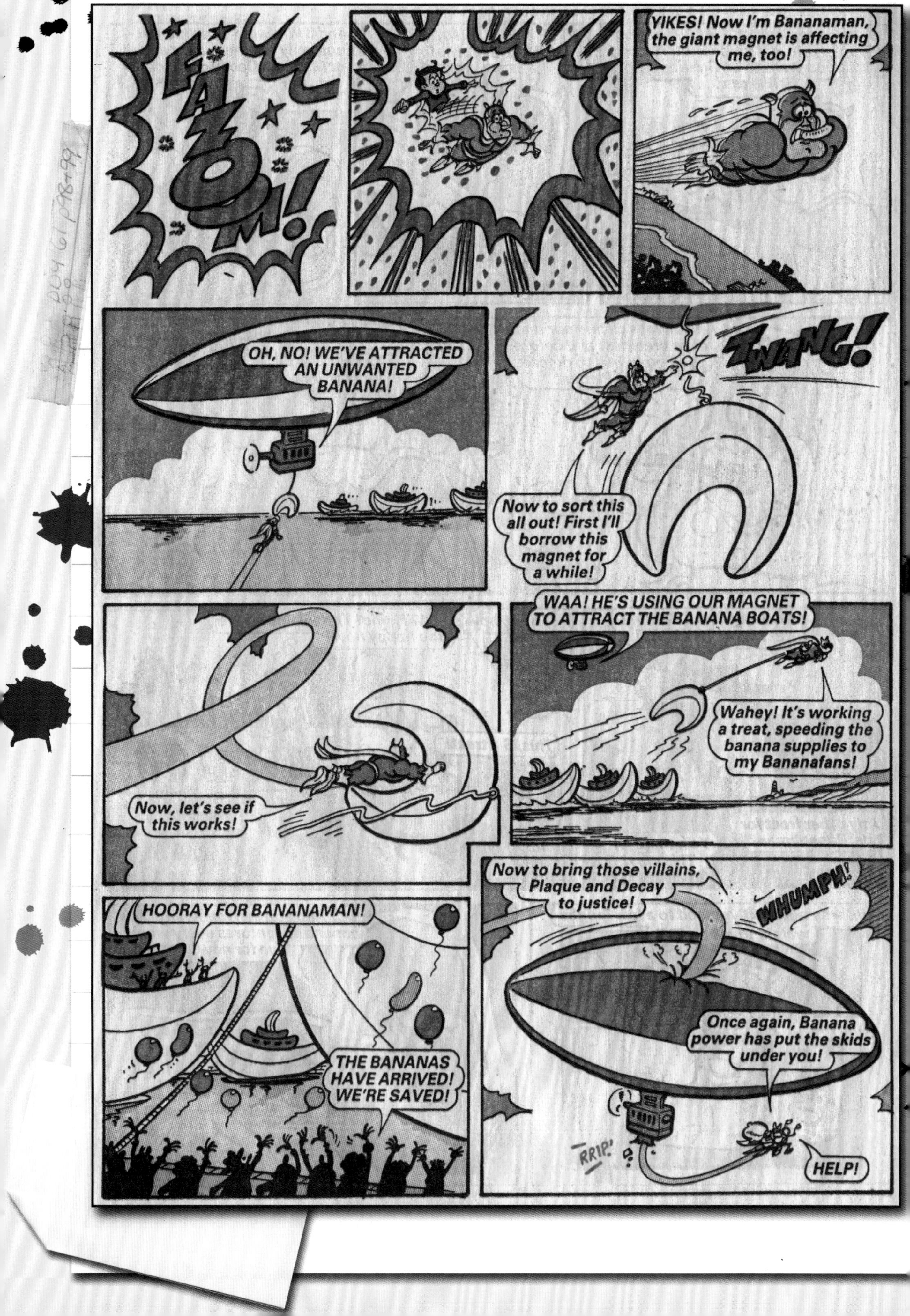
FAZOOM!
YIKES! Now I'm Bananaman, the giant magnet is affecting me, too!
OH, NO! WE'VE ATTRACTED AN UNWANTED BANANA!
TWANG!
Now to sort this all out! First I'll borrow this magnet for a while!
Now, let's see if this works!
WAA! HE'S USING OUR MAGNET TO ATTRACT THE BANANA BOATS!
Wahey! It's working a treat, speeding the banana supplies to my Bananafans!
HOORAY FOR BANANAMAN!
THE BANANAS HAVE ARRIVED! WE'RE SAVED!
Now to bring those villains, Plaque and Decay to justice!
WHUMPH!
Once again, Banana power has put the skids under you!
RRIP!
HELP!

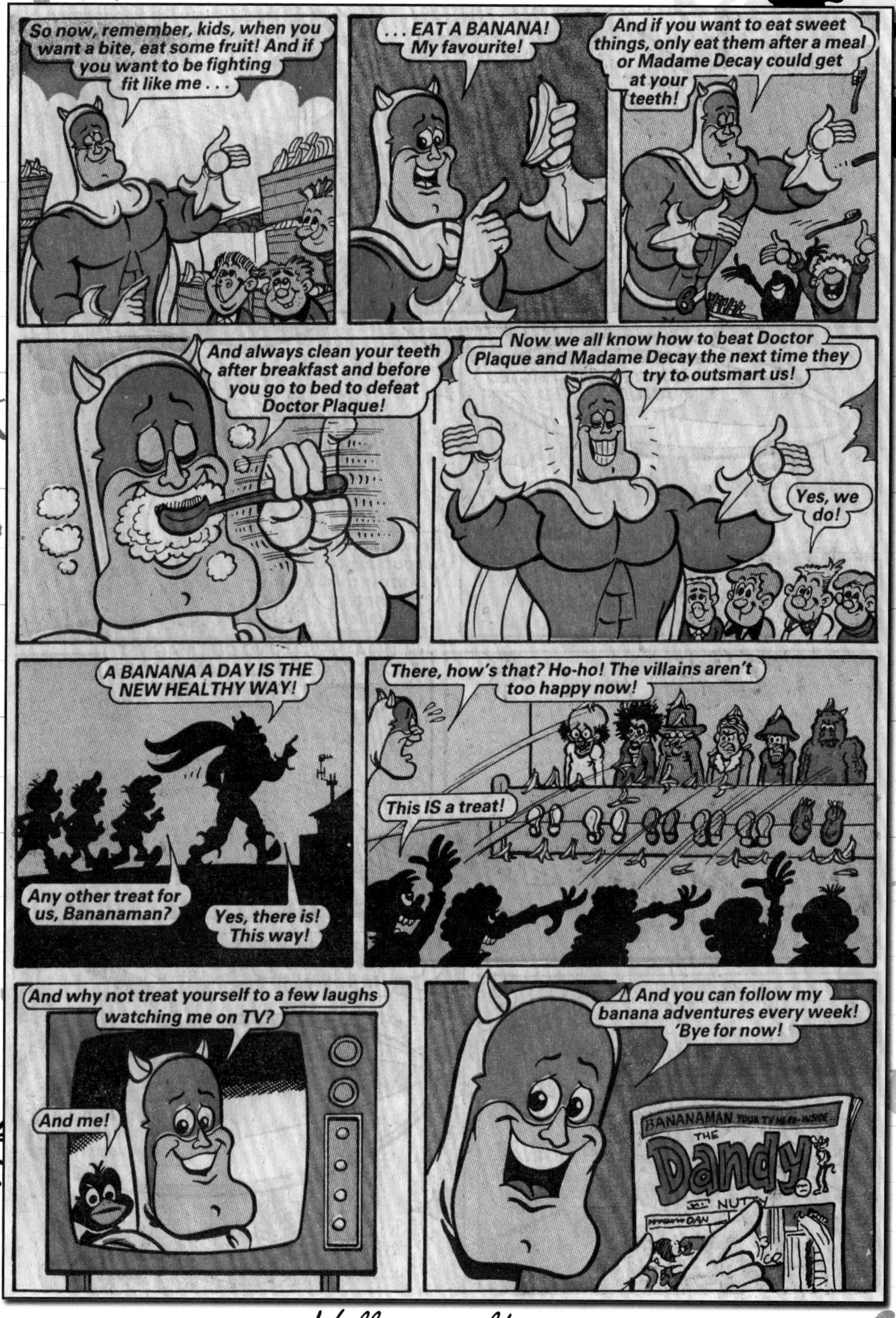
So now, remember, kids, when you want a bite, eat some fruit! And if you want to be fighting fit like me . . .
. . . EAT A BANANA! My favourite!
And if you want to eat sweet things, only eat them after a meal or Madame Decay could get at your teeth!
And always clean your teeth after breakfast and before you go to bed to defeat Doctor Plaque!
Now we all know how to beat Doctor Plaque and Madame Decay the next time they try to outsmart us!
Yes, we do!
A BANANA A DAY IS THE NEW HEALTHY WAY!
Any other treat for us, Bananaman?
Yes, there is! This way!
There, how's that? Ho-ho! The villains aren't too happy now!
This IS a treat!
And why not treat yourself to a few laughs watching me on TV?
And me!
And you can follow my banana adventures every week! 'Bye for now!
BANANAMAN
THE Dandy!

Well, you could in 1985.

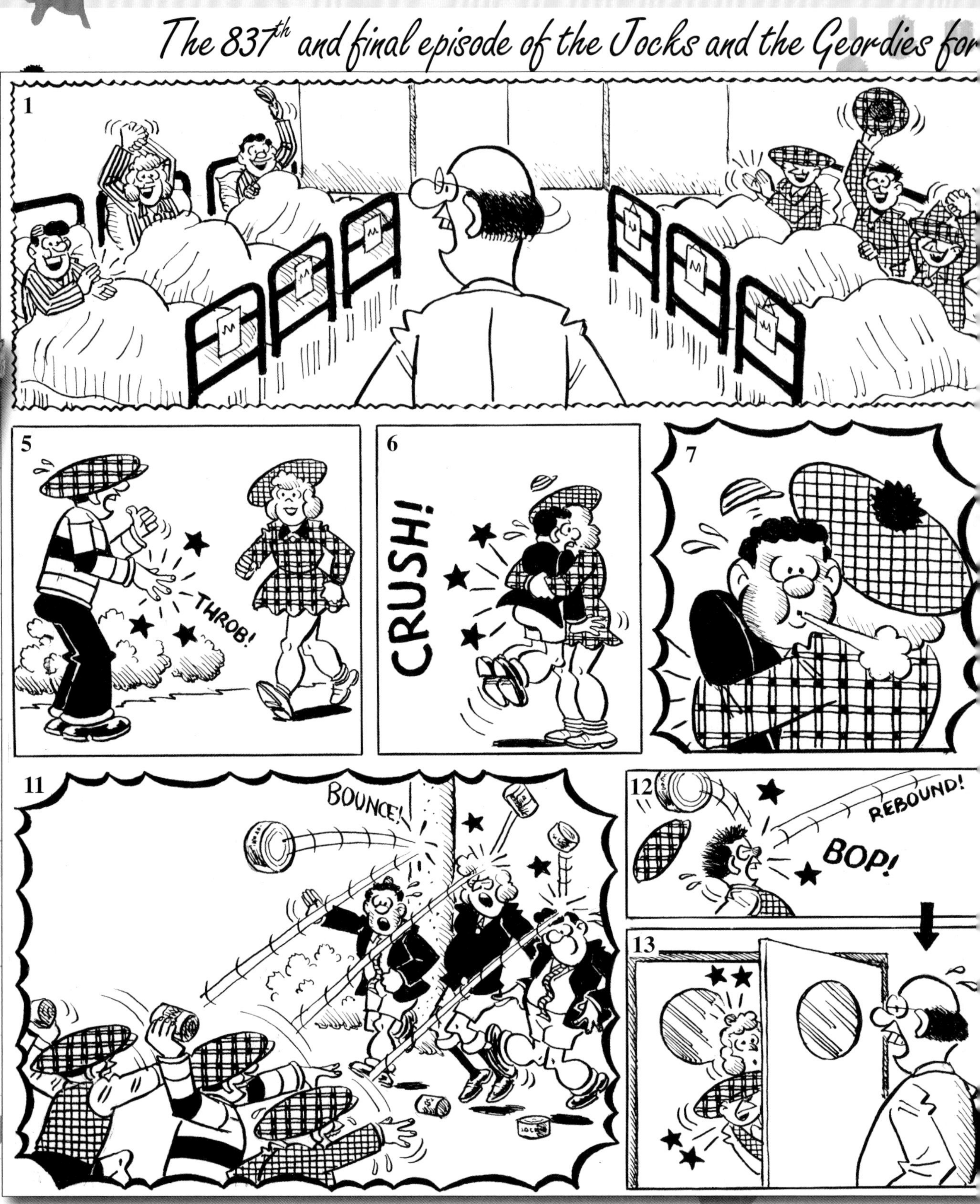

The 837th and final episode of the Jocks and the Geordies for
1
5
THROB!
6
CRUSH!
7
11
BOUNCE!
12
REBOUND!
BOP!
13

JOCKS AND GEORDIES SCRIPT : BEING FRIENDS

1. The Jocks and Geordies have been fighting again and one is in hospital. A doctor is discharging them.
Doctor – You can go back to school but I don't want to see you again.
Jocks – Hurrah!"

2. Doctor sees them out.
Doctor – Be friends with one another.
Sidney Geordie – Why aye, man.

3. Big Jock and Sidney are puzzled.
Jock – What do friends do?
Sidney – Dunno. We've always fought.

4. Sidney shakes Big Jock by the hand – very firml
Big Jock howls in pain.
Sidney – I know friends shake hands.
Jock – OOYAH!

5. Big Jock is nursing his sore hand when Agnes Jo
comes along.
Jock – Sidney's friendly handshake has crushed my fingers.
Agnes – I'm going to see him.

6. Agnes gives Sidney a hug.
Agnes – Friends give each other hugs.

The Dandy. The pages never made it into print – until now.

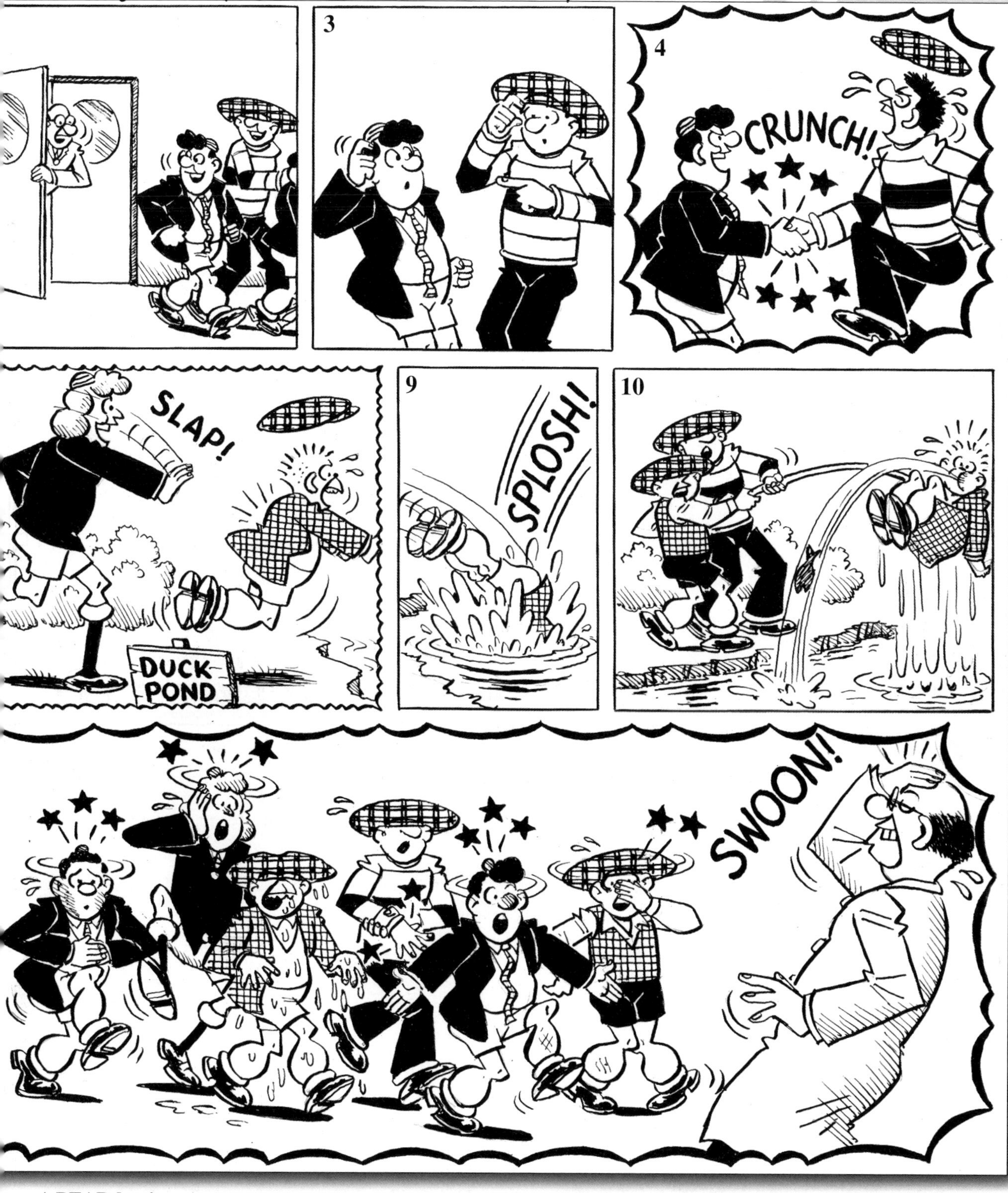
3
4
CRUNCH!
SLAP!
DUCK POND
9
SPLOSH!
10
SWOON!

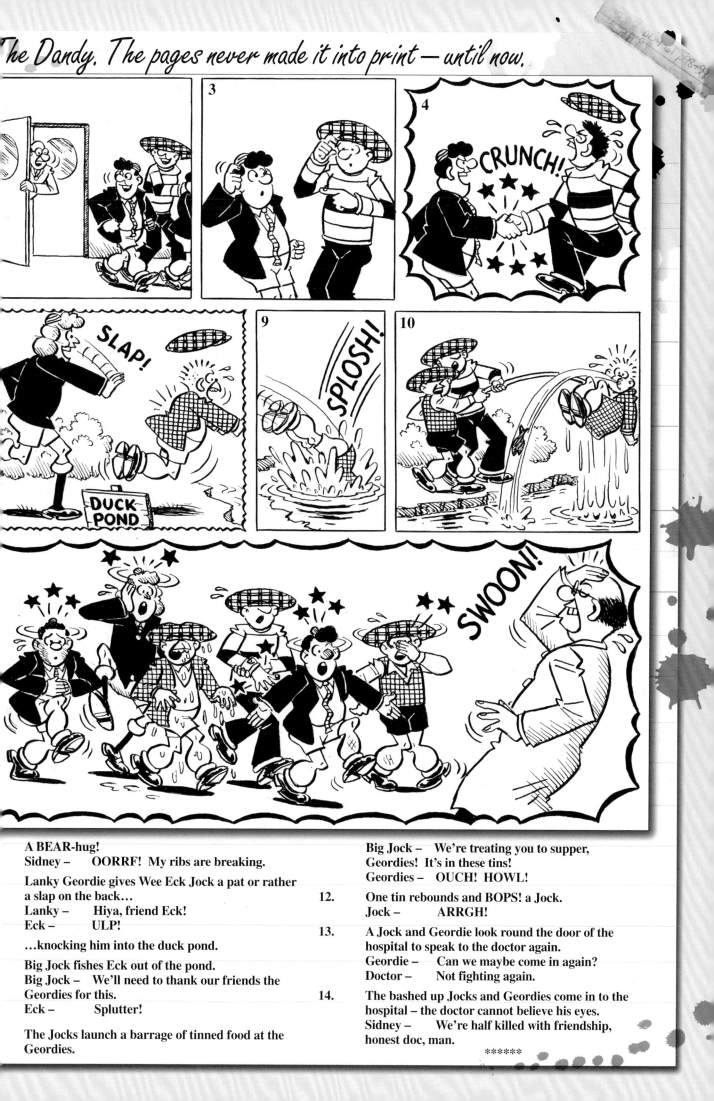

A BEAR-hug!
Sidney – OORRF! My ribs are breaking.

Lanky Geordie gives Wee Eck Jock a pat or rather a slap on the back…
Lanky – Hiya, friend Eck!
Eck – ULP!

…knocking him into the duck pond.

Big Jock fishes Eck out of the pond.
Big Jock – We'll need to thank our friends the Geordies for this.
Eck – Splutter!

The Jocks launch a barrage of tinned food at the Geordies.

Big Jock – We're treating you to supper, Geordies! It's in these tins!
Geordies – OUCH! HOWL!

12. One tin rebounds and BOPS! a Jock.
Jock – ARRGH!

13. A Jock and Geordie look round the door of the hospital to speak to the doctor again.
Geordie – Can we maybe come in again?
Doctor – Not fighting again.

14. The bashed up Jocks and Geordies come in to the hospital – the doctor cannot believe his eyes.
Sidney – We're half killed with friendship, honest doc, man.

******

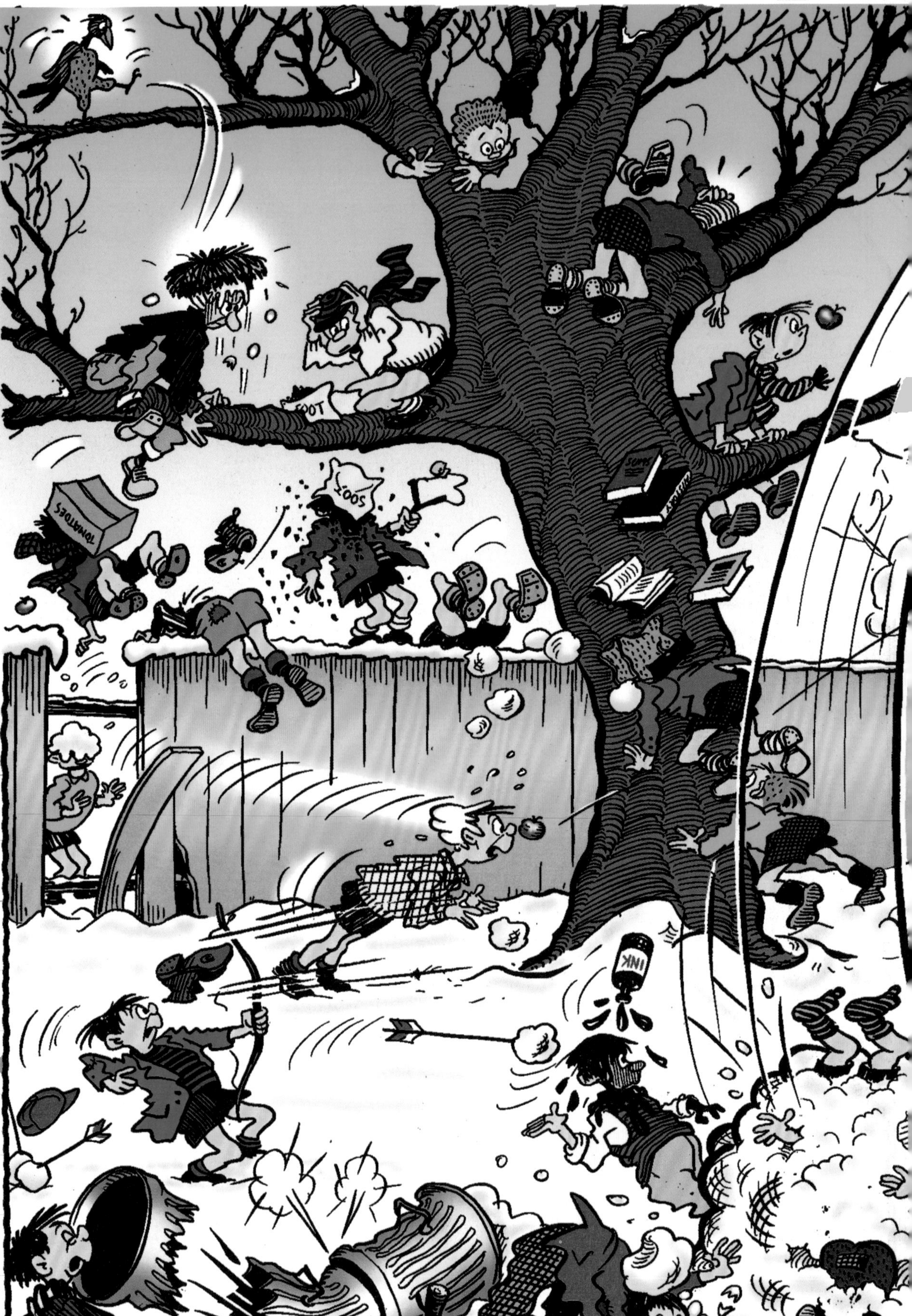
SOOT
TOMATOES
SOOT
INK
ROTTEN EGGS

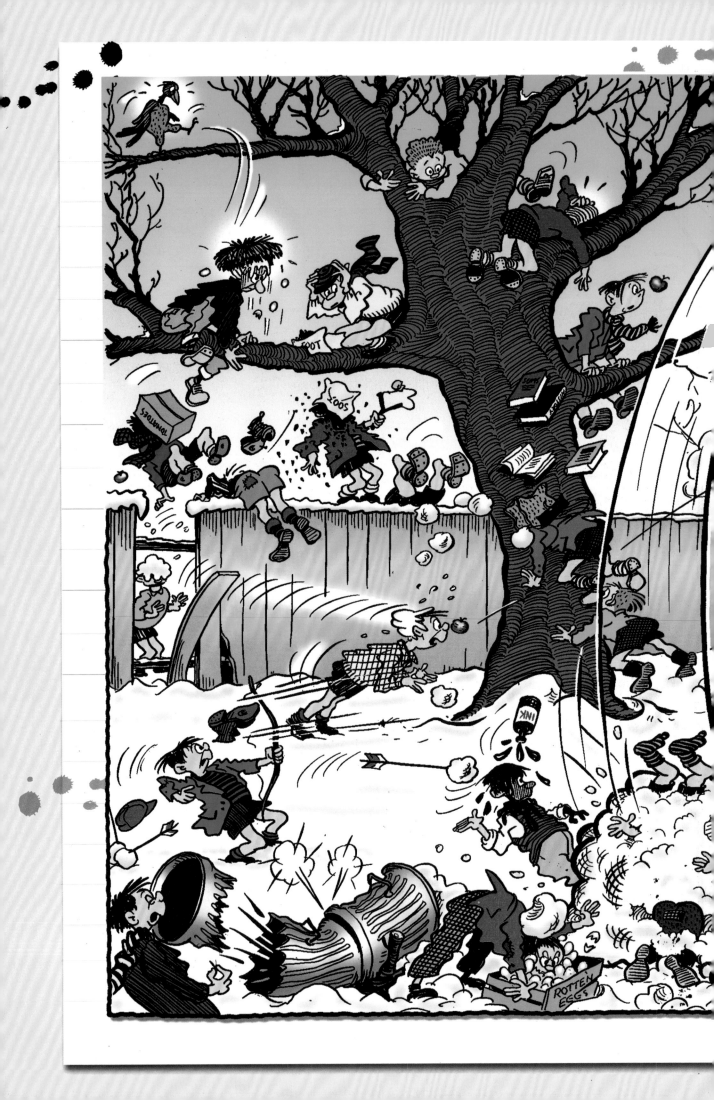